A

DISSERTATION

ON THE

Nature and Character

OF THE

CHINESE SYSTEM OF WRITING,

IN A LETTER TO JOHN VAUGHAN, ESQ.

By PETER S. DU PONCEAU, LL.D.,

President of the American Philosophical Society, of the Historical Society of Pennsylvania,
and of the Athenæum of Philadelphia ; Corresponding Member of the Institute
of France, &c. &c.

TO WHICH ARE SUBJOINED,

A VOCABULARY OF THE COCHINCHINESE LANGUAGE,

By Father JOSEPH MORRONE,

R. C. Missionary at Saigon,

WITH REFERENCES TO PLATES, CONTAINING THE CHARACTERS BELONGING TO EACH WORD,
AND WITH NOTES, SHOWING THE DEGREE OF AFFINITY EXISTING BETWEEN THE
CHINESE AND COCHINCHINESE LANGUAGES, AND THE USE THEY RESPEC-
TIVELY MAKE OF THEIR COMMON SYSTEM OF WRITING,

By M. DE LA PALUN,

Late Consul of France at Richmond, in Virginia ;

AND

A COCHINCHINESE AND LATIN DICTIONARY,

IN USE AMONG THE R. C. MISSIONS IN COCHINCHINA.

PUBLISHED BY ORDER OF THE AMERICAN PHILOSOPHICAL SOCIETY, BY THEIR HISTORICAL
AND LITERARY COMMITTEE.

PHILADELPHIA:
PUBLISHED FOR THE AMERICAN PHILOSOPHICAL SOCIETY,
BY M'CARTY AND DAVIS, 171 MARKET STREET.

1838.

I. ASHMEAD AND CO. PRINTERS,
PHILADELPHIA.

OFFICERS

AMERICAN PHILOSOPHICAL SOCIETY,

FOR THE YEAR 1838.

PATRON,

His Excellency the Governor of the State.

PRESIDENT,

Peter S. Du Ponceau.

VICE PRESIDENTS,

Nathaniel Chapman,   R. M. Patterson.
Joseph Hopkinson,

SECRETARIES,

Franklin Bache,   Alexander D. Bache,
John K. Kane,   J. Francis Fisher.

COUNSELLORS, ELECTED FOR THREE YEARS.

In 1836,
{ William Short,
George Ord,
William H. Keating,
Clement C. Biddle.

In 1837,
{ Nicholas Biddle,
James Mease,
Thomas Biddle,
Gouverneur Emerson.

In 1838,
{ Robert Hare,
William Hembel, jun.
Charles D. Meigs,
William Meredith.

CURATORS,

Franklin Peale,   Isaac Hays.
Isaac Lea,

TREASURER,   **LIBRARIAN,**
John Vaughan.   John Vaughan.

LIST

OF THE

OFFICERS AND MEMBERS OF THE HISTORICAL AND LITERARY COMMITTEE.

OFFICERS.

Peter S. Du Ponceau, *Chairman.*

Job R. Tyson, *Secretary.*

MEMBERS.

Nicholas Biddle,
Nathaniel Chapman,
Benjamin H. Coates,
Thomas Cooper, *Columbia, S. C.*
Robley Dunglison,
J. Francis Fisher,
James Gibson,
Joseph Hopkinson,
Charles J. Ingersoll,
John K. Kane,
William H. Keating,
Charles D. Meigs,
William Meredith,
Benjamin R. Morgan,
Joseph P. Norris,
Eugenius Nulty,
George Ord,
Robert M. Patterson,
John Pickering, *Boston,*
Condy Raguet,
Joseph Reed,
John Sergeant,
Thomas Sergeant,

William Short,
John Vaughan,
Robert Walsh,
Samuel B. Wylie.

DECEASED MEMBERS.

B. Allison,
Nicholas Collin,
Zaccheus Collins,
Joseph Correa da Serra, *Lisbon*,
John E. Hall,
David Hosack, *New York*,
Thomas C. James,
Thomas Jefferson, *Monticello, Va.*
George Izard, *Arkansas*,
George Logan, *of Stenton*,
William Rawle,
Charles Smith,
Isaiah Thomas, *Worcester, Mass.*
William Tilghman,
Caspar Wistar.

INTRODUCTION.

It is a just and true remark of the Rev. M. Gutzlaff, that
"nothing has so much *puzzled* the learned world in Europe
as the Chinese language."* We need not go very far to find
out the cause of this embarrassment. It is produced, like
many other difficulties that occur in almost every science,
by the abuse of words, by the use of metaphors instead of
plain intelligible language, and by looking beyond nature
for the explanation of her most simple operations.

The learned writer above cited does not tell us what he
means by the words "the Chinese *language*." If he meant
the *spoken* idiom, (as it is affected to be called,) there does
not appear any difficulty or cause of embarrassment. The
Chinese language (properly so called) is a simple idiom,
and, peculiarly the Kou-wen, or ancient language, essentially elliptical; its words are monosyllabic, and its syntax
chiefly consists in the juxtaposition of those words, aided
by a certain number of particles, which stand in the
place of our grammatical forms and inflexions. A great
number of those words are homophonous, but they are distinguished by accents and tones; and, upon the whole, the
people who speak this language find no difficulty in understanding each other. It is perhaps more elliptical than any
other; more is understood by it than is actually expressed;
but no difficulty arises from it. Ideas and perceptions are
awakened by the Chinese monosyllables, as well as by

* Post, p. 15.

B

those grammatical forms which may be called the *luxury* of our idioms.

Here, then, is nothing that can *puzzle* the philologists of Europe. But if, by the Chinese *language*, the learned author meant the written characters, (and in that sense only I can understand him,) he says what is unfortunately too true; and by the use which he makes of the word *language*, he shows that he has not yet discovered the true cause of the embarrassment which he very properly notices, and which must strike every one who has attended to the subject.

The Chinese characters do not, more than any other graphic system, constitute *a language* in the proper sense of the word. Metaphorically, indeed, they may be so called, and so may the groups formed by the letters of our alphabets. We do not read by letters; we read by groups of those little signs, representing words and sentences. No one, who is not in his A B C, will spell a word when he reads, or even think of the sounds of its component figures. This is so true, that there are words, such as the word *awe*, in which not a single one of the sounds attached to the three letters that compose it, is heard when it is read. In the word *ought*, none is heard but that of the letter *t*. Our eye catches the group, and our mind the sound and sense of the written·word, all at the same moment; it does not stop to take notice of each letter; the physical and mental processes are performed at the same instant, with the rapidity of thought, which is exceeded by nothing that we can form an idea of. These groups, therefore, might also receive the name of ideographic signs or characters, and their aggregate and various combinations might be called a written *language*. But every one will understand that this word, so applied, would only be metaphorical.

To apply these principles to the Chinese system of writing, is the object of the following dissertation. All those

(I believe I may say almost without exception*) who have written on the subject, have represented the writing of the Chinese as a separate, independent language, unconnected with the sounds of the human voice, and consequently with speech; a language acting *vi propriâ*, and presenting ideas to the mind directly through the eye, without passing through the mental ear, in which it is said to differ from our alphabetical system. Hence it has been called *ideographic*, and the language properly so called, the *oral* language, is represented as nothing more than the *pronunciation* of that which has usurped its name and its place.

In proof of these assertions, it is said that the Chinese writing is read and understood by nations who cannot speak or understand one word of the spoken idiom, but who make use of the same characters. How far this is founded in truth, the subjoined vocabularies of the Cochinchinese language, which employs in its writing the Chinese characters, will, I think, sufficiently show. However it may be, it will not affect the principles on which I intend to demonstrate that the Chinese graphic system is founded; nor will it in the least support its pretended extraordinary, and I might say almost miraculous properties.

I endeavour to prove, by the following dissertation, that the Chinese characters represent the *words* of the Chinese language, and ideas only through them. The letters of our alphabet separately represent sounds to which no meaning is attached, and are therefore only the elements of our graphic system; but, when combined together in groups, they represent the words of our languages, and those words represent or recall ideas to the mind of the reader. I contend that the Chinese characters, though formed of different

---

* Dr. Morrison is the writer who has said the least upon the subject. He has been more cautious than his brother sinologists. He does not, however, contradict the opinion that is generally received.

elements, do no more, and that they represent ideas no
otherwise than as connected with the words in which language has clothed them, and therefore that they are connected with sounds, not indeed as the letters of our alphabet
separately taken, but as the groups formed by them when
joined together in the form of words.

There are two species of what are called *alphabets*,
among the different nations who inhabit the earth; the one
is syllabic, and the other I would call *elementary*. Each
character of the first represents a syllable, generally unconnected with sense or meaning. This system has been
adopted by those nations whose languages consist of a small
number of syllables; such as the Cherokee, which has only
eighty-five, and the Japanese, that has no more than forty-
seven, with an equal number of characters to represent
them. These characters are few, and may be easily retained in the memory; it has not, therefore, been thought
necessary to carry analysis farther. Syllabic alphabets,
besides, have considerable advantages over those that we
make use of; they do not require spelling, and a great
deal of time is saved in learning to read. The process of
writing is also quicker, and the writing itself occupies less
space.

But those nations whose languages will not admit of a
syllabic alphabet, on account of the too great number of
their consonants, are obliged to proceed further in their
analysis of sounds; and, having discovered that the number
of the primary elements of speech, which we call letters, is
comparatively very small, they have adopted the system
which prevails in Europe and Western Asia, and which we
also call *alphabetical*, though we have properly no name to
distinguish it from the *syllabic*.

The Chinese, when they invented their system of writing,
found themselves possessed of a language composed entirely
of monosyllables, each of which was a word of the idiom,

so that they could, by the same character, recall a word
and a syllable at the same time. They also found that each
of those words represented an object or an idea, so that
they could present to the mind through the eye, at the same
moment, a syllable, a word, and an idea. It is no wonder,
therefore, that they did not look further, and that their first
endeavour was to affix a sign to each word, by means of
which they would recall the idea at the same time. But
the idea was only to them a secondary object; it was attached to the word, and could not be separated from it.

All savage nations, in their first attempts to communicate
with each other by writing, have begun with rude pictures
or delineations of visible objects. The original forms of a
number of their characters show, that the Chinese began in
the same manner. But that could not carry them very far;
yet it may have served their purpose while civilization had
not made much progress among them. Afterwards they
tried metaphors, which they probably found of very limited
use. At last, as they advanced in knowledge and civilization, they fell upon a system, which they have preserved
during a period of four thousand years, and with which they
appear to be perfectly satisfied. It is to that system that
philologists have given the name of *ideographic* writing.

In forming this system, they invented a certain number
of what I should call primary signs, which they applied to
an equal number of words. Some of those signs were
abridged forms of their original pictures and metaphors,
but so altered as to be no longer recognised. The number
of those primary or simple characters is not known; it is
to be presumed that it was not greater than could be easily
retained in the memory. The Chinese grammarians, under
the name of keys or radicals, have reduced them to the
number of two hundred and fourteen; but of these several
are compounded, so that the number was probably still
smaller. Be that as it may, two hundred words, more or

less, having signs or characters to represent them, by joining two, three, or more of them together, and using them as
catch words to lead to one that had no sign to represent it,
could produce an immense number of combinations; and
a still greater one by joining to these, and combining with
them, the new compounds; and so they might proceed in
the same manner *ad infinitum.* By means of that system,
with some modifications, the Chinese succeeded in representing all the *words* in their language. The ideas were only
an ingredient in the method which they adopted, but it was
by no means their object to present them to the mind un-
accompanied by the word which was their model, and
which, if I may use a bold metaphor, sat to them for its
picture; a picture, indeed, which bore no resemblance to
the object, but which was sufficient to recall it to the memory.

From this general view of the Chinese system of writing,
it is evident that the object of its inventors was to recall to
the mind, by visible signs, the words of which their language
was composed, and not to represent ideas independent of
the sounds of that language. But the number of those
words being too great to admit of merely arbitrary signs,
the forms of which could not easily be retained without
some classification to help the memory, they thought of
some mode of recalling at the same time something of the
meaning of each word, and that was done by combining
together the signs of several of them, so as to make a kind
of definition, far, indeed, from being perfect, but sufficient
for the purpose for which it was intended. And that is
what the Chinese literati, and the sinologists after them,
have been pleased to call *ideographic writing;* while, instead
of ideas, it only represents words, by means of the combination of other words, and therefore I have called it *lexigraphic.*

To make this still clearer, I shall add here the explana-

tion given by the Chinese themselves of their system of
writing, for which we are indebted to Dr. Morrison, in his
Dictionary, and M. Abel Remusat, in his Grammar of the
Chinese language.* I believe it will fully confirm the representation that I have made of it.

The Chinese divide their characters into six classes,
which division they call *Lou-chou* according to Remusat,
and *Luh-shoo* according to Morrison's orthography. As
these two writers do not agree as to the order in which
these classes are placed, I avail myself of the same privi-
lege, and place them in such order as I think best calculated
to give a clear idea of the whole. The three first relate to
the external forms of the characters, and the three last to
the manner in which they are employed, in order to produce the effect required. We shall now examine them
separately.

I. The *Siang-hing*, (R.) or *Hing-seang*, (M.) M. Remusat calls these characters *figurative*, as representing as much
as possible the forms of visible objects. Thus the sun is
represented by a circle, with a dot in the middle; the moon
by a crescent; a man, a horse, a dog, the eye, the ear, &c.
by linear figures, representing or attempting to represent
the different objects, the names of which they recall to memory. The Chinese writers, says Dr. Morrison, assert that
originally those figurative characters composed nine-tenths
of their alphabet, which is difficult to believe, unless the
alphabet itself is very limited; but the Doctor adds that
they give but very few examples of them, which is much
more credible.

Be that as it may, those characters, if ever they existed
to any considerable extent, have long ceased to be in use.
The Chinese themselves admit it; and the reason they give

* Morrison, Introd. p. 1. Remusat, p. 4.

for it, according to Dr. Morrison, is, that "they were abbreviated for the sake of convenience, and added to for the
sake of appearance, so that the original form was gradually
lost;" no trace of it now remains. The characters, as they
are at present formed, present nothing to the eye but linear
and angular figures, quite as insignificant as the letters of
our alphabet, otherwise than by being connected with the
words of the language as those are with its elementary
sounds, and when grouped together with the words themselves. Therefore, as they now appear, those signs can in
no manner be called *ideographic*.

II. The *Tchi-sse*, (R.) or *Che-khe-sze*, (M.) M. Remusat
calls them *indicative*. They are an attempt to recall, by
figures, ideas that have no figure. Thus the numerals one,
two, three, are represented by horizontal lines, as in the
Roman arithmetical characters they are by vertical ones;
the words *above* and *below*, are represented by short vertical lines above or below horizontal ones; and the word or
the idea of *middle*, by an oblong square, with a vertical line
passing through the middle of it. It is evident that there
can be but few such characters; I have seen none cited,
except those above mentioned. Whatever may be said of
them, there are not enough to characterize a system.

· III. The *Tchouan-tchu*, (R.) or *Chuen-choo*, (M.) M. Remusat calls them *inverted*. They are an attempt to represent things by their contraries. Thus a character representing a fork, with three prongs and a crooked handle, the
prongs turned towards the right, stands for the word *left*,
and for the word *right*, if the prongs are turned the other
way. M. Remusat quotes four others, intended to represent the words *standing*, *lying*, *man*, and *corpse*; but in my
opinion they represent nothing to the mind through the eye,
and they must be absolutely guessed at. M. Remusat says

that their number is very small, (très peu considérable,) and it is easy to conceive why it should be so.

These three first classes of characters are the only ones, the ideographic nature of which is said to be inherent to their external form. It has been seen that the first has long been entirely out of use, and is now superseded by arbitrary signs, which have no connexion with ideas, except by re-calling to the mind the words by which the ideas are ex-pressed. The two others, ingenious as they are, are too few, and too vague and uncertain in their expression, to give a name, much less a descriptive character to the Chi-nese system of writing. We shall now pass to the three other classes, which have nothing to do with the external form of the characters.

IV. The *Kia-tsei*, (R.) or *Kea-tseay*, (M.) which in the Chinese language signifies *borrowed*. M. Remusat defines it thus :* " To express abstract *ideas*, or acts of the under-standing, they (the Chinese) have altered the sense of those simple or compound characters which represent material objects, or they have made of a substantive the sign of a verb, which expresses the corresponding action. Thus the *heart* represents the *mind*; a *house* is taken for *man*; a *hall* for *woman*; a *hand* for an *artificer* or *mechanic*, &c." Un-fortunately for this theory, the sense of the characters (as corresponding with the words) has not been in the least altered; it is the sense of the words that has been changed, and the characters have followed. In the Chinese *spoken* language, a sailor is called a *ship-hand*, a monk a *reason-house*, or house of reason, &c., and the writing only applies the appropriate character to each of these words. The language is full of similar metaphors: *east-west* signifies a thing or something; *elder brother* with *younger brother*, signify simply brother, without distinction of age, &c.†

* Gram. Chinoise, p. 3.   † Ibid. pp. 108, 109.

c

The writing does no more than represent these words by the characters appropriated to each; the metaphor is in the *language*, not in the *writing*.

Dr. Marshman[*] wonders that he has never seen a Chinese treatise on the grammar of the spoken idiom. The reason is obvious. The Chinese affect to ascribe every thing to their system of writing, which they would have us believe to be an admirable philosophical invention, independent of, and unconnected with the language, which they consider only as the oral expression of the characters, while the reverse is the exact truth. That a vain, ignorant nation should entertain such notions, is not at all to be wondered at; but that grave and learned European philologists should adopt them without reflection, is truly astonishing. The reader will see in the following dissertation, what strange opinions have been entertained on this subject, by men of the most profound knowledge and the most eminent talents.

There is nothing, therefore, in these *borrowed* characters, as they are called, that entitles them to form a class in the Chinese system of writing. They are, like all the others, but the representatives of certain words.

M. Remusat includes in this class the character representing the verb *to follow*, which, he says, is formed by the images of three men placed behind one another. I shall not inquire how distinctly these images are to be seen in the character *suy*, to follow.[†] It seems to be one of the old obsolete metaphors. This is what M. Remusat calls changing substantives into verbs, and it is the only example of it that he produces.

V. The *Hoëï-i*, (R.) or *Hwuy-e*, (M.) This class and the following appear to me to embrace the whole graphic sys-

---

[*] Clavis Sinica, p. 185.
[†] Morrison's Anglo-Chin. Dict. verbo *follow*.

tem of the Chinese. The first class (so called) is interesting only to antiquaries, the second and third relate only to the form of a few characters, and the fourth has been shown to be fallacious. These two last, therefore, claim our principal attention. I shall attend, in the first place, to the fifth class.

This class is formed of a combination of two or more characters, each of which represents a word, to represent another word of the language. M. Remusat calls it *combined*. Dr. Morrison, in his Chinese Dictionary, in which the words are classed in the order of our alphabet, explains *Hwuy-e'* (No. 4560) to mean "association of *ideas* in compounding the characters." The learned Doctor here, it seems, merely translates a Chinese definition of that word. We take the liberty to define it thus: "The association or combining of several words in their appropriate characters to represent another word." Thus we combine the letters of our alphabet to give them a meaning which, separately, they have not. The Chinese combine their *significant* characters to give to the groups thus formed a meaning which none of them possess separately. The meaning is in the words to which the characters are applied, and that meaning they only hint at by the association of other words represented by their appropriate signs.

M. Remusat gives us six examples of these combinations. They are the word *light*, represented by the words sun and moon, placed next to each other; the word *hermit*, by man and mountain; *song*, by bird and mouth; *wife*, by woman, hand and broom; the verb *to hear*, or hearing, by ear and door; and the substantive *tear*, by the words eye and water. All these words are, of course, represented by their signs, which bear no resemblance to the objects signified, whatever they might originally have done.

The characters are sometimes placed above, below, or by the side of each other, in their separate forms. Sometimes they are joined together with various alterations, so as to form but one character, in which last case they are not always easy to be recognised. Two hundred and fourteen of them, of which a few are compounds, but the rest simple characters, have been selected for the sake of method, and called *roots* or *keys*. They serve in the dictionaries to class the words by their analogies: every word is placed under some one or other of them. This concerns only the method or arrangement of the alphabet, but is no part of the system of writing, except so far, that a certain number of simple characters was indispensably required to form the basis of a combination system, which otherwise would have been impossible.

It results from the above, that the graphic system of the Chinese, generally considered, consists in this:

1. A certain number of arbitrary signs (say two hundred) to represent an equal number of words, which may be called the *nucleus* or foundation of the whole.

2. An indefinite number of characters to represent all the other words of the language, which characters are formed by the combination of those primitives with each other, and with the new characters formed by that process also combined together, so as to have a distinct letter, character or sign for every word in the language. The separate meaning of the words thus combined, or the *ideas*, as the Chinese express it, are only an auxiliary means to aid in the recollection of the word to which is attached the idea which is to be conveyed. It very often happens that those combinations are mere enigmas, and present no definite idea to the mind, and sometimes one entirely contrary to its object; but they serve the purpose, precisely as our groups of letters when they represent different sounds from those attached to the separate characters.

I have explained this system more fully in the following dissertation, to which I must refer the reader.

VI. The *Hing-ching*, (R.) or *Heae-shing*, (M.) Although words expressive of moral sentiments, of actions and passions, and of numerous visible objects, may be represented or recalled to the memory by combining and placing together other words, which, by their signification, may serve as definitions or descriptions, or rather as *catch words*, to lead by their meaning to the recollection of the one intended to be represented,—it is very difficult, when there are a great number of objects of the same kind, all of which have specific names, but whose differences cannot be explained or even guessed at by the aid of a few words. Such are trees, plants, herbs, fruits, birds, fishes, and a great number of other things. Here the system of catch words could not be applied; and the Chinese invented this class, or rather this special combination of characters, to represent those kinds of specific names.

A certain number of characters, all, in their common acceptation, representing words of the language, are set apart to be used with regard only to their sounds, independent of their meaning; and, joined to the character which represents the name of the *genus*, they indicate the sound of the name of the species to be represented. Thus, if the name of an apple be *ping*, though that monosyllable may signify twenty other things, each of which has an appropriate character, any one of those characters, simple or compound, provided it be within the selected list, joined to the word *fruit*, or the word *tree*, signifies either an apple or an apple-tree, as the case may be. This class of characters the Chinese admit to be phonetic, or representative of sound, but they deny it as to all the rest, because they ascribe to the character the sense which is attached to the significant syllable, and which the written sign only reflects.

The Chinese have other modes of employing their characters to represent the sounds of words or proper names of foreign origin; but they are not included in the above six classes. They are fully explained in the following Dissertation, in which I have endeavoured to prove that the Chinese system of writing is essentially phonetic, because the characters represent words, and words are *sounds;* and because, if not connected with those sounds, they would present to the mind no idea whatever.

The Chinese characters have been frequently compared to our arithmetical figures, and to the various signs employed in algebra, pharmacy, &c., and therefore they have been called *ideographic*, or representative of *ideas*. The comparison is just in some respects; because ideas being connected with the words of the language, and those characters representing words, they may be said at the same time to represent the ideas connected with them. But the comparison does not hold any further. The numerical figures express ideas which in every language are expressed by words having the same meaning, and though their sounds be different, the idea is the same; the other signs are abbreviations, applied to particular sciences, and understood only by those who are learned in them. There is no doubt that if all languages were formed on the same model, and if every word in all of them expressed with precision the same idea, and if they were all formed exactly like the Chinese, the Chinese characters might be applied to all in the same manner as our numerical figures; but that not being the case, those characters are necessarily applied to a particular language, and therefore, their object not being to represent ideas independently, but at second hand, through the words of that particular idiom, they are not entitled to the name of *ideographic*, which has been inadvertently given · to them.

If this theory be found consistent with reason and sound sense, there will result from it a clear and natural classification of the systems of writing now known to exist on the face of the earth. The elements of language are words, syllables, and the simple sounds represented by the letters of our alphabets. Those three elements are all produced by the vocal organs; and, as all writing is made to be read by all who understand the language to which it belongs, and to be read aloud as well as mentally by all in the same words, and in the same order of words, it seems clear that the written signs must represent or recall to the mind some one or other of those three elements; and hence we have three graphic systems, distinct from each other, but formed on the same general principle—the *elementary* or alphabetic, the characters of which, called *letters*, represent singly the primary elements of speech, which are simple sounds; the *syllabic*, that represents syllables which, for the most part, have no sense or meaning, but only serve as elements in the composition of polysyllabic words; and lastly, the *lexigraphic*, which, by means of simple or combined signs, represent the words of a language in their entirety; and this last mode seems to be more particularly applicable to monosyllabic languages, in which every syllable has a sense or meaning connected with it, which supplies a method for the formation of the characters, the multiplicity of which otherwise might create confusion. Nothing deserves to be called writing which does not come within some one or another of these three classes. It might be otherwise, if all men were born deaf and dumb; but since the habit of speaking, acquired in their infancy, has given body and form to their ideas, every thing which is not a representation of those forms, can, in my opinion, only be considered as an abortive attempt to make visible supply the place of audible signs, which may have served some limited purposes, but never deserved to be called writing. In the following dissertation I have considered in this point of view the hieroglyphics of ancient Egypt, and the paintings of the Mexicans. I will not anticipate here what I have said on those subjects. The result is, that an *ideographic* system of writing is a creature of the imagination, and that it cannot possibly exist concurrently with a language of audible sounds.

Another object of this publication is, to discover what ground there is for the popular notion that several nations, entirely ignorant of each other's oral language, communicate with each other in writing by means of the Chinese characters. As it regards nations whose languages, like the Japanese, are polysyllabic, and have inflections and grammatical forms, I think I have sufficiently proved that it is impossible that they should understand the Chinese writing, unless they have learned the Chinese language, though they may not be in the habit of speaking it. But it may be otherwise with respect to those nations whose languages are monosyllabic, and formed on the same model with the Chinese, and who have adopted the same system of writing. It cannot be denied, that to a certain extent, that is to say, as far as words, having the same meaning in both languages, are represented by the same characters, they may so far, but no farther, communicate with each other in writing. How far that can be the case, can only be shown by a comparison of their languages, and of the manner in which they make use of their written signs. For this purpose, I wish we had a more extensive vocabulary than the one here presented, which contains only three hundred and thirty-three Cochinchinese words, with their corresponding signs; but I hope it will be followed by others more copious and complete. It is much to be regretted that the English East India Company declined publishing the Dictionary offered to them by the Vicar Apostolic of Cochinchina, which probably was that composed by the venerable Bishop of Adran.* I am not, however, disposed

---

* See post, p. 101.

to blame them for this refusal. It is well known that that illustrious body is not deficient in liberality, and that they have expended very large sums* in the publication of Dr. Morrison's excellent Chinese dictionaries, for which science will ever owe them a debt of gratitude; it is not astonishing, therefore, that they should not be willing, at least for the present, to incur farther expense. But we must not despair of seeing the book published; there are Asiatic societies at Paris and London, under whose auspices many valuable philological works have been brought to light; and there is no reason to suppose that they will not still pursue that meritorious course. It would be worthy of them to republish the Anamitic grammar of Father de Rhodes.† It seems now well ascertained, that the language of Tonquin and that of Cochinchina are nearly if not entirely the same; and with that book, and the two vocabularies here published, a pretty clear idea might be formed of the nature and character of the Anamitic dialects.‡ But to return to our question.

On examining Father Morrone's Vocabulary, here subjoined, (No. II.) it cannot but be observed, that in adopting the Chinese alphabet, the Cochinchinese appear frequently

* M. Remusat understood, in 1822, that the publication of Dr. Morrison's *Dictionary* would cost £10,000 sterling. (Mélanges Asiatiques, vol. ii. p. 25.) The Doctor published *several* dictionaries, and other valuable works, so that the whole must have cost a great deal more.

† See p. 87.

‡ There seems to be very little difference between the Anamitic spoken in Tonquin and that of Cochinchina. In Father Morrone's Vocabulary we find the word *troi* for heaven, while M. Kraproth gives us *bloi* in Tonquinese for the same word. Thus he gives us *blang* for moon, while in the Cochinchinese Vocabulary it is *trang*. But the Dictionary which follows gives us *troi* and *bloi*, and *trang* and *blang*, as synonymous words. So that the Tonquinese words appear to be also in use in Cochinchina. Whether the reverse also takes place, we do not know. After all, there seems to be but a trifling difference of pronunciation between them.

to have paid more attention to the sound than to the meaning of the Chinese words to which the characters belong. Thus the character *san*, (Plate No. 14) which in Chinese means *drizzling rain*, is applied in Cochinchinese to the word *sam*, thunder; the character *chouang*, white frost, (19) to *suong*, the dew; *ko*, a lance, (37) to *qua*, yesterday; *kin*, metal, (232) to *kim*, a needle; *po*, to bring a ship to shore, (236) to *bac*, silver; *tchy*, fetters, (227) to *choi*, a broom,— and many others of the same kind. It shows how natural it is to consider written characters as representative of sound.* This, I am well aware will hardly be credited by those sinologists who consider ideas to be inseparably inherent in the Chinese characters. The learned M. Jacquet, to whom I communicated some of these examples, appears disposed to consider those anomalies as resulting from the addition or subtraction of some strokes in the running hand of the Cochinchinese, so that the characters might always be found to be bad imitations of some which have in Chinese the same meaning as in Cochinchinese; he, however, can-

---

* We are informed by M. Remusat, (Mélanges Asiat. vol. ii. p. 98,) that even among the Chinese many homophonous characters, though different in their meaning, are employed one for the other, and pass for various forms of the same character; which, he says, occasions much confusion in reading. This is in printed books. Elsewhere, the same writer tells us that the merchants and mechanics of China, in their ordinary writing, employ but one character to represent all the words of their language that have the same sound. (See post, p. 64.) Can there be stronger proof that those characters are considered by the Chinese themselves as *phonetic*, and that in their common writings they often attend more to the sound than to the sense?

The Chinese literati have multiplied their characters to the immense number which they at present exhibit from motives not difficult to be guessed at. When science is connected with political power it must have its *arcana*, to keep it beyond the reach of the common people. The same thing happened in ancient Egypt; the priests tried to involve their graphic system in mysteries, but necessity compelled the people to simplify it.

didly acknowledges "que c'est plutôt trancher la difficulté que la résoudre," in which I entirely agree with him. At the same time I must say, that the specimens I sent him were too few to enable him to form a decided opinion, and that he pointed out among them some affinities which have escaped our friendly annotator, M. de la Palun; as, for instance, that the character *thanh*, (Plate No. 86) which in Cochinchinese means *a city*, has the same meaning in Chinese, though it also signifies *walls*.* He has moreover observed, that the character *ben*, (89) which in Cochinchinese means *la partie du nord, de l'est*, &c., is the same with the Chinese *pien* or *pian*, latus, ora, terminus, (De Guignes, No. 11,169.) But these few observations, however just they appear, do not solve the question before us. Independent of those characters which I cannot consider otherwise than as expressive of the Cochinchinese sounds, without regard to the meaning which they have in China, it is evident that there are many others, which, though Chinese in their origin, are combined together in a manner peculiar to the Cochinchinese language; so that, upon the whole, I cannot resist the conviction that forces itself upon me, that the inhabitants of Anam cannot read Chinese books, or converse in writing with others than their countrymen by means of the Chinese characters, except to a very limited extent, unless they have made a special study of those characters as applied to a different language than their own; or, in other words, unless they have learned Chinese.

The Cochinchinese themselves make a distinction between the Chinese characters and their own. They call the former *Chu nho*, and the latter *Chu nom*. These the authors of the Cochinchinese and Latin Dictionary (No. III.) define thus: "Litteræ Annamaticæ ad exprimendas vulgares voces, seu

* In Cochinchinese, the word *thanh*, a city, signifies also *walls*. See the Dictionary, *hoc verbo*, p. 346.

ad referenda Annamitica verba."[*] Like the Italians, and
as was common through all Europe some centuries ago,
they call their language the *vulgar tongue*, (lingua vulgaris,)[†]
which implies that the Chinese to them, as the Latin to us,
is the learned or the classical language. They call the characters, it is true, " Sinico-annamitici," but I understand
them to mean the system of writing, which in both countries is the same, though the characters frequently differ in
their application or in their forms. A scholar with them
must be skilled in the Chinese and in the Anamitic.[‡] It is
no wonder, therefore, that men who have been taught in
that manner can understand each other without speaking.
As the characters in both languages are *lexigraphic*, each
being the representative of a word, it is not perhaps so necessary that they should remember the Chinese sounds,
particularly as the two languages appear formed on the
same grammatical system, though it appears to me that the
Cochinchinese is more elliptical than the Chinese, as I do
not find in it the connecting particles of the *Kwan-hoa*, or
modern Chinese. But of these details I do not find myself
competent to speak. I submit them to the investigation of
the learned.

I had adopted, without sufficient reflection, the popular
opinion that the Cochinchinese (spoken) language was a
dialect of the Chinese; but, on further examination, it does
not appear to me to be the case. By far the greatest number of the Cochinchinese words appear to differ entirely
from the Chinese. In the numerals particularly, which in
the Indo-European, and in the Oceanic languages, show so
great an affinity between the different idioms, there is none
to be observed when compared with those of the language
of China. In the Dictionary (No. III.) a very few words

---

[*] See Dict. post, p. 311, verbo *nho*, and p. 314, verbo *nom*.
[†] Ibid.   [‡] Ibid.

are said to be "Vox Sinico-annamitica," and, as far as I can judge by the means of comparison within my reach, it rather appears to me that those two languages are not derived from each other. M. Klaproth, in his Asia Poly-glotta,* has given us a tabular view of one hundred and forty-eight Chinese and Anamitic words. Out of this number thirty-nine only show more or less affinity between the two languages. To thirty-three out of the remaining one hundred and nine he has joined in italics the Chinese to the Anamitic word, as if both were in use in the Anamitic countries, which may possibly be the case, in consequence of the great intercourse that exists between the two nations; but those Sinico-anamitic words, if they are really in use, do not belong to the original language, and therefore cannot be cited as proofs of affinity between the two idioms. This is another subject, in my opinion, well deserving investigation. The comparative study of languages has hitherto been confined to polysyllabic idioms. The monosyllabic languages of Asia offer, perhaps, a no less interesting object to the lovers of that science.

I think proper to mention here, that somewhere in the following Dissertation† I have expressed a doubt of the correctness of Captain Beechy's opinion that the language of the Loo-choo Islands is polysyllabic, and a dialect of the Japanese. Further examination has satisfied me that that gentleman had good grounds for advancing that opinion, and it is with great pleasure I take this opportunity of doing him the justice to which he is entitled. At the same time it is right that I should observe, that this admission does not in the least militate against the principles which I have laid down; and that if the Loo-chooans, as appears probable, speak a polysyllabic Japanese dialect, they do not apply the Chinese characters to it otherwise than the Japanese

* Page 368.   † Page 96.

themselves. On this subject I must refer the reader to what I have said in my Dissertation, and in my letter to Captain Basil Hall,* where I think I have sufficiently proved that the Japanese do not make use of the Chinese characters to represent the words, but only the syllables of their vernacular language; and there is no reason to suppose that the Loo-chooans have done otherwise. If, therefore, they can read and understand the Chinese writing, it appears to me that no reason can be given for it than that they have learned that language, as is done by so many other nations who have adopted the religion, the manners, and the literature of the celestial empire.

Thus much, I have thought proper to say, by way of introduction to the Dissertation which immediately follows, in order to prepare the reader for the further developments that it contains. I have taken this opportunity to present some views of the general subject, which either were omitted in my letter to Mr. Vaughan for brevity's sake, or which did not occur to me at the time. I have done the same in the Preface to Father Morrone's Vocabulary. I hope the reader will excuse this defect in point of method, which should not have taken place if I had not, as I proceeded, found a wider field than I had at first contemplated, and if I had not been afraid of extending my Dissertation to too great a length, not leaving sufficient room for the important documents that are subjoined, and which are the principal objects of this publication.† The form of a letter to a friend, which I adopted, will show that I did not at first contemplate treating the subject so much at large as I have done;

* Post, pp. 60, 85, 114.

† It was at first intended for the sixth volume of the American Philosophical Transactions, now in the press, which could not have afforded room for a long Dissertation to be added to the Vocabularies. When the Society ordered it to be published separately, it was too late to write it over again.

and yet I am far from having exhausted it. New views are constantly presenting themselves to me, which I must leave to others, to whose minds I have no doubt they will also suggest themselves. I hope that at some future day this subject will be resumed by an abler hand. It appears to me to involve some of the most important principles of the philological science.

On the whole, by the publication of this book, I have had in view to establish the following propositions:

1. That the Chinese system of writing is not, as has been supposed, *ideographic*; that its characters do not represent *ideas*, but *words*, and therefore I have called it *lexigraphic*.

2. That ideographic writing is a creature of the imagination, and cannot exist, but for very limited purposes, which do not entitle it to the name of writing.

3. That among men endowed with the gift of speech, all writing must be a direct representation of the spoken language, and cannot present ideas to the mind abstracted from it.

4. That all writing, as far as we know, represents language in some of its elements, which are words, syllables, and simple sounds. In the first case it is lexigraphic, in the second syllabic, and in the third alphabetical or elementary.

5. That the lexigraphic system of the Chinese cannot be applied to a polysyllabic language, having inflections and grammatical forms; and that there is no example of its being so applied, unless partially or occasionally,* or as a special, elliptical and enigmatical mode of communication, limited in its uses; but not as a general system of writing, intended for common use.

* In our alphabets we have single letters which represent words, as A, E, I and O, in Latin; A and I, in English; E and O, in Italian; U, in Low Dutch; Y, in Spanish and French, &c. These are at the same time elementary, syllabic, and lexigraphic. In the ancient Egyptian system of writing, there are lexigraphic characters; but see what I have said on that subject, post, p. 129.

6. That it may be applied to a monosyllabic language, formed on the model of the Chinese; but that it will necessarily receive modifications and alterations, which will produce material differences in the value and significations of the characters between different languages, however similar in their original structure; and therefore,

7. That nations, whose languages like the Japanese, and, as is said, the Loo-chooan, are polysyllabic, and have inflections and grammatical forms, although they may employ Chinese characters in their alphabet, cannot possibly understand Chinese books and manuscripts, unless they have learned the Chinese language; and that if those nations whose languages are monosyllabic, and who use the Chinese characters *lexigraphically*, can understand Chinese writings without knowing the language, it can only be to a limited extent, which it is one of the objects of this publication to ascertain.

Although strongly impressed with the conviction of the truth of these propositions, it is nevertheless with great deference that I submit them to the judgment of the learned.

P. S. D.

Philadelphia, 12th February, 1838.

LETTER

FROM

PETER S. DU PONCEAU

TO

JOHN VAUGHAN, Esq.,

ON

THE NATURE AND CHARACTER

OF THE

CHINESE SYSTEM OF WRITING.

Read before the American Philosophical Society 2d of December, 1836, and referred by them for publication to their Historical and Literary Committee.

1

No. I.

Letter from Peter S. Du Ponceau to John Vaughan, Esq., on the Nature and Character of the Chinese System of Writing.

My dear Sir,

I beg leave to present through you to the American Philosophical Society two manuscript vocabularies of the Cochinchinese language, which, if published under their auspices, will in some measure contribute to the advancement of comparative philology. The languages of Tonquin and Cochinchina, and in general of the ultra-Gangetic idioms, are very little known in Europe,* and even in British India, and we know still less of them in this country. The Tonquinese and Cochinchinese are sister languages to

---

* I find in the *Journal des Savans* for March last, that a grammatical sketch of the Burman language has been lately published in French at Hesse Darmstadt, by Mr. A. A. E. Schleiermacher, privy counsellor to the grand duke of that principality. It is introduced as an appendix to a dissertation on a philological problem proposed in 1824 and 1825 by the Volney Commission of the French Institute, and which received a premium, which, by the analysis that M. Silvestre de Sacy has given of it in the journal above mentioned, it appears to have justly deserved. The author, who does not profess to be a grammarian or a linguist, has shown himself entitled to the praise of both—and moreover, to that of a clear, logical, and profound reasoner. I do not find that that interesting work has yet made its way into this country.

the Chinese, which they not only resemble in the derivation
of their words, but in their monosyllabic character and
grammatical structure; and their graphic system is evidently
borrowed from that of China. A comparison of those languages, therefore, as spoken and as written, is a subject of
considerable interest. One of these vocabularies has the
written characters prefixed to the words; and both, I hope,
will be favourably received by the learned world.

A fortunate circumstance brought these manuscripts into
this country. In the year 1819, two vessels sailed from the
port of Salem, in Massachusetts, on a commercial voyage
to the China Seas, and touched at Cochinchina. They
were, it is said, the first American ships that ascended the
Don-nai river, and displayed the stars and stripes before the
city of Saigon. On board one of those vessels was Lieut.
White, of the United States' navy. During his stay in that
capital, he became acquainted with Father Joseph Morrone,
an Italian missionary, who made him a present of the above
mentioned vocabularies, the one Cochinchinese and French,
consisting of 333 words, with the appropriate characters
prefixed to each; the other more voluminous, Cochinchinese
and Latin, in the alphabetic form of a dictionary, but without the characters. The first, in two columns, (the second
column being a comparison of the Cochinchinese with the
Chinese, by a French sinologist,) is here presented in an
English dress; the other in the original state. I believe no
similar work has yet been published in Asia or Europe.

I have never been able to bring my mind to concur in
the opinion so generally entertained, that the characters
which the Chinese employ in their writing, and of which
the Cochinchinese and other nations also make use, are
what is called *ideographic*, that is to say, that they present
to the mind ideas unconnected with vocal sounds, so as to
make what is called an ocular language, of which words
are only the *pronunciation;* and consequently, (for the con-

sequence appears to me necessarily to follow,) that it is a system of *pasigraphy*, to be read alike in all languages, which absurd consequence appears now to be abandoned by philologists. But the fact of the Chinese characters being read and understood by the Cochinchinese, Japanese, and other nations, speaking different languages and ignorant of that of China, is to this moment asserted by missionaries, travellers, and even learned philologists in Asia and Europe, so that logic is forced to yield to the weight of authority. The manuscripts accompanying this letter will, I hope, go a great way towards deciding this question, which I think has not been sufficiently investigated. As introductory to them, I wish to submit to the Society the views which I entertain of the nature, genius, and character of that Chinese system of writing to which such wonderful effects are attributed, and I beg you will follow me in that discussion, which I shall endeavour, though not an easy task, to make as brief as possible.

I do not pretend to be a sinologist in the legitimate sense of the word. It never was my intention to penetrate into the depths of Chinese literature, to read and understand the works of Confucius and Meng-Tseu. I never attempted to commit to memory, to any considerable extent, either the characters or the words of the Chinese language. The study I have made of it has been directed to a single object, which was, to become acquainted with the grammatical structure of that idiom, and the principles of its graphic system. It is not, therefore, without the greatest diffidence, that I venture to advance my opinion upon it. But the science of general and comparative philology is so extensive, as it embraces all human languages, that those who apply themselves to it cannot be expected to possess, I do not say all, but any considerable number of the idioms of which it treats; otherwise, there would be an end of the science.

This is my apology, and the only one that I have to offer: I hope it will be received with indulgence.

Perhaps it is fortunate for me that I have not learned the Chinese language, and have not read in the original tongue the encomiums of the Chinese writers upon it. I might have imbibed that enthusiasm, "so difficult," says M. Remusat, "to moderate when one begins that study."[*] I feel no such enthusiasm; nor have I, on the other hand, any prejudice against the Chinese[†] or their idiom: my judgment is free to act without bias on either side. Without further preface, therefore, I shall enter at once upon my subject, dividing it into short sections for the sake of method and clearness, and in order to give you intervals to breathe; for although it is my intention to make this letter as short as possible, I fear I may be drawn by my subject to a greater length than I contemplate. I shall, however, do all in my power to be brief, even at the risk of deserving the reproach of being obscure, which I shall, nevertheless, also endeavour to avoid, steering as well as I can between the two rocks which I too clearly perceive standing in my way. But I must proceed.

[*] Un premier enthousiasme, difficile à modérer quand on commence l'étude du Chinois. *Essai sur la langue et la littér. Chinoise*, p. 10.

[†] Unless my opinion of their national suavity (in which, perhaps, they are not singular) should be construed into prejudice.

SECTION I.

When in the last century the Chinese language, through the writings of the Catholic missionaries, became known to the learned of Europe, great astonishment was excited by its simple, ungrammatical structure, by its complicated graphic system, and by the small number of its monosyllables, compared with the immense quantity of the characters employed in writing.* Every new and extraordinary object must, with the mass of mankind, be a *monster* or a *miracle;* the latter was preferred.† Admiration succeeded surprise, and then imagination did its work. The Chinese writing was called *hieroglyphic, ideographic,* and said to represent ideas entirely independent of speech. It was almost exclusively considered as *the* language, and the spoken words were called its *pronunciation,* as if they were only a secondary mode of communicating ideas, and dependent upon the ocular method. At last, it was said that the Chinese characters were read and understood as in China, by nations entirely ignorant of the spoken idiom. In short those visible signs were held up by enthusiasts as a model for an universal language which should reach the mind through the eyes, without the aid of articulate sounds.

These enthusiastic opinions were introduced into Europe by the Catholic missionaries, about the middle of the last century. Those venerable men imbibed them from the

---

* M. Remusat (Gram. Chin. 33) states the number of syllables of the Chinese language to be 450, which, by the variation of tones or accents, may be increased to 1203. The number of written characters (Ibid. 22) he computes to be 33,000. They have been said to amount to 80,000. Dr. Marshman gives 31,214 as the number of those that are to be found in the Imperial Dictionary, (Gram. p. 31.) He does not much differ from M. Remusat.

† Maluit esse Deum. Hor.

Chinese literati, whose national vanity is without bounds. They were received as sacred oracles, and spread rapidly among the learned, who, like other men, are apt to be smitten with the wonderful.* Even in this enlightened age these opinions are yet supported, to a greater or lesser extent, by men whose judgment in other matters is entitled to the respect of all.

I might here quote numberless passages from the writings of the missionaries, to show the wild ideas which they entertained of the Chinese writing, but I wish not to exceed reasonable bounds. One example, I think, will be sufficient. *Ab uno disce omnes.*

A French missionary, Father Cibot, thus wrote from Pekin, under the assumed name of Father Ko, a Chinese Jesuit, in an Essay on the Antiquity of the Chinese Nation, which is published in the first volume of the Mémoires concernant les Chinois: "The Chinese characters," says he, "are composed of symbols and images, unconnected with any sound, and which may be read in all languages. They form a kind of intellectual, algebraical, metaphysical and ideal painting, which expresses thoughts, and represents them by analogy, by relation, by convention," &c.†

These opinions were adopted without discussion by the learned, not only in France, but in all Europe. M. Fréret, a distinguished member of the Academy of Inscriptions and Belles Lettres, thus expresses himself on the subject: "The

* Il y a un certain éclat dans les idées extraordinaires, qui les rend propres à séduire quelquefois les esprits les plus judicieux. Remusat, Recherches sur les langues Tartares, p. 29.

† Ils (les caractères Chinois) sont composés de symboles et d'images, et ces symboles et images ne tenant à aucun son, peuvent être lus dans toutes les langues, et forment une sorte de peinture intellectuelle, d'algèbre métaphysique et idéale, qui rend les pensées, et les représente par analogie, par relation, par convention, &c. Mém. conc. les Chin. vol. i. p. 22.

Chinese characters are immediate signs of the ideas which they express. One would think that that system of writing was invented by mutes, ignorant of the use of speech. We may compare the characters of which it is composed to the algebraic signs which express relations in our mathematical books. Let a geometrical demonstration, expressed in algebraic characters, be presented to ten mathematicians of different countries, they will all understand it alike, and yet they will not understand the words by which those ideas are expressed in speech. The same thing takes place in China; the writing is not only common to all the inhabitants of that great country, who speak dialects different from each other, but also to the Japanese, the Tonquinese, and the Cochinchinese, whose languages are entirely distinct from the Chinese.*

These wonderful descriptions of another hieroglyphical system of writing, naturally led the minds of the learned to that of the ancient Egyptians, which was then and is still considered as *ideographic*, in the same sense with the Chinese. Father Kircher was no more, and Young and Champollion had not yet appeared. Mr. Needham, an English-

---

* Les caractères Chinois sont signes immédiats des idées qu'ils expriment. On dirait que cette écriture aurait été inventée par des muets qui ignorent l'usage des paroles. Nous pouvons comparer les caractères qui la composent avec nos chiffres numéraux, avec les signes algébriques qui expriment les rapports dans nos livres de mathématiques, &c. Que l'on présente une démonstration de géometrie exprimée en caractères algébriques aux yeux de dix mathématiciens de pays différents; ils entendront la même chose: néanmoins ces dix hommes sont supposés parler des langues différentes, et ils ne comprendront rien aux termes par lesquels ils exprimeront ces idées en parlant. C'est la même chose à la Chine; l'écriture est non seulement commune à tous les peuples de ce grand pays, qui parlent des dialectes très différents, mais encore aux Japonais, aux Tonquinois, et aux Cochinchinois, dont les langues sont totalement distinguées du Chinois.—*Réflexions sur les principes généraux de l'art d'écrire, &c.*, par M. Fréret, in the Memoirs of the Academy of Inscriptions and Belles Lettres, vol. vi. p. 609.

2

man, being at Turin, saw in the museum of that capital
some Egyptian characters, which he conceived to have a
resemblance to those of China. He communicated his discovery to the Royal Society of London, of which he was a
member; and they thought it sufficiently important to take
upon it the opinion of the Catholic missionaries in China.
The Egyptian and Chinese symbols were sent to them, and,
after due examination, they sent their answers through Father Amiot, which is also recorded in the first volume of the
Mémoires concernant les Chinois. It was decided that there
was no affinity between the Chinese and the Egyptian cha-
.racters, and no reason to infer from them that the two nations were connected together. As far as relates to the
question submitted, the arguments of Father Amiot are extremely judicious, and he appears to have been a man of
sound sense, when certain superstitious notions did not lead
him astray.* On the subject of the Chinese writing, however, he adopted the opinion of his brother missionaries.
" I define," says he, " the Chinese characters, such as I conceive them in their origin, to be images and symbols, unconnected with any sound, *and which may be read in all languages.*"†

It is now well understood that there is no connexion between
the Chinese writing and the Egyptian hieroglyphics, but the
doctrine advanced by the Catholic missionaries in the eigh-
teenth century is still maintained in the nineteenth, by some

* The French missionaries at that time thought they saw in the Chinese
characters typical signs, connected with the mysteries of the Christian religion, and some of them were prophetic, announcing the future coming
of the Messiah. De Guignes saw in them Phenician Letters, borrowed from
the Egyptian hieroglyphs. Remusat, in Mémoires de l'Acad. des Inscrip.
vol. viii. new series, p. 11.

† Je définis les caractères Chinois, tels que je les conçois dans leur origine, des images et des symboles, qui ne sont liés à aucun son, et peuvent
être lus dans toutes les langues. Mém. conc. les Chin. vol. i. p. 282.—
The words *dans leur origine*, qualify this opinion in some degree.

of the most eminent philologists of Europe, and has given rise to opinions of such a strange character, as can hardly be believed to have been entertained by learned and judicious men in this enlightened age. Permit me to give you some examples in proof of this bold assertion, and to show how far the imagination of men, gifted with the most acute and discriminating minds, can mislead them, when once they have adopted an opinion on the authority of others, and without sufficient examination.

If the Chinese characters are an original language, unconnected with sound, and conveying ideas to the mind through the eyes, without the intervention of any other medium, the first question that arises is how, by whom, and by what process was it invented? "We can hardly imagine," says Dr. Marshman, "that while most of the languages, formed on the alphabetic plan, bear evident marks of being formed rather by accident than design, a number of Chinese sages should have sat *in deep divan*, in order to select certain objects as the basis of the imitative system; yet we shall find that these elements include most of the objects of sense, which are remarkably obvious, few being omitted which from their form or frequent use might be likely to attract notice," &c. The Doctor proceeds to point out the difficulties that must have attended the formation of the 214 radicals of the Chinese alphabet, but comes to no conclusion on the question that he has raised.[*]

But M. Remusat, one of the most learned sinologists of Europe,—one whose loss is regretted by all who could appreciate his talents and his virtues, and by none more than myself, whom he honoured with his esteem,—that great man, while he admits the force of the negative proposition of Dr. Marshman, undertakes to decide the question in such a manner as must excite astonishment in every reflecting

* Clavis Sinica, p. 18.

mind. Unable to account, on rational principles, for the origin of a system of writing unconnected with sounds, he falls upon the notion that that system was invented before an oral language was adapted to it, which is not very far from the general proposition that writing preceded language, and that men wrote before they spoke. But let us hear him. "Some writers," says he, "among whom Fourmont holds the ·first rank, have considered the Chinese *language* (he means the *writing*) as being the invention of some philosophers, who afterwards communicated the use of it to their nation; and considering the characters as anterior to the words, and consequently writing as existing before speech, they have made of the words of the spoken language the expression of the characters or their *name*, if I dare thus to speak: in this those authors appear to me to have inverted the natural order. Indeed, if things had so happened, it would not be astonishing that the whole language should be composed of monosyllables, since every part of it would have been formed by men of learning according to the principles which they thought the fittest. But who will believe that any language was formed in that manner, or that a language thus formed should have been adopted by the people?"*

M. Remusat here speaks like a philosopher, and his reasoning is conclusive on all points. But who will believe that this eminent and justly celebrated sinologist, after thus demolishing the system of M. Fourmont and others, contradicts in the same breath all he has said, by the conclusion which he draws, which is quite as fanciful as that of the writers whom he censures? "Is it not," says he, "much more likely to suppose that there was among the Chinese, prior to the invention of the characters, a popular language composed of words, if not all monosyllabic, at least very short,

* Mélanges Asiat. tom. ii. p. 52.

as they are found among many barbarous nations? This language will have been *adopted* by the inventors of the writing, to serve as a *pronunciation* to the characters, and that the learned might communicate with the common people. One is inclined to believe that things must have so happened, when one considers," &c.* Here M. Remusat attempts to support his conjecture by arguments derived from the peculiar structure of the Chinese language, which it is unnecessary to repeat.†

Do not believe, my dear sir, that I mean here to detract from the well earned reputation of our much regretted associate, Abel Remusat, whom I justly consider as one of the first philologists of his age, and one whose labours have greatly contributed to the advancement of science. In this case he only partook of a general error, spread all over

* N'est il pas beaucoup plus vraisemblable de supposer qu'il y avoit chez les Chinois, avant l'invention des caractères, une langue populaire, composée de mots, si non tous monosyllabiques, au moins très courts, comme on les trouve chez beaucoup de nations barbares? Cette langue aura été adoptée par les inventeurs de l'écriture pour servir de prononciation aux caractères, et pour que les gens instruits pussent s'entendre avec le vulgaire. On est porté à croire que les choses ont du se passer ainsi, quand on considère, &c. *Mélanges Asiatiques,* vol. ii. p. 52.

† A similar opinion was entertained by the once celebrated orientalist Golius, who flourished about the middle of the seventeenth century. "Il croyait," says Leibnitz, "que la langue des Chinois est artificielle, c'est à dire qu'elle a été inventée toute à la fois par quelque habile homme pour établir un commerce de paroles entre quantité de nations différentes qui habitaient ce grant pays: que nous appellens la Chine." *Nouveaux Essais sur l'entendement humain,* L. iii. c. 1, § 1, in Raspe's edition, p. 232.

Thus the wildest opinions are reproduced from age to age, and will probably continue to be so until the end of the world. The great Leibnitz gravely proposed an universal philosophical language, founded on the principles of mathematical science, by which all truths could be demonstrated, and all errors detected. Almost all the errors of mankind may be traced to celebrated philosophers; such is the weakness of our nature, and it shows how little respect is due to authority, in matters that depend on reason and common sense.

Europe at the time when he wrote, and supported by such
respectable authority that it would have appeared presump-
tuous at that time to controvert it. You can easily see by
the passage which I have quoted, that his mind was not entirely free from doubt and hesitation, since he advances propositions in evident contradiction to each other. I shall
show, in its place, that at a subsequent period he was among
the first who successfully combated the opinion that the
Chinese writing was read and understood by nations who
were ignorant of the spoken language. As to its ideographic
character he appears not to have varied; but this notion
was not peculiar to him or to his country; it was entertained, as I have said, by the learned of all Europe. The
celebrated Adelung thus speaks in the Mithridates of the
graphic system of the Chinese: " It differs from all others in
this; that it neither consists of natural or symbolic hieroglyphics, nor of an alphabet of syllables or letters, but represents
whole ideas, each idea being expressed by its own appropriate sign, without being connected with speech. It speaks
to the eyes as the arithmetical figures of Europe, which
every one understands, and pronounces after his own manner. Thus it may be learned, without knowing a word of
the language."* Mr. Adelung, however, does not go so far as
to say, that the Chinese characters were invented before a
language or pronunciation was applied to them; but we find
that idea entertained by men of learning not only in France,
but also in England.

* Sie (die Sinesische Schrift) unterscheidet sich von den übrigen
Schriftarten dadurch, dass sie weder natürliche noch symbolische Hiero-
glyphik, noch Sylben noch Buchstaben Schrift ist, sondern ganze ausgebil-
dete Begriffe, und zwar jeden Begriff durch sein eigenes Zeichen aus-
druckt, ohne mit der Sprache in Verbindung zu stehen. · Sie spricht zu
dem Auge, wie die Europäischen Zahlzeichen, welche jeder verstehet,
und auf seine Art ausspricht. Man kann daher Sinesisch lesen lernen,
ohne ein Wort von der Sprache zu verstehen. Mithrid. vol. i. p. 46.

An anonymous writer in the London Quarterly Review, who, I am told, is believed to have been a celebrated philologist whose name I do not feel at liberty to mention, goes even farther that M. Remusat, who only supposed that after the invention of the characters, an *existing language* was sought to be applied to them as a pronunciation; but the writer I speak of presumes that a language was made, and words invented, for that purpose. He instances the two words *sun* and *moon*, which, joined together in a group, signify *splendour* or *brilliancy.* "It was necessary," says he, "*to give a name to this new compound,*"* and he proceeds at great length to show by what combinations of sounds and ideas the Chinese succeeded in finding a *word* to serve as a *pronunciation* for the sign. From these strange theories it would seem that words were made to represent signs, and not signs to represent words. This shows how difficult it is, even for learned and intelligent men, to get over ancient and deeply rooted prejudices.

Such were the ideas generally entertained by learned sinologists, respecting the graphic system of the Chinese, so late as the beginning of the present century; and although the principles of that method of writing are now better understood than they were at that time, the science is nevertheless still overshadowed with much prejudice, and many vague, unsettled notions, because those principles have not been philosophically investigated and clearly traced to their origin. A recent writer on China, the Rev. Mr. Gutzlaff, a protestant missionary, who has resided in that country, and is well acquainted with its language, expresses himself in these words: "Nothing," says he, and he speaks the truth, " has so much puzzled the learned world in Europe, as the Chinese language. To express so many ideas as arise in the mind by 1445 intonated monosyllables—to substitute a

* Quarterly Review, vol. v. (May, 1811) p. 390.

distinct character for a simple alphabet, was undoubtedly a gigantic effort of human genius. But the Chinese have effected what we might have deemed impossible."* Here this author only shows his admiration of the Chinese system of writing, in comparison to which he considers the oral language to be imperfect, and tells the old story of the Chinese having recourse to writing when they cannot express themselves by words. But afterwards, in a communication to the Royal Asiatic Society of Great Britain and Ireland on the language of Cochinchina, so late as the year 1831, he goes much farther, and asserts the pretended pasigraphic character of the Chinese writing. " It is generally known," says he, " that neither sound nor tone is inherent in the Chinese characters, but that they are read in different ways, whilst the significance of the character remains the same in all the countries where the Chinese way of writing is adopted."†

This appears to me to be going as far as any Catholic missionary ever did, and is sufficient to show that the true principles on which rests the graphic system of the Chinese are yet far from being clearly and correctly understood.

When such opinions are advanced by men of real learning, and who are practically as well as theoretically acquainted with the Chinese language, it is not astonishing that it should be still maintained that Chinese books and other writings are understood by nations who speak different idioms, and are unacquainted with that of China. Even at this day, this is asserted as a fact by men of respectability, and who speak of their own knowledge, as I shall show in its proper place before I conclude this letter. This arises from the false notion that the Chinese characters are unconnected with words. And to bring this matter still nearer to

---

* History of China, ch. iii.

† Trans. R. A. S. of Great Britain and Ireland, vol. iii. p. 296.

the present time, and to show how vague and unsettled are
the opinions *now* entertained on this subject, I need only refer to an article, which has at this moment caught my eye,
in the Edinburgh Review for the month of October last, and
in which I find the Chinese system of writing thus described:
" The Chinese have for ages employed a multitude of *ideagraphic* (*sic*) characters, derived by composition and otherwise from a limited number of elementary pictures or repre-
sentations of external objects called keys, without making
the least step towards an alphabet." And further: " The
Egyptians seem likewise to have remained contented with
their hieroglyphic system, or at least not to have advanced
a step beyond it." Here the writer speaks of *ideographic*
and *hieroglyphic* characters as opposed to *alphabets,* by
which last word he clearly understands those signs which
represent the *primary* elements of sounds, and which we
call consonants and vowels. He seems to forget that other
sounds may be represented by characters or letters, however these may be shaped, whether in the forms of living
objects or otherwise, and his distinction appears founded on
the *ideagraphic* character, (as he calls it,) of the Chinese and
Egyptian signs and our *elementary* system, which alone he
seems to consider as *phonetic;* yet in another place, when
commenting on Bishop Warburton's opinion that the hieroglyphs of Egypt constituted a real written language, applicable to all kinds of civil as well as of religious matters, he
very justly observes that such a system of writing must have
been in connexion with the spoken language,* which is what
I mean to prove to you and to the Society, and to show, as
far as is in my power, how this connexion is formed, particularly in the Chinese, and that the word *ideographic* is
improperly applied to that system of writing. The writer
of this article does not appear to entertain perfectly clear

* Edinb. Rev. Oct. 1836. Art. iv.

3

ideas upon this subject, which, as I have said before, has not
yet been sufficiently investigated.

To explain and fully to develop the views which I entertain upon what is called *ideographic* writing would require
a large work, a task which I have neither the time nor the
inclination to undertake. But, as connected with the main
object of this letter, which is to bring before the learned
world the question how far the Chinese written character
can be understood by nations speaking a different idiom, I
hope, my dear sir, you will permit me to state as briefly as
I can the opinions that I have formed of the Chinese language and, its graphic system, and to explain the reasons
which make me differ from those who consider the latter as
a distinct language, which they call *ideographic*, and assert
it to be unconnected with sounds and independent of speech.
I hope, on the contrary, to be able to show that the Chinese
characters are the representation of the *words* of the oral
language, which, like the groups formed by letters of our
alphabets, they recall to the mind of the reader, and ideas
only through them; the only difference lies in the method
pursued, but the object and the effect are precisely the
same.

SECTION II.

The Chinese language, with a few exceptions that do not
at all bear upon my argument, is essentially monosyllabic.
I do not mean that by the junction of its component monosyllables, polysyllabic words cannot be formed; but I think I
may safely say, that, with few exceptions, every syllable is
significant, and constitutes what we call a *word*. These syllables may be united in speech, as in *welcome, welfare, house-
hold,* or in the French word *bienfait;* or they may be sepa-

rated, as in *well done, well made, bad work,* or in the French phrase, *C'est bien fait.* The difference does not appear in the rapidity of speech, we are only aware of it by the typographical arrangement of the syllables. It is therefore of no consequence whether the Chinese language, as spoken, be called monosyllabic or polysyllabic, but it is important to know that every one of its syllables is a *word,* and as each character represents a syllable, which is called its *pronunciation,* it necessarily follows that each character represents a *word.*

It is not true, therefore, that the Chinese characters are unconnected with sounds, unless it should be contended that a syllable is not a *sound.* But the syllabic alphabets of Japan and of Citra-Gangetic India have never been considered otherwise than as the representation of sounds, and it has never been pretended that they are not *phonetic.* A syllable, indeed, may by analysis be reduced to more simple elements; but though composed of those elements, it is still a reverberation of the human voice, produced at once and in the same breath by the organs of speech. If, then, syllables are *sounds,* monosyllabic words are so likewise; and the characters which represent them cannot be said not to be connected with them *as such.*

There is no character in the Chinese alphabet (if I may be permitted so to call it) that does not represent a syllable, and consequently a *word;* nor is there a word in the language without a character to represent it. For this we have the authority of M. Remusat, and a better one could not be desired. " The written and spoken language," says that celebrated author, " are distinct and separate, yet every word of the one answers to the sign of the other which represents the same idea, and reciprocally."* And

* La langue parlée et la langue écrite sont distinctes et séparées: toutes fois chaque mot de l'une répond au signe de l'autre qui représente la même idée et réciproquement. Gram. Chin. p. 1.

elsewhere: "Each character answers in the oral language to a word that has the same signification; the character awakens in the mind of him who sees it the same idea as the word, if it should be heard."[*]

Here let us pause for a moment. Each character represents a word, and each word has a character to represent it. This cannot be denied; all the sinologists agree to it. How comes it, then, that there should be eighty, forty, or thirty thousand written characters, and less than two thousand words, including all the differences of tones and accents? This is a curious question, though not of much consequence to my argument. No sinologist has yet said that there are characters without meaning, except those, the signification of which has been lost by the lapse of time; none has said that there are characters which are not the expression, or, to speak more properly, the representation of some word in the language. The characters, therefore, which exceed in number the words of the idiom must necessarily be superabundant, and it is not difficult to account for their existence; we need only look at home. The Portuguese orthography was once exclusively used to represent the sounds of the Chinese words by means of the letters of our alphabet, and it was adopted and understood by all, until national vanity and individual caprice interfered. Not only every nation, but every sinologist has his own mode of spelling Chinese words. The English, the French, and the Germans, have each adopted a mode of spelling suited to their own language. But the evil does not stop here; every writer has a spelling of his own; Morrison does not spell like Marshman, nor Remusat like De Guignes. Where will this confusion end? For my part, I adopt in this disquisition the spelling of the writer that first comes to

* Chaque charactère Chinois répond, dans la langue orale, à un mot qui a la même signification; le caractère éveille dans l'esprit de celui qui le voit, la même idée que le mot, si l'on vient à l'entendre. Ibid. p. 23.

hand. I shall certainly not try to reconcile them, or show a preference to one over the other. I only wish that the old fashioned Portugueso mode of spelling had been preserved; or that the alphabet of my learned friend Mr. Pickering was as generally adopted by the learned of Europe and America, as it is by our missionaries in the South Sea Islands and elsewhere.

This example is sufficient to show why there are so many synonymous characters in the graphic system of the Chinese. They are only different manners of spelling the same words, every writer having thought his method superior to that of the others. I shall explain hereafter in what that method consists, and you will easily understand how it came to be applied in different ways to the formation of a variety of characters intended to represent the same words.

After all, a great many of those characters are out of use, and the number of those which are commonly employed is comparatively small. It is only among the learned that a variety of characters is employed.

But the difference, in point of numbers, between the written and spoken words of the Chinese language, is not so great as is generally imagined. In the first place, there are a great number of homophonous words, which being pronounced alike are, as I presume, in calculating the numbers of those significant syllables considered as one and the same *pronunciation* of different characters, and not so many different words in relation to their sense. It is the same as if, in our language, we should consider as one the words *fain, fane,* and *feign,* because pronounced alike, although they differ in meaning widely from each other. There is another mode of computation which is directly the reverse of this. Because the monosyllables of the Chinese language are significant, they alone have been honoured with the name of *words,* and their numerous compounds have been left out of view. I have said above, that those monosyllables might be compounded, precisely as those of our own language in *welcome, welfare*, &c.; and I may add here, that the greatest part of the Chinese idiom is formed of those compounds, which are separated only by the manner in which they are exhibited to the eye when written. Thus, in our dictionaries, *shoemaker* is found as a polysyllabic word, while *pear tree* is not, but each of its component syllables must be looked for in its proper place, according to the alphabet. And yet it would seem that *peartree* is as much a word in English as *shoemaker, shipwright*, and so many others. There are English words which in Chinese are expressed by five significant monosyllables, such for instance as the word *puberty*, which is called *fa-shin-tsih-she-how.* I am not sufficiently versed in the Chinese language to explain the meaning of each of these five monosyllables; I leave the task to sinologists. But it is evident, that nothing is wanting but to give to the Chinese compounds the denomination of *words*, to make that language as rich, perhaps, as those whose composition is disguised by the foreign origin of the monosyllables, or the more artificial manner in which they are joined together.

Dr. Morrison has rendered a great service to philology by his alphabetical dictionaries of the Chinese (spoken) language, the one Chinese and English, and the other English and Chinese. He would have rendered a still greater, if he had explained the meaning of each of the characters that are grouped together to represent a word compounded of several others, as those which are employed to express the English word *puberty*, which I have mentioned above. But the learned Doctor wrote for merchants and missionaries, and not for philologists; and his works were intended for practical use, and not to aid philological disquisitions, to which nevertheless they are of great advantage, and for

---

* Morrison's English and Chinese Dictionary, verbo *puberty*.

which the author is justly entitled to our thanks. But let us return to our subject.

It is, as I have just shown, a fact not to be denied, that each Chinese character has a word to represent it, and *vice versâ*. Here is, therefore, a close connexion between the writing and the language, and they cannot be said to be independent of each other. I must now prove that the writing was made for the language, and for no other purpose than to recall its words to the memory of the reader. To be convinced of this, it is sufficient to observe that the characters follow servilely the spoken words, and the ideas which these express, in the order in which they are explained. Thus a *glove*, which in our language expresses a compound idea in one word, is called in Chinese *show-taou*, hand covering,* and there is a character for each of these words. If, as in German, the language had said *hand-shoe*, the writing would have the character which stands for *shoe* instead of that which represents the word *covering*. In the same manner a sailor is called *ship-hand;* a library, *book-house;* a monk, *reason-house* (the house of reason); a physician, *medicine-house.* The abstract idea of a *thing* is quaintly expressed by the words *east-west;* and that of a *brother* indefinitely by two monosyllables, one of which signifies *elder brother*, and the other *younger brother.* In representing all these compounds, and a multitude of others, of which the language is full, the writing does not attempt (if I may use the expression) to *think* for itself, and to represent ideas after a manner of its own, but follows the spoken language step by step, word for word, and echoes it through the eye to the mental ear. Perhaps it will be said, that it is not the writing that follows the language through its various combinations of ideas, but on the contrary that it is the language which is the echo of the characters; but that would lead us to the

* Morrison's English and Chinese Dictionary, verbo *glove.*

absurd conclusion of the pre-existence of the latter, which I think I have already sufficiently exposed.

The learned authors of the historical and descriptive account of China, which is a part of the collection called "The Edinburgh Cabinet Library," are therefore under a mistake, when they say that "the idea of making the written subservient to the spoken language, seems never once to have occurred to the mind of a Chinese."* On the contrary, it is clear that the primary, and indeed the sole object of the inventors of the writing, was to give representative signs to the words of the oral idiom, and consequently to make their graphic system subservient to it, as in fact it is and ever will be. That the literati of China should entertain a different opinion, and "consider speech as an altogether secondary and subordinate mode of communication,†" is not at all to be wondered at; their excessive vanity led them into this prejudice, and maintains them in it.

So far, at least, no sign appears of an *ideographic* language, as the Chinese writing has been called. Its object, as far as we have seen, is not to recall ideas to the mind abstracted from sounds, but the sounds or words in which language has clothed those ideas. The written signs do not, indeed, represent sounds in the elementary form of letters, but in the compound form of syllables and words. They have precisely the same effect as our groups of letters, and do not advance a step farther into the ideal world. Then we may say that it is not an idea that each character represents, but a *word;* and if it represents the idea at all it is through the word which it calls to mind; and such is the operation of our alphabetical writing. The five letters which, placed next to each other, form the word *horse,* present to our minds the idea of the animal so called, quite as

---

* Edinb. Cab. Libr. China, vol. ii. p. 20. This book was published in 1836. † Ibid.

well as the horizontal and perpendicular strokes of the Chinese character answering to the same word. That group of letters might also be called *ideographic*, when, in fact, it is but the sign of a spoken word.

Man spoke before he wrote, and languages were fixed before any system of writing was invented. Before the invention of their characters, the Chinese communicated by means of *knotted cords*, like the Quipos of the Peruvians.* They might be yet in a savage state when they invented their writing, but nevertheless they spoke and understood each other. Their ideas, then, had received an external shape, the impression of which was made through the sense of hearing, and therefore they were not driven, like those born deaf and dumb, to give them an original form, derived only from their sensations. Where a solitary language exists, be it ocular or auricular, ideas present themselves to the mind clothed in the forms that that language has given them. The deaf and dumb man, before he has learned to read, thinks in the visible signs by means of which he communicates with his fellows: when, by the art of De l'Epée and his followers, he has learned to understand some written language, he thinks in the groups of letters or characters the meaning of which he knows, and which memory presents to his recollection through the mental eye. Without these helps his ideas would be vague and confused, having nothing on which to fix themselves; and they would be reduced to the feeling of present sensations and the recollections of the past. We, who are possessed of the art of writing, do not think in groups of alphabetical characters, but in combinations of spoken words, because we have learned the words before the figures, and the impression that they have made is more deeply fixed in our minds. Thus it must have been with the Chinese, when they invent-

* Morrison, Chinese Dict. in order of radicals, Introd. p. 1.

4

ed their art of writing; they thought in words, and their ideas had no shapes but those that the words had given them.

That the Chinese alphabet is ingenious, I am by no means prepared to deny; my object is only to show, that it was made to represent the significant syllables which constitute the language and recall them to the mind, and through them the ideas which they were intended to awaken; but that it is not, as enthusiasts have pretended, a language of ideas, abstracted from and unconnected with any sounds or audible signs. I shall show presently how the Chinese came to this ingenious method to *peindre la parole*, as the French poet elegantly expresses it, and by that means to *parler aux yeux*. I shall compare this invention with analogous ones of other nations, and endeavour to point out some advantages which philology may derive from the comparison. But I must at present pursue my argument.

The Chinese characters, ingenious as they are, paint the words, and when read, are read in the words which they represent, and in no others. It is true, that etymologically, or, if you will permit me to coin the word, *etymographically* considered, they may recall not only the compound idea which each word represents, but some of the accessary ideas which enter into its composition; as, for instance, if the characters that form the group which represents the word *clock* or *watch*, should be formed by the junction of the two characters *time* and *piece*, and thus might be read *time-piece*. But in reading, the Chinese, any more than we, do not think of etymology. Whether we say a *time piece* or a *clock*, the idea presented to the mind is the same; and in the first case, we do not think separately of *time* and of *piece*, but of the machine which the words signify. When we say a *square*, we do not always think of a quadrangular figure, but the word represents to us, according to the context of the sentence where it is placed, either an open space of ground, or one of the divisions of our city, or a rectangular instrument employed in certain mechanical operations; and, *vice versâ*, when that instrument is exhibited to us it is the word "square" as applied to it, and not the idea of a *right angle*, that presents itself to our mind. When we say *hand maid*, we think of a female servant, not of the part of the body called the *hand*. When we say *Bridewell*, we neither think of a *bride* nor of a *well*, much less of St. Bridget or St. Bride, after whom the place was denominated; we think only of a house of detention. When we say a *hogshead*, (meaning a cask to contain liquor,) we do not think of the animal called *hog*, nor of any part of his body. When we speak of the *hands* of a ship, we think of the men, not of their hands. It is the same with the Chinese. The word *she* or *chi*, which signifies *time*, is represented in writing by a group of three characters, which severally signify the *sun*, the *earth*, and a *measure*; as who should say, "the sun measuring the earth," or in plainer language, "the revolutions of the sun round the earth;" a very just and ingenious metaphor. But, though these three characters separately represent the several words affixed to each, and through them the ideas which those words contain; when grouped together they only bring to mind the word *she*, and the abstract idea of *time*.*

But it will perhaps be said, that those characters are *paintings*, that they present to the eye directly or metaphorically, the figures of visible objects, and that their impression is stronger upon the mind, than that of spoken words. *Segniùs irritant*, &c. Horace may be quoted here to advantage. But the fact is otherwise. It is true, that in the

---

* However complicated any character may appear, still the compound, though it embrace six or seven characters, like compounds in Greek and Sungskrit, expresses only one idea, and still remains an adjective, a substantive, a verb, &c., as capable of union with other characters, as the simplest character in the language. Marshm. Clavis Sinica, p. 4.

origin of Chinese writing, the painting of natural objects was, to a certain extent, adopted as its medium; thus the sun was represented by a circular figure, the moon by that of a crescent, &c.; but since the adoption of the square characters, those images have vanished, and the Chinese writing exhibits at present to the eye only arbitrary signs, which method has saved from confusion, as will be hereafter explained. A single glance at a Chinese dictionary will convince the reader that the characters, as at present formed, are no representation to the eye of natural objects; as to moral sensations, it is well known that they cannot be painted. The whole system, therefore, consists in representing a *word*, sometimes by a single character, which also serves as an element wherewith to form others, but most frequently by a combination of those signs, recalling two, three, or more words, which together, as the significant syllables in our compounds, bring to mind the word to be represented. The knowledge of these combinations is in China a science, analogous to what in our own language is called *etymology*. The knowledge and the history of these combinations is the principal study of the Chinese philologists. They love to trace the origin of their characters, principally of those that are obsolete and no longer in use; to follow and describe their successive variations and their different forms. They have an immense number of what I would call etymological dictionaries, in the study of which they spend many years. That, and the knowledge of the books of Confucius and other moralists, is the sum of the learning of a Chinese *savant*, and what entitles him to admission to the highest offices in the empire.

Of this learning, as it may be supposed, they are excessively proud; they consider a system of writing, which has cost them so much pains to investigate and trace to its original sources, as the most admirable invention of man; they attribute to it a divine, or what to them is the same, an imperial origin; they consider it as the basis of the language, or rather as the language itself, to which words are only accessary and made for the use of the vulgar; they consider signs which represent only words, as representing ideas, and they believe their writing to be what we call *ideographic*. No doubt they believe it to be so; their long and profound studies have left impressions on their minds, which, with national pride, are the source of those illusions, which nothing can eradicate. To form an idea of them, we need only hear them speak. "The Chinese," say they, "lay the stress on the characters, not on the sounds. The people of *Fan* (their Tartar neighbours who have syllabic alphabets) prefer sounds, and what they obtain enters by the ear; the Chinese prefer beautiful characters, and what they obtain enters by the eye."*

It is no wonder, therefore, that those Europeans who first studied their language, participated in their illusions, and communicated them to others. M. Remusat, in the first flight of his enthusiasm, thus exclaims: "It is impossible," says he, "to express in any language, the energy of those picturesque characters, which present to the eye, instead of barren conventional signs of pronunciation, the objects themselves, figured by all that is essential in them, so that it would require many sentences, to exhaust the signification of a single word."†

I acknowledge I cannot perceive those picturesque beauties, and that I am rather inclined to compare them to those of Father Castel's ocular harpsichord. But it may

* Morris. Dict. Introd. p. vii.

† Il me semble, en effet, impossible de rendre dans aucune langue, l'énergie de ces caractères pittoresques, qui présentent à l'œil, au lieu de signes stériles et conventionnels de prononciation, les objets eux mêmes, exprimés et figurés par tout ce qu'ils ont d'essentiel, tellement qu'il faudrait plusieurs phrases, pour épuiser la signification d'un seul mot. Essai sur la langue et la littér. Chin. p. 11.

be owing to my ignorance of the Chinese language. I am
persuaded that those beauties exist in the minds of Chinese
scholars; such is the force of imagination and of the associations that it brings forth, after the long study and contemplation of a favourite object. I shall, therefore, leave
the sinologists in the enjoyment of it, and content myself
with endeavouring to prove that the Chinese writing is not,
as it is called, *ideographic*, and that it does not represent
ideas, but syllables and words, all of which come within
the general denomination of *sounds*, and therefore, that it
belongs to that class of graphic systems, to which philologists have given the name of *phonetic*, though the sounds
which its characters represent are not, with very few exceptions, the *primary* elements of which our alphabets are
composed.*

The ancients called the simple sounds of which human
language is composed, *elementa*, in Greek ςοιχεῖα, and the
letters which represent them they called *literæ* and γράμματα.
Their writers, however, by a kind of metonymy, frequently
employed one of those expressions for the other, and at last
used them indifferently. In our modern languages, we
hardly ever apply the word *sound* to the elements of speech,
we almost always designate them by the word *letters*. Thus
we say that a Delaware Indian cannot pronounce the *letter*
F, meaning the *sound* which that letter represents. This
confusion of language produces a confusion of ideas, and
our word *alphabet*, formed of the names of two elementary
sounds, represented to the eye by the signs A and B, adds
to its effect on the mind. Although we know that there are
systems of writing in India, the characters of which represent *syllables*,† and though we call the series of those cha-

* There are a few Chinese words which consist of one single vowel
sound.

† The Japanese have an alphabet of 47 syllables, which they call *I-ro-
fa*, from the names of the three first letters, which, as our A, B, C, are

racters a syllabic *alphabet*, yet, when we use that word abstractedly, those characters are hardly ever present to our minds, and we only think of alphabets of elementary sounds, like our own, much less do we think of any sounds consisting of more than one syllable. Hence it follows, that when in the Chinese characters or Egyptian hieroglyphics, we look for the signs that we call *phonetic*, we are disappointed unless we find such as represent the most simple elements of speech.

I say the *most simple*, because I do not believe that what may be properly called the *elements* of language, consists only of the sounds separately represented by the signs which we call *letters*. The word *element* is relative, and is susceptible of various significations. In one sense, it means all the parts of which a thing is composed, which parts may be resolved into more minute elements, until analysis can go no farther. Then not only what we call *letters*, but syllables, words and even sentences, are to be included among the elements of speech; and the most minute are called the *first* elements, *prima elementa*, which name has been applied to letters by ancient writers.* *Les premiers élémens* is a familiar expression in the French language, which may be applied to any subject.† In our language, the word *elements* is also a generic term. We say *the elements of a science*, not restricting the word to the *first* elements.

In this sense, I have no doubt, Clement of Alexandria used these words in the celebrated passage of the fifth

no others than the sounds of the syllables which they represent. Gram. Japon. du P. Rodrigues. Paris, 1825.

* An Philippus, Macedonum rex, Alexandro, filio suo, *prima* litterarum elementa tradi ab Aristotele voluisset.—Quintil. Inst. Orat. l. 1. c. 1.

    Ut pueris olim dant crustula blandi

    Doctores, elementa velint ut discere *prima*.

                                Hor. l. 1. Sat. 1.

† Dict. de l'Acad.

chapter of his *Stromata*, which has occasioned so much discussion among the learned. In his description of the hieroglyphic characters of the Egyptians, he says there are two among them that he calls *kyriological*, which present objects or ideas to the mind, the one by an imitation or picture of the object, (κατὰ μίμησιν) the other by means of the first elements (διὰ τῶν πρώτων ϛοιχείων) by which, as the words are applied to a system of writing, he must be understood to have meant the *first* or simplest elements of speech, or in other words, the letters of the alphabet. The discoveries of Young and Champollion, have proved beyond the possibility of doubt, that the Egyptian hiero-. glyphs were employed in that manner, and in that case they are called *phonetic*, that is to say representing *sounds*.

The celebrated Hellenist, M. Letronne, consulted by his friend Champollion, as to the precise meaning of the words τὰ πρώτα ϛοιχεῖα, interpreted them exactly as I have done.* Afterwards, however, he doubted the correctness of this interpretation and attempted others, in which, in my opinion, he was not so successful.† Men of eminent talents are too apt to be dissatisfied with themselves, and to find faults in their works, which others cannot perceive, and which do. not exist in reality.

In making these observations, I have not meant to draw your attention to the Egyptian hieroglyphics, of which I shall speak more at large in another part of this letter. My object has been to show how vague are the ideas generally entertained as to what constitutes the *elements* of speech, by which I understand all its constituent parts without exception. Sentences are elements in relation to discourse, words to sentences, syllables to words, and simple sounds or letters-are either syllables or the elements of syllables.

---

* Champol. Précis, 1st Edit. p. 329.
† See the second edition of the same work.

These are the elements of speech; and writing, I believe, may be so contrived as to represent all or any of them.

When, towards the close of the revolutionary war, I held the office of under Secretary in the Department of State, then called the Department for Foreign Affairs, having been successful in deciphering an intercepted letter written in cipher by Gov. Haldimand of Quebec, to Sir Guy Carleton, at New York, I was desired to devise a new cipher for the use of our diplomatic correspondence. I did so, and made the cipher on the principles that I have above explained. It was extremely simple, and yet it abounded in combinations. Every word might be written either entire, by a single sign, or each syllable and each letter might be represented by a modification of that sign. When I say every word, I mean about one thousand, as it would have been impossible to insert all the words in the Dictionary. There were also signs for whole sentences, such as the formula "By the United States in Congress assembled," and others that occurred most frequently in our correspondence. The cipher was adopted; it was found easy in practice, and was long in use; whether it is so at present, I cannot tell.

I hope you will not ascribe to vanity my having mentioned this circumstance of my early life. There is no great merit in inventing a diplomatic cipher. Since the time I am speaking of, the art has been carried to its highest degree of perfection, and it is the fault of cabinets, if their letters are deciphered. But I meant to show by this example, that words and even sentences may be represented by written signs, as well as syllables and elementary sounds, and that they are all elements of that admirable gift, whether mediate or immediate, of the divinity called *language*, by which man is distinguished from the brute creation. When, therefore, we are considering a graphic system, the principles of which are unknown to us,

5

we should take into view all those elements and try to find out which of them the signs are intended to represent or recall to the mind. The pictures of objects, and graphic symbols and metaphors, can serve but a very limited purpose, unless connected with speech; and if they represent ideas, it can only be in the forms in which language, spoken language, has clothed them.

It is for not attending to this comprehensive meaning of the word *sound*, as applied to language, and confining it exclusively to its primary elements, or at most to insignificant syllables, that sinologists have been led to conclude that the Chinese writing is an ocular language, independent of speech, representing ideas, *and addressed wholly to the eye.* Dr. Marshman, in his otherwise excellent Grammar of the Chinese language, advances this proposition in the broadest terms. "The sound of no character," says he, "is inherent therein: it may be totally changed without affecting the meaning of the character. Thus to the character *yin*, a man, might be affixed *tao* or *lee*, or any other name, and the character would still convey the same idea, *because the written language speaks wholly to the eye.*" And in proof of his assertion, he adds: "Some characters have *two* names widely different from each other."[*]

But the Chinese characters representing words, do not speak more exclusively to the eye, than our letters or groups of letters representing elementary sounds. They both are addressed through the eye to the mental ear. And if some of them represent more than one word or one sound, it is an anomaly from which no general principle is to be deduced. There are anomalies in grammar, in pronunciation, in orthography, in every existing language, whatever may be the nature of its graphic system. In our own idiom, letters and groups of letters often represent dif-

* Clavis Sinica, p. 81.

ferent sounds. The group *ough* is pronounced differently in the words *ought, bough, dough, through* and *enough*, the sound of the letter *a* is different in *grace*, in *bad*, and in *all;* and of course the same thing may happen with the Chinese characters. And if this fact proves any thing, it is rather in opposition to Dr. Marshman's principle, than in favour of it; for it proves that the characters thus varying their pronunciation may represent different words, precisely as our letters represent different elementary sounds.

If the Chinese writing were, as it is called, *ideographic,* or, as it is asserted to be, a complete ocular language, independent of the oral mode of communication and unconnected with it, it would have its poetry and its prose, and a style peculiar to itself. It would be translated, not read. But how does the fact stand? The poetry of the Chinese is addressed to the ear. It is measured, and has even recourse for its harmony to the jingle of rhyme.* How could a poem be read if every character did not represent a single word, and if those characters and the words which they are intended to express were not placed in the same order of succession? And as to prose. There are some who believe that there are beauties in the selection and in the arrangement of the characters in the formation of a period. As to the selection; if the character from among which one is selected represent or recall the same word, which they must necessarily do, I have shown that their etymography can have no effect upon the mind of the reader, which seizes upon the word, and through it receives the idea. As to a different arrangement of signs representing different words, as the syntax of the Chinese language depends chiefly on their juxtaposition, it would create a cacophony in reading that would, to the hearer, make the sense of the characters

* Morrison, Chinese Grammar, 273. Remusat, Grammaire Chinoise, p. 171.

perfect nonsense. It is impossible, therefore, to accede to such a supposition; the writing must servilely follow the words spoken, otherwise there will be two different languages, and one must be translated into the other. But this is not pretended. Besides, prose as well as poetry is written for the ear and not for the eye. There is a harmony of sounds which every writer is bound to attend to, and to attempt to combine it with a supposed harmony of signs, would be a task, in my opinion, beyond the power of talent and of genius, however exalted, to compass.

From all that I have said, I conclude that the Chinese system of writing is improperly called *ideographic;* it is a *syllabic* and *lexigraphic* alphabet. It is *syllabic,* because every character represents a syllable: it is *lexigraphic,* because every syllable is a significant word. I do not know of any other denomination that can be properly applied to it, and this appears to me to be sufficiently descriptive. I submit it, however, to the judgment of those who are better acquainted with the subject.

SECTION III.

I perceive that this letter is already drawn to a great length, and yet I am sensible that my ideas are too much condensed, and need greater development, particularly in the way of examples and illustrations. It will not mend the matter when I tell you that I have not yet done with the Chinese language and its graphic system; I wish to present them in a more general and more enlarged point of view, and to touch on the relation that they bear to other analogous idioms. How far that will lead me, it is impossible to tell.

Brevity and clearness are difficult to be reconciled. I shall do my best, however, to compass that object, and in the meanwhile I entreat your further indulgence.

All the languages that exist upon earth are divisible into four component parts:

1. Sentences or propositions.

2. Words and their various forms.

3. Syllables.

4. Elementary sounds, which we generally designate by the name of letters, and which the ancient grammarians called, as I have remarked above, *elementa* or *prima elementa; στοιχεῖα* or *τὰ πρῶτα στοιχεῖα*.

When, at the confusion of tongues,* the primitive language was forgotten and entirely obliterated from the minds of men, and they were left to their own resources to invent new ones, the descendants of Noah had a difficult task to perform, as at the same time they were dispersed through the different parts of the world. They could not, therefore, agree upon an uniform system, and it is probable that every family had its own. They proceeded separately to the formation of their idioms.

The task they had to perform was, to express their ideas in words and sentences, for which, their materials were syllables and elementary sounds. But there were no philologists among them, and they had not analysis for their guide. Anxious to make themselves understood, some of

* The poet Dante will have it that the primitive language was entirely lost, even before the attempt to erect the Tower of Babel, which produced the confusion of tongues. In his vision of Paradise, he relates a conversation between him and the father of mankind, in which, to the question what language he spoke in Paradise, Adam answers him as follows:

> La lingua ch' io parlai fu *tutta* spenta,
> *Innanzi* che all' ovra inconsumabile
> Fosse la gente di Nembrotte attenta.
>
> PARADISO, Canto xxvi.

them attempted to express the sense of a whole proposition by a single word. Some ancestor of the Delaware Indians, being invited by his neighbour to partake of some food, said, *Nschingiwipoma,* and made him understand by signs that it meant "I do not like to eat with you." To his mistress he said, *Kduhoatel,* and that was to say, *I love you;* to which she doubtingly answered, *Mattakdahoaliwi,* you do not love me. Thus, by endeavouring to say a great deal at once, a polysynthetic language was formed, which, in the course of time, was regularized by method; for without some method in language, it would be impossible for men to understand each other.

In some other country, say in China, or in the country of the Othomi Indians, whether from the difficulty of articulating sounds, or from some other cause, men stuck to syllables, and conveyed their ideas successively, affixing to each a simple or compound articulation; that is to say, a simple elementary vocal sound, or a syllable. Thus were formed monosyllabic languages.

Between these two opposite systems many others arose, participating more or less of the one or of the other. Then, for the sake of method, grammatical forms were invented, such as the juxtaposition of words to determine their sense; particles prefixed, suffixed, or introduced into the middle of a word, as in the Mexican and its cognate languages; inflexions of various kinds, accents, and tones, and all the multitude of audible signs of discrimination between words, which distinguishes from each other the numerous languages existing on the face of the earth.

Whatever form or system was adopted in the first formation of a language, was, by the spirit of imitation natural to man, continued, with occasional modifications, until the idiom attained its highest degree of perfection. Nations frequently adopted words from their neighbours; rarely grammatical forms. Hence we see, that the Chinese has remained monosyllabic during the space of four thousand years; while the polysyllabic Sanscrit, in the various dialects derived from it, retains its primitive forms to a greater or less degree, but does not deviate into the monosyllabic system. There is a tendency in languages to preserve their original structure, which cannot escape the eye of the philological observer.

But men were not satisfied with communicating with each other by word of mouth. As they advanced in civilization, they felt the want of an ocular system to interchange their sentiments with the absent, to impart to distant friends the knowledge of facts, and preserve the memory of them to their posterity. Even savage nations felt the want of such a mode of intercourse, to inform their friends of their warlike and hunting movements, and to warn them against those of their enemies. Self-preservation was the first cause that produced this feeling.

The first mode of effecting their object that presented itself to their minds was *painting;* and the first ocular communication between men, next to audible and visible signs between persons present, was the representation of natural objects by rude figures, to which a particular sense by tradition was affixed, or the meaning of which was easily penetrated by their keen, unsophisticated, and I might say, virgin minds. Every one knows the figures which our northern Indians carve or paint on the bark of trees, to give notice to their friends of facts important for them to know. "But this," says Champollion, "and even painting by the best artists, does not deserve the name of writing. It is incapable of expressing the most simple proposition; even the crayons of Raphael, coloured by Rubens, will always leave us in ignorance of the names of the personages, of the time, and the duration of the action, and will never give to any individual, except the painter himself, a complete idea of the fact; painting representing only an instantaneous mode of being, which always requires in the spectators some preliminary notions."*

The art of painting is unconnected with oral language. It is evident, that without such a connexion it cannot serve the purpose of writing to any considerable extent. How far the Mexicans, who, being more civilized, have made a more extensive use of pictures than our northern Indians, have contrived to establish such a connexion, if such should exist, it is impossible for us to know, in the present state of the information that we possess upon the subject. On inspection, it would seem that the use they made of those paintings was very limited; and that however tradition might have come in aid of them, they could hardly have served the purposes of writing, which is to be read, and not to be guessed at. Tradition, indeed, is absolutely necessary to make pictures intelligible; among us they generally represent historical scenes, scenes taken from ancient mythology or the sacred records of our religion, with all which we are well acquainted; but how can tradition supply the intelligence of facts unknown, and which have never been heard of? Certain conventional signs may supply this defect, but always imperfectly, unless connected with sounds; and when that connexion has taken place, the system may be called *writing*, and not before.

Those signs, at first view, (with very few exceptions,) do not appear to exist in the Mexican paintings. Yet if we believe the writers who have treated of this subject, there was much more in them than meets the unexperienced eye. It may not be out of place to put here together the facts asserted by those writers, in a connected point of view.

"The Mexicans," says Baron Humboldt, "had annals which went back to the sixth century of the Christian era.

* Précis du Syst. Hier. 2d Bd. p. 328. When this work is quoted generally, it is always with reference to the second edition.

There were found the epochs of migrations, the names of the chiefs issued from the illustrious family of Citin, who conducted the northern tribes to the plains of Anahuac. The foundation of Tenochtitlan falls into the heroic times, and it is only since the twelfth century that the Aztecan annals, like those of the Chinese and Tibetans, relate almost without interruption the secular feasts, the genealogies of kings, the tributes imposed on the vanquished, the foundations of towns, the celestial phenomena, and even the most minute events which had an influence on the condition of the rising societies."*

"We know by our *books*," said the Emperor Montezuma to Cortez, "that I, and all those who inhabit this country, are not its original inhabitants, but that we are foreigners, who came from a great distance. We also know, that the chief who brought our ancestors hither, went back for some time to his own country; and that on his return, he found those whom he had left married to native women, and having a numerous posterity. They had built towns, and would no longer obey their former master; so that he left them, and returned home alone." This fact is related by Baron Humboldt, who took it from the letters of Fernando Cortez.†

Besides these relations of historical facts, it is said that they had geographical maps;‡ reports or statements of tributes paid to their sovereign by the conquered nations;§ descriptions of the manners, usages and customs of their country;‖ calendars, genealogies;¶ a code of laws;** and lastly, pleadings or memorials for courts of justice, which M. de Humboldt calls *pièces de procès*, of one of which he

---

* Vue des Cordillieres, vol. i. p. 36. Purchas Pilg. vol. iii.
† Humb. Ibid. p. 113. ‡ Ibid. p. 135.
§ Purchas, vol. iii. ‖ Ibid.
¶ Humb. Vue des Cord. vol. i. p. 169.
** Ibid. 171.

gives a fac simile, handsomely engraved and coloured.* He says that those documents were, *long* after the conquest, exhibited in the Spanish tribunals; and that it was thought indispensable that there should be advocates who could *read* them.†

We learn from the same authority, that the Mexicans had religious books; but whether ritual, liturgical, historical, or merely devotional, is not ascertained. The manuscript preserved in the Library of the Vatican, and on that account called *Codex Vaticanus,* and that kept at Velletri, are believed by Zoega, Fabrega, and other learned archæologists, to be what they call a *ritual almanac,* combining the indication or descriptions of religious rites, with astronomical computations showing when they are to be performed.‡ Another book is mentioned by the same learned author, (which, however is now lost,) called the *divine book,*§ which was written so early as the year 660 of the Christian era. It is said to have contained the Mexican cosmogony, their mythology and system of morality; the whole in regular chronological order.‖ It is difficult to conceive how all these things could have been transmitted from generation to generation by means of mere paintings, or signs expressive only of *ideas.*

It is said, moreover, that the Mexican books were written or painted on durable and portable materials. Those were, cotton stuffs prepared for that purpose,¶ tanned deer skins, or paper fabricated with the leaves of the maguey, (Agave Americana.)** "They supplied pretty well, (*assez bien,*)" says M. de Humboldt, "the want of books, manuscripts, and

---

* Humb. Vue des Cord. vol. i. p. 160.

† Ibid. 171.   ‡ Ibid. p. 234.

§ Teaomoxtli. *Amoxtli,* in Mexican, means a *book.*

‖ Humb. Vue des Cord. vol. i. p. 249.

¶ Lienzos de algodon, que tenian prevenidos y emprimados para este ministerio. Anton. de Solis, Conquista de Mexico, l. 2.

** Humb. Vue des Cord. vol. i. p. 194-5.

alphabetical characters. In the time of Montezuma, thousands of persons were employed in composing or copying pictures;[*] in short, those paintings, folded and arranged in a certain manner, were preserved in the form of books, the *tout ensemble* of which offered the most perfect resemblance (*la plus parfaite ressemblance*) to our bound volumes."[†]

We have but little information as to the system on which the Mexicans proceeded in the application of those paintings to the purposes of writing. Some light, though very faint, is however thrown upon the subject by different writers. "Those things," says Acosta, "which had a visible form or figure, were directly represented by their images; and those that had none, were represented by characters signifying them; and by that means they figured and *wrote* all that they pleased."[‡]

"We know beyond a doubt," says again the learned Humboldt, "that besides their pictures of visible objects, the Mexicans had simple hieroglyphics, by means of which they recalled the ideas of divers objects that are not susceptible of being painted. Such are the air, fire, water, day, night, midnight, speech, motion. They had also numeric signs for the days and months of the solar year. We even find among them traces (*des vestiges*) of those hieroglyphics which are called *phonetic*, and which show a relation (*annoncent des rapports*) not with the thing, but with the *spoken language*. They expressed by that means the names of towns, and those of their sovereigns, which in general were significant."[§]

According to Antonio de Solis, they went even beyond that; and their pictures, like those of the Egyptians, began to assume the form of writing. "They also had," says

[*] Humb. Vue des Cord. vol. i. p. 194-5.
[†] Ibid. 190, 196.
[‡] Hist. de Indias, l. 8.
[§] Humb. Vue des Cord. vol. i. p. 190.

this historian, "signs of explication; for the painters employed by Teutile, to give to Montezuma a full knowledge of what concerned the Spaniards, added to their pictures in various places certain characters, which, to appearance, were designed to explain the meaning of what was painted."*

And lastly; among the fac similes of Mexican paintings, given by Baron Humboldt in his Vue des Cordillières,† there is one, copied from a manuscript in the Royal Library of Dresden, the figures of which are of a peculiar character, which makes the learned author hesitate to say whether they are hieroglyphics or a kind of cursory writing, (*des caractères cursifs*.)‡ It is much to be regretted that the Spanish priests destroyed so many of those precious manuscripts. Why should religion be an enemy to science?

It is to be added, that, like the Egyptians, the Mexicans employed colours in their paintings; but whether for the mere purpose of ornament, or as a part of their graphic system, is, I believe, yet unknown.

This is, I think, all that is known with respect to the Mexican paintings, unless some late discovery has been made that throws more light upon the subject. If we are to believe all that is said above; if neither the conquerors nor the conquered have exaggerated facts; if it be true that thousands of persons were employed in composing or in multiplying copies of those pictures, and that they served as a regular mode of written communication; if, besides the figures and symbols, they had explanatory signs to connect the discourse, (which, however, I have not been able to discover in the pictures that I have seen,) their system was not very different from that of the Egyptian hieroglyphics, and

* Iban poniendo á trechos, algunos caracteres, con que, al parecer, explicaban y daban significacion á lo pintado.   Conq. de Mex. l. 2.
† Vol. ii. p. 268.   ·   ‡ Ibid. p. 271.

it must necessarily have been connected, by tradition or
otherwise, with the spoken language. Its polysynthetic
forms, however, are a great difficulty in the way of this
hypothesis. I am, nevertheless, inclined to believe in its
possibility; and I would recommend to those who may devote themselves to the study of the Mexican paintings, to
found their investigation on a full knowledge of the words
and structure of the Mexican language.

If we admit the Mexican paintings to have been a system
of writing, we must also acknowledge, as I have said before, that it bears no small resemblance to the hieroglyphs
of ancient Egypt. It does not appear, however, that the
Mexicans made use, like the Egyptians, of their painted
figures to represent elementary sounds. If their proper
names of persons and places were, as is said, significant,
they had little use for this manner of writing, which a more
extended intercourse with other nations would have made
necessary, nay, indispensable to them. They were, to all
appearance, in a state of transition between the rude paintings of the savages, and the more perfect system of the
Egyptians. Had they been left to themselves, they would
in time have improved that which they possessed, as the
Egyptians and Chinese have done. A learned Mexican,*
well acquainted with that idiom, and who resides in the city
of Montezuma, is at present employed in investigating this

* Don Manuel Naxera, author of the Dissertation on the Othomi Language, published in the fifth volume of the new series of our Transactions.

subject. He thinks he has already discovered the distinctive signs between substantives and verbs. Success to his labours!

The graphic system of the Egyptians, notwithstanding the important discoveries of Young, Champollion, Salt, and other learned men, is yet involved in much obscurity. Its connexion with the spoken language is only partially developed. But I have no doubt that it exists, and that the hieroglyphic figures do not represent abstract ideas, but the words of the oral idiom. This is, I know, reasoning *à priori*; but *à priori* reasoning is sometimes admissible. It is so, when the adverse proposition to that which is maintained is not only improbable, but may be said to be impossible. Now I cannot conceive the possibility of the existence of what is called an *ideographic* system of writing; and that such was not that of the Egyptians, any more than that of the Chinese, I hope I shall be able to demonstrate.

Every system of writing, deserving the name, is made to be read; not mentally alone, but *vivâ voce*, and by all in the same words, otherwise it cannot serve the purpose for which it was intended. I would ask how, in a country civilized as Egypt is acknowledged to have been, a herald could have proclaimed an edict of the sovereign, if it had been written in *ideographic* characters, which every one might have interpreted as he pleased, according to the greater or lesser knowledge that he possessed of the strength and value of words in the spoken language? Heralds or public criers are not, in general, excellent grammarians. How could a contract between individuals have been drawn up by the most experienced scribe, with the precision required to make its clauses and stipulations sufficiently clear and void of ambiguity? Oral language itself is ambiguous enough; there is no idiom that expresses the ideas of men with perfect precision. The greatest number of the questions which arise in the law-suits that are brought into our courts of justice, have their source in the imperfection of language, and the different interpretations that are put upon words. Is it to be supposed, that writing would have been so contrived as to increase that ambiguity? The moment you admit any system of writing to be a language, and not the representation of a language, you introduce two languages into the nation that makes use of it, the most perfect of which is the most fugitive, because its errors may be instantly corrected; whereas the other is permanent, and if two parties are interested in its construction, and happen to differ about what it expresses, it can no more be altered than a man's will after his death, and remains for ever a source of contention. It appears to me impossible to believe that a civilized nation ever adopted such a system, to any considerable extent.

Again. M. Champollion tells us, that the priests of Egypt wrote in *hieroglyphics* (mind, he does not say in the *demotic*, or epistolographic character,) the sacred rituals, those relating to funerals, treatises on religion and the sciences, *hymns* in honour of their gods, or the praises of their kings, while all the classes of the nation used the demotic character in matters relating to their private affairs.* M. Champollion does not quote any authority for these facts; but he surely would not have asserted them without some sufficient warrant.

Here, then, we have liturgies, religious treatises, nay *hymns*, which we may reasonably believe to have been poetical,† written in an ocular language of abstract ideas!

* Les prêtres écrivaient en caractères *hiératiques*, les rituels sacrés, les rituels funéraires, des traités sur la religion et sur les sciences, des *hymnes*, à la louange des dieux ou les louanges des rois, et toutes les classes de la nation employaient l'écriture *démotique* à leur correspondance privée et à la rédaction des actes publics et privés qui réglaient les intérêts des familles. Précis, p. 423-24.

† I have read somewhere, that the ancient Egyptians had no poetry, because none has been found among the papyri that have been hitherto dis-

I have already shown, with respect to the Chinese, what cacophony would ensue in attempting to execute such poetical melodies. Only represent to yourself our hymn books and metrical psalms to be written *ideographically*, and to be sung *ad libitum*, like musical *cadenzas*, or variations on a given theme. A congregation of poets would be at a loss to find a harmonious reading, and the hymns could only be sung in a translation, which should be either learned by heart, or written in a different character, to connect it with the spoken language. It is impossible to conceive that such things ever existed.

Such, however, would have been an *ideographic* mode of writing, in the sense that is generally ascribed to it. For, let it be understood, that it is not with the word that I find fault, but with its meaning. I care very little about words, except when they lead us into false notions; and such has been the effect of the word *ideographic*. When writers, even the most enlightened, speak of the Chinese and Egyptian systems of writing, they say that they represent *ideas*; when of a particular character, that it represents such or such an idea; whereas they should say such or such a word or part of a word. It will be said, that the view of the Egyptian graphic system, to which I am opposed, was that of the Egyptians themselves; and Horapollo will be cited as an authority, to which there is no reply. But I mistrust the vanity of the Egyptians, as much as that of the Chinese.

covered. This hasty mode of reasoning is too common among the learned. The same writer perhaps will tell us, that among *all* nations poetry has always preceded prose writings, because it happens to have been the case among the Greeks. But the Mohawks and Algonkins never had any poetry, and we know them to be very eloquent in prose. It is never safe to generalize from insulated facts. Nature delights in variety, and from that variety proceeds the pleasure that we feel in the contemplation of her works. But our theorists would regulate every thing by the square and compass, and can see perfection only in dull uniformity.

Both wished to make their system of writing appear as something mysterious, and as a great effort of the human mind; and they trusted to the credulity and indolence of mankind to make them believe in those absurdities. When Horapollo* tells us that the figure of a bee meant in their language *a people obedient to their king*, and that a *vulture* represented the abstract idea of *maternity*, and a *bull* that of *strength* combined with *temperance*, I cannot give my unqualified assent to these propositions, and believe that those signs might be read by every one as he pleased, provided he did not lose sight of the general idea. I believe that each character or sign had not merely its ideal, but its vocal representative, either in elementary sounds, or in syllables, or in words, or, perhaps, in a limited number of cases, in whole sentences, as we have &c. for *et cætera*, and other abbreviations of a similar kind. I believe that there was a method taught in the schools at Thebes, Memphis and Alexandria, by which every one could read the hieroglyphic as well as the demotic writing aloud, and in the same words, without the variation of a syllable. Without that there would be no reading, properly so called; there would only be *translating*.

When I speak of hieroglyphics, I do not mean to include the *anaglyphs* or monumental hieroglyphs, mentioned by Champollion as a secret sacerdotal writing.† These might be more elliptical than the rest, a kind of short-hand or lapidary, and, to a certain extent, enigmatic style, which tradition enabled the priests alone to understand. There is

* I quote this writer at second hand, from Champollion's *Précis*, 340. I have not been able to procure that work from Europe. My Hamburg correspondent wrote to me that no such book was to be found in the shops. I presume that all the copies of it are in public or private libraries, and I regret it exceedingly.

† *Précis*, p. 427.

7

nothing extraordinary in that; and we know too little about
it to make it a subject of discussion. It might not have been
intended to be read aloud, but only to be understood by the
initiated. On this subject we are left entirely to conjectures.

It seems certain, however, that many of those inscriptions were part of the mysteries of the Egyptian religion,
and had a recondite sense not accessible to every one.
Those were probably the *enigmas* mentioned by Clement
of Alexandria. Among them I place the celebrated one in
the temple of Thebes, as given to us by the same writer.* A
child, the symbol of birth; an old man that of death; a hawk
for God; a fish for hatred,† and a crocodile for impudence,
all put together, signified, "Ye who are born and die," (in
other words, "Ye mortals,") "God hates impudence."‡
It is well known that this symbolical method of expressing
religious and moral sentences, was a part of their theological system, known only to the initiated. "All their theology," says Plutarch, "contains, under enigmatical words,
the *secrets* of knowledge."§ So, it would seem, there were
enigmatical *words* as well as signs. Clement of Alexandria
tells us, that those enigmas were, as to their secret and con-
cealed meaning, similar to those of the Hebrews.‖ It is to
be observed, that the fifth book of the *Stromata* is dedicated
to religious mysteries, and is intended as an apology for the
Christians, who at that time had also their own; for it was
then believed that no religion could exist without mysteries

* Stromat. V. p. 566. Sylburg's edit. Colon. 1688.
† The priests of Egypt would not eat fish, for various reasons, mentioned
by Plutarch, *De Iside et Osir.* Baxter observes, that Plutarch might have
added to those reasons, that fish is very unwholesome in hot countries.
‡ Ω γινόμενοι καὶ ακογινόμενοι, Θεὸς μισει 'αναίδειαν.
§ *De Iside et Osir.*
‖ Ομοια τοις Ε'βραιοις κατὰ γετην ετίαρυψιν τὰ τῶν Αιλυπτιων
αινίγματα. Clem. Alex. Ibid.

and secret initiations. The theological science was taught among the Egyptians by means of enigmatic symbols, which could be understood only by means of sacerdotal traditions. Thus Clemens[*] tells us, that some represented the sun by the figure of a crocodile, which meant, in enigmatical language, that the sun, in its course through the air, generated time ;[†] and this, says he, is according to one of their sacred histories.[‡] These sacerdotal enigmas, therefore, should not be confounded with the Egyptian system of writing, although there is no doubt that it borrowed many of those symbols to represent words, it being most probable that the symbols were invented by the priests, as part of their mysteries, before the art of writing became general, and was reduced to a system. But surely afterwards, books, edicts, laws, histories, contracts, and familiar correspondences, intended to be read and understood, could not be written in symbols and *enigmas*. The Rosetta inscription was an edict of the sacerdotal body, and so we must conclude that even the *hieroglyphic* part of it was so written as to be understood by all; otherwise, what purpose could the enigmas have answered? Besides, we know from Clement, that this mode of writing was taught in the schools.

I do not mean to deny, that the graphic signs or characters of the Egyptians were formed on a kind of ideographic system; but that was only a mnemonic contrivance, by which they recalled the memory of *words*, through the medium of images; and that was the only method they could adopt, to avoid confusion, when they had not an alphabet of syllables or elementary sounds. But the ideas or images were only their means to arrive at the vocal sounds, not

[*] Clem. Alex. Ibid.

[†] The sun was represented by other figures; but it seems that that of a crocodile was enigmatic, and to be taken only in the sense which the author explains.

[‡] Δια τινα ιεραντιην ιστοριαν. Ibid.

their end. In that limited sense, the word *ideographic* may perhaps be used, but not with the more extensive meaning that has been given to it. When, for instance, Mr. Salvolini, in his learned and ingenious letters to the Abbate Gazzera,* speaks, in almost every page, of Egyptian characters representing *l'idée jour* and *l'idée mois*, we are led to believe, by this mode of expression, that the words *day* and *month* are out of the question; whereas it was those words, and those words alone, that the signs were intended to call to the memory, by means of signs which may perhaps, in some respects, be called *ideographic*, but never in the sense of their representing ideas independently of sounds; and by sounds, I mean the words of the oral language.

The illustrious Champollion himself is not free from the prejudice I am combating. He always applies the Egyptian characters to ideas and not to words, except when employed as letters of an elementary alphabet. Thus, when Horapollo tells us, in terms sufficiently clear, that when the Egyptians write (the word) *mother*, they paint the figure of a vulture, which appears to me to be the same as saying that the vulture is the orthography of the word *mother*, M. Champollion expresses a different opinion, and says that he has found that the vulture is *always* symbolic, and represents the *idea* signified by the word *mother*, (*l'idée mère.*) But he gives no instance of its being employed otherwise than to represent that *word*, by which alone I am convinced that it is to be read, and not by any of its compounds or derivatives, or by any word, other than the word *mother*, bearing any relation to the abstract idea of *maternity*, which Horapollo is reported to have said to be its meaning, but certainly not in the sentence quoted by M. Champollion.†

§ Des principales expressions qui servent à la notation des dates sur les monuments de l'ancienne Egypte. Two pamphlets, Paris, 1832, 1833.

† Horapollon nous apprend que pour *écrire* mère, les Egyptiens peignoient un vautour. Précis, p. 122. Then the vulture was the character employed to *write* the word mother, and not to represent *l'idée mère.*

But M. Champollion does not stop here. Who will believe that this great man saw ideographic characters even
in the *statues* of the ancient Egyptians? When observing
upon the imperfection of their forms, as compared with
those of the Greek artists, he accounts for it by saying that
those of Egypt had not in view to reproduce and perpetuate
the beautiful forms of nature; but that their art was dedicated to the *notation* of *ideas*, rather than to the representation of objects. Sculpture and painting never were any
thing in Egypt but *branches* of their system of writing.* It
would be more natural to say that their writing was a branch
of their imitative arts. Men of genius cannot be too much
on their guard against the sallies of their imagination; their
ideas are greedily swallowed by the small fry of writers,
and it is difficult always, and sometimes dangerous, to contradict them.

The study of the writing of ancient Egypt has hitherto
been principally directed to the elucidation of the history
and chronology of that interesting country. To reconcile
Manetho, Diodorus, Julius Africanus and George Syncellus
with each other, and all with the Table of Abydos, and with
historical truth, has been the great object of modern Egyptologists, and they have pursued it with remarkable success.
But another object, not less important, claims our attention;
I mean the advancement of general philology. It is greatly
to be wished that this curious graphic system should be
studied with a view to that science, and as a branch of the
history of the human mind.

With a view to the object that I have mentioned, it was
natural that Egyptologists should turn their first attention

---

* Cet art (la sculpture) semble ne s'être jamais donné pour but spécial
la reproduction durable des belles formes de la nature; il se consacra à
la *notation des idées* plutôt qu'à la représentation des choses. La sculpture
et la peinture ne furent jamais en Egypte que de véritables *branches de
l'écriture.* Lettres à M. le Duc de Blacas, première lettre, pp. 9, 10.

to the hieroglyphic characters in monumental inscriptions, where they were most likely to find the names and titles of the successive sovereigns of Egypt, and the epochs, with perhaps some of the principal events of their reigns. But I doubt whether it is the best course to be pursued in the study which I have recommended. We are informed by Clement of Alexandria, that the Egyptians were instructed first of all (πρῶτον πάντων) in the *epistolographic* character; that is to say, in the *popular*, or, as we would call it, the *running hand*, which of course was the easiest to be acquired. From thence they proceeded to the *hieratic*, and last of all, the *hieroglyphic* character.* I am inclined to believe that the course of study which was the easiest for the Egyptians, would be so likewise for us, and therefore I venture to recommend it, though not without the greatest diffidence. As far as I am able to learn, it seems that there is no deficiency of materials, as besides the *enchorial* inscription on the Rosetta stone, with its Greek and hieroglyphic counterparts, numerous rolls of papyrus have been discovered in the catacombs of Thebes and elsewhere, among which are bilingual documents in Coptic and Greek. Enough remains of the ancient idiom to aid us in that investigation, and I have no doubt that, if zealously pursued, the success that it would meet with would amply reward the labour bestowed upon it.

We are informed by M. Klaproth, that Messrs. Silvestre de Sacy and Akerblad, in France, and Dr. Young in England, were once employed in the study of this style of writing; and he adds, that they pursued it with *perseverance*.† No trace of their labours, however, remains, which is greatly to be regretted, and particularly that they suffered themselves

---

* Stromat. 5. p. 555.

† Les écritures cursives étaient à cette époque (about 1820) l'objet de travaux poursuivis avec persévérance par plusieurs savans, tels que MM. Silvestre de Sacy et Akerblad en France, et Dr. Young en Angleterre. Klaproth, Examen critique des travaux de feu M. Champollion, p. 3.

so soon to be discouraged; for their *perseverance* does not appear to have lasted a great while.

Dr. Seyffarth informs us, that in the Royal Library of Berlin there are no less than fifty-seven rolls of papyrus, written of course in the ancient Egyptian language and character, some of which are not less than thirty feet in length, with few exceptions closely written, so that it is difficult to find in any other writing so many ideas and words brought together in so small a compass.* Some are in the hieroglyphic, others in the hieratic and in the enchorial character. However it may be, I think no one will pretend that those characters, not sculptured on monuments, but written on rolls of paper, represent abstract ideas in the shape of metaphors and enigmas, and not in the forms given to them by the articulate sounds of the spoken language. To work, then, noble Prussians; sagacious, learned and indefatigable Germans! Cease to look in those writings for *ideographic* signs, which present nothing definite to the mind of the reader, and apply yourselves to finding out the connexion between the writing and the language, for such a connexion must and does certainly exist. Do not be frightened by the obstacles which a learned writer, indeed, but too intent on depreciating the labours of his great rival, Champollion, has placed in dread array before you.† The task is difficult, but success is not impossible. To work, then, ye Germans, and may God prosper your labours!

I have been led, my dear sir, much farther in this disquisition than I at first intended, and yet I am not willing to drop it. I must demolish entirely, if I can, the still prevailing notion of an universal system of writing, of ideographic characters presenting a complete language to the mind without the intervention of articulate sounds, nay, without any

* Bemerkungen über die Ægyptischen papyrus in der K. Bibliothek zu Berlin, p. 1.

† Klaproth, ibid. p. 148.

connexion with them in the shape of words or otherwise. I must show, by multiplied examples, that words, articulated words, are the foundation of all writing; and that whatever graphic system, figurative or otherwise, may be adopted, its only object is to express or represent words, and through them ideas, in the forms which spoken language has invented. This I meant originally to do only through the comparison of the Chinese and Cochinchinese, by means of the documents submitted; but·as, in the course of my discussion, the Egyptian has intruded upon me, I cannot avoid strengthening my argument by comparing its system with that of the Chinese, and showing that they have both proceeded to obtain the same object by the same road, as far as the structure and genius of their respective languages permitted them so to do. Again, therefore, let me request your further indulgence.

SECTION V.

In the first place it must be observed, that the Chinese, and the Coptic or ancient Egyptian, differ essentially in their structure, the former being monosyllabic, and the latter polysyllabic. Some writers, and among them some of the most eminent philologists,* have conjectured, I think without sufficient foundation, that all languages, and especially the Coptic, were originally monosyllabic. I do not

* The learned Eichhorn, who maintains this doctrine, infers from it that the *primitive* language consisted only of monosyllables. *Geschichte der neuern Sprachenkunde*, p. 17. I can perceive no reason for such a supposition. The name of the first man, *Adam*, is dissyllabic; and the word *Adomah*, from which it is said to be derived, has three syllables. The most ancient names in profane history are also, for the most part, polysyllabic. As in religion, there are superstitions in science.

coincide with them in that opinion, being a believer in the permanency of grammatical forms; but as this has nothing to do with our discussion, I shall not say any thing more about it.

The Coptic language, notwithstanding its polysyllabic character, is well adapted to the graphic system commonly called *hieroglyphic*, which it once adopted. Its grammatical forms, by which the ideas of gender, number, case, persons, tenses, moods, &c., are conveyed to the mind, do not, like those of the Greek and Roman languages, consist of inflexions, by which the sounds of the radical words are varied, and sometimes obliterated; but they are represented by particles prefixed or affixed, or (as in our Indian languages) infixed in the middle of the principal word, which remains unchanged, and therefore can be easily separated from them. Father Kircher, in his short Coptic Grammar, gives us examples of about one hundred and thirty-five of those particles,* and explains their use. Hence it follows, that the written characters may, without the least inconvenience, represent each a radical word, a noun or a verb, or one of those prepositions or qualifying particles, and that, I am inclined to think, is the ground of the system. M. Champollion, with great sagacity, has discovered a great number of those particles in the Egyptian writing.† This discovery has been contested by some learned writers, as not sufficiently proved;‡ but it appears to me that he has made it out in a clear and satisfactory manner.

As a matter of curiosity to us Americans, showing the similarity of some of the Coptic forms with those of our Indians, permit me to add, from the book above cited,§ the declension of a noun, with the possessive pronouns inter-

---

* Prodrom. p. 32.   † Précis, chap. v.

‡ Klaproth, Examen critique des travaux de feu M. Champollion, Paris, 1832. L'abbé Affre, Nouvel Essai sur les hiéroglyphes. Paris, 1834.

§ Kircher, Prodrom. p. 304.

8

fixed. It has also double plural forms; but that is found likewise in the Hebrew, and other Oriental languages, and therefore is not more particularly noticed.

The word *Pos*, Lord, or the Lord, is thus declined:

Singular.

P*aos*,	my Lord
P*ekos*,	thy Lord (masc.)
P*eos*,	thy Lord (fem.)
P*ephos*,	his Lord
P*esos*,	her Lord

Plural with Singular.

P*enos*,	our Lord
P*etenos*,	your Lord
P*owos*,	their Lord

Double Plural.

Here N is substituted for the P initial.

N*aos*,	my Lords
N*ekos*,	thy Lords
N*ephos*,	his Lords
N*esos*,	her Lords
N*enos*,	our Lords
N*etenos*,	your Lords
N*owos*,	their Lords

It would seem that *os* is the root of this word, and that P is a prefix indicating the sex or gender; for in the feminine, my lady or mistress is *taos*, and T is known to be the sign of the feminine, as P of the masculine gender.*

So far the Chinese and Coptic languages resemble each other, and if they differ in any thing, that difference is not

*Kircher, Prodrom. p. 305.

material to my argument. The Chinese words are all monosyllabic, and the particles which express the different relations are so likewise, and are in fact *words;* * they have
their appropriate signs or characters, as well as the principal locutions, because they are or may be entirely separated
from them. For, as M. Remusat well observes,† it is only
in writing that they are separated; and who can tell how
it would be under a different graphic system? In speaking,
the particle and the word which it qualifies may be considered as one. The Coptic has existed under two different
graphic systems. With the alphabetic characters introduced
by the Greeks, the particles and the words to which they are
attached appear as one polysyllabic word; under the figurative system it might have been otherwise, though the particles do not all appear of themselves to be significant, yet
they might have been separately represented. In this power
of separation consists the similarity between the two languages.

Supposing that the particles are always considered as
parts of the words to which they belong, it is enough that
they be separated by a mental operation, to justify and indeed
to suggest the application of different characters to them.
In this last supposition I should not call the Egyptian writing, as I have done the Chinese, *lexigraphic.* I would try
to find some more appropriate epithet whereby to distinguish it, which, however, cannot be done until we are better
informed of the nature and character of this graphic system,
and of the method which it employs to represent the sounds
of the language, whether in the form of words, of syllables,
or of other component parts of speech, or by a mixture of
several of those forms; a study well worthy the attention
of the philologist, and which the discoveries of Champollion
and his fellow labourers give us reason to hope will be suc-

* Remus. Chin. Gram. p. 144.
† Mélanges Asiat. vol. ii. p. 47.

ceeded by others, by means of which the great problem will
at last be completely solved, and the writing of the ancient
Egyptian fully understood.

Let us now see how the Chinese and the Egyptians, possessed of such languages as I have described, may be presumed to have proceeded, in order to recall to the mind,
by means of written signs, the sounds of those languages as
they were combined in the form of words.

Had those nations possessed inflected languages, like the
Greek and Latin, their task would have been much more
difficult to perform. I am strongly inclined to believe, that
it was the difficulty of representing, by ocular signs, the
various and complicated grammatical forms of certain languages, which led to the discovery of the syllabic proper
and of the elementary alphabets. The multitude of words
which those forms presented to the ear, made the nations
who spoke them despair of recalling them to the mind
through the organs of sight, in any other manner than by
analysing their sounds, and affixing a character to each
element. Some stopped at syllables, probably in languages
where they were not exceedingly numerous, as we have
seen it to be the case in the Cherokee, and as it is in the
Japanese, which has only forty-seven syllables;* others, on
on the contrary, when, by the intermixture of vowels and
consonants, syllables appeared to exist in too large numbers
to be easily arranged into an alphabetical system, proceeded further in their analysis, and no doubt were greatly
astonished when they discovered the very small number of
pure elementary sounds of which human language is composed. This led them naturally to the formation of elementary alphabets. It was not the case, however, with all
nations; for we find that the Mexicans, with a language so

* Gramm. Japon. de Rodriguez, trad. par Landresse; Introd. par Remusat, p. xv.

compounded as to be properly called *polysynthetic*, and consisting of words of an immense length, have proceeded no farther than to a system, analogous, as far as we know, to that of ancient Egypt. But to inquire into the causes of these various results would lead us too far from the subject I am treating of.

There is no doubt that alphabetical writing is, for certain purposes, the most adequate method of representing or recalling to the mind, through the eye, thoughts or ideas already fixed by oral sounds. In proof of this assertion, it is sufficient to instance proper names of persons and places, and those of the numerous species and varieties of natural objects, which can only be represented by signs or characters indicative of simple sounds. Hence we find, that both the Chinese and Egyptians were obliged to have recourse to that method; but they fell upon it at an advanced stage of civilization, and too late to make them abandon their former system, to which they had long been accustomed, except when absolute necessity compelled them to it. They were misled at first by the apparent facility of adapting the *pictorial system* to languages, composed of short words, which they thought susceptible of being easily represented by figurative signs. At the same time, it cannot be denied that the lexigraphic system is well adapted to the structure of their language, and that it is only deficient with respect to proper names or new objects, and the representation of the sounds of foreign idioms.

Such was the case with the Chinese and the Egyptians. They both began, like all savage nations, with rude pictures of visible objects. But those kyriologic signs, κατὰ μίμησιν, as Clement of Alexandria calls them, which expression I would render by *mimic signs*, could not carry them very far; for visible objects of various kinds have often the same form, and it is no easy matter to distinguish them to the eye. The sun and the moon are round, but so are nuts,

apples, and a multitude of other things.* Hence they were
soon compelled to have recourse to allegories, metaphors,
and a variety of other figures; and to invent a system, by
means of which they might make them subservient to their
purpose. Although their idioms resembled each other, as I
have shown, in a most important feature, yet in the details
they differed, and those differences, though they pursued the
same general system, led them into different roads. This
requires some explanation.

The Chinese language, and particularly the *Kou-wen*,
which was first in use, is essentially *elliptical.* It wants
grammatical forms to express the various shades of ideas,
and leaves them to be gathered from the relative position of
the words, and the sense of the context. This ambiguity,
as to us it appears to be, who are accustomed to more precise forms of language, is increased by the great number of
homophonous words, not even varied by their accents.
This has led sinologists to believe, that the Chinese writing
was intended to correct that ambiguity, and it has been
said that so insufficient are the words to convey ideas, that
the Chinese are often obliged to explain their meaning by
tracing characters with their fingers in the air. That this
may happen, sometimes, as in our languages we spell one
out of several homophonous words to specify its meaning,
may perhaps be believed; but it must be a thing of very
rare occurrence. Besides, the Chinese have a very easy
way, which I shall presently mention, of explaining verbally
the meaning of their ambiguous words, without being obliged
to trace figures in the air. And here I cannot help observing, how easily men of learning are imposed upon by travel-

---

* The arms of the Penn family are three nails, the round heads of which
alone appear on the scutcheon. Hence they are generally taken to be
balls, like the *palle* of the Medicean family. But the motto of the old Ad-
miral sufficiently explains what they are, *Dum clavum teneam,* "While
a single nail remains, I will not give up the ship."

lers and other dealers in wonders. The Chinese understand
each other when speaking, quite as easily as other people.
Their language, like all others, was made to be understood,
otherwise it would not be a language. I have known Chinese, and heard them converse with each other with the
greatest fluency. I asked them whether they found any
difficulty in conveying by speech any idea they thought
proper; they answered me, not the least. I frequently
asked the same question of our Indians, who uniformly answered in the same manner.

The system adopted by the inventors of the Chinese mode
of writing, as it now exists, was that of recalling the words
of the language to the memory of the reader by signs, descriptive, as much as possible, of their signification. By
this method, they gave an advantage to writing over speech;
for while the language was filled with homophonous words,
the signs which represented them were not (if I can use the
expression) *homomorphous*, and the eye could distinguish
them from each other, though the ear could not. This advantage, however, has been greatly exaggerated. M. Remusat contends, that it is from it that the Chinese language
derives all its clearness.* It is precisely as if one were to
say, that the clearness of the English language is derived
from our various modes of spelling homophonous words;
as, for instance, *bow* (arcus) and *beau; bow* (signum reverentiæ) and *bough*, &c. This may be pleasing to the eye,
but has nothing to do with the clearness of the language.
He who understands it when he hears it spoken, may also
understand it when he hears it read, and consequently when
he reads it himself. All our homophonous words are not
distinguished in writing by a different orthography; the

* Les monosyllables de la langue parlée des Chinois tirent toute leur
clarté des intraduisibles caractères auxquels ils tiennent lieu de prononciation. *Recherches sur les langues Tartares*, p. 134.

word *sound*, for instance, when used as a substantive, means
the effect produced by noise, or the name of an arm of the
sea; as an adjective, it means healthy, right, proper; in
theology, it means orthodox; and lastly, as a verb, it means
to produce noise, to try depth, to endeavour to discover the
sentiments of others; yet in all these cases the word is spelt
in the same manner, and no confusion ensues. Nor would
it in the Chinese, if one character only was employed to
represent all the words which are pronounced in the same
manner. M. Remusat himself gives us a fact in support of
this proposition, too strong to be omitted. He says, that at
this time the merchants, mechanics, and other unlettered
men in China, paying very little attention to the symbols, are
contented with making use of one single character for each
pronunciation, in whatever sense the syllable may be used,
while the literati write them with different characters.*

Now, nothing can be more plain, than that if any thing
peculiarly requires clearness in the mode of writing, it is the
contracts of merchants and mechanics, and their correspondence on matters of business. This fact appears to me sufficient to settle the whole question.

Then the Chinese might as well, as far as clearness was
concerned, have affixed a single sign or character to each
syllable or word of their language. The same rules of syntax which enable the hearer to understand words spoken,
would have helped him to their meaning when written.
But the number of monosyllabic words was too great to
admit of their being represented by arbitrary signs, which
memory could not easily have retained, and which would
not have been susceptible of classification. For the sake of

* Actuellement même, les marchands, les artisans et autres hommes
illettrés, se contentent de savoir un seul caractère, pour chaque prononciation, et ce caractère leur sert pour toutes les acceptions de la même
syllabe, qui, chez les gens instruits, s'écrivent avec autant de caractères
différents. Ibid. pp. 72, 73.

method, therefore, they fell upon their present system, which
is as well adapted to the nature of their language as that of
the Egyptians to their own. Whenever a word wanted a
sign to represent it, they had nothing to do but to write two
or more other words already provided with signs, to recall,
by a kind of definition, the memory of that for which a character did not yet exist. Thus, if they want to represent
the word *foo* or *fou*, which means a married woman, they
write in the appropriate characters the words *woman, hand,
broom*, as much as to say, a woman who keeps her house
clean, a matron, a housekeeper; but that group of characters is not read literally; it is read *foo*, and means a *married woman*. The words *sun* and *moon*, grouped together,
are read *ming*, which signifies light; *man* and *mountain*, are
read *hermit; mouth* and *bird*, are read *song; ear* and *door*,
to hear; *water* and *eye*, a tear or tears.* It must not be
believed that the Chinese read those definitions even mentally, any more than we advert to the etymology of our
compound words; this manner of distinguishing the characters has only served the inventors as a method to avoid
the confusion of mere arbitrary signs, and their grammarians afterwards have classed them into families of roots or
radical signs or characters, as they are called, by means of
which they are able to find them easily, in a kind of regular
order, in their dictionaries, thus supplying the want of an
alphabetical method.

A Chinese writer, in a short essay of two pages, which
Dr. Morrison has published at the head of his Anglo-Chinese
Dictionary, under the title of "Brief explanation of an alphabetic *language* (system of writing) as exemplified by the
English," has come very near to the opinion which I have
expressed. Dr. Morrison has not subjoined a translation to
that paper; he has published it only in Chinese. But M.

* Remus. Gramm. p. 2.

9

Remusat, in his Mélanges Asiatiques, has given us an extract from it, sufficient to make us know the sentiments of the author. The title of this essay, as translated by him literally, is, " A short introduction to the knowledge of the letters of the kingdom of England." The author institutes a comparison between the alphabetical system, generally considered, and that of his own country. " There are," he says, " but two systems of writing; the one which represents the *sounds* of the *words*, and the other their *meaning*."* Among the former he includes the syllabic alphabets of India and the elementary alphabets of Europe, and among the latter the Chinese writing and the hieroglyphics of ancient Egypt. He admits that it is difficult to decide as to the preference to be given to one over the other, as they both have their advantages and disadvantages. " The characters," says he, " which represent the meaning, do not express the sounds, and yet both must be *committed to memory*." This truth is incontestable. " Besides," continues he, " this faculty of representing the *meaning*, is not applicable to the ideas which the mind conceives, independently of the existence of things; those which designate material objects have, on the other hand, a great advantage."†

It is evident this author well understood that the Chinese

* Mélanges Asiat. vol. ii. p. 213.

† Ils (les systèmes d'écriture) se réduisent à deux, l'un qui représente les sons des mots, et l'autre qui en exprime le sens. Parmi les premiers on cite les caractères *fan* ou Sanskrits, ceux mandchoux, ceux des *ying* ou Anglais, et ceux des autres Royaumes occidentaux de l'Europe. Quant à ceux qui expriment le sens des mots, ce sont les anciens caractères du Royaume de *Yi-tchi-pi-to* (Egypte) et les caractères anciens et modernes de la Chine. On serait assez embarrassé de déterminer la préférence à accorder à l'un de ces systèmes, qui ont leurs avantages et leurs inconvénients. D'ailleurs cette faculté représentative du sens, ne s'applique pas aux idées conçues, par l'esprit, indépendamment des choses. Ceux qui désignent les objets matériels ont, d'un autre côté, un grand avantage.— Remusat, Ibid.

characters represent *words* and not *ideas.* "Ideas," he says, "cannot be represented by written signs, as they appear to the mind;" from whence it follows, that they can only be represented in the forms in which words have clothed them. "The characters," he says further, "do not present the *sounds* of the words, but their *meaning.*" What he calls their *meaning,* is expressed by characters formed of the words which the signs represent, and not by external forms, which present nothing to the mind except the words to which they apply; as to simple characters, which are comparatively few, they also present nothing to the memory but the sounds of the words they are meant to express, precisely as our letters represent the *elements* of those sounds. To those characters alone which designate material objects, that is to say, to *picture writing,* he allows the advantage; and it is clear that he had then in view the hieroglyphs of Egypt, or some of the ancient Chinese signs now out of use, as he well knew that the forms of the present characters no longer represent the figures of visible objects. On the whole, these admissions of a Chinese writer, those lights which shine in the midst of his native prejudices, I cannot but consider as a powerful support to my argument.

It is remarkable, that while in the last century the learned were expatiating on the wonderful properties of the Chinese system of writing, an illustrious philosopher, ignorant of the language, and who does not appear to have paid any particular attention to the subject, by the mere force of his genius penetrated into the true character of that system, and described it in a few words, to which no attention seems to this moment to have been paid. I mean the celebrated J. J. Rousseau, of Geneva. That great man, it is true, too often suffered his eccentric imagination to carry him beyond the bounds of reason and even of common sense; but, in the midst of those aberrations of his powerful mind, he scattered here and there some profound thoughts, of the value of which he was not himself sensible, but which, if developed and diluted into volumes, would establish the reputation of an intelligent and skilful plagiarist.

Such is the description which he gives of the Chinese writing, in his essay on the origin of languages; a work, it is true, like those of Plato, full of wild and fanciful ideas; but also, like those of the Greek philosopher, full of admirable truths. Thus, while speaking of languages, he tells us, in one of his romantic flights, that the first words spoken in the northern regions were *aidez moi*, and in southern climes *aimez moi*,* in the same work he throws carelessly, as it were, and in a few words, a flood of light on the nature and character of the Chinese system of writing.

He divides the graphic systems in use among mankind into three classes. The first is the hieroglyphic, of which he speaks like those who preceded him; and the third is the alphabetical, of which he says nothing worthy of remark. The second is the Chinese, and on this we must hear him speak.

"The second method," says he, "is that of representing *words* and *propositions* by conventional signs, which can only be done when the language is entirely formed, and when a whole people are united by common laws; for there is here a two-fold agreement. *Such is the writing of the Chinese*, and that is truly to paint *sounds*, and speak to the eyes."† Let us dwell upon this for a few moments.

1. *The Chinese characters paint sounds and represent words.* This is precisely what I have been labouring to

* Essai sur l'origine des langues, ch. x. *in fin.*

† La seconde manière est de représenter les *mots* et les propositions par des caractères conventionnels, ce qui ne peut se faire que quand la langue est tout à fait formée et qu'un peuple entier est uni par des lois communes; car il y a déjà ici double convention; telle est l'écriture des Chinois, c'est là véritablement peindre les *sons* et parler aux yeux. Ibid. ch. v.

prove. Rousseau does not speak of *ideas;* his intuitive genius told him that ideas could not be painted.

2. *They also represent propositions.* So do the groups of characters which distinguish homophonous words from each other. I have instanced the character *foo,* a married woman. It is formed of three others, those of *woman, hand,* and *broom,* therefore the group represents in elliptic form the proposition *a woman holding a broom.* I have explained the object of this mode of discrimination; it is the orthography of the Chinese.

3. *This mode of writing is only suited to a language entirely formed.* Therefore language preceded the writing, and writing was made to represent the sounds or words of which language is composed, and not ideas abstracted from them.

4. *And to a people united by common laws;* that is to say, to a civilized people. Savages could not have invented this system of writing.

5. *There is here a two-fold agreement.* This is very clear; the language was first agreed upon, and the writing afterwards. They could not have both been invented at the same time, much less the latter before the former.

Here, then, all that I have been endeavouring to prove in this long letter, appears to have been expressed in a few words by an illustrious philosopher, whose intuitive mind perceived, at a single glance, the nature of a system which others were labouring to involve in mystery, and to explain by opinions opposed to every principle of reason and common sense. His lucid exposition was not noticed, or perhaps was smiled at by the philologists of his day. I hope their successors will do him justice. Let us now return to the Coptic.

SECTION VI.

This language, which M. Quatremère* has clearly proved to be the ancient Egyptian, has not come down to us entire, but much mixed with Greek words and locutions. Even Greek adverbs and particles, such as αλλα, γαρ, χωρις, have crept into it, which makes me believe that it became at last a partially mixed idiom, like the German in the interior of Pennsylvania, which is not only spoken, but written in newspapers and in translations from the English. Nevertheless, in the state in which we possess it, the structure of the language does not appear to have suffered any material alteration, any more than that of the German in our country, which is still preserved, nothwithstanding the introduction of English words. The same may be said of the French in Canada and Louisiana; and it corroborates my opinion of the tendency of languages to preserve their original structure.

I have been asked how it happened (if my theory be correct) that the Latin language has lost so many of its forms, in the modern Italian, as well as in the French, Spanish, Portuguese, and other languages derived from it. I do not mean to deny the power of invasion and conquest; it may modify the forms as well as the words of a language; nay, it may destroy it altogether. The Coptic language has vanished before the Arabic, and is no longer in existence. But these are the effects of force, which do not in the least militate against my theory; it remains unimpeached, whenever violence has not interfered, and even in many cases when it has. The Basque language, for instance, driven from Spain and Aquitain, and perhaps from several other parts of Europe, has taken refuge in the Pyrenean moun-

* Recherches critiques et historiques sur la langue et la littérature de l'Egypte, par Etienne Quatremère. Paris, 1808.

tains, where, after many ages, it still preserves its original structure. Many other similar examples might be adduced.

We may, therefore, have a correct idea of the grammatical character and forms of the ancient Coptic; it indeed adopted Greek words, but we find in it none of the inflexions of the Hellenic idiom, and nothing of its manner of compounding words by altering the syllables of the component parts. The Coptic appears to be formed on the model of the Hebrew, Chaldaic, Arabic, and other neighbouring languages. If I should be asked why all those nations having languages formed on a similar or analogous system, did not all adopt the same mode of writing, I can only conjecture that the Egyptians invented their own, and the Hebrews, Chaldeans and Arabs received theirs from other nations, or, perhaps, discovered sooner the defects of the mimic, or, as it is called, hieroglyphic writing, and rejected it before long habit had endeared it to them, and made it a kind of second nature. Although the different forms of their languages led the Egyptians and Chinese into different roads, while they agreed in the general principle of their graphic system, it does not follow that the various structure of languages was the only, or even perhaps the principal cause that induced nations to adopt a particular system of writing in preference to another. It is very seldom, if ever it happens in human affairs, that effects are produced by a single cause, and the same cause does not always produce similar effects. The road of conjecture is dark and intricate, and when I presume to offer mine, it is always with due diffidence, and I am far from wishing to have them considered as axioms.

Although we are sufficiently acquainted with the ancient Coptic language to form an idea of its structure and grammatical character, it is not so with its graphic system, before it adopted and substituted for it the letters of the Greek alphabet. The Rosetta inscription, and the discoveries to which it has led, have thrown some light upon it, but still

it is no more than a glimmering light. It would rather
seem that it did not adopt the Chinese plan of stringing two
or three words together, in order, by a kind of lame definition, to recall the memory of a third or fourth. The Chinese words when spoken are simple, when written compound; while, on the contrary, the spoken words of the
Egyptian are compounded in the same manner as the Chinese characters, and their graphic signs, as far as we know,
represent words singly, and not by means of a compound
form. M. Champollion is of opinion that those groups of
signs which, in the Chinese, represent a word by attempting
to define it, are not found in the Egyptian writing ;* so that
it would appear, that a word might be represented by a
compounded character; as, for instance, when the word
day is represented by an open oblong square and a closed
semicircle,† but that the two signs thus grouped together
should be only metaphorical, and not intended to define the
word day by the signs of two other words. This opinion of
M. Champollion is not without plausibility, because the Coptic
language, not consisting, like the Chinese, of great numbers
of homophonous monosyllables, there seems to have been no
necessity to explain their meaning by verbal definitions, as
the sense of each word was sufficiently understood by the
analogies of the language, without having recourse to that
method. Nevertheless, we have not yet sufficient facts before us to enable us to form a decided opinion upon this
question. The system of *definitions* might have been adopted by the Egyptians as well as by the Chinese, for the sake
of method, and to avoid confusion. Mere arbitrary signs,
and even pictures, when numerous, are difficult to be classed
and to be retained in the memory.

It is curious to observe that the Chinese, in forming their
system of writing, followed the same plan in representing

* Précis, p. 346.   † Salvolini, Letter I. p. 12.

by signs the monosyllabic words of their language, which
has been universally adopted in the formation of the words
of polysyllabic idioms; that is to say, by so compounding
them, as by the composition to define their meaning. Thus
the Latin word *concordia*, formed of the words *with* and
heart, represents the *union of hearts*, which is nothing else
than a definition of the compound word. In our modern
languages, derived from the Latin, Greek, Saxon, &c., these
definitions can, in most cases, only be perceived by recur-
ring to the etymology of the compound; but they nevertheless exist, and it is evident that without them no polysyllabic
language could have been formed. To illustrate this view
of the subject, permit me to place here some examples of
the Egyptian compound words, compared with the Chinese
written representation of their spoken monosyllables.

COPTIC WORDS,

From Champollion's Précis, p. 336.

HET signifies *heart.*

Hetshem	(little heart)	signifies	cowardly
Harshhet	(slow, heavy heart)	"	patient
Shashet	(high heart)	"	proud
Shabhet	(weak heart)	"	timid
Hetnasht	(hard heart)	"	not clement
Hetsnaou	(two hearts)	"	undecided
Tamhet	(close heart)	"	obstinate
Womnhet	(eating *his* heart)	"	repenting
Athhet or Athet	(without heart)	"	foolish
Eihet	(heart come up)	"	to reflect
Thothet	(heart mix)	"	to persuade, concili-
Kahet	(place *one's* heart)	"	to trust [ate
Tihet	(give *one's* heart)	"	to observe, examine

10

Djemhet	(find by heart)	signifies	to know
Mehhet	(fill heart)	"	to satisfy

CHINESE WORDS DEFINED BY WRITING.

From Marshman's Grammar, p. 53 et seq.

Chinese.	English.	Groups of characters.
tshin	keen, acute	heart gold
hhoh	to collect, unite	man one mouth
chhoong	a species of bamboo	straight reed
Lee	ingenious, intelligent	profit man
Lee	whiskey	profit wheat

It would be easy to collect an immense number of these forms, as the great mass of the Chinese characters is thus compounded, but these will be sufficient for my purpose. It is often difficult to find the chain of ideas which has led to the formation of these characters.

These facts have not escaped the observation of the sagacious Champollion; but the inference that he draws from them, and which he applies to *all* hieroglyphic characters, or, as he calls them, *caractères figuratifs*, though I do not mean to contest its application to the Chinese method of writing, is perhaps too general; because, I must here again repeat it, it is *sounds* or *words* that those characters are intended to recall to mind, and ideas only through them. " In *those systems* of writing," says the illustrious author, " the order of nature in forming oral languages is necessarily followed. For instance; as languages begin with *onomatopeias* or imitations of sounds, ocular systems begin with the direct representation of visible objects, whence they proceed to allegories, metaphors," &c.*

I shall not inquire into the correctness of this principle,

* Précis, p. 333.

as applied to the Egyptian hieroglyphics; it does not appear to me by any means to be proved. I am rather inclined to believe, by the comparison of the graphic systems of China and Egypt, that those nations do not pursue entirely the same road, and that the genius and grammatical forms of their languages required, or at least produced, different methods of presenting the words to the eye. Thus the Chinese define their monosyllables, and explain their meaning, by combining the signs of other monosyllables, which is exactly the counterpart of the system of the Egyptian spoken language, in which the polysyllabic words define themselves, exactly as the Chinese characters define their monosyllables. But it is not yet clear that the Egyptians, in their system of writing, have followed the same course, though I do not mean to deny it; it is not impossible that they may have done it *partially*.

If the Egyptians had meant to adopt as a general principle that on which is founded the graphic system of the Chinese, they would, for instance, in order to represent the compound word *heavy heart*, which we translate by *patient*, have grouped together the sign or character representing the word *heavy* and that of the word *heart*, or presented them successively. Whether they have done so or not does not yet appear. It is worth the inquiry of philologists, and the solution of this question may be the means of further progress in the deciphering of the Egyptian inscriptions and manuscripts. In this attempt, the language and its grammatical structure and forms should never be lost sight of; nor should it be forgotten, that the object of all graphic systems is to represent words and not ideas, and that the figures and other imitative signs that are employed for that purpose are only the means and not the end. Even the rude pictures of savage nations differ only from the more perfect systems in being more elliptical. They bring to the mind a few catch words, out of which a sentence is formed; but they can never serve for any extensive purpose of written communication. It appears to me indispensably necessary to a system of writing, that it should be in some way or other connected with the sounds of the language, whether in the form of words, syllables, or primary elements.

But here a difficulty occurs, even in our own alphabetical method. There is no language on the face of the earth that possesses all the sounds that can be uttered by the human voice. The *phonetics* of nations differ as much as their countenances and external appearance. In vain we may invent new signs and new characters, to represent sounds to which our ears and our vocal organs are not accustomed; in vain we may adopt for that purpose new systems of orthography; we may multiply accents, apostrophes, and other designations of such sounds, we only torture the eye, without conveying any thing to the ear. All such attempts appear to me to be idle, and can only gratify the vanity of authors. All that we can obtain, by our utmost efforts, is a certain approximation, and with that we ought to rest contented. We have long been accustomed to the name of *Mahomet*, but we have now twenty ways of writing it, in order to display the Arabic learning of the inventors of the new orthography. We have been long satisfied with the Alcoran, but now we have the Koran, the Khoran, the Qoran, the Koraun, the Korân, and what not?* When will pedantry be banished from the republic of letters?

The same difficulty occurs in the Chinese and Coptic systems of writing, and to a greater extent, because they want the proper signs of elementary sounds. It is curious to compare those nations in their efforts to overcome this difficulty.

* The reason which is generally given for saying the *Koran*, and not the *Alcoran*, is, that it is to avoid an unnecessary duplication of the article. But how is it in *almanac, algebra, alkali*, &c.; must we also contract these words? *O vanæ hominum mentes!*

The Egyptians represent each elementary sound by the sign of some word beginning with it; as for instance, the sign of the word *lion*, whether it be the figure of the animal or some other allegorical or metaphorical sign, will stand for the letter L; the sign of the word *onion*, or that of *ostrich*, for the letter O, and so forth. M. Champollion tells us, that these alphabetical signs or characters constitute two-thirds at least of the *language*,* as he calls it; by which I understand, that in a page of writing, two-thirds at least of the figures or characters are used alphabetically, or *phonetically*, as Egyptologists express it; which I am very much inclined to believe, as their hieroglyphics, not defining, as we suppose, like the Chinese character, the word which they represent by the combination of the signs of other words, too large a number of them would have created confusion and occupied an immense space, and therefore they were sooner obliged to have recourse to an alphabet. Whether the method they employed was convenient or not, it is not for us to inquire, as it has nothing to do with the present discussion.

The Chinese have two modes of alphabetical writing; the one syllabic, the other elementary. The first, called *Hing-ching*, is principally employed to express the specific names of animals, plants, minerals, and other objects. The syllabic character is joined to the generic name, without regard to what it is singly meant to express. Thus the word *pe* singly signifies white, and it also signifies the tree called *cypress*. In the latter case, the character will be composed of the sign of the word *tree*, and of that of the adjective *white*; but it will not be read *tree-white*, but *cypress*. It is the same with the specific names of birds, fishes, &c.; the

* Précis, pp. 102, 125. Elsewhere, p. 447, he says: Les caractères figuratifs et les caractères symboliques sont employés, dans tous les textes, en moindre proportion que les caractères *phonétiques*.

sign of the word *bird* or *fish* is joined to that of any monosyllable, whatever may be its meaning, that is homophonous
with the name of the fish or bird which is to be recalled to
the memory. M. Remusat says, that the words thus sylla-
bically expressed form at least *one-half* of what he calls the
written language.[*]

· With regard to foreign names or words which do not occur in their own language, they have a different method,
which is more complicated, but which, however, serves
their purpose. The Chinese language abhors syllables
ending with a consonant; all those of which it is composed
are formed of a consonant and a vowel sound, either simple
or nasal, such as *ko*, *lee*, *ching*, *foong*, &c. When they have
to write a foreign name or word alphabetically, they begin
by dividing it into syllables to suit their pronunciation. The
word *Christus*, for instance, they will divide in this manner,
ke-le-se-too-se, and write down each syllable as follows:
They take two Chinese syllables or words, without regard
to the meaning, one of them beginning with the consonant,
and the other with the vowel of the syllable to be expressed.[†] For the first syllable of *Christus*, divided as above,
they will write *ko-le*, which two words will signify, if you
please, the one *cabbage*, and the other *pumpkin*, and add
a character which means *divide*.[‡] The reader is thereby
informed that he must read alphabetically. He will take
the *k* from *ko* and the *e* from *le*, and read *ke*, and so on with
the other syllables, until he has made out the whole word.
There is a certain number of characters specially applicable
to that purpose, some of them intended to represent or indicate the initial, and others the final sound, of the syllable
meant to be expressed.[§]

The Chinese have a particular mode of representing

---

* Gramm. Chin. p. 4.
‡ Ibid. p. 2.
† Morrison, Chinese Gramm. p. 1.
§ Marshm. Clavis Sinica, p. 88.

the sounds of foreign names, the component syllables of which exist in their own language. It is by writing successively the syllables of which the name is composed, without regard to their meaning. Thus they will write in this manner the name of Washington.

WA	which means a *brick*
SHING	the name of a measure for grain and liquids
TUN*	grass growing

But in that case they will, like the Egyptians, surround the name so written with a frame, which the French call *cartouche*, in order to inform the reader that nothing but sounds is meant to be represented.

The Egyptians, as I have said before, represent elementary sounds by figures, the names of which, written alphabetically, begin with the letter or sound to be represented. Thus a lion or a lamb will stand for the letter *l*, a mountain or a mouse for *m*, &c. But whether, like the Chinese, they have a mark or sign, (other than the *cartouche*, which they also make use of for proper names,) to inform the reader that the characters are alphabetical, does not yet appear. "Almost nothing of the kind," says Champollion, "is observed in the hieroglyphic texts of the Egyptians."† Until this fact is ascertained, we cannot expect to make much further progress in the deciphering of the Egyptian hieroglyphics.

But it is time that I should leave this long digression, and proceed as fast as I can to the conclusion of this letter, which already exceeds all reasonable bounds.

---

* These three syllables or words will be found in Morrison's Chinese and English Dictionary, in which the words are classed in the order of our alphabet.

† On n'observe, en général, presque rien de semblable dans les textes hiéroglyphiques Egyptiens. Précis, p. 346.

SECTION VII.

I find, my dear sir, that I have gone through a wide field
of discussion. I have wandered from the Chinese to the
Mexican, from that to the Egyptian, and back again to the
Chinese, and yet I have not touched on the main subject of
this communication, which is to consider whether and how
far the Chinese writing is read and understood by nations
who speak different languages from the Chinese, and who
cannot either speak that idiom, or understand it when spoken.
I cannot close this letter without saying something upon this
interesting question, which I submit, however, to the further
investigation of the learned; and, to assist them in it, I present to the Society the two annexed vocabularies.

That a language may be read and understood, and even
written by persons who cannot speak it, or if they do speak
it, who cannot understand each other, because of the difference in their mode of pronunciation, is a fact so common,
that examples of it need hardly be adduced. An Englishi-
man and a Frenchman, both good classical scholars, cannot,
without great difficulty, understand each other when speaking Latin. I believe there is not an orientalist in the uni-
versities of Europe, who, unless he has resided some time
in the East, can hold a conversation in Arabic or Persian;
and there are excellent translators of modern European
languages who cannot speak a word of the idiom that they
translate from. I have been assured that M. Le Tourneur,
who translated into French Young's Night Thoughts and
all Shakspeare's plays, was quite a stranger to the English
spoken language. He had learned to read and to understand the meaning of the groups of letters, to which he applied the sounds of his native tongue. He did not consider
those groups as images or symbols of ideas, but as the representatives of words, which he understood, but could not

pronounce so as to be comprehended by a native Englishman; nor were his ears so accustomed to the sounds of the
language, as to enable him to understand it when spoken.

It may also be observed, that those nations who speak
sister languages, or languages derived from the same stock,
understand a great deal of each other's written dialect. As
the English has borrowed much from the French language, a native of France will understand all the French
words in an English book, except when used in a different
sense from that to which he is accustomed. No doubt, all
these things must operate among the nations bordering upon
China, particularly those whose languages are monosyllabic
and dialects of the Chinese; but I am of opinion, that as in
our languages, these causes can only operate to a certain
extent, and that the Asiatics are not more assisted by the
form of the Chinese characters, than Europeans are by the
appearance of the groups formed by the letters of our
alphabet.

But that is not what is meant by the enthusiasts of the
Chinese system of writing. They ascribe every thing to
the *magical* characters, (if I may so express myself,) and
overlook the plainest and most obvious natural causes. Dr.
Marshman, observing that there are numerous different
dialects spoken in the empire of China, and yet that they all
understand the pure style of writing which is called the
Kwan-hwà, or Mandarin tongue, accounts for it in this manner. "One effect," says he, "resulting from the *written*
language being thus *unconnected* with the colloquial, is
however worthy of notice; it has conferred on the former
a character of *permanent perspicuity*, which renders it
equally intelligible to the inhabitants of the most distant provinces in that vast empire, and even to those of Cochinchina
and Japan; while the latter has assumed a greater variety
of forms than the colloquial dialects of ancient Greece and
of India, with this exception, that these varieties of dialect

11

(like those in the various counties of England,) are *confined
to conversation*, because incapable of acquiring that permanent character, which their connexion with the written medium has conferred on those of Greece and India."[*]

Now see, my dear sir, how far enthusiasm has carried
this learned sinologist. He represents the Chinese dialects,
light words, as they are called, ("Επεα πτερόεντα,) as not
written, and as used only in colloquial discourse. He very
justly compares them to the provincial dialects of England,
which he says are also unwritten; yet, though he cannot
but see that the two cases are exactly similar, since the pure
English is read in the provinces as well as in the capital, he
must find a different cause for that of the Chinese, and that
is what he calls the *permanent perspicuity* of its system of
writing.

The venerable Doctor is not quite correct in supposing
that the Chinese dialects, and those of England and other
countries of Europe, are not written. If he means that they
are not *cultivated*, and that they have not what is called a
literature, I am disposed to agree with him; but that they
are, or at least may be written, is a fact too notorious to be
denied. I have seen a great number of popular books, in
verse and in prose, written in the different *patois* of France.
I have in my possession a collection of *Noels* (Christmas
carols) in that of *Poitou*; and there is one, in another dialect,
in the Congress library at Washington. I have not seen a
book in an English dialect, but I have seen provincial words
written in philological essays, and enough may be seen in
Fielding's Tom Jones of the patois of Somersetshire. In
fact, every language may be written with the letters of our
alphabet. There are sounds, it is true, which they cannot
represent; in that case new characters must be invented,
or the old ones somewhat altered, as is done in the Polish

* Clavis Sinica, p. 558.

and other languages of Europe, and as is also done, by an analogous process, in the Indo-Chinese countries.

Thus the provincial dialects in China are written, by applying to their words and sometimes misapplying the characters of the national alphabet, or by altering them or inventing new ones when found necessary, of which the Doctor himself gives us several examples.* Why, then, does he represent those dialects as *unwritten*, as it were to increase our astonishment at the fact, that the Chinese characters are generally read and understood? Does he wish to make us believe that those characters speak to the mind of the reader *vi propriâ*, by means of their *permanent perspicuity?* No; the learned author does not wish to deceive, but he deceives himself, and his language bears the stamp of the strong impressions which have taken hold of his prejudiced mind.

It is of little consequence whether provincial dialects are or not *light* or *flying languages;* but in this the Chinese, who give them that contemptuous name, and the sinologist who repeats it after them, are alike mistaken. It is a well known fact in Europe, that the *patois*, or peculiar dialects of provinces, preserve their words and their forms longer than cultivated languages. If we wish to have an idea of the language that was spoken in England several centuries ago, it is not to London, but to Yorkshire or Lancashire that we must go to find it; and the dialect of Provence remains the same at this day that it was in the time of the Troubadours, while the old French idiom is still preserved in the Walloon countries of the Netherlands. A cultivated language, on the contrary, continually varies according to the caprice of the writers, who think they are fixing it; but the works of the authors of a succeeding generation show them to have been mistaken. The language of Chaucer,

* Clavis Sinica, p. 560.

and a great deal of that of Shakspeare, can now only be
found in some counties where the words are still retained.

The Mandarin dialect of China is not more permanent, as
a spoken or written language, than those of the provinces.
The only difference is that it is preserved in books, which the
others are not. This may be called *permanency* in a certain sense; that is to say, so far that the memory of the recorded language is preserved even after it has ceased to be
in popular use, but it cannot be understood in the sense of
duration; for the Basque language, spoken by a few thousand men in a corner of Europe, has lasted longer than any
of the cultivated idioms of that part of the world.

As to the Chinese writing, its immense number of super-
fluous signs, invented and added from time to time by the
literati, show any thing but permanency, and may well be
compared to the changes that we perceive from time to
time in the orthography of our languages.

But what has the permanency, real or pretended, of the
Mandarin dialect, or of its writing, to do with the reason
of its being generally read or understood throughout the
Chinese empire? Why should sinologists seek for the cause
of that fact in the superiority of one system over another,
when it may be accounted for in a much more simple and
natural manner? The reason that this dialect is generally
read and understood in China, while the others remain local,
is, that it is the only one which is taught in the schools;
precisely as in England the pure English, and not the northern or southern dialects, and in France the pure French,
and not the patois of Languedoc or Provence, are taught,
and consequently read and understood every where in those
countries. It may be added, that the knowledge of the Mandarin dialect and of its graphic system, is the only means
by which local as well as national offices can be obtained
in the Chinese empire. Therefore, it is no argument in
favour of the pretended ideographic character of the Chi-

nese writing, to say, that it is read and understood by all in China who have learned to read and write. I am almost ashamed to have to answer such arguments, and yet they are urged by men to whose opinions, on other subjects, I would submit with respect. Such is the force of prejudice, which even in enlightened minds is so difficult to be conquered.

We know very little of the dialects of the Chinese empire, as we are not permitted to penetrate into that country, or even to land on their coast, except at the port of Canton. Dr. Marshman has given us some interesting particulars respecting the dialect of that province,* from which we find that it differs very little from the court dialect. It is, like that, monosyllabic, and destitute of grammatical forms. The difference lies in some words, and in some peculiar modes of expression; but on the whole it is the Chinese, read and pronounced as Chinese with a few exceptions, which have necessarily occasioned some alterations in the character, which are the provincial orthography. The Mithridates gives us also a brief account of the dialect of the province of Fo-kien, extracted from a grammar and dictionary preserved in manuscript in the Royal Library of Berlin. The grammar, it appears, has been printed in Bayer's *Museum Sinicum*, which book I have not seen. On the whole, it differs from the pure Chinese, pretty much in the same manner as the Canton dialect;† and Dr. Marshman presumes that it is much the same in the other provinces.

But it is said that not only the inhabitants of the provinces of China, who speak different dialects, read, write and understand the Chinese written language, but that the same thing takes place in Tonquin, Cochinchina, the Loo-choo Islands, and other countries, where the languages are

* Clavis Sinica, p. 560.   † Mithrid. vol. i. p. 54.

monosyllabic dialects of the Chinese, and also in Japan, the
vernacular idiom of which country is known to be polysyllabic, and to differ entirely in etymology and grammar from
that of China. If this were stated merely as a fact, without
attaching to it any particular importance, it might easily be
credited, as there is certainly nothing in it to excite our wonder. Thus, if a Chinese should say that he saw in Europe men
of different nations conversing with one another in writing,
in a language called the *La-tin*, though they could not understand each other's native idiom, nor even converse together in that language, because of the difference of their
pronunciation, he would easily be credited, and no more
would be said about it; all the inference that would be
drawn from the fact would be, that both had learned the
Latin language, but could not converse in it, because they
pronounced it differently. But it is not so that our enthusiasts wish to be understood. They wish it to be believed
that there is something *magical* in the Chinese writing,
something out of the ordinary course of things, by which
ideas are conveyed from eye to eye, and through the eyes
from mind to mind, without the intervention of articulate
sounds; so that each person may read the characters in his
own language, however it may differ from the Chinese in
words or in form. To such a broad assertion it is impossible for a rational man to give his assent.

If the language of those who thus read the Chinese without being able to speak it, should be formed precisely on the
model of that idiom as to its grammatical structure, and
should use the same characters to represent corresponding
words, the fact might easily be believed; but that is a thing
not to be expected, since even in China the dialects differ
from each other. If the resemblance should extend only to
a certain number of words and of characters, to that extent
the parties might understand each other, but no farther. If,
however, the difference were total, as between the Japanese

and the Chinese, I cannot conceive how two men, thus circumstanced, can converse together in writing in the Chinese character, unless they both should have learned it, not as an ideographical character, but as the representation of a spoken idiom; in short, as *Chinese*. That they should not both pronounce it alike can make no difference; their vocal organs might not be accustomed to utter its sounds, or they might not have been in the habit of speaking it, and could not find the words when they wanted them.

This is a natural explanation of a natural fact; but *miracles*, such as the enthusiasts would have us believe, cannot be explained. We have disposed of the Chinese provinces; let us now see how the fact stands in other countries, and to what causes it is to be attributed.

We know that the monosyllabic family of languages extends beyond the limits of the Chinese empire. All those languages, as far as we are informed, appear to be derived from the same stock; but which of them is the mother tongue, it is impossible to tell. The Chinese is the most cultivated, but that does not give it the *droit d'aînesse*. Of all those languages we have but a few words, scattered here and there in the works of philologists. Of one of them only, a dictionary and a short grammar exists in Europe. It is the Anamitic, or, as some write it, *Annamitic*, the language of the country of *Anam*, which is said to include Tonquin and Cochinchina. The book is entitled *Alexandri De Rhodes Dictionarium Annamiticum*, and was printed at Rome, in 1651, in quarto.[*] Such rare books are not to be obtained in this country. It does not appear whether the written characters are given with the words; I rather presume that they are not.

It is known also, that those nations make use of the Chinese characters in writing their several idioms, but in what man-

* Mithrid. vol. i. p. 88.

ner, and with what alterations or modifications, is entirely unknown. I am informed that there are several Tonquinese manuscripts in the Royal Library at Paris, but that the characters are so altered or so abbreviated, which in part perhaps arises from their peculiar calligraphy, that the sinologists have hitherto been unable to decipher them. Of the Cochinchinese graphic character, nothing that I know of has yet appeared in Europe. Father Morrone's Vocabulary, now presented to our Society, will be the first printed specimen of the Chinese system of writing, applied to another monosyllabic language. It may help to decipher the manuscripts in the Royal Library at Paris. There is reason to believe that the Tonquinese and Cochinchinese, with little variation, are the same language.

It is therefore from this Vocabulary, and from it alone, that we can at present form an idea of the manner in which the Chinese system of writing is applied to a monosyllabic language other than the Chinese. I can do little more than produce the document, as it is not in my power to institute a comparison between the Chinese and Cochinchinese languages, and to explain the practical use which they respectively make of the same graphic system. The observations of M. de la Palun are not intended to instruct his brother sinologists, but to facilitate their labours. To them the question before us, as it respects monosyllabic idioms, must ultimately be submitted.

In this Vocabulary any one may observe that there are a number of genuine Chinese characters applied to words corresponding in sense, though often differing in sound. So far, it must be acknowledged that the two nations may communicate with each other in writing, though they might not orally. But it will be seen also, that this correspondence does not exist throughout, and that the same character in the two languages often represent what the sinologists would call *ideas*, totally different, and sometimes opposite to each other. Neither is the combination of the characters always the same in the two idioms. And lastly, it will be perceived, that there is a great number of characters, which M. de la Palun could not find in the printed Chinese dictionaries. They may be abbreviations of Chinese characters peculiar to the Cochinchinese, or perhaps they are among the multitude of obsolete signs known only to the literati, and therefore which can be of little service in common use. All these things, no doubt, will be duly weighed by the sinologists of Europe, if the subject should be thought worthy of their attention.

But I will not anticipate on the labours of the sinologists, who are much more able to investigate this subject than I am, and to whom I am happy to have furnished a subject on which to exercise their sagacity, aided by knowledge which I do not possess.

On the whole it must be acknowledged, that, to a certain extent, the Chinese and Cochinchinese may communicate in writing without knowing each other's spoken language. How far it is in their power so to do, I leave to those better able to decide it than myself. I must now proceed to the polysyllabic languages.

It is unfortunate, that of the polysyllabic languages which are said to make use of the Chinese characters in their writing, there is but one, the Japanese, with which we are sufficiently acquainted to be able to form a judgment on the question before us. We have a grammar of this language, written in Portuguese by Father Rodriguez, and translated into French by M. Landresse.* To this work is added a

* Elémens de la Grammaire Japonaise, par le P. Rodriguez; traduits du Portugais sur le manuscrit de la Bibliothèque du Roi, et soigneusement collationné avec la Grammaire publiée par le même auteur à Nagasaki en 1604, par M. C. Landresse, membre de la Société Asiatique. Précédés d'une explication des *syllabaires* Japonais, et de deux planches, contenant

12

preface, and an explanation of the two syllabic alphabets of the Japanese, by which we are enabled to understand their graphic system; and the grammar lets us fully into the structure of their vernacular language, which is polysyllabic, and in its words as well as in its grammatical forms differs entirely from the Chinese. This language is called the *Yomi;* it is the idiom of the country, not a *patois,* solely in use among the 'vulgar and illiterate. In this language, says M. Remusat, are written novels, poems, and other works of light literature.*

The alphabet of this idiom consists of forty-seven characters, each of which represents a syllable. Those characters are Chinese, but which do not here represent words, or, as the sinologists would say, *ideas,* but only syllabic sounds. There are two such alphabets, one called *Kata Kana* and the other *Firo Kana,* but they are in fact one and the same; the only difference between them is, that one of them is formed of the *running hand,* and the other of the square characters of the Chinese. Both are written in an abridged form, and are joined together in various ways, which it is unnecessary here to mention. It is evident that those who know only this language, cannot communicate with the Chinese, either orally or in writing.

But the Chinese is also used in Japan. It is there a learned language, in which are written works of history, philosophy, and the higher literature.† The notes are usually written in the Yomi, as notes to Latin books with us are sometimes written in English. Sometimes the two languages are mixed, which it would seem can only be for those who are acquainted with both, that is to say, the literati. It is not presumable that the mass of the people possess this

les signes de ces syllabaires, par M. Abel Remusat. Ouvrage publié par la Société Asiatique. Paris, Dondey Dupré, 1825.

* Elémens, &c. p. xiv.   † Ibid. p. xiii.

knowledge. The pure *Koye*, says Father Rodriguez, is no other than the Chinese.*

The words, or, as sinologists would say, the *pronunciation*, of this language, are the same as the Chinese, with some trifling difference, arising principally from that in the vocal organs of the two nations, as several of the Chinese sounds are wanting in the Japanese. The people of Japan, for instance, want the letter *l*, and substitute for it the letter *r*, and *f* for *p*, which they also want. They omit the nasal sounds, which they cannot articulate. M. Remusat gives us some examples of these differences.

For Thian or Teen	(heaven)	the Japanese say	Ten
Youei	(moon)	"	Goua
Foung	(wind)	"	Fou
Ping	(ice)	"	Fiao
For Jin	(man)	"	Nin
Koung	(prince)	"	Koo
Fo	(Buddha)	"	Bouts
Pe	(white)	"	Fak
Wang	(king)	"	Oo
Li	(place)	"	Ri
Seng	(religious)	"	Soo, &c.

It is probable, therefore, that those Japanese who have learned the *Koye*, that is to say, the Chinese language, though they pronounce it differently, as Europeans do the Latin and the Greek, may communicate in writing with the Chinese, though they may not understand each other when speaking; while those who have learned only the *Yomi*, cannot make themselves understood, either by writing or by word of mouth. In all this there is nothing wonderful or

* Gramm. Japon. p. 104, § 109.

miraculous, nor any thing that tends to prove the ideographic character, or, as Dr. Marshman calls it, the *permanent perspicuity* of the Chinese system of writing.

———

Conclusion.

Such were my sentiments upon this subject in the month of December, 1827, when I had the pleasure to become acquainted with Captain Basil Hall, of the Royal British Navy. I had read his voyage to the Loo-Choo Islands, in which he had stated as matter of fact, that the inhabitants of China, Corea, Japan and Loo-Choo, understood each other by means of *common written characters*, though they could not understand each other's languages. I took the liberty, in the course of a conversation that I had with him, to express a different opinion, and to offer some arguments in support of my sentiment. Captain Hall candidly acknowledged that he had received his information at second hand, and that it was possible that he had been misinformed. There the matter rested until the latter end of June, in the year following, when Captain Hall being at New York, on the point of embarking for his native country, reminded me by letter of our conversation, and requested that I should send to him in England a statement of the facts and arguments on which was founded the opinion that I had advanced. This I promised to do, and he departed.

Shortly after his departure I performed my promise, and wrote him the letter which you have seen,* containing a summary of the arguments and facts by which I supported

my opinion, and which I have explained here more at large.
The season being fine, and I in want of exercise and relaxation from my professional labours, I took a trip to New York, and carried the letter with me, in order to put it on board one of the packets about to sail for England. While in that city I accidentally met with the latest number of Baron Ferussac's Bulletin des Sciences Historiques, &c.,* that had reached this country, in which, in a pretty long notice of a philosophical work, then lately published in Germany, I read the following paragraph:

"The author (M. Windischmann) is in an error, when he believes that the Chinese writing might become a *pasi-graphy*, which all the world might make use of, even without knowing the oral language; for the characters which represent sound, the *hing-ching*, constitute almost three-fourths of the writing; and it is even this difficulty which has induced the Coreans, the Japanese, and the Cochinchinese, to change that system more or less, in order to adapt it to their languages. We find all the details relative to this alteration, which, at the same time, shows the passage from the ideographic to a system of syllabic and alphabetical writing, in the Memoir of M. Abel Remusat, inserted in the eighth volume of the Memoirs of the Institute, (Academy of Inscriptions and Belles Lettres, pp. 34—59.)"

I was as much surprised as delighted in reading this paragraph. I had always considered M. Remusat as the most formidable of my adversaries. I could not but remember that he had said, that the inhabitants of Japan, Tonquin, Cochinchina and the Loo-choo Islands, though they did not understand one another when speaking, could hold a con-

---

* It is much to be regretted that this excellent periodical has been discontinued, as well as the *Revue Encyclopedique*, which was conducted by M. Jullien, at Paris. Their loss, at least to my knowledge, has not yet been repaired.

versation in writing, and read the same books.* But that was in 1811, when he was yet fresh from the reading of the Chinese authors, and his mind biassed by their opinions, which no one at that time could have contradicted without being stigmatised as a rash innovator and a fanciful theorist. But more extensive studies, and his own excellent judgment, had at last brought him to a clearer and a more rational view of the subject.

I was so delighted with this discovery, that I immediately informed Captain Hall of it in a postscript to my letter, which was not yet sealed up; it was done in such haste, that I called the article on M. Windischmann's book a *short* notice, and told him that it was written by Champollion, junior, which I really believed when I wrote, but which I have since found to be a mistake. The article is anonymous, and signed S.

Shortly after my return to this city, our Society received the eighth volume of the Memoirs of the Academy of Inscriptions, and I received M. Remusat's Memoir from the author himself. I cannot express with what pleasure I perused it. I found in it all my ideas, but much better expressed than I could have done. I recommend to you to read it with attention; you will find in it a full and clear refutation of the opinion which has too long prevailed of the almost universality of the Chinese characters.†

I should not have entered into this discussion, considering the question to be put at rest by M. Remusat's learned and

---

* De sorte que quoiqu'ils ne se comprenerent pas en parlant, ils peuvent cependant converser par écrit, et lire les mêmes livres. C'est cette propriété de la *langue* Chinoise, qui a fait desirer à quelques missionnaires, qu'elle fût cultivée dans le monde entier, parce qu'alors, le Nouveau Testament étant traduit en Chinois, tous les peuples pourdient le lire sans apprendre la langue et *sur la seule inspection des caractères.* Essai sur la langue, &c. p. 35.

† See Appendix, B.

elegant Memoir, if, notwithstanding the strength and clearness of his arguments, the opinion which he supports, and which has been ascribed exclusively to me, had not been repeatedly contradicted in such a manner as to require on my part to be noticed. An anonymous writer in the Canton Register rebuked Captain Hall in a severe, and, I might say, illiberal manner, for having yielded his opinion to mine, and asserted that he had himself interchanged thoughts in the Chinese character with the Cochinchinese, Japanese, and Loo-chooans, without understanding their respective languages; and that it would be to be regretted, if that fact should lose its hold on the mind of any *Christian* philanthropist by the confessions of Captain Hall. You will find a copy of the whole article here subjoined.*

I cannot understand how *religion* comes to be called in aid of any man's opinion in a mere question of fact. I should think that it may be decided without appealing to Moses or the prophets. I never suspected before that the Chinese characters involved a religious dogma, which cannot be contradicted without danger to the Christian faith.

Not long afterwards, a more liberal antagonist presented himself in the person of Captain F. W. Beechey, of the Royal British Navy. That gentleman, in the narrative of his voyage to the Pacific and Behring's Straits, relates, that he found in the Loo-choo Islands many people who understood the meaning of the Chinese characters, but who could not give the Chinese pronunciation of the word; and he adds, that the language of Loo-choo is not monosyllabic like the Chinese, but is, like the Japanese, polysyllabic.†

I do not mean to contradict the gallant Captain in any thing that he asserts from his own knowledge. He has seen Loo-chooans who could read the Chinese character, and yet could not converse with him in Chinese. Be it so; I

* Appendix, C.   † Appendix, D.

hope I have shown above how this may have happened, without affecting the principles on which I found my doctrine. I am not so well convinced that the Loo-choo language is polysyllabic; in this I fear Captain Beechey will find himself mistaken.

The interesting question, therefore, *how far* the Chinese character may serve as a common medium of communication between nations who speak different languages, and cannot communicate orally with each other, may be considered as still *sub judice;* and documentary evidence tending to its solution, cannot be unworthy of the attention of a philosophical society. On one side are arguments which, to every unprejudiced mind, appear to be conclusive; on the other, are facts attested by witnesses worthy of credit. Surely the science of philology never presented a subject more deserving of full and complete investigation.

I can easily comprehend how Chinese books and writings may be read and understood by those who cannot speak the language. Such is the case, as I have observed before, with the sinologists and orientalists in Europe, who have never visited the countries the languages of which they have learned, would be greatly embarrassed were they to be suddenly transported into the city of Pekin or Cairo, to ask even for the common necessaries of life. It is the same with other languages, which are read and understood when written, by those who can neither speak nor understand them when spoken. There are many persons in this country and elsewhere, who can read French, Italian or German, without being able to converse in those idioms. The fact is, that the groups of alphabetical letters which form our written languages are quite as *ideographic* as the characters of the Chinese, and the proof is, that they can be read and understood by persons born deaf and dumb, and who never had the least idea of sounds. They understand the meaning of those groups by means of their analogies, precisely as the Chinese characters are read. Those analogies in polysyllabic languages consist in the frequent occurrence of the same prefixes, affixes, and inflexions of words, in the Chinese, in the juxtaposition and combination of the signs of words explanatory of each other, but not in the mimic forms of the signs themselves, as representing natural or allegorical objects.

So far there is no difficulty. If we consider the Chinese as a predominant or a learned language, taught in the schools of Cochinchina and other countries as a necessary part of education, we may conceive how it can be read and understood by educated persons, and to a certain extent be written by them, though it cannot be spoken; but if we are to understand that each nation only learns to read the Chinese character as written at home, and as applied to her own language, the question becomes much more difficult, and it must be acknowledged that it requires further investigation.

I should not, however, have addressed either the Society or yourself upon this subject, but should have left it to take its chance, if I had not expected to throw some new light upon it by the communication of Father Morrone's Cochinchinese Vocabularies. I was informed of their existence by reading Lieutenant White's Voyage to the China Sea. I found in it a short extract from the Cochinchinese and French Vocabulary, containing twenty-five words of that language with the Chinese characters prefixed, and the corresponding Chinese word added by way of comparison, by a learned gentleman of Boston.* The greatest number of the Cochinchinese words, though different in sound, agreed in signification with the Chinese; but several were of quite another meaning. I found, for instance, that the character which in Chinese stood for *kettle*, in Cochinchinese signified

* The Rev. William Jenks, D. D.

13

lead; the Chinese character *po,* to land, in Cochinchinese meant *silver,* &c. I was so struck with this, that I mentioned it in the preface to my translation of Zeisberger's Delaware Grammar,* and expressed a hope that the Academy of Arts and Sciences at Boston would publish it in their valuable Memoirs. In this, however, I was disappointed. In the mean time, M. E. Jacquet, a distinguished member of the Asiatic Society of Paris, and a pupil of Abel Remusat, who had read the account I had given of that document in our transactions, expressed the wish to see it entire, and recommended that we should either publish it here, or transmit it to him to be published under the sanction of the Asiatic Society. The manuscript had been deposited by Lieutenant White in the library of the East India Marine Society at Salem, in Massachusetts. I made application to that Society for permission to take a copy of it. With the greatest liberality that respectable institution, through their president, William Fettyplace, Esq., sent me the original manuscript, and with it another, of the existence of which I had no knowledge, and which is the one in Cochinchinese and Latin, which, on account of its larger size and alphabetical arrangement, I have called a Dictionary. Of this last I immediately caused a copy to be made, which you have here enclosed.

On examining the former, I mean the Cochinchinese and French Vocabulary, with the Chinese characters prefixed, I found that it had not the addition of the Chinese words, as in the extract published by Lieutenant White. I was not then sufficiently acquainted with Dr. Jenks to take the liberty of asking him to undertake that labour. I was at a loss what to do, when I fortunately made the acquaintance of M. de la Palun, who was then consul of France at Richmond, in Virginia, and is now in the same capacity at Caracas, in

* Transact. A. P. S., vol. iii. N. S. p. 72.

the republic of Venezuela. That gentleman, also a pupil of Abel Remusat, and well versed in the Chinese language, readily undertook to compare each Cochinchinese word with the Chinese word represented by the same character, and to commit to writing the result of his inquiry. This work he completed before his departure, not without much haste, as he did not expect so soon to be removed. He gave it to me in his passage through this city, on his way to New York, where he embarked for the place of his destination. I regret that I had not sufficient time to confer with him on some points, which perhaps would have required a fuller explanation.

Lieutenant White, in his book, makes no mention of the authorship of those two documents, and only says that they were given to him by Father Joseph Morrone, at Saigun, and that he is the eldest of the Italian missionaries there. We are therefore left to conjecture who are the authors of those two Vocabularies.

As to the first, I mean the one which has the Cochinchinese characters annexed to it, I believe it to have been compiled by the good father himself. It is written entirely in his own hand, and the translation of the Cochinchinese words is in indifferent French. For instance, he writes *la claive*, I presume from the Latin *clavis*, instead of *la clef*, (the key,) and there are other indications which show him not to be very familiar with the language in which he wrote, though Lieutenant White says that he speaks it fluently. I therefore believe that I may publish this Vocabulary as the work of Father Morrone, as I see no reason to suppose that it is that of a French missionary. It is true, that the Cochinchinese words are written with the Portuguese orthography, but that may be in common use among the missionaries there. In translating the Cochinchinese word which means *a goose*, he uses the French word *canard*, but not being sure of it, he explains it by the Italian word *oca*, which shows that he wrote in a language in which he was not perfect.

As to the second manuscript, (the Cochinchinese and Latin Dictionary,) I am of a different opinion, and believe it to be only a copy of the work of some other person. M. Jacquet, whom I consulted on the subject, wrote to me as follows: "As to the Vocabulary No. 2, I do not believe it to have been composed by Father Morrone. For more than two centuries, there has been in the missionary establishments in Cochinchina, a Cochinchinese and Latin Vocabulary, without the Chinese characters, which every new missionary copies on his arrival at the mission, and adds to it his own observations, if he is able to make any. In this manner there are several copies, differing in the details, though the ground work is the same. The celebrated Bishop of Adran, M. Pigneaux,* undertook, about fifty years

* Lieutenant White calls him Bishop Adran, mistaking the name of his episcopal see for his proper name. The account he gives of him is interesting. "At the period of the rebellion," (1774) says he, "there resided at court a French missionary of the name of Adran, who called himself the apostolic vicar of Cochinchina. The king held him in such great consideration, as to place under his tuition his only son and heir to the throne. After the rebellion was ended, the bishop became the oracle and guide of the king. Under his auspices the country was greatly improved; and during a short peace, he established a manufactory of salt-petre, opened roads, held out rewards for the propagation of the silk-worm, caused large tracts of land to be cleared for the cultivation of the sugar-cane, established manufactories for the preparation of pitch, tar, rosin, &c.; opened mines of iron; constructed smelting furnaces and foundries for cannon. Adran translated into the Onam language a system of European military tactics, for the use of the army. Naval arsenals were established, and a large navy, principally consisting of gun-boats, galleys, &c., was built and equipped. Under his direction, reformation was effected in the system of jurisprudence; he abolished several species of punishments that were disproportionate to the crimes to which they were annexed. He established public schools, and compelled parents to send their children to them at the age of four years. He drew up commercial regulations; built bridges; caused buoys and sea marks to be laid

ago, to compile all those Vocabularies into one, which should be the *Dictionnaire de l'Académie* of Cochinchina. He was, during fourteen years, engaged in that work, and compiled at the same time a Latin and Cochinchinese Dictionary, and wrote a grammar of that language. His labours, yet unpublished, were lately presented to the Asiatic Society of Calcutta, with a request that the British government in India should be invited to publish them, at the expense of the East India Company, either at the printing office of Penang or at that of Calcutta. After a pretty long negotiation, the government made known to the Asiatic Society their refusal to undertake that publication, which would have cost only twelve hundred rupees. Application has since been made to the Translating Committee at London; the result is not yet known."

In the Journal of the Asiatic Society of London for January, 1836, p. 54, I read the following paragraph: " A letter from the Vicar Apostolic of Cochinchina was read, requesting the Society to forward the specimen of *his* Dictionary, which he regretted to hear could not be printed in Calcutta, to the Oriental translating fund in England, in case that body should be inclined to patronise its publication."

Nothing has been heard about it since that time; and it is feared that this application has been as unsuccessful as the former. The United States, therefore, will have the honour of being the first to publish authentic documents respecting the language of Cochinchina, and to introduce that curious idiom to the literary world.

down in all the dangerous parts of the coast, and surveys to be made of the principal bays and harbours. The officers of the navy were instructed in naval tactics by Frenchmen; his army was divided into regular regiments; military schools were established, and the officers taught the science of gunnery. Unfortunately for the country, the death of Adran occurred shortly after this; and with him expired many of the wholesome laws, institutions and regulations established by him." See White's Voyage to the China Seas, pp. 89, 93. Boston edition.

This publication will not fail to excite interest in the other hemisphere. There is none in Europe in any way relating to the Cochinchinese idiom, except the *Dictionarium Annamiticum* of Father De Rhodes, which I have already mentioned, and which is very rare. The Anamitic language of which it treats is that of Tonquin, but there is reason to believe that it does not differ much from that of Cochinchina. Lieutenant White calls the latter the language of *Onam*, by which the Tonquinese is also known; and he calls the Cochinchinese the Onamese flag. The Anamitic words given by Mr. Klaproth, in his Asia Polyglotta, are pure Cochinchinese.

It is said also, that about two hundred years ago the Tonquinese invaded Cochinchina, and drove away the former inhabitants from the country; and that, it is also said, is the origin of the present population.* In that case, the language must be very nearly if not entirely the same.

I have not pretended to enter into the comparison of the Cochinchinese languages and their system of writing, because I do not feel myself competent to it, and because the task will be much better performed by the sinologists of Asia and Europe, to whose judgment I shall cheerfully submit.

I am, very sincerely,

Your friend and humble servant,

PETER S. DU PONCEAU.

Philadelphia, 24th November, 1836.

* White, p. 82. Morrison's View of China, p. 80.

APPENDIX

A.

Letter from Peter S. Du Ponceau to Captain Basil Hall,
R. B. N.

PHILADELPHIA, 7th July, 1828.

My DEAR SIR,

Our mutual friend, Mr. Vaughan, has handed me your polite letter of the 29th ult. I was much surprised, and at the same time highly flattered, to find that the few observations I took the liberty to make to you on the writing of the Chinese, when we last met at Dr. Gibson's, had left an impression on your mind; as I had no expectation, amidst the many objects with which you were surrounded in your peregrinations through this country, of leaving even a trace in your remembrance. It is therefore with great pleasure that I comply with your request, in giving some further development to the ideas which I then threw out to you, and which derive all their value from your having thought them worthy to be kept in mind.

Having for many years devoted my leisure moments to the study of the philosophy of language, the Chinese idiom and its peculiar system of writing could not escape my attention. I was at first astonished at the wonders which are ascribed to this mode of ocular communication, which appeared to me to be greatly exaggerated, and I determined

14

to pursue the subject as far as my means would permit me. The result of my investigations does by no means agree with the opinion that is generally entertained. I do not pretend to know the Chinese language; therefore those who have learned, and consequently can read and understand it, have a great advantage over me in a discussion in which I attempt to controvert even the opinions of profound sinologists. I have, however, studied the elementary and other works which treat of that idiom, in order to acquaint myself with the curious structure of that language, and the principles of its graphic system; and have possessed myself of a sufficient number of facts to enable me to form logical conclusions. This is all that can be expected of a general philologist; if it were otherwise, that science must be entirely abandoned, as it is impossible for any one man to know more than very few of the unnumbered and perhaps innumerable languages that exist on the surface of the earth.

The general opinion which prevails, even among those who are the most proficient in the Chinese idiom, is, that the system or mode of writing which is in use in that country, and which they call the *written* in opposition to the *spoken* language, is an ocular method of communicating ideas, entirely independent of speech, and which, without the intervention of words, conveys ideas through the sense of vision directly to the mind. Hence it is called *ideographic,* in contradistinction from the *phonographic* or alphabetical system of writing. This is the idea which is entertained of it in China, and may justly be ascribed to the vanity of the Chinese literati. The Catholic at first, and afterwards the Protestant missionaries, have received it from them without much examination; and the love of wonder, natural to our species, has not a little contributed to propagate that opinion, which has at last taken such possession of the public mind, that it has become one of those axioms which no one will venture to contradict. It requires not a little boldness to fly in the face of an opinion so generally received, and which has so many respectable authorities in its support, and none against it but those of reason and fair logical deductions from uncontroverted facts. As you have, however, in a manner challenged me to produce the proof of my assertions, I do not hesitate to do it, in the spirit of humility which becomes me, and submitting the whole to your candour and better judgment.

This opinion has naturally led to that of the Chinese writing being an universal written language conveying ideas directly to the mind, and which might be read alike in every idiom upon earth, as our numerical figures and algebraic signs are. This idea has been carried so far, that some missionaries have wished that the Chinese *written language*, as it is called, should be cultivated through the whole world ; for then the New Testament, being translated into Chinese, all nations might read it, without learning the spoken idiom, and on a mere inspection of the characters.* And as a proof that this might be done, it has been alleged that the Japanese, Coreans, Cochinchinese, and other nations, could read Chinese books without knowing or understanding the oral language of China. But these are not the only wonderful systems to which this opinion has given rise.

This writing having been formed, as is supposed, without any reference to, or connexion with, spoken language, a question might naturally arise, which of the two was first invented ? Nobody, to be sure, has ventured to say that writing existed before speech; yet if that proposition has not been directly advanced, I must say that sinologists have come very near to it. For instance, they affect to call the monosyllabic words of the Chinese language the *pronuncia-*

* Remusat, Essai sur la langue et la literature Chinoise, p. 35.

tion of the characters, which leads to the direct inference that the words were made for the signs, and not these for the words. A justly celebrated French sinologist, M. Abel Remusat, does not indeed believe that a language was invented to suit the written characters after they were formed; but he supposes that some then existing popular idiom was *adopted,* to serve as a *pronunciation* to the graphic signs.* One step more, and hardly that, and written characters must have been invented before men learned to speak.

The English sinologists, Sir George Staunton, the Rev. M. Morrison, and others, represent the Chinese writing much in the same point of view, of which you may convince yourself by referring to their works. And by way of proof, it is every where repeated that the Chinese writings are read alike by different nations who do not understand the spoken idiom.

No philosopher that I know of has yet attempted to reduce these vague notions to a rational standard. I have stated them candidly, as they appear in the works of the missionaries, travellers, and sinologists, and I must own that they never satisfied my understanding. I have taken great pains to come at the real truth, and I shall now proceed to communicate to you the result of my inquiries.

The Chinese language, I mean as it is spoken, for I do not call any writing a *language*, except metaphorically, is, as you well know, monosyllabic; that is to say, every one of its syllables (with very few exceptions) is a word, and has a specific determinate meaning; in which it differs from our languages, which consist for the most part of unmeaning syllables, or of syllables which, if they have an appropriate meaning, have no connexion with the words of which they make a part. Take, for instance, the word *con-fir-ma-*

* Mélanges Asiatiques, vol. ii. p. 52.

tion; the first and the two last syllables have no meaning whatever; the second, *fir*, by itself means a kind of tree, but it has no relation to the word in which it enters. It is otherwise with the Chinese language; every syllable of it is significant, and is never employed but in the sense of its meaning. There may be compound words in the Chinese, but as in our words *welfare, welcome,* each of their component syllables preserve their proper signification.

Every one of these significant syllables or words has one or more characters appropriate to it, and every character has a corresponding word.* If two Chinese read the same book, they will read it exactly alike; there will not be the difference of a single syllable. Were it otherwise, the Chinese writing would be translated, not read. Notwithstanding what the sinologists tell us of the beauty of the Chinese poetry, and even of their prosaic style, *to the eye,* it is certain that the metre and rhythm of their verses are addressed to the ear. Their versification is measured, and their poetry is in rhyme, and they have also a measured prose.† All this is written in the pretended ideographic character, word for word, exactly as it is spoken; and no two readings can absolutely take place. It seems therefore evident, that the characters were invented to represent the Chinese words, and not the ideas which these represent, abstractedly from the verbal expression.

It is true, that in the grouping of characters to represent single words, the inventors have called to their aid the ideas which the words express. Thus the character which answers to the word *hand,* is grouped with those which answer to words expressing manual operations. But this was not done with a view to an ideographic language; it was merely an auxiliary means to aid in the classification of the numerous signs which otherwise the memory could not

---

* Remusat, Grammaire Chinoise, p. 1. † Ibid. p. 171, &c.

have retained. The sinologists see great beauties in these associations, of which I am not competent to speak. I suspect, however, that there is in that more imagination than reality.

Be this as it may, as the Chinese characters represent the words of the language, and are intended to awaken the remembrance of them in the mind, they are not therefore independent of sounds, for *words are sounds.* It makes no difference whether those sounds are simple and elementary, as those which our letters represent, or whether they are compounded from two or three of those elements into a syllable. There are syllabic alphabets, like that of the Sanscrit and other languages, and it has never been contended that they do not represent *sounds.* And it makes no difference that the Chinese syllables are also *words,* for that does not make them lose their character of sounds. But, on account of this difference, I would not call the Chinese characters a *syllabic,* but a *logographic* system of writing.

This being the case, it seems necessarily to follow, that as the Chinese characters are in direct connexion with the Chinese spoken words, they can only be read and understood by those who are familiar with the oral language. I do not mean to say that they cannot be applied to other monosyllabic idioms, (and they are, in fact, applied even to polysyllabic languages, as I shall presently show,) I only contend that their meaning cannot be understood alike in the different languages in which they are used.

You very well know, my dear sir, how various are the forms of human languages. You know that, even in the same language, there are not two words exactly synonymous; *a fortiori,* it must be so in two different idioms. Take the word *grand,* for instance, which belongs to the French and to the English languages. Though its general meaning be the same in both idioms, yet how strong are the shades which distinguish the ideas they particularly represent! Now let us suppose that England is in possession of a logographic system of writing. Will the character representing the word *grand* be clearly understood by a Frenchman who does not know the English oral language? Will an Englishman understand the French character *j'aimerais*, without knowing the French mode of conjugating verbs? How would a Latin phrase be understood by an Englishman or a Frenchman, merely by means of signs appropriate to each word? Our ideas, independent of speech, are vague, fleeting, and confused; language alone fixes them, and not in the same manner with every nation. Some languages take in a group of ideas, and express them in one word; others analyse a single idea, and have a separate word for each minute part of which it is composed. Some take an idea as it were in front, others in profile, and others in the rear; and hence the immense variety of forms and modes of expression that exist in the different languages of the earth. All languages abound in metaphors and elliptical modes of speech, which vary according to the genius of each particular idiom. In no language are these figures more frequent than in the Chinese, which is admitted to be elliptical in the highest degree, and is full of far-fetched metaphorical expressions. For instance, the grandees of the empire are called *the four seas*, (*quatuor maria*,) to express which the Chinese writing has two characters, one for *quatuor* and the other for *maria*, which is very distinct from the idea of *superiority* or *greatness*. I ask how these characters can be understood or read in a language that has not adopted the same mode of expression? Again: the English phrase, " *I do not expect it*," is rendered in Chinese by " *how dare!*" and the sentence, " *What you are alarmed about is not of much importance*," is thus expressed; " *You this one bother not greatly required.*"* It would be difficult

* Morrison's Chinese Dialogues, vii. 197.

to read this intelligibly in any language but the Chinese, or one formed exactly on the same model, and in every respect analogous to it. Nor could the corresponding literal English phrases be read intelligibly in Chinese, for want of similar turns of expression and grammatical forms.

A purely ideographical language, therefore, unconnected with spoken words, cannot, in my opinion, possibly exist. There is no universal standard for the fixation of ideas; we cannot abstract our ideas from the channel in which language has taught them to run; hence the Chinese writing is and can be nothing else than a servile representation of the spoken language, as far as visible signs can be made to represent audible sounds. I defy all the philosophers of Europe to frame a written language (as they are pleased to call it) that will not bear a direct and close analogy to some one of the oral languages which they have previously learned. It will be English, Latin, French, Greek, or whatever else they may choose; but it will not be an original written idiom, in which ideas will be combined in a different manner from those to which they have been accustomed.

This reasoning, you will say, may be perfectly correct; but what if, in spite of your theory, Chinese books are understood in Japan, Corea, and Cochinchina, even though the people do not understand the spoken idiom of China? This is, indeed, a pressing argument; but was the child born with a golden tooth?

It is a pretty well ascertained fact, that in Tonquin, Laos, Cochinchina, Camboje and Siam, and also Corea, Japan, and the Loo-choo Islands, the Chinese is a learned and sacred language, in which religious and scientific books are written; while the more popular language of the country is employed for writings of a lighter kind. It is not therefore extraordinary, that there should be many persons in those countries who read and understand Chinese writing, as there are many among us who read and understand Latin;

and many on the continent of Europe, and also in Great
Britain and the United States, who read and understand
French, although it is not the language of the country.
In many parts of the world there is a dead or living language, which, from various causes, acquires an ascendancy
among the neighbouring nations, and serves as a means of
communication between people who speak different idioms
or dialects. Such is the Arabic through a great part of
Africa; the Persian in the East Indies; the Chinese in the
peninsula beyond the Ganges; and the Algonkin or Chip-
peway among our north-western Indians. This alone is
sufficient to explain why Chinese books and writings should
be understood by a great number of persons in those countries, and why they should smile at an *unlettered* foreigner
who cannot do the like. But it must not be believed that
they read those writings as a series of abstract symbols,
without connecting them with some spoken language. If
their language be a dialect of the Chinese, varying only in
the pronunciation of some words; and if it be entirely
formed on the same model, there is no doubt but that the
two idioms may be read with the same characters, as their
meaning is the same in both; but if there is any material
diversity between the two idioms, it is impossible that the
Chinese character should be understood, unless the spoken
language of China be understood at the same time; and
this may be proved by well ascertained facts.

In Cochinchina, the language commonly spoken is a dialect of the Chinese, monosyllabic like the mother tongue,
and formed on the same grammatical principles. In writing
this language, the Chinese logographic character is exclusively used; but it does by no means follow, that a Cochinchinese book would be understood in China, or *vice versâ.*
For although, in both languages, each character represents
a single word, yet the words so represented are not always

15

the same in sound or in sense. Thus the character which in Chinese represents the word *tăn*, (a plain,) in Cochinchinese signifies *dât*, (the earth.) The character *kin*, (metal,) in Cochinchinese is read *kim*, (a needle); Chinese *y*, (kettle,) Cochinchinese *chi*, (lead) ; Chinese *pŏ*, (to land,) Cochinchinese *bac*, (silver.)* It is evident that the same book or manuscript could not be read or understood alike by a Chinese and a Cochinchinese.

I cannot omit here an observation which appears to me to be peculiarly striking. If the Chinese writing be really *ideographic;* if it represents *ideas* and not sounds, how does it happen that the same character is used in different languages to signify things that have no kind of connexion with each other; as for instance, the verb *to land*, and the substantive *silver?* It is difficult to think even of a distant metaphor that will apply to both these subjects.

In Japan, there are two languages in general use. The *Koye*, which is no other than the Chinese, with some variation in the pronunciation of the words, arising probably from the difference of the vocal organs of the two nations; and the *Yomi*, which is the most popular language, the former being devoted to religion and science. The Yomi is polysyllabic, and has declensions, conjugations, and other complex grammatical forms, which the Chinese has not. Therefore, it cannot be written with the Chinese character *logographically*, any more than the Greek or Latin could; yet the Chinese character is used in writing that idiom. From a selection of those characters a syllabic alphabet has been made, which is in common use.† From a similar selection, says M. Remusat, the Coreans have made a monophonic alphabet of nine vowels and fifteen consonants,‡

* White's Voyage to the China Sea. Boston: ed. 1823.
† Grammaire Japonaise de Rodriguez.
‡ Recherches sur les langues Tartares, p. 81.

with which they write their language. At the same time they can read and understand the Chinese, in which their sacred and scientific books are written.

We know very little of the language of the Loo-choo Islands. Father Gaubil (the French missionary) says, that they have three different idioms; others say that they speak a language compounded of the Chinese and Japanese. But little reliance is to be placed in these reports. It is probable that the Chinese is read and understood there also as a religious and scientific language, or perhaps as an auxiliary means of communication.

I have said enough, I think, to show, that if the Chinese writing is read and understood in various countries in the vicinity of China, it is not in consequence of its supposed ideographic character; but either because the Chinese is also the language or one of the languages of the country, or because it is learned, and the meaning of the characters is acquired, through the words which they represent. Without a knowledge of these words and of their precise signification, according to the genius, syntax, and grammar of the language, it would be impossible to understand or remember the signification of the characters. If those characters could be read into languages which, like the Yomi and the Corean, differ in their forms from the Chinese, or in the meaning and sound of the words which the signs represent, they might be read alike in English, French, Latin, Greek, Iroquois, and in short in every existing idiom upon earth, which I think I have sufficiently proved to be impossible, according to the plainest deductions of simple logic.

I have been carried further by my subject than I intended; but as I do not believe that it has yet been presented in this point of view, I thought that I should not be sparing of a few words in order to make myself clearly understood. With what success I have made out my argument, I leave you entirely to judge. At any rate, I rejoice in the opportunity which it gives me of expressing to you the sentiments of sincere respect and esteem with which I am, dear Sir,

Your most obedient, humble servant,

PETER S. DU PONCEAU.

Capt. Basil Hall, R. B. N., F. R. S., &c. &c.

New York, 14th July.

P. S.—Since my arrival in this town, whither I have come on an excursion of pleasure, I have been agreeably surprised to find, by an article in the Baron Férusac's *Bulletin des Sciences Historiques, Philosophiques*, &c. for the month of March last, that the opinion I have expressed on the subject of the Chinese writing, begins to prevail among the learned of Europe. The article I allude to is a short notice (p. 258) by M. Champollion, the elder, of a work on the History of Philosophy, published last year at Bonn, by M. Windischman, a German writer, who, as usual, represents the Chinese character as a sort of *pasigraphy*, which may be read alike in every language. M. Champollion very properly combats this opinion, and observes, (as I have done,) that the Japanese, Cochinchinese, and other nations, have been obliged to modify that system of writing, to adapt it to their own languages. He adds, that the details of those alterations are to be found in a late memoir of M. Remusat, inserted in the eighth volume of the Memoirs of the Institute of France, (Academy of Inscriptions and Belles Lettres,) pp. 34—69. Thus I have the good fortune to have M. Champollion and M. Remusat on my side, to some extent at least, though to *what* extent I cannot exactly tell, as the volume of the Memoirs of the Institute above referred to has not yet reached this country, at least that I know of. I am very anxious to see it, as I have no doubt that the subject will have been treated in a very profound and scientific manner, by so able and learned a writer as M. Remusat. I beg leave to refer you to it, for further information on this interesting topic.   P. S. D.

————

B.

Translated extract from M. Abel Remusat's Memoir, entitled Remarques sur quelques écritures syllabiques, tirées des caractères Chinois, &c. See the Memoirs of the Academy of Inscriptions and Belles Lettres, vol. viii. New Series, p. 34 et seq.

The first missionaries who spoke of the Chinese language have said,—and it has been repeated after them in all relations or narratives, and in all treatises of geography, general or particular,—that the Chinese characters, indifferent to all pronunciation, were understood by all the nations neighbouring upon China, notwithstanding the difference of their idioms; so that the Tonquinese, the Cochinchinese, the Coreans, the Japanese, read and pronounced them in their own way; and that all those nations who cannot communicate orally either with the Chinese or with each other, could nevertheless correspond by writing, and read the same books, because they attached the same signification to the characters. This idea naturally brought us to that of *pasigraphy*, or universal writing, and it was strengthened by the example of the Arabic figures, which, as I have already said, are to a certain degree analogous.—But, without losing ourselves in vain speculations, the fact itself, such as it has been advanced, would be to us a considerable subject of astonishment. Indeed, it would be necessary that the idioms of the nations in the vicinity of China should bear a great analogy to that of the Chinese, to have made the former adopt, without any alteration, the characters of the latter, so as to be able to read, in their own language, books written in a different idiom; the structure of both languages, the syntax, the order in which the words are placed, the inversions, the metaphors, should be exactly the same; the particles and signs of relation should always be employed on the same occasion, and put in the same place; all these analogies would suppose a complete similarity in the genius of all those languages, and that would be a phenomenon which the difference between the words would render still more difficult to explain. It will not therefore excite surprise, to find, on examination, that things are not exactly as has been supposed, which it will be easy to demonstrate.

The books of Confucius, and the other classical works, which are required to be understood by all who occupy places in the countries submitted to the institutions of China; the imperial calendar, received by all the tributary nations, are the only books generally read and understood out of China, by all who pretend to the title of a man of letters (*un lettré*): *but it is false that they read those books in their own language.* The pronunciation which they apply to each word is taken from that of the Chinese themselves, and does not differ more from it than that of certain provinces of the empire differs from that of the Mandarin language. When read by the literati of Cochinchina or Japan, the Chinese of those books is altered and corrupted, but it is still Chinese. The phraseology does not want to be changed; the grammar remains the same: but then that is a *learned language*, which is specially studied, and is not understood by the mass of the inhabitants, except a small number of words, which are common to them and the Chinese; some techni-

eal terms, some names of natural objects or articles of mer-
chandise, and some consecrated formulas or proverbs, which
have passed into universal usage.

On the other hand, in Tonquin, Japan or Corea, some
persons may write, in imitation of those books, Chinese
sentences or characters, which will be read and understood
in China, if they are regularly composed; and it is what is
often done by the *learned* of those countries, particularly in
Japan. But, in that case, they make use of characters
which are foreign to them, and of a language and grammatical system which are not those of their maternal idiom.

[The learned author expatiates much further upon this
subject, and illustrates it by a variety of examples, drawn
from the Anamitic and other languages. We can only refer our readers to that excellent Memoir, which is well
worthy of their attention.]

C.

*Extracted from the Canton Register, No. 6. Wednesday, 17th
March,* 1830.

Captain Basil Hall's Travels in North America.—In the
second volume of this work, at the 369th page, there are
some remarks concerning the Chinese language, being the
result of a conversation which the Captain had with Mr.
Du Ponceau, of Philadelphia, "one of the most learned
philologists alive." Hall says, that he himself had published
the opinion "that in China, Japan, Corea and Loo-choo,
though the spoken languages were different, the written

character was common to them all; and consequently, that when any two natives of the different countries met, though neither could speak a word of the other's language, they would readily interchange their thoughts by means of written symbols." "Before Mr. Du Ponceau had proceeded far in his argument," (says the Captain,) "he made it quite clear that I had known little or nothing of the matter; and when at length he asked why such statements had been put forth, there was no answer to be made but that of Dr. Johnson to the lady who discovered a wrong definition in his Dictionary—Sheer ignorance, Madam." "Seriously, however," (continues Hall,) "it is to be regretted that an error of this magnitude in the history of language should still have currency; and I have done, by way of reparation, what obviously presented itself at the time;" which was, that Mr. Du Ponceau should give the Captain his arguments in writing, that he might print them, which Du Ponceau did. Unfortunately, however, the Captain has not published his friend's reasoning, but only his conclusions. Those who desire to see the reasoning, are referred to the Annals of Philosophy, for January, 1829.

In a former number we noticed the boldness of Captain Hall's assertions in reference to Loo-choo in the presence of Bonaparte, which assertions Sir Walter Scott repeated in his Life of Napoleon. Our author was not more bold then, than he appears timid on the present occasion; for whatever the arguments or theory of his "good humoured" friend may be, there is not, we are convinced, any material error in Captain Hall's first assertion. That in every one of those countries, China, Japan, Corea and Loo-choo—not, as Du Ponceau says, in Camboje and Siam—but in the above named nations, the Chinese written language is very generally understood by all who can be said to read and write; and not in the limited manner that a "learned and sacred language may be supposed to be understood." And it is equally certain, that "when any two natives who can write the Chinese character meet, though neither could speak a word of the other's language, they can readily interchange their thoughts by means of the Chinese written symbols." The writer of this has interchanged thoughts with Cochinchinese, Japanese, and Loo-chooans, by means of the Chinese characters, although he could not understand one word they uttered, nor could they understand his speech. Therefore, for all practical purposes, whether of religion, science or commerce, it is difficult to see wherein Captain Hall's first assertion is erroneous.

But Mr. Duponceau, the President of the American Philosophical Society, says: "It must not be believed that they (the several nations alluded to) read those writings as a series of abstract symbols, without connecting them with some spoken language." Again: "If there is any material diversity between the two (or the many) idioms, it is impossible that the Chinese character should be understood at the same time." Page 372.

As Captain Hall's book does not contain the theory nor argument of the President Du Ponceau, it is difficult to say what he is combating. But that the inhabitants of China, Cochinchina, Corea, Japan and Loo-choo, can, when totally unintelligible to each other orally, communicate their thoughts by means of the Chinese character—that is, the Chinese character is understood at the same time—is perfectly true. That the Chinese character is thus generally understood by five nations, whose spoken languages are unintelligible to each other, is an important fact; and "seriously would it be to be regretted" that this fact should lose its hold on the mind of any Christian philanthropist, by the confessions of Captain Hall before the President of the American Philosophical Society.

.   16

D.

*Extract from the book entitled " A Narrative of a Voyage to
the Pacific Ocean and Behring's Strait, to co-operate with
the Polar Expeditions performed in his Majesty's ship
Blossom, under the command of Captain F. W. Beechey,
Royal Navy, F. R. S., &c. &c., in the years 1825, 26, 27,
28." Published by authority of the Lords Commissioners
of the Admiralty.* London, printed : Philadelphia, reprint-
ed : 1832.

While upon this subject I must observe, that the idea of
Mr. P. S. Du Ponceau, " that the meaning of the Chinese
characters cannot be understood alike in the different languages in which they are used," is not strictly correct, as
we found many Loo-choo people who understood the meaning of the character, which was the same with them as the
Chinese, but who could not give us the Chinese pronunciation of the word.   And this is an answer to another observation which precedes that above mentioned, viz. that " as
the Chinese characters are in direct connexion with the
Chinese spoken words, they can only be read and understood by those who are familiar with the spoken language."
The Loo-choo words for the same things are different from
those of the Chinese, the one being often a monosyllable,
and the other a polysyllable; as in the instance of *charcoal,*
the Chinese word for it being *tan,* and the Loo-chooan *cha-
ehee-jing,* and yet the people use precisely the same character as the Chinese to express this word; and so far from its
being necessary to be familiar with the language to understand the characters, many did not know the Chinese words
for them.   Their language throughout is very different

from that of the Chinese, and much more nearly allied to the Japanese. The observation of M. Klaproth, in *Archiv für Asiatische Litteratur*, p. 152, that the Loo-choo language is a dialect of the Japanese, with a good deal of Chinese introduced into it, appears to be perfectly correct, from the information of some gentlemen who have compared the two, and are familiar with both languages. The Vocabulary of Lieutenant Clifford, which we found very correct, will at any time afford the means of making this comparison.

No. II.

VOCABULARY

OF THE

COCHINCHINESE LANGUAGE.

Quan Maria

BY THE REV. JOSEPH MORRONE,

MISSIONARY AT SAIGON.

WITH NOTES,

SHOWING THE AFFINITY OF THE CHINESE AND COCHINCHINESE
LANGUAGES, AND THE MANNER IN WHICH THOSE TWO NATIONS
MAKE USE OF THE SAME SYSTEM OF WRITING.

BY M. DE LA PALUN,

Late Consul of France at Richmond, in the State of Virginia; now holding
the same office at Caraccas, in the Republic of Venezuela.

PREFACE,

BY PETER S. DU PONCEAU.

———

The pious and learned Warburton was the first who discovered that the inscriptions on the Egyptian obelisks were
not a secret and mysterious writing, but that they were intended to be read and understood by all. He was the first
who discovered (before Young or Champollion was born)
that the characters called hieroglyphic were employed by
the Egyptians as the signs of elementary sounds, or in other
words, as letters of an alphabet.* He made these discoveries by the force of his intuitive genius, and by a clear and
correct understanding of the famous passage of Clement of
Alexandria, which philologists in Europe have since taken
so much pains to torture and render unintelligible. He
made all these discoveries, but has not received for them
the credit to which he is entitled. Young and Champollion
only proved by facts that his theory was correct. His superiority over them is that of the mind, which soars above
the clouded atmosphere of human intelligence, and pene-
trates into the unknown, over the patient labour, aided by
sagacity, that investigates details. To Warburton, therefore, is due the honour of having first of all the moderns,
discovered and understood the true system of the ancient

* Divine Legation of Moses, book iv. sect. 4.

Egyptian writing, and manifested it to the world by a clear and luminous course of reasoning, founded on the nature of things, and to which every reasonable man is forced to give his assent.

These were great and important discoveries for the time when they were made; but unfortunately the learned prelate stopped there, and did not proceed further. The Egyptian writing was connected with the subject he was treating of; the Chinese was not, and much less the paintings of the Mexicans. With respect to those, he adopted the generally received opinions. Therefore, he considered the art of writing as confined to two systems, the one representing or recalling to the mind *ideas*, (as he conceived the Chinese characters to be, and the Egyptian symbols to have been in their origin,) the other representing sounds. But by the word *sounds*, he understood only the primary and secondary elements of speech, which we call *letters* and *syllables;* it does not appear to have occurred to him that *words* also were *sounds*, and might be represented *as such* by graphic signs.

The President Debrosses, who, in his Traité de la formation mécanique des langues, adopted all the Bishop's opinions on this subject, and whose chapter on the different systems or modes of writing is but a paraphrase of what is said in the Divine Legation, entitles that chapter "De l'écriture symbolique et littérale," (Of symbolic and literal writing,) thus taking it for granted that no other system than these two did or could exist. This Vocabulary I hope will show, that there is also a *lexigraphic* system, by which *words*, that are also elements of speech, are recalled to the mind by means of written signs or characters, and which is therefore a *phonetic* system as much as our alphabets; and that the only difference between it and those which represent the more minute elements of human language, is in the method pursued, arising from the great number of words of which languages are composed, which could not be conveniently represented by characters purely arbitrary.

If this theory be founded on rational principles, there will arise out of it a system of classification of the different modes of writing, which appears to me to be consistent with itself and with the nature of things. Written languages, then, (I am willing to use the expression,) will be divided into three classes, to wit:

1. The *lexigraphic*, which represents *words*.

2. The *syllabic*, which represents *syllables*.

3. The *elementary*, which represents the primary sounds or elements of speech, which we call *letters*.

In the first of these classes I would place the writing of the ancient Egyptian, as well as that of the Chinese, and its affiliated languages.

I do not mean to say that one of these forms is exclusively adopted in any one language. They may be found mixed, as has been shown to be the case in the Egyptian and the Chinese. There is nothing in this world which is not composed of various elements, but there is generally one which predominates.

As to *ideographic* writing, as it is called, I am willing to admit that it may exist as abridged forms, and as auxiliary to other systems. Thus we have our arithmetical and algebraical figures, and in our almanacs we see the planets, the phases of the moon, and the signs of the zodiac, represented by peculair characters. But I cannot believe that there can be an entire language so composed, as I have endeavoured to prove in my letter to Mr. Vaughan.

As to the Mexican paintings, we know too little about them to make them the basis of a system. We must wait until more light shall be thrown upon the subject. Until then, conjectures can lead to no result. I believe them to have been connected with the spoken language, but I confess that I cannot administer the proof of it.

17

I find by Dr. Young's Rudiments of the Egyptian Language, annexed to Mr. Tatam's Coptic Grammar, which has but lately come to my hands, that great progress has been made in deciphering the demotic manuscripts, a fact of which before I had no knowledge. The discoveries that have been made go far to confirm my theory. I hope this study will be pursued.

I have not yet seen the work on Egyptian hieroglyphics, ascribed to M. Spineto; but from references made to it I observe that the learned in Europe are now looking more for *words* than for *ideas* in the hieroglyphic characters. Thus my theory is at least adopted in practice. I see also that this author has found characters representing those particles that take the place of our inflected grammatical forms, which corroborates M. Champollion's opinion, contradicted with so much levity by M. Klaproth,* and shows the Egyptian writing to have been in part syllabic. I have seen also, from those few quotations, that the Egyptians had characters to represent words of more than one syllable, as *soten*, king, and *noyte*, God; from which it appears, that the lexigraphic system is not confined to monosyllabic languages, like the Chinese, as might perhaps have been supposed. Upon the whole, I would conclude that the Egyptian system was mixed, and partook of the lexigraphic, syllabic, and elementary character, with symbolic abbreviations, (the remains of a former imperfect system,) such as we ourselves use in our almanacs, &c. These, probably, were chiefly employed on religious subjects.

It is much to be regretted that literary intercourse is not more frequent and more regular between this country and Europe. Many valuable books do not come to us until long after they have appeared abroad. Thus American writers

* See above, p. 57.

may be taxed with pretending to have discovered what had been discovered before. Our celebrated Rittenhouse for a long time believed that he was the inventor of fluxions. He did not know that Newton and Leibnitz had been contending for the merit of the discovery. That was in early colonial times, but we may be said to be yet in a great measure *colonial* in that respect. I hope the learned of both hemispheres will unite their efforts to produce a state of things more favourable to science.

These remarks will perhaps be considered as out of place, and as foreign to the Vocabulary which this preface is meant to introduce. I am willing to confess that they are. A twelvemonth has elapsed since my letter to Mr. Vaughan was written, and further reflection has convinced me that the system which I have presented in it might have been much more fully developed, and that it is fruitful of consequences that may perhaps extend the bounds of philological science. It appears to me that the art of writing, in its different forms, deserves to be separately investigated; it not being less important to consider how men have proceeded in inventing different modes of communicating their ideas by writing, as in forming their oral languages. This branch of science might be called *graphology*, or by any other name that should be thought more appropriate.

It is but lately that the idea occurred to me of dividing the different systems of writing into classes, as I have attempted to do in this preface. This classification is a natural consequence of my general theory, and I have thought I might, without too much impropriety, introduce it here, with a few more observations that occurred to me as I wrote. I have however to say, by way of apology, that the question which this Vocabulary is intended to aid in solving is intimately connected with the system that I have exposed, and that its solution appears to me in a great measure to depend upon it.

That question, restricted within its proper bounds, is no other than " Whether, and how far, the Chinese characters can serve as an ocular medium of communication between two nations who do not understand each other's spoken language, and who have not learned to read that character as Chinese, and as connected with the Chinese oral idiom?"

Two nations are here presented (the Cochinchinese and the Chinese) who appear to have originally made part of the same people, who both speak monosyllabic languages, formed on the same grammatical system, and appearing to be dialects of each other, or of some other language formerly common to them both. Those nations have, with some modification, the same religious principles, the same form of government, the same habits, manners and customs, and that common stock of ideas, which constitutes a family of nations, and greatly facilitates their communications with each other. If it should be found and decided that two nations, thus circumstanced, cannot communicate together in writing by means of a common graphic system, it will be clear that no others can do the same; if otherwise, it will prove nothing as to nations whose oral languages differ essentially in their structure, and to which the same system of writing cannot be applied; as, for instance, the Japanese and the Chinese, on whom I have sufficiently expatiated.

This Vocabulary will not only aid in the solution of that important philological question, but I think it will throw some light on the early history of the Chinese and Cochinchinese people in relation to each other. Languages are acknowledged to be a source of history. The same, I believe, may be said of the graphic characters of the Chinese and Cochinchinese. Let me be permitted to give here an example of it.

In the Chinese language the sun is called *ji*, and the moon *youei* (I use M. Remusat's orthography); each of these words has a character to represent it, which was originally meant as a picture of the object. A month, which in that language is called *a moon*, has the same name as the planet, and is represented in writing by the same character. Now let us see how it is in Cochinchinese.

In that language the sun is called the *face in the heavens*, or, in their abridged form of speech, *face heavens*. The moon is called *white face* or *moon face;* for the word *trang*, which signifies *white*, used singly, means also *moon*.* The words *sun* and *moon*, or rather *face heavens*, and *face white* or *face moon*, are each represented by two groups of characters, placed one under the other, according to the Chinese custom. (See plates Nos. 7 and 8.) So that the Cochinchinese have not, like the Chinese, a single word to express the *sun* or the *moon*, nor have they a single character or group to represent either. Those two great luminaries, however, strike the senses at first sight; and almost every nation has a separate name, consisting of a single word, for each of them, without having recourse to a periphrasis for either.†

From these facts I am inclined to infer, that the Chinese and Cochinchinese had been long separated, before the latter received the art of writing from the former, and that their spoken idioms had at that time considerably diverged; so that it may be fairly presumed that the Chinese were a civilized nation long before the people of Cochinchina.

Many more such facts, no doubt, will strike the minds of those who are better acquainted than I am with the Chinese

* *Thang* is the word for *month;* the character is the same as for *white*. (See plates, Nos. 8 and 26.)

† Some of our Indians call the moon the sun or the star of the night, (l'astre de la nuit,) but such instances are rare.

language and character, and to them I commit the subject with great pleasure. On these various grounds I hope that this Vocabulary, and the Dictionary which follows it, will not be thought devoid of interest by the learned world.

The Vocabulary was written by Father Morrone, in the French language; I have only added to it the English signification of the words, that it might be more generally understood. M. de la Palun's Notes, and his Preliminary Observations, were also written in French; I have, with his permission, translated them into English, and added a few occasional remarks, particularly references to the Cochinchinese and Latin Dictionary,* (which M. de la Palun had not before him when he wrote his annotations,) and some other references. Those additions are enclosed between brackets []; all else is a faithful translation of M. de la Palun's text. The asterisks, (*) which indicate that the Cochinchinese characters could not be found in his Chinese dictionaries, are exactly in the places which he assigned to them.

The Dictionary, or Lexicon, as it is entitled, was written in Cochinchinese and Latin, as it now appears; nothing has been changed or altered in it. It is published (except the title) exactly as it was received. The alphabetical order does not appear to have been very carefully preserved; but it has been thought best not to make any alteration in it. The accents, and the signs indicating the tones, have been omitted, both in the Vocabulary and the Dictionary, as useless to the object of this publication, which is not to teach the pronunciation of the Cochinchinese language. The system of writing is the principal object in view.

The characters in the plates have been lithographed from the copy made of them by M. de la Palun; they are more legible than those in the original manuscript.

* Post, No. III.

M. de la Palun's manuscript is preserved in the library of the American Philosophical Society. The original Vocabularies will be returned to the East India Marine Society at Salem, by whom they were kindly lent to us for publication.

Philadelphia, 14*th Nov.* 1837.

POSTSCRIPT.

Since this Preface was written, and part of it being already in type, I have received from Lieutenant Godon, of the United States' navy, lately returned from a three years' cruise in the Indian Sea, with the squadron under the command of Commodore Kennedy, to be presented to the American Philosophical Society for their library, a valuable collection of printed Missionary Tracts and translations, and several Manuscripts, in the languages of the different countries bordering on that sea, of which I think it right to mention here the most important, for the information of American philologists. I stop the press to insert this short notice.

Amongst other donations of the same kind are the following:

1. A religious Tract in the Siamese language and character. The Siamese is classed by Adelung* among the the monosyllabic languages; the characters do not show it to be so; they are to all appearance alphabetical, probably syllabic. The words are separated as in our languages; some words have more than twenty letters.

2. A Manuscript in the same language, being several leaves taken from a book on Astrology. It is written on the leaves of the Tallipot, a species of Palm tree. The wri-

* Mithrid. vol. i. p. 92.

ting is elegant; the characters are the same with those in the printed tract, but their form is more acute. This was obtained by Lieutenant Godon with great difficulty, not without the aid of money.

3. A Manuscript Book in the same language. The subject of it is unknown, but it is of a popular character, and is supposed to be a tale, a kind of reading which the Siamese are very fond of. It is written on a single sheet of thick paper, but not stiff, like pasteboard, so that it may be folded without breaking. The sheet is of the length of twenty-two feet four inches, and thirteen inches in breadth (English measure.) It is black on both sides, and the writing is white; the letters appear as if written with chalk, but Lieutenant Godon says it is done with a pencil. The writing is beautiful; it has the appearance of our most elegant *script* calligraphy, much like what the French call *écriture bâtarde*, and the characters are not acute as in the other manuscript. The book, thirteen inches long and four inches broad, is only eleven inches in thickness. It is made up by folding the sheet like the leaves of a fan. Each fold contains two pages, of which this volume has sixty, being folded thirty times. It is so that popular books are written and made up, and Lieutenant Godon says they are very common. He saw several persons engaged in writing them.

3. Another Manuscript, writen on Tallipot leaves, and in the *Pali* or *Bali*, the sacred language of ultra Gangetic India. Of this language very little is yet known. Messrs. Burnouf and Lassen, in a learned and interesting Essay, have shown it to have great affinity with the Sanscrit, and have expressed the hope " that it will soon become an important branch of the studies respecting Asia, which now engage the attention of the learned of Europe.*"

* Essai sur le Pali, langue sacrée de la presqu'ile au delà du Gange. Par E. Burnouf et Chr. Lassen. Ouvrage publié par la Société Asiatique. Paris, 1826.

4. A Missionary Tract in the Birman language. Of what part or what dialect of the Birman country is not known; but it is presumed to be that of Ava, as the characters resemble those of which samples are given in Carpanus's Alphabetum Barmanum.* It is hoped, that now that the English are in possession of a great part of the Birman country, they will make us better acquainted than we are with their languages.

5. A religious Tract in the language of the *Bugis*, a people as yet very little known. They are the same people whom Adelung calls the *Buggese*,† (die Buggesen,) and Malte-Brun *les Boughièses*.‡ They are said to be a savage people, who reside on the Bay of Bony, in the Island of Celebes, in the Indian Archipelago. I believe this is the first specimen that we have of their language. It was received from an American missionary at Siam. I have not time to examine the character and compare it with others. It is evidently alphabetical, and probably syllabic.

I do not speak of the Tracts, &c., presented by Lieutenant Godon, in languages that are better known; such as the Hindoostanee, Malay, &c. That officer deserves the thanks of the friends of science, for the zeal which he has displayed in its cause. In general, the officers of our navy have shown the greatest disposition to promote it.

The missionaries also are entitled to thanks. It is only to be regretted that, too exclusively intent on the great object of their mission, they do not give to their books a greater circulation, by sending some copies of them to be sold in

---

* Alphabetum Barmanum seu Romanum regni Avæ finitimarumque regionum. Romæ, 1776. Typis Sacræ Congregationis de Propaganda fide. This work is very rare; the writer is indebted for a valuable collection of the publications of the Propaganda, to the kindness of the Prince of Musignano, which he takes this opportunity to acknowledge.

† Mithrid. vol. i. p. 598.

‡ Précis de la Géographie Universelle, vol. iv. p. 297.

18

the great capitals of America and Europe; or if, as is believed, they despise gain, present some at least to the principal libraries. It is wished also that they should devote a page or two in the English, or some other known language, to let us know the subject of their publications, and the language they are written in. If, as in most cases, they are translations, it would be of great advantage to philologists to refer them to the originals: the additional expense would be but trifling. It is hoped that this suggestion will be taken in good part by the venerable men to whom it is addressed.

PRELIMINARY OBSERVATIONS,

BY M. DE LA PALUN.

The text of Father Morrone occupies the left hand column in each page of this Vocabulary. We have thought it our duty to make no alteration in it, except correcting some faults in the orthography of French words, very excusable in a person who writes in a foreign language, in a distant country, where he has not the help of books.

The order of the Vocabulary has been followed, and the Cochinchinese words have been successively numbered, in order to facilitate a reference to the plates. The letters A, B, C, D, serve to designate the characters in the order in which they are placed under each other.

The asterisk (*) in the right hand column shows that the character designated by the number opposite to it is not found in the Chinese Dictionaries that we have consulted.

The letter M. designates some one or other of Morrison's Chinese Dictionaries. When it is followed by a single figure, it indicates the number affixed to each character in the Chinese and English Dictionary, in which the Chinese words are arranged in alphabetical order; when followed by two or three figures, the reference is to the Dictionary in which the characters are placed in the order of radicals; the first figure refers to the volume, the second to the page, and the third to the column.

The letter G. indicates a reference to the Chinese Dictionary of Father Basil de Glemona, translated from the Latin into French, and published at Paris in 1813, by M. de Guignes. The figure which follows indicates the character referred to.

We have referred only to Morrison's and Glemona's Dictionaries, although we are possessed of several in the Chinese language; such as the *Choue wen Kiai Tseu*, the *Tchhouen tseu wei*, the *Thseng pou hiouan kin tseu wei*, the *Tching tseu thoung*, the *K'hang Hi tseu tien*, &c. Time did not permit us to go into this laborious investigation; the sinologists of Europe will be able to supply what is wanting in this hasty sketch, made when we were on the point of leaving this country (the United States) for the Republic of Venezuela, to which we have been ordered by our government.

M. Remusat, in his remarks on some syllabic writings drawn from the Chinese characters, (p. 46,) observes, that the calligraphy of the Cochinchinese essentially differs from that of the Chinese, and that the former inclines its characters from right to left as those we call italic. We have not been able to discover that difference in the manuscript of Father Morrone. The writing of that missionary is very bad; his characters are ill formed, and with a rapidity which has not permitted us to decipher them all. We have not been able to employ much time in the study of Chinese calligraphy; we therefore have to solicit indulgence for our inelegant manner of writing the Chinese characters. We have no pretention, in this respect, than to represent exactly the number of strokes of which they are composed, and in a manner sufficiently distinct, that they may be known without hesitation by any one who is in the least acquainted with the language of Confucius.

Father Morrone has prefixed the characters to each word in his Vocabulary, written horizontally in succession from left to right, in the same manner as Dr. Morrison has done

in his Anglo-Chinese Dictionary; we have thought it best
to write them separately in columns, marked with successive numbers, by which we refer to them in the Vocabulary.
The columns are arranged so as to be read from left to
right, in the European manner.

Father Morrone indicates the pronunciation of the Cochinchinese vowels by three kinds of accents:

The first (ă) shows that the syllable is to be pronounced
short.

The second (â) that the vowel is open.

The third (ŏ) placed on the vowel *o*, shows that it is to be
pronounced like the French *œ*, (perhaps he means *eu*);
on the letter *u*, that it is to have the sound of that letter in
French.

The *o* without an accent, as in *long*, the heart, has the
sound of *ao*, probably as *ow* in the English word *now*; sometimes it has the sound of the French diphthong *au*, as in
ngon, finger.

He also says that the Cochinchinese language is sung,
and that it has different tones like the Chinese. According
to him, there are six tones in the pronunciation of that language, which he distinguishes by the signs (.) (`) (´) (2) (–).
The first of these tones, which serves as the basis of the
tonic scale, has no sign to distinguish it. We have omitted
these last signs in copying the Vocabulary.

We can hardly believe the Cochinchinese have *six* tones.
The missionaries of Peking had carried to five the number
of those of the Chinese language, because they did not examine with sufficient care the assertions of the Chinese
grammarians, who have sought differences in intonations
which escape the delicate ear of poets, and which consequently, if they are real, can only exist for purists, and are
of no kind of use.

We have not copied two Cochinchinese phrases, of which
Father Morrone has endeavoured to represent the pronun-

ciation by means of the notes of our musical scale. It has
been long since demonstrated that those notes cannot represent the pronunciation of any language, and that it is in vain
that missionaries have endeavoured to show an analogy
between two systems that have nothing common between
them.

VOCABULARY.

VOCABULARY

OF THE

COCHINCHINESE LANGUAGE,

WITH MARGINAL NOTES,

SHOWING ITS RELATION TO THE CHINESE.

I.—OF THE HEAVENS.

Cochinchinese.

Chinese.

1. Troi.
Les Cieux.
The Heavens.

* This character is formed out of two Chinese characters; the four strokes at the top are the Chinese character *tien*, heaven [G. 1798]; the three lower ones are the character *chang*, which means above, superior. [G. 7. Thus it might be read in Chinese *Tien-chang*, Heaven above.]

M. Klaproth (Asia Polygl. 369) writes this word [in the Anamitic language] *bloei.*

2. Dui chua troi.
Dieu.
God.

A. Chinese *te*, virtus, beneficium. G. 2719.

[The first syllable *dui*, according to the Cochinchinese and Latin Dictionary which follows, is ge-

Cochinchinese.	Chinese.

neric for all the virtues. Thus, *Dui lin*, faith; *dui cau bang*, justice, &c. It is also used as an adjective for *most excellent*.]

The second syllable is represented by the Chinese character *tchu*, dominus, (G. 35,) and has the same signification.

For the third syllable *troi*, see above, No. 1.

[Thus God is called " the most excellent Lord of heaven."]

The Court of Rome has decided that *thian* or *tien tchu* (the Sovereign of heaven) is the most suitable way of expressing in Chinese the idea of God.

Theological expressions in this Vocabulary may be generally considered as devised by Europeans.

3. Thien dang.
Le Paradis.
Paradise.

A. *Tien*, Heaven. G. 1798.

[Mr. Morrison writes it T'hëen. M. 576.]

B. *Thang*, a hall, a temple. G. 1633.

[*Thang*, a dignified, honourable mansion; a palace; a temple; a court or hall of justice; a hall or public room. M. 512.

These words mean, therefore, " The palace or the temple of heaven." The Chinese say the *garden*, M. verbo *Paradise*.]

Cochinchinese.	Chinese.

4. Thien Than.
Les Anges.
Angels.

A. See above, No. 3.

B. *Chin*, [or *Shin*,] a spirit. G. 7025. [M. verbo *angel.*] It is the expression used by the Jesuits in China.

.5. Thanh.
Les Saints.
The Saints—Christians.

This appears to be an abbreviation of the character *Ching*, by which the Christians in China express the same idea. G. 8360. [M. verbo *Saints.*]

6. Dui chua ba.
La mère de Dieu.
The Virgin Mary.

For A and B, see No. 2.

C.* *Pha*, a woman's name. M. 1. 610. 2.

[In Cochinchinese *Ba* signifies Queen. See the Dictionary. So the Virgin Mary is here called " The most excellent Lady and Queen."]

In some Chinese books, the Virgin is designated by the words *Ching mou*, the Holy Mother.

7. Mat troi.
Le Soleil.
The Sun.

[*Mat*, face; *troi*, the heavens; the face in the heavens.]

A * is composed of the 176th Chinese radical *mian*, a face; and the 75th *mou*, a tree or wood. This last appears to be intended to indicate the pronunciation. [B. See No. 1. A.]

Klaproth (Asia Polygl. 369) *nhot, nhit.* Balbi (Atlas) *mat bloi* (the sun.)

8. Mat trang.
La Lune.
The Moon.

[*Mat*, face; *trang*, white; the white face.]

[A. See above, No. 7. A.]

Cochinchinese.	Chinese.

B.* This character is composed of the 74th Chinese radical *youei*, the moon; and the Chinese character *ling*, high, eminent. G. 1777.

[The Cochinchinese Dictionary has the following, verbo *trang:* Trăng *vel* blăng, *Luna*.

Trăng, *albus, a, um;* the latter has an acute accent on the *n*, which the first has not.

The word *trang*, variously accented, has several other significations. See the Dictionary.]

Klaproth, *blang;* Balbi, *mat blang.*

9. Ngoi Sao.
Les Etoiles.
The Stars.

A. Chinese *wei*, a high hill. M. 2. 46. 2.

B. *Sing*, the stars. G. 3900.

10. Anh Sang.
Les rayons du soleil.
The Sun's rays.

A. Chinese *Han*, to dry by the fire. G. 5521.

B. Perhaps *tchhouang*, to begin. G. 829, or a sharp sword. G. 743.

11. Sang.
La Lumière.
The light.

* [Chinese *kwang*. Same meaning, character different. M. 6707. Also, in Anglo-Chinese Dictionary, *verbo* light.]

12. Khi.
L'air.
The air.

Chinese *khi*, the air. G. 4828.

13. Moi.
Les nuages.
The clouds.

* This character seems composed of the 173d Chinese radical, *tu*, rain; and a group which is pronounced *mey*. See G. 11973.

This explanation, however, is only conjectural. Klaproth gives *mua*, in Anamitic for *the clouds.*

Cochinchinese.	Chinese.

14. Sam set.
    Le tonnerre.
    Thunder.

A. *Tsan* or *San*, drizzling rain. **M.** 3. 655. 2.

B.* Klaproth, *Sam*, thunder.

15. Chop.
    La foudre.
    The thunderbolt.

* The 173d radical *tu*, rain, and the group *Cho* or *Tsuh* [to lay hold of, to catch.] M. 1178.

16. Gio.
    Le vent.
    The wind.

* The group is pronounced *yu.* G. 250. Klaproth, *djo.*

17. Thuyet.
    La neige.
    The snow.

Siouei [the snow.] G. 11948. Klaproth, *thouyet.*

18. Mua.
    La pluie.
    Rain.

* The same as No. 13, with part of the radical 162.

[This radical, in Remusat's Chinese Grammar, is *tchho*, to walk (marcher); in Marshman's Clavis Sinica it is *Vih*, a city.]

19. Mu Suong.
    La rosée.
    The dew.

A. *Fuh*, a rainy appearance. M. 3. 643.

B. *Chouang*, a white frost. G. 11984.

II.—Of Time.

20. Khi.
    Le temps.
    Time.

K'hi, to despise. G. 4613.

In Chinese time is called *chy.* G. 3376, 3914. [But the character is different. M. 435.]

21. Doi.
    Le siècle et la vie.
    The age and the life.

Tay, generation. G. 112.

22. Doi Doi.
    L'éternité.
    Eternity.

* [*Ages-Ages.* A word probably coined by missionaries.]

Cochinchinese.	Chinese.

23. Nom.
Un an.
A year.

* This is composed of two Chinese characters. That on the left, which is pronounced *nan*, means the *south;* that on the right, *hian*, means *a year.*

24. Nom truoc.
L'an passé.
The last year.

A. See No. 23.

B. Appears to be a different form of G. 6217. [*Lio*, modicum, parùm; terminus, as who should say, the year now ended or terminated.]

25. Nom sou.
L'an prochain.
The next year.

I can only find this character as a group with the 66th radical, in *Sou* [or *Soo*] to reckon, to count, to number. G. 3769. M. 9521.

26. Thang.
Le mois.
The month.

This group in Chinese is pronounced *Shang.* The 74th radical, *youei*, which signifies *moon*, or month, has been added to it.

This group is often employed for the character *Tang*, companions. G. 13152.

27. Ngai.
Le jour.
The day.

* This group is pronounced *gai.* M. 2793. [The character on the left hand is the Cochinchinese form of the Chinese radical 74, *youei*, the moon. On the right is the character *gai* or *gae*, an impediment, probably to indicate the pronunciation. M. 2795.]

28. Tuan le.
La semaine.
The week.

A. *Siun*, a period of ten days. G. 3869.

B. *Ly*, a rite, usage, custom. G. 6992.

Cochinchinese.	Chinese.
29. Khae. Un quart d'heure. *A quarter of an hour.*	*Khe,* the eighth part of the Chinese hour (fifteen minutes.)
30. Gio. Les heures. *The hours.*	*Kwei,* light. M. 2. 308.
31. Lat. Un moment. *A moment.*	* The first character is probably an abbreviation of the second, which in Chinese is pronounced *la.*
32. Som mai som. De bon matin. *Early in the morning.*	A. *Khin,* [to grasp or hold in the hand.] M. 3. 558. 2. B. *May,* to conceal. G. 1610. [C, is A repeated.]
33. Nua ngai. Midi. *Noon.*	A. *Pwan,* a woman during the period of her monthly courses. M. 1. 621. 2. This group is composed on the left of the 38th radical, *niu,* a woman, probably to indicate the pronunciation. On the right is the Chinese group *Pouan,* which signifies *half.* G. 1001. B. This group is pronounced *gai.* [On the left, 74th radical, *youei,* the moon; on the right, *gae,* to hinder. M. 2824.]
34. Chieu. Le soir. *The evening.*	*Chao,* the morning. G. 4046.
35. Dem. La nuit. *The night.*	*Tien,* a shop. G. 2509.

Cochinchinese.	Chinese.

36. Bua hom nai.
Aujourd'hui.
To day.

A. *Po,* [waves, to move, to agitate.] G. 4924.

B. *Hin,* to rejoice. G. 4624. [But see No. 37.]

C.* Probably *Na,* [to press hard with the hand.] G. 3413.

[In the Dictionary we find *ngay hom; nay,* hodiè, which would seem the better mode of expression. *Ngay* signifies *day.* See above, No. 27. The Dictionary gives *hom* vesperè, and *nay* appears to be the pronoun *this; dem nay,* hâc nocte; *mon nay,* hoe anno. *Bua,* in the Dictionary, accented as in this Vocabulary, is rendered by *negotia.*]

37. Hom qua.
Hier.
Yesterday.

A.*

B, 62d radical, *ko,* a lance, (arma.) [*Hom,* vesperè; *qua,* transire. See the Dictionary, *his verbis.*]

38. Hom kia.
Avant hier.
The day before yesterday.

A.* [See above, No. 37.]

B. *Ky,* he, his, this, (pronoun.) G. 618.

39. Den mai.
Demain.
To-morrow.

A. *Tien,* law, rule, precept. G. 620.

B. Same as No. 32 B.

40. Den mot.
Après demain.
The day after to-morrow.

A. Same as No. 39 A.

B. *Mie,* bamboos divided into small sticks. G. 7571.

It might be the same group with the 140th radical, *thsao,* [a plant.]

41. Ngai le.
Le jour de fête.
A holiday.

A. Same as No. 27.

B. Same as No. 28 B.

Cochinchinese.	Chinese.

42. Ngay sinh nhot. A. [Same as No. 27 and 41 A.]
Le jour de noël. B. 100th radical, *seng,* to be born.
Christmas day. C. 72d radical, *ji*, the day.

43. Ngay phue sinh. A. [Same as 42 A.]
Le jour de pâques. B. *Fo,* again, to return. G. 2708.
Easter day. The Jesuits in China express Easter day by *Fou ho,* to live again. G. 4972.
C. [Same as 42 B.]

44. Ngay diu minh. A. [Same as 41, 42, 43, A.]
Le Dimanche. B.* The group in Chinese is pronounced *tieou,* with the 54th and 162d radicals.
Sunday. C. *Ming,* pure. G. 3890.
The Jesuits in China translate the word Sunday by *tchu yi,* the Lord's day.

45. Mua dong. These two characters appear ill written.
L'hiver. A. Should be written like No. 46 A.
Winter. B. The 15th radical, *ping,* ice or frost, appears to be wanting to this character. As it is, it is pronounced in Chinese *toung,* and signifies *the East;* as it seems it should be written, it is also pronounced *toung,* but signifies *to freeze.* G. 701.
Klaproth gives *D'on,* Anamitic, for *winter.*

46. Mua he. A. The 110th radical, *meou,* a halbert, indicates here the pronunciation.
L'été. B. *Hia,* summer. G. 1780.
Summer. Klaproth, *he,* summer.

20

Cochinchinese.	Chinese.

47. **Mua xuan.**
Le printemps.
The spring.

A. [Same as 46 A.]
B. *Tchun*, the spring. G. 3903.
Klaproth, *muan*.

48. **Mua thu.**
L'automne.
The autumn.

A. In this character, the 110th radical is probably omitted by error. See above, No. 46 A.

B.* The autumn, *thsieou*, is written differently in Chinese. G. 7125. Instead of the 76th radical, [*khian*, expiration, insufficient,] it has the 86th, [*ko*, fire.]

49. **Ngay nang.**
Un jour de chaleur.
A warm day.

A. [See above, 41—44.]
B.* The group is pronounced *nang*.

50. **Ngay lanh.**
Un jour de froid.
A cold day.

A. [Same as 41 A.]
B. *Leng*, cold. G. 676.

51. **Ngay xau.**
Un jour de mauvais temps.
A day of bad weather.

A. [Same as 50 A.]
B.*

52. **Ngay tot.**
Un beau jour.
A fine day.

A. [Same as 51 A.]
B. *Tsou*, to finish. G. 1008.

III.—OF THE WORLD, &c.

53. **The gian.**
Le monde.
The world.

Chi kian, the world.
[A. *She*, the world of human beings, the present state of existence. M. 475. 2.
B. *Wan*, to ask, to inquire, to investigate. M. 11613.

Cochinchinese.

Chinese.

Chi kien or *she keae,* is the Chinese pronunciation (as it is called) for the *world.* See M. *verbo world,* p. 475, 2.]

54. Dat.
La terre.
The earth.

Tan, flat, even, [ample, spacious.] G. 1578.

55. Non nui.
Une montagne.
A mountain.

A. The group is pronounced *nun.*
B.* The group is pronounced *nouy.*
Klaproth, *mi.*

56. Rong.
La campagne.
The country (rus.)

* I consider this group as an abbreviation of the 212th radical, *loung,* [a dragon.]

57. Vuon.
Le jardin.
The garden.

A.*
B. *Youen,* round. G. 1542. *Youen,* a garden, G. 1541, has a different character.
Klaproth, *Uoeu.*

58. Cay.
Les arbres et les bois.
The trees and the woods.

He, the stone or seed of a fruit. G. 4214. [M. 242, verbo *kernel.*]

59. Re.
Une racine—radix.
A root.

*

60. Goe.
Le tronc.
The trunk (of a tree.)

Ouo or *wo,* a house; [to dwell.] G. 2246.
O or *uh,* a wooden screen. M. 2. 258.

61. Nhanh.
Les branches.
The branches.

Seems to be a variation of the Chinese *ting,* which has the same meaning. G. 4258.

62. La.
Les feuilles.
The leaves.

*

Cochinchinese.	Chinese.
63. Hoa. Les fleurs. *Flowers.*	*Houa.* G. 8844.
64. Hot giong. La semence. *The seed.*	A. *He,* a thick silk thread. G. 7755. B. *Tchong,* a seed. G. 7206.
65. Da. Une pierre. *A stone.*	*
66. Dang. Chemin, rue. *A way, a street.*	*Tang,* the name of the imperial dynasty from the year 618 to 907 of the vulgar era ; [also, the aisles or walks in ancient temples, (viæ in avorum templis.) G. 1276.]
67. Rung. Forêt—silva. *A forest.*	*Ling,* an angle; a square piece of wood. G. 4320.
68. Vuon nho. Jardin de vignes. *A vineyard.*	A. *Youen.* See No. 57 B. B. *Mei,* the trunk of a tree. G. 4138. C.* Probably a variation of B.
69. Buong nho. Raisin. *Grapes.*	A. *Wang,* a name of wine. M. 3. 549. In the MS. the two dots below the group are wanting. B.* Same as No. 57 B. and 68 A.
70. Chuoi. Figues. *Figs.*	*Tchy,* shackles (compedes.) G. 4232
71. Suoi. Une fontaine. *A fountain.*	*
72. Giang. Puits—puteus. *A well.*	*King.* M. 2. 458. But the group without the radical is pronounced *tsing,* and signifies *a well.* G. 70.

Cochinchinese.	Chinese.

73. Song.　　* Might be *Shing*, the name of a
　　Rivière.　　　river. M. 9303.　See No. 56.
　　A river.　　[The two characters are the same,
　　　　　　　　one to signify *the country*, the
　　　　　　　　other *a river.*]

74. Bo song.　　*Po*, a hillock, a mound of earth for
Les bords d'une rivière.　a sepulchre.　G. 1574.
The banks of a river.

75. Bien.　　　* See No. 82.
　　La mer.
　　The sea.

76. Song.　　　*
　　Les vagues.
　　The waves.

77. Bai.　　　*
　　La rade.
　　The road.

78. Phong ba.　　A. is the 182d radical [*foung*, wind.]
　　La tempête.　　B.*
　　The storm.

79. Chiec tau.　　* The group is pronounced *tchi*. [It
　　Le vaisseau.　　has on the left the 137th radical,
　　The ship.　　*tcheou*, ship.]

80. Ghe.　　　*
　　Un petit bateau.
　　A small boat.

81. Cheo.　　　*
　　Les rames.
　　The oars.

82. Cua bien.　　A.* The 169th radical [*men*, door]
　　Le port.　　　never has a group to the right.
　　The port.　　B. See No. 75.

83. Cu' lao.　　A. *Kiu*, a bank to confine water.
　　Une ile.　　　M. 6084.
　　An island.　　B. *Lao*, to labour.　M. 6925.

Cochinchinese.	Chinese.

84. Nuoc.
Un royaume.
A kingdom.

Hvuls, the sound or noise of water. M. 2. 483.

85. Xa.
Une province.
A province.

This character has some resemblance to *tchu,* to dwell, to tarry; also, a place, a region. G. 9361.

86. Thanh.
Une ville.
A town.

Tching, walls. G. 1613.

87. Lang.
Un village.
A village.

Hiang, Pagus, territorium. G. 11251.

88. Que.
La patrie.
The fatherland (patria.)

Kwei, a kind of sceptre. M. 1. 481. 2.

89. Ben bai.
Le partie du nord.
The north.

A.*
B. *Pe,* the north. G. 953.

90. Ben dong.
La partie de l'est.
The east.

A.*
B. *Tong,* the east. G. 4108.

91. Ben nam.
La partie du sud.
The south.

A.*
B. *Nan,* the south. G. 1010.

92. Ben tang.
La partie de l'ouest.
The west.

Si, the west. G. 9852.

IV.—OF MANKIND.

93. Don ong.
Un seigneur.
A lord.

A.*
B. *Ong,* a name of honour given to old men. G. 8231. [Senior, Signor, Seigneur, &c.]

Cochinchinese.	Chinese.
94. Don ba.	A.*
Une dame.	B. The second character only is
A lady.	found as a group with the pronunciation *pa*. [See above, No. 6.]
95. Nguoi ta.	A. *Gai*, some impediment. M.2793.
L'homme.	B. *Sie*, a little, not much. G. 74.
A man.	
96. Loai nguoi ta.	A. *Luy*, a class, species, sort, kind.
Le genre humain.	M. 7431.
Mankind.	B. C. See No. 95.
	[The honourable class or species.]
97. Cha.	*Tcha*, to be angry, to scold. G. 1147.
Le Père.	[No resemblance to the Chinese *foo*,
Father.	father.]
98. Me.	*Mai*, a woman of an elegant figure
La mère.	and pleasing countenance. M. 1.
Mother.	665.
99. Con.	*Kouen*, the elder child (natu major.)
Les enfants.	G. 3883.
Child.	
100. Con trai.	[A. See 99.]
Un garçon.	B.* The group on the right is pronounced *lai*.
A male child, a boy.	
101. Con gai.	[A. See 99.]
Une fille.	B. *Hoo*, good and beautiful. M. 1.
A female child, a girl.	607.
102. Con it.	[A. See 99.]
Un enfant.	B. This looks like the 5th radical,
A child.	*y* [or *yih*] one, unity.
103. Con nho.	A. See 99.
Un mourrisson.	B. *Iu*, milk, woman's breast. G. 56.
A nursling, a child at the breast.	

Cochinchinese.   Chinese.

104. Con tre.   *
Un jeune homme.
A youth.

105. Gia.   *
Un vieillard.
An old man.

106. Chong.   The character on the right hand is
Le mari.   the same as the Chinese *Chang-
Husband.   foo,* husband. [M. verbo *husband.*]
                          That on the left hand is probably
                          to indicate the pronunciation.

107. Vo.   * Character unknown. The pro-
La femme.   nunciation does not much differ
Wife.   from the Chinese *foo* or *fou* [or *foo*]
                          above cited.

108. Dong trinh.   A. *Tong,* childhood. G. 7372.
Une vierge.   B. *Tching,* upright and firm (moral-
A virgin.   ly speaking.) G. 10410. *Thoung
                          tching,* a virgin.
                          [Thus a virgin in Chinese is called
                          thoung-tching, as who should say
                          a virtuous child, and the same in
                          Cochinchinese. This reminds us
                          of the Delaware word *pilape,* a
                          chaste or innocent man, meaning
                          a *youth* under fifteen.]

109. Ba hoa.   A. See No. 94.
Une veuve.   B.*
A widow.

110. Chau.   *Tchao,* to call somebody by making
Le neveu.   a sign with the hand. G. 3316.
Nephew.

111. Ba con.   [Woman-child, or lady and child.
La famille.   See Nos. 94 and 102.]
The family.

Cochinchinese.	Chinese.
112. Ho hang. Les parents. *The kindred.*	A. is the 63d radical, *hou,* a door. B. is the 144th radical, *hing,* to advance (progredi.)
113. Dian. Le peuple. *The people.*	*Min,* the people, the subjects. G. 4822.
114. Vuo. Le roi. *The king.*	*
115. Hoang hau. La reine. *The queen.*	(G. 6491.) *Hoang Heou,* the empress. G. 1143. [A. *Hvang,* a title of high dignity. M. 4378. B. *Heou,* prince, king, queen. G. 1143.]
116. Quan. Les ministres. *The ministers.*	*Kouan,* a common appellation for magistrates. G. 2116.
117. Ten linh. Les soldats. *The soldiers.*	A. *Sien,* before. G. 580. B. *Ling,* another. G. 1112.

V.—OF THE HUMAN MIND AND BODY.

118. Xac. Le corps. *The body.*	*
119. Dau. Le tête. *The head.*	*Teou,* [the head.] G. 1222).
120. Toc. Les cheveux. *The hair.*	*

Cochinchinese.

Chinese.

121. Thi.
L'intelligence.
Intelligence, under-
standing.

Tchy, wisdom, prudence. G. 3949.

122. Y muon.
La volonté.
The will.

A. *Y,* an act of the will. G. 2958.
B. *Men,* sad, (tristis.). G. 2887.

123. Su nho.
La mémoire.
Memory.

A. *Sse,* business, affair, thing, occu-
pation. G. 64.
B. This character, very ill drawn,
has some resemblance to that
which is pronounced *ngo* or *'o,*
(I, ego.) G. 3177.

124. Linh hon.
L'ame.
The soul.

125. Oc.
Le cerveau.
The brain.

Ouo [or *wo*] fat (pingue.) G. 8545.

126. Tran.
Le front.
The forehead.

Thheou, the front. M. 3. 693.
[In his Anglo-Chinese Dictionary,
Dr. Morrison gives *gih* for forehead, with a character that resembles only in part the Cochinchinese. Under the word *front*
(outside surface) he gives the
word *fan meen,* with two other
characters.]

127. Chan may.
Les sourcils.
The eyebrows.

A. *Tching,* felicity, happiness. G.
7071.
B. *Mao,* inundation. G. 5116.

128. Con mat.
Les yeux.
The eyes.

A. See No. 99.
B. *Mo,* dim-sighted eyes, (oculi ob-
scuri, caligantes,) G. 6627, is
composed of the same group and

Cochinchinese.	Chinese.
	the same radical, but in an inverted order. See above, No. 7.
129. Tai.	*
Les oreilles.	
The ears.	
130. Mat.	* See Nos. 7, 8, and 128.
La face.	
The face.	
131. Ma.	*
Les joues.	
The cheeks.	
132. Mui.	*
Le nez.	
The nose.	
133. Mei.	* The group is pronounced *mei.*
Les lèvres.	
The lips.	
134. Rang.	Appears to be a variation of *ngo,*
Les dents.	*bang ngo,* the space in the mouth
The teeth.	between the upper and the nether lip. G. [13280,] 13281.
135. Luoi.	*
La langue.	
The tongue.	
136. Nou.	*
Le palais.	
The palate.	
137. Mieng.	*Haou,* the roar of a wild tiger. M. 1. 380.
La bouche.	The Cochinchinese character is
The mouth.	formed of the 30th radical, which signifies *mouth,* and of the 108th, *ming,* [a porringer,] to indicate the pronunciation.

Cochinchinese.	Chinese.
138. Hong. La gorge (guttur.) *The throat.*	*Heung,* the breast. M. 3. 99.
139. Tieng. La voix. *The voice.*	*
140. Rou. La barbe. *The beard.*	*Fa,* the hair of the head. G. 12679.
141. Co. Le col. *The neck.*	*Kou,* ancient. G. 1110.
142. Vai. Les épaules. *The shoulders.*	*Wei,* the light of the sun. M. 2. 310.
143. Lung. Les reins et le dos. *The reins of the back.*	* The group is pronounced *ling.*
144. Tai. Les mains. *The hands.*	It is an ancient form of *y,* to remove. M. 2. 208.
145. Tai mat. La main droite. *The right hand.*	A. See No. 144. B. See Nos. 7, 8, 128, 130.
146. Tai trai. La main gauche. *The left hand.*	A. See No. 115. B. *Tchay,* debt, debtors. G. 410.
147. Mach. Le pouls. *The pulse.*	*Me,* [the pulse.] G. 8499.
148. Ngon tai. Les doigts. *The fingers.*	A.* B. See above, 144.

Cochinchinese.	Chinese.
149. Ngon tai cai.	[A.*]
Le gros doigt.	[B. See 144.]
The thumb.	C. *Kay*, to beg, (mendicare.) G. 11.
150. Ngon tai tro.	[A.*]
[L'index.	[B. See 144.]
The fore finger.]	[C.*]
151. Giua ngon.	* [There are here four characters;
[Le doigt du milieu.	but the last being a repetition of
The middle finger.]	the first, it is omitted in the
	plate.]
152. Ngon nhan.	*
L'annulaire.	
The ring finger.	
153. Ngon ut.	A.*
Le petit doigt.	B. See No. 102, where this charac-
The little finger.	ter has the pronunciation *it*. [In
	Father Morrone's Cochinchinese
	Dictionary, *it* is explained by pa-
	rum, modicum ; and he adds, *mot*
	it, mot chut, idem est. So that *it*,
	ut, chut, imply the idea of little-
	ness, and *con it* is a *little child*.]
154. Mong tai.	A. *Mang*, to gather. M. 2. 251.
Les ongles.	B. See 144.
The nails.	
155. Ngue.	*Py*, the stomach. G. 8523.
La poitrine.	
The breast.	
156. Mo ac.	A. may be *mei*, pregnancy. M. 3.
L'estomac.	108.
The stomach.	B.*
157. Long.	*
Le cœur.	
The heart.	

Cochinchinese.	Chinese.

158. Bong. · *
   Le ventre.
   The belly.

159. Run.   * It may be an abbreviation of *kien,*
   Le nombril.   an empty space below the ribs.
   The navel.   G. 8571.

160. Trai ve.   A.* The group is pronounced *lai.*
   La cuisse.   B.* The group is pronounced *wa.*
   The thigh.

161. Qui.   *Kouey,* to bend the knee. G. 10686.
   Les genoux.
   The knees.

162. Chon.   *Tchin,* true, [straight, neat, perfect.]
   Les pieds.   G. 6628 [somewhat varied.]
   The feet.

163. Trai chon.   A. *Luy,* the skin rising. M. 3. 105.
   Les jambes.   B. See above, 162.
   The legs.

164. Bon chon.   A.* See below, 242.
   La plante des pieds. B. See above, 162.
   The sole of the feet.

165. Than.   The first character is the 158th ra-
   Les membres.   dical, *chin,* the body. Father
   The limbs.   Morrone has probably forgotten
   to give its pronunciation. The
   second character is pronounced
   pen, [ignorant, coarse.] G. 164.
   It is vulgarly employed for *thy,* the
   members of the body. G. 12651.
   These two characters together
   are pronounced in Chinese *chin-
   pen,* and signify, as in Cochinchinese, *the members of the body,* or
   the *limbs.*

Cochinchinese.	Chinese.

166. Mau.
Le sang.
The blood.

Maou, the name of a river. M. 2. 460.

167. Gan cot.
Les nerfs.
The nerves.

A. *Kin*, the nerves. G. 7447.
B. is the 188th radical, *kou*, bone.

168. Gan.
Les veines.
The veins.

See No. 167 A.

169. Ruot.
Les entrailles.
The bowels.

＊

170. Dia.
Le peau.
The skin.

Pe, flesh. M. 3. 97. But the group is pronounced *pi*, and signifies *skin.*

171. Xuong.
Les os.
The bones.

＊ The group is pronounced *tchhung.*

VI.—OF CLOTHING.

172. Ao.
L'habit.
The coat.

Yaou, the earth producing things out of season. M. 2. 770.

173. Ao trong.
Les habits de dessous.
The under clothes.

[*Tchong*, an infant, (parvulus.)— *Tchong-tchong*, hanging ornaments, (dicitur de ornamentis pendulis.)] G. 672.

174. Ao ngoai.
Les habits extérieurs.
The outward clothes.

A. See above, 172.
B. *Ouay*, [or *way*,] without (foras.) G. 1786.

175. Non.
Le chapeau.
The hat.

＊

Cochinchinese.	Chinese.

176. Khon. *Tchong*, within, (intùs.) G. 26.
Le mouchoir ; tous les
  linges.
The handkerchief and
  all other linen.

177. Quan. The group is pronounced *kouan*,
  Les culottes. [kwan.]
  The breeches.

178. Giay. *Khiay*, coarse silk. M. 3. 23.
  Les souliers.
  The shoes.

179. Nut. *Chi*, the end or head of an arrow.
  Les boutons. M. 3. 23.
  The buttons.

VII.—Of the House.

180. Nha. *Ju*, to eat. G. 8925.
  La maison.
  The house.

181. Nha tho. [A. See 180.]
  L'église. B.* The group is pronounced *tou.*
  The church.

182. Nha quan. [A. See above, 180, 181.]
  L'hospice et l'hôte. B. See No. 116.
  The house and its
    master.

183. Nha bep. A. See above, No. 182.
La cuisine et le cuisi- B.*
  nier.
The kitchen and the
  cook.

Cochinchinese.	Chinese.
184. Nha ruong. Maison de campagne. *A country house.*	A. See above, No. 180. B.* The group is pronounced *kouang*. [See above, No. 56, where the word is written *rong*.]
185. Voch. Les murailles. *The walls.*	The same group in Chinese, with the 90th radical, *tchouang*, [a bed,] signifies *walls*, and is pronounced *tsiang*. G. 5619.
186. Cua. La porte et le port. *The door and the port.*	This is the 169th Chinese radical, *men*, [door.]
187. Cot. Une colonne. *A column.*	*Koue*, a stake, a small column. G. 4503. The same character, with only a small variation.
188. Thong. L'escalier. *The stairs.*	*Yang*, [oziers or twigs, (vimina.)] G. 4369. In some compositions it is pro- nounced *tang*.
189. Phong. La chambre. *The room or chamber.*	*Fang*, a dyke or embankment, (agger.) G. 11756.
190. Moi. Le toit. *The roof.*	These two characters having but one pronunciation, it is probable that the Cochinchinese used indif- ferently the one or the other. A. *May*, to purchase. G. 10437. B. *May*, to sell. G. 10486. [These characters are evidently applied to the sound.]
191. Ngai. Les tuiles (canales.) Probably *the gutters*.	* To this pronunciation are prefix- ed the two characters which ac- company that of the following number; there is probably an error.

Cochinchinese.   Chinese.

192. Truoc y.   *
    La chaise.
    The chair.

193. Kiuh.   * This character calls to mind *king*,
    Un miroir.   term, end, confines, limits, G. 7366,
    A mirror.   which is employed to indicate the
              pronunciation in *king*, a mirror.
              G. 11565.

194. Anh.   *Yng*, a shadow. G. 2669.
    L'image.
    The image.

195. Giu ong.   A.*
    Un lit.   B. *Tchouang*, a bed. G. 2500.
    A bed.

196. Nem.   *Men*, a rope or cord of bamboo.
    Une couverture.   G. 7885.
    A bed cover; a blanket.

197. Mong.   *Mong*, a dream. G. 1793.
    La courtine.
    The curtain.

198. Goi.   *Hoey*, to paint. G. 8036.
    Les oreillers.
    The pillows.

199. Giay.   *Sie*, to tie, (ligare.) G. 7823.
    Le papier.
    Paper.

200. Long ga.   A. is the 196th radical, *niao*, [a bird.]
    La plume.   B. is the 124th radical, *iu*, [feathers.]
    The pen.

201. Muc.   This is an abbreviation of *ne*, black.
    L'encre.   G. 1709. It also signifies *ink*.
    Ink.

202. Xe.   Radical 159. *Kiu*, [a car or car-
    Une voiture.   riage.]
    A carriage.

Cochinchinese.	Chinese.

203. Binh muc.
L'encrier.
The inkstand.

A. This character, says Mr. Morrison, occurs in an ancient work; but neither the sense nor the sound is known. M. 3. 563. The group is pronounced *ping*.

B. See No. 201.

204. Sach.
Un livre.
A book.

Tse, a book. G. 636.

205. Sach kinh.
Un livre d'oraison.
A book of prayers.

A. See above, No. 204.

B. This appears to be *king*, (liber classicus,) the name of the five classical books, of which an ancient form is given by Morrison. M. 3. 15. It has besides much resemblance to the Cochinchinese character.

206. Sach truyen.
Un livre d'histoire.
A book of history.

[A. See 204.]

B. *Tchouan*, traditions. G. 408.

207. Den.
La lampe.
The lamp.

* This group is in part composed of the 102d radical, [clavis agrorum,] which is pronounced *tien*, but its meaning has no connexion with that of the Cochinchinese word.

208. Chon den.
Le chandelier.
The candlestick.

A. See above, 162.

[B. See above, 207.]

209. Diou.
L'huile.
Oil.

Yeou, oil. G. 4899.

210. Sap.
La cire.
Wax.

La, wax. G. 9616.

Cochinchinese.

Chinese.

211. Hom.
Une caisse.
A box.

Se or *tse*, a wood fit for making the wheels of a large carriage. M. 2. 388.

212. Khoa.
La clef.
The key.

* [Father Morrone wrote this word *la claive* instead of *la clef.* M. de la Palun read it *le glaive.* It is believed that *la clef* is the better reading.]

213. Diao.
Un couteau.
A knife.

18th radical, *tao*, [a knife.]

214. Diao got.
Un rasoir.
A razor.

A. See above, No. 213.
B. This, with a small variation, is the character *ko*, a boiler; pronounced at Canton *wo*. M. 6427.

215. Guom.
Une épée.
A sword.

Kiun. M. 3. 559.

216. Sung.
Fusil.
A musket.

Tchong, a cannon, (tormentum bellicum.) G. 11442.

217. Keo.
Les ciseaux.
Scissors.

Composed of three radicals: 167, [*kin*, gold;] 111, [*chin*, an arrow;] and 68, [*kou*, a measure of capacity.]
Han, to contain as any vessel. M. 3. 569.

218. Hop.
Une tabatière.
A snuff-box.

219. Thuoc.
Le tabac.
Tobacco.

Tung-fung, the name of a plant found in Canton province. M. 3. 172. Chinese radicals 73, 75.

220. Hit thuoc.
Tabac à priser.
Snuff.

A.*
B. See above, 219.

Cochinchinese.	Chinese.
221. Hut thuoc. Tabac à fumer. *Smoking tobacco.*	A.* B. [See above, 219.]
222. Bi. Un sac. *A sack or bag.*	* The group is pronouced *pi.*
223. Lua. Le feu. *Fire.*	*Lo*, to burn. M. 2. 539. 2.
224. Khoi. La fumée. *Smoke.*	One single pronunciation for two characters. A.* The group of this character, with the 86th radical, *ho*, fire, is pronounced *hay*, and signifies *to burn.* B. This group is in part composed of the 194th radical, *kouei*, manes or shades of the dead; probably to indicate the pronunciation.
225. Than. Les charbons. *Coal.*	This character appears to be a variation or abbreviation of *tan*, coal. G. 5408.
226. Tro. Les cendres. *Ashes.*	* Perhaps *han*, to burn. M. 2. 534.
227. Choi. Balai. *A broom.*	*Tchy*, fetters, impediments, (compedes.) G. 4232.
228. Diu. .Un parasol. *An umbrella.*	* The group is pronounced *teou.*
229. Diay. Une corde. *A rope.*	* The group is pronounced *ti.*

Cochinchinese.	Chinese.

230. Dinh.
Un clou.
A nail.

Ting, a nail. G. 11381.

231. Bua.
Un marteau.
A hammer.

* May pass for a variation of *poo*, a metal plate. M. 3. 560.

232. Kim.
Une aiguille.
A needle.

167th radical, *kin*, metal.

233. Chi.
Le fil.
Thread.

Su, the beginning of a thread. G. 7930. The group is pronounced *tche.*

234. Noi.
Une casserolle.
A stew pan.

* The group is pronounced *nei.*

235. Chuong.
Une cloche.
A bell.

* The group is pronounced *tchoung.*

236. Bac.
L'argent.
Silver.

Po, to land, to bring a ship to shore. G. 4912.

237. Vang.
L'or.
Gold.

Hoang, a large bell. G. 11576. [It is used also, though improperly, for *hoang*, the sound of bells. G. 11510.]

238. Dong.
L'airain.
Brass.

Tong, copper. G. 11444.

239. Sat.
Le fer.
Iron.

Tchy, [to sew clothes.] G. 11419. But this character is also used for *tie*, iron. G. 11593.

240. Thiet.
Le fer blanc, (stannum.)
Pewter or tin.

To, the end of a cart axle-tree. M. 3. 577.

Cochinchinese.	Chinese.

241. Chi.
Le plomb.
Lead.

Y, a sort of kettle. G. 11407. The 65th radical on the right is pronounced *tchi,* but is unconnected with the sense. It means a *branch.*

VIII.—Of the Table, &c.

242. Bon.
La table.
Table.

* See above, No. 164 A.

243. Chia.
La fourchette.
Fork.

This is the same character as No. 241, with a different meaning and pronunciation.

244. Dia.
Les plats.
The dishes.

*

245. Chen.
Le verre.
A glass to drink out of.

* The group is pronounced *tchen.*

246. Bat.
Une tasse de terre.
An earthen cup.

A. *Tchouen,* baked bricks. G. 1684.
B.* The group on the right, which is the numeral 8, is pronounced *pa.*

247. Va.
Une bouteille.
A bottle.

The group appears to be written in a running hand; it is thought useless to hazard conjectures.

248. Va chai.
Bouteille de cristal.
A glass bottle.

*

249. Va lanh.
Bouteille de terre.
An earthen jug.

*

Cochinchinese.	Chinese.
250. Muong. Une cuiller. *A spoon.*	* The group is pronounced *meng*.
251. Banh. Le pain. *Bread.*	* It is to be remarked that the characters G. 12348 and 12377 are pronounced *ping*, and signify *bread.*
252. Ruou. Le vin. *Wine.*	* Perhaps a variation of *liou*, a name of liquor. M. 3. 546. 2.
253. Diam. Le vinaigre. *Vinegar.*	* The group is pronounced *ting*.
254. Nuoc. L'eau. *Water.*	* The group is pronounced *so.*
255. Thit. La chair. *Flesh or meat.*	*Thian*, fat. M. 3. 98. 2.
256. Ca. Le poisson. *Fish.*	*
257. Trai. Les fruits. *Fruit.*	*Ko*, fruit. G. 8991.
258. Cam. Les oranges. *Oranges.*	*Kan*, a kind of sweet orange. G. 4161.
259. Com. Le riz. *Rice.*	* The 69th radical on the right, which means *sweet*, and is pronounced *kan*.
260. Ot. Le poivre. *Pepper.*	A. *Ngan*, hard. G. 4125. B.*

Cochinchinese.	Chinese.
261. Muoi. Le sel. *Salt.*	* The group is pronounced *mei.*
262. Dano. Le sucre. *Sugar.*	In Chinese, sugar is called *tang*, and is written with the same group, either with the 119th or the 164th radical.
263. Mot. Le miel. *Honey.*	* It is a variation of *mi*, honey. M. 7666.
264. Mut. Les confitures. *Sweetmeats, preserves.*	*
265. Tra. Le thé. *Tea.*	*Tcha*, tea. G. 8923.
266. Dot long. Le dejeuner. *Breakfast.*	A.* The group is pronounced *io.* B. *Loung*, to play, trifle with; [but used to denote performing, acting, or doing any business or work.] M. 3. 7896.
267. An bua trua. Le diner. *Dinner.*	A.* The group is pronounced *an.* B.* The group is pronounced *pou.* C. *Thian*, fat, rich soup. M. 3. 106. 2.
268. An bua thoi. Le souper. *Supper.*	A.* B.* [A. B. See 267.] C. *Tsouy*, much, (valdè.) G. 4024.

IX.—OF ANIMALS.

269. Cam tu. Les animaux. *The animals.*	A. *Hoey*, all (omnes); [to collect, assemble, unite.] G. 4025. B. *Cheou*, quadrupeds. G.* 5870.

23

Cochinchinese.	Chinese.
270. Chim.	* The group is pronounced *chin.*
Les oiseaux.	
Birds.	
271. Con ngua.	A. [Nomen genericum.] *Kouen*, all,
Un cheval.	similar. G. 3883.
A horse.	B.*
272. Con bo.	A. See 271.
Un bœuf.	B.* The group is pronounced *pou.*
An ox.	
273. Con bo cai.	A. B. See 271.
Une vache.	C.* The group is pronounced *kai.*
A cow.	
274. Con ga.	A. See 271.
Une poule.	B. *Ky*, a hen. G. 12990.
A hen.	
275. Con bo.	A. See 271.
Un cochon.	B.* The group is pronounced *hiao.*
A hog.	[In the original, the character B is duplicated.]
276. Con chien.	A. See 271.
La brebis.	B. *Y*, name of a sheep. M. 3. 57. 1.
An ewe.	
277. Con ong.	A. See 271.
Les abeilles.	B.* The group is pronounced *oung.*
The bees.	
278. Con lua.	A. See 271.
Un âne.	B. Probably an abbreviation of *lu*,
An ass.	[an ass.] G. 12591.
279. Con voi.	A. See 271.
Un éléphant.	B.* The group on the left hand is
An elephant.	pronounced *siang*, and means an *elephant;* that on the right is pronounced *pei.*

Cochinchinese.	Chinese.

280. Con su tu.　　A. See 271.
　Un lion.　　　　B.*　C.*
　A lion.　　　　*Sse theu,* in Chinese, signifies *lion.*

281. Con bo du.　　A. See 271.
　Un taureau.　　　B. See 272 B.
　A bull.　　　　C. *Te,* a victim.　G. 5665.

282. Con eho.　　　A. See 271.
　Un chien.　　　　B.* The group is pronounced *tchu.*
　A dog.

283. Con soi.　　　A. See 271.
　Un loup.　　　　B.*
　A wolf.

284. Con hum.　　　A. See 271.
　Un tigre.　　　　B.*
　A tigre.

285. Con nai.　　　A. See 271.
　Un cerf.　　　　B.* The group is pronounced *ni.*
　A deer.

286. Con ran.　　　A. See 271.
　Un serpent.　　　B.* The group is pronounced *lin.*
　A snake.

287. Con sau.　　　A. See 271.
　Les vers.　　　　B.* It resembles in part 286 B.
　The worms.

288. Con vit.　　　A. See 271.
　Canard (oca.)　　B.*
A duck or goose, but most
　probably a goose.

289. Con chuot.　　A. See 271.
　Les rats (mus.)　　B.* The group is pronounced *tso.*
　The rats.

290. Con khien.　　A. See 271.
Les fourmis (formica.)　B. See *tching,* a kind of oysters, G.
　The ants.　　　　　9462; [and *tching,* a kind of small

Cochinchinese.	Chinese.

oyster, G. 9590; from which part of this character seems to have been borrowed.]

291. Con bau cau.
La colombe.
The turtledove.

A. See 271.
B.* The group is pronounced *po.*
C.* The group is pronounced *keou.*
In Chinese, *pau-kieou.*

292. Trung.
Les œufs.
Eggs.

＊

X.—Of Numbers.

293. Mot.
Un.
One.

* See No. 303 B.

294. Hai.
Deux.
Two.

This character is composed of the Chinese No. 2; on the right; and on the left that of *tay,* high, eminent. G. 1121.

295. Ba.
Trois.
Three.

* The Chinese No. 3, with a group which is pronounced *pa.*

296. Bon.
Quatre.
Four.

* The Chinese No. 4, with a group which is pronounced *pen.*

297. Nam.
Cinq.
Five.

The numeral 5, with a group pronounced *han.*

298. Sau.
Six.
Six.

* The numeral 6, with a group pronounced *tseou.*

299. Bay.
Sept.
Seven.

＊

Cochinchinese.	Chinese.
300. Tam. Huit. *Eight.*	* The numeral 8, with an abbreviation pronounced *tang*.
301. Chin. Neuf. *Nine.*	* The numeral 9, with a group pronounced *tchin*.
302. Muoi. Dix. *Ten.*	*
303. Muoi mob. Onze. *Eleven.*	A.* B. *Mei*, twigs. M. 7596. [See No. 293.]
304. Muoi hai. Douze. *Twelve.*	* [Ten-two (ten and two.) See 302 and 294.]
305. Hai muoi. Vingt. *Twenty.*	* [Two-ten (twice ten.) See 294 and 302.]
306. Ba muoi. Trente. *Thirty.*	* [Three-ten. See 295 and 302.]
307. Mot tram. Cent. *A hundred.*	A. [*Mot*, one, above. See 293.] B.* The Chinese numeral 100, with a group pronounced *lin*.
308. Mot ngan. Mille. *A thousand.*	[A*. See above, 307.] B.* The numeral 1000, with a group pronounced *ngan*.
309. Mot muon. Dix mille. *Ten thousand.*	A.* [See above, 307.] B.* The numeral 10,000, with the 169th radical, *men*, door.
310. Mot hai muon. Vingt mille. *Twenty thousand.*	* Literally one-two (twice) ten thousand. [See above, 293, 294.]

Cochinchinese.	Chinese.

311. Muon muon.
Innumerable.

* [Thousand-thousand; as it were thousands without number.]

312. Muon van.
Un million.
A million.

[A. See No. 308.]
B. *Ouan,* ten thousand.   G. 9037.

313. Tien.
La monnaie.
Money.

Abbreviation of *tsien,* money.   G. 11490.

314. Mot dong.
Une sapèque.
One sapek.

[A. See 293.]
B. *Tong,* copper.   G. 11444.

315. Mot tien.
Soixante sapèques.
Sixty sapeks.

* [See Nos. 293, 313.]

316. Mot quan.
Dix tien.
Ten tien.

A. See No. 293.
B. See No. 116.

317. Mot chuc.
Dix quan.
Ten quan.

A. See No. 293.
B.* The group is pronounced *chou* [or *shoo.*]   See 318 B.

318. Hai quan.
Vingt quan.
Twenty quan.

A.* See No. 294.
B.* See No. 317 B.

319. Mot tram chuc.
Mille quan.
A thousand quan.

* See Nos. 293, 307 B, and 317 B.

XI.—Of Various Things.

320. Quot.
L'éventail.
A fan.

* The group is pronounced *ko.*

Cochinchinese.	Chinese.

321. Nhan. *
L'anneau.
A ring.

322. Sam truyen.   A. *Tsan,* to testify. G. 10301.
La Bible.   B. *Tchouen,* libri sapientium. G.
The Bible.   408.

323. Hat boy.   A. *Yae* or *ho,* a shout, an exclama-
La comédie.   tion. M. 1. 411. 1.
Comedy.   B.* The group is pronounced *po.*

324. Iu rac.   A. *Tsieou,* a jail or prison. G. 1509.
La prison.   B.*
The jail.

325. Die ngue.   A. *Ti,* earth or ground. G. 1557.
L'enfer.   B. *Yo,* prison. G. 5804.
Hell.

326. Ma qui.   A. *Mo,* demons. G. 12768.
Le diable.   B. *Kouey,* a spirit, 194th radical,
The devil.   *mo-kouey,* the devil.

327. Toi loi.   A. *Tsouy,* sin. G. 8150.
Le péché.   B.*
Sin.

328. Phuoc duc.   A. *Fou,* virtue. G. 7063.
La vertu.   B. *Pou,* to publish, to sacrifice. G.
Virtue.   2407.

329. Di diao.   A.* The group is pronounced *tchi.*
Aller à la promenade. B. *Tao,* way. G. 11117.
To go to walk.

330. Di ngu.   A.* See above, 329.
Aller dormir.   B.*
To go to sleep.

331. Thuc diay.   A. *Tchi,* to remember. M. 3. 384. 2.
S'éveiller.   B. *Y,* to draw, to lead. G. 4016.
To awake.

Cochinchinese.	Chinese.
332. Toi to. Un serviteur. *A servant.*	A.* [*Toi*, ego, meus, a, um. See Dictionary.] B. *Tso*, to assist. G. 162.
333. Rua mat. Se laver le visage. *To wash one's face.*	A.* B. See No. 7.

霚　霙　解　29
　　霜　暑　刻
5　　　　26
　　20　　30
嵗　　解　暟
星　欺　婁　31
　　21　26
至　　　㳠
6　靁　腯　漱
　　　　27
　　16　　32
德　　　鈙
主　霝　腯　埋
妃　　28　鈙
7　17　旬　33
桶　雪　礼
坴　18
8　　遷　解
桶　19　24
胺

爔　創　代
11　12　代
創　氣　22
　　13
　　　代
　　　代
　　　23

辡	38	42	45	49	53	圓
胯	歆	胯	冷	胯	世	
34	其	生	東	爆	間	68
朝	39	日	46	50	54	楂
35	典	43	務	胯	乚旦	59
店	理	胯	夏	冷	55	枞
36	40	復	47	51	崇	60
坡	典	生	務	胯	岗	楎
歆	簋	44	春	乜	56	61
37	41	胯	48	52	滝	梃
歆	胯	咄	冷	胯	57	62
戈	礼	明	秋	卒	稛	菙

2

尋旹　昆妳　軝　招　皇后　遨　125

94　102　106　111　116　121　腥

吒　昆乙　軝　妃昆　官　智　頭　126

97　103　107　112　117　122　禛眉　127

媄　　猵　户行　先另　意悶　昆相　128

99　昆乳　童貞　113　118　123

昆　104　109　民　壱　事仅　聰　129

100　　妃过　114　119　124

昆躰　昆祂　110　希　頭　灵魁

101　105　　115　120　120

					136	142	147	151	栖	160

136 脪　142 曬　147 脈　151 钟　栖　160 㦸
137　143　148　珤西　156　肮
叩　暖　珤　手西　156　161
139　144　栖　152　䏠　跪
胸　栖　149　珤　腸　162
139　145　珤　习　157　真
啃　栖　栖　153　悉　163
140　㯱　丐　珤　158　腺
髟　146　150　乙　腠　真
141　栖　珤　154　159　164
古　債　栖　檬　朕　盟

169 袄 鈇 短 楊 夗

170 脾
外 180 184 189 193
股 175 茹 茹 防 竟
171 繢 181 185 190 194
髖 176 茹 曠 檀 影
172 中 祿 墙 檀 196
袄 177 182 186 191 糀
173 襸 茹 門 丁 庠
袄 178 官 187 夗 196
冲 緒 183 撇 192 總
174 179 茹 188 丁 197

197 夔

車

207 畑

錺

218 鈐

223 烙

霏

198 繪

203 鈄

213 刀

鈐

烙

229 綉

199 線

鈄黑

208 真畑

214 刀鎬

219 枼

嗨燼

釘

200 鳳羽

204 冊

209 沺

215 鈞

220 嗽枼

225 燄

231 錫

201 黑

205 冊縫

210 蠟

216 銃

221 哭枼

226 炶

232 金

202

206 冊傳

211 檺

217 銂

222 綏

227 娌

228

233 緒

234

234	240	246	250	256	埖	267
圽	鐅	塼圦	鑖	齵	262	唠
235	241		251	257	磄	餡
鏈	鈘	247	餇	菓	263	肵
236	242	塄	252	258	寳	268
泊	壺	248	醅	柑	264	唠
237	243	鵰	253	269	饙	餡
鑛	鈘	砇	酊	鉗	265	最
238	244	砮	254	260	茶	269
銅	扒	249	湝	栁	266	魯
239	245	攜	255	楬	餔	猷
鉄	墩	垗	鮕	261 弄	弄	270

270	274 昆	昆	特	妣	卒 294
鵾	昆鷄	驦 279	282	286	昆 台二 295
271 昆	275	昆	昆主	昆蛥	昆蜆 巴三 296
驤	昆	象盃	283	287 291	罘 297
272 昆	醫 280	昆	昆弉	昆蛛 昆鯆	鼎五 298
捕	昆羖	師	284 288	昀句	赴六
273 昆	276	子 281	昆贙	昆鳥 292	罸七 299
捕丐	昆蠣 278	昆捕	285 289	293	
			昆 昆	沒	

萬 | 305 台辵 | 309 茨齋 | 313 錢 | 317 茨聯 | 321 勾 | 地欵 | 髟導

330 髟旿

306 巴辵 | 310 茨台齋 | 314 茨銅 | 318 台瞋 | 322 識傳 | 326 廥皀

327 罪弃福布

331 識

307 茨森 | 311 齋齋 | 315 茨錢 | 319 茨森瞋 | 323 喝倍 | 328 因

332 砥佐

308 茨彥 | 312 齋齋 | 316 茨官 | 320 撒 | 324 因 | 325 客 | 329

333 冶榀

LEXICON

COCHIN-SINENSE LATINUM

AD USUM MISSIONUM.

A R. P.

JOSEPHO MARIA MORRONE,

Catholicæ Romanæ Ecclesiæ Missionum in Cochin-Sina

MINISTRO

ET ILLIC IN URBE SAIGON COMMORANTE

CIVI AMERICANO JOHANNI WHITE

PERBENIGNE DONATUM.

AMERICANÆ PHILOSOPHICÆ SOCIETATIS JUSSU

TYPIS EXCUSUM.

24

LEXICON

COCHIN-SINENSE LATINUM.

[Signa tonorum, ad elevandam vel deprimendam vocem in pronunciatione syllabarum, hc, tanquam inutilia, omittuntur.]

A.

A. Instrumentum rusticum triangularè ad secandum paleas aptum.

A. Soror major natu. Co a, Famulæ vel concubinæ mandarinorum. Chi a, Apud sorores religiosas est secunda in conventu.

Ac. Ludere simpliciter. Ac nghiep, vel choi ac, Ludere turpiter. Lain nghe choi ac, Exercere res turpes. Chim ac, Corvus. Mo ac, Pulsus pectoris.

Ach. Jugum. Ach nan, vel tai ach, Calamitas. Ach nuoi, Calamitas totius regni. Phat ach, Morbus, qui spiritum semper sursum agit.

Ai. Quis? Ai lay, Quis accepit? Istud relativum, quis, quæ, quod, si jungatur aliis nominibus, mutatur in vocem nao, et semper postponitur nominibus, ut ng nao, quis homo? vel quæ mulier? Su nao, Quæ res, &c. Ai ai, vel He ai ai, Quicumque. He ai ai muon de roi chon thi tri het ph' biet tao Catholica, Quicumque vult salvus esse, antè omnia opus est ut teneat Catholicam fidem.

Ai nay. Non propriè quidem, sed ex usu concionatorum nunc invalescente evadit in secundam personam pluralem; ut ai nay ph' biet, Vos debetis scire. Ai phue vel che phue, Vestis lugubris. Cung ai, Tono lugubri. Ai mo, Vehementer amare.

Ai. Corruptio lignorum, vestium, &c. eâdem sua formâ subsistente dicitur ai; sed quando aliquid corruptum et in partes confractum est, dicitur nat: D. J. C. chiu danh don nat het thit ra, Dominus Jesus flagellatus est usque concisionem totius carnis.

Ay. Terra sterilis. Ay, Ille, illa, illud. Ay no, Ecce ille. Pronomen ille, illa, illud, semper debet postponi substantivo; ut ng ay, Homo ille, illud negotium.

Am. Locus vel ædicula dicata idolo vel mortuo. Tumulus bonziorum.

Am. Dicitur de fuligine vel fumo quando alicui adhærent rei. Qui am, dæmon obsidet. Nguoi qui am, Obsessus a dæmone.

Am. Gestare infantem in sinu.

Am. Ista vox apud annamitas variè significat et apponitur litteræ duong: undè am duong, est luna et sol; mulier et vir; aer humidus et calidus; par et impar: undè xem vel xin am duong, sortilegium scrutare. Biu am, Æstus solis sine splendore.

Am cai am. Lebes vel ahenum ad calefaciendum aquam. Dicitur etiam de aere temperato à frigore. Nhieu ao thi am, Multæ vestes temperant à frigore. Dam am, suavitas aëris tempore veris.

Am. Humidus, a, um. Am am, Sonitus.

An vel *yen.* Pax, tranquillitas. Nguoi Anam, Annamita. Nguoi Anan, Tunkinum. An ui, Consolari. Yen khau, ephippium equinum.

An. Scriptum ad cautelam. Lap an, Conficere scriptum ad cautelam. Dieu an, Deferre ejusmodi scriptum ad judicem. Nguoi luy an, Homo facinorosus, qui multis ejus-

modi scriptis est notatus. Huong an, Incensi altare apud
Ethnicos.

A-ng. Genus vasis.

A-ng na. Pater et mater; non est in vulgari sermone.

An. Manducare, cibum capere. An trom, Furari. An cuop,
Diripere. Ke trom ke cuop, Fures et raptores. An o,
Conversari, gerere se, rem cum viro aut muliere habere.
An noi, Loqui. An muoy, Mendicare. Manducare pro
personis honoratis dicitur xoi. Xin cu di xoi com. Digneris Pater ire manducatum oryzam. Vox vero regalis est
com vong, vel com thue.

Anh, Frater major. An hem, Fratres. Anh, Imago.

Ang. Ponitur cum yen; ut yen ang, Silentium, Silere.
Anh mat bloi, radii solis.

An. con an, an tiu, Sigillum. An bau, Sigillum regale.
Dan han, Sigillum imprimere. Dao an, sigillum fabricare. Sap an, Inchoantur feriæ. Khai an, Desinunt feriæ. An xuo, Deprimere.

An. Abscondere se. An nih tren rung, Abscondere se in
silvis. Abscondere alias res, dicitur Giau. Giau boi troi
nih, Occultare pecuniam in pectore.

Ao. Piscina vel stagnum.

Ao. Vestis. Ao dai, Vestis talaris. Ao chen toy, vestis
strictioris manicæ. Cao mu dai ao, Dicitur de illis qui
affectant sæculares dignitates in biretis et vestibus ob-
longis.

Aong, vel ao, apes. Tieng ao tieng ve, Balatus apum et
cantus cicadarum, metaphoricè pro molestis querelis.

Ao ao, Murmur multorum clamantium.

At. Noi at ng ta di, Contradicere et conari verbis cæteros
prævalere.

Ap. Fovere. Au lo, Mestus. Cai au, Vasculum.

Ap vao, Applicare. Ap, propè. Au, castanea.

Ap lai, vel ap viu. Præses operis.

At la, vel hla au la, Certè, sine dubio.

Ay la, illud est.

An nan, Pœnitere. An nan toi, contritio.

Aт, vel at la. Certè.

B.

Bᴀ. Tres. Ia ba ba, testudo.

Bᴀ. Venenum quo canes à furibus enecantur. Ao ba, genus telæ sericæ.

Bᴀ, avia. Diu ba, regina. Ista vox etiam sumitur pro omni personâ honoratâ feminini sexûs, ut Ba thanh Ine, Sancta Agnes. Diu ba, apud Christianos per antanomasiam nominatur Beata Virgo. Anh Diu Ba, Imago Beatæ Virginis. Ba nay, Ista Domina.

Ba tri ba, Dignitas quædam. Ba, vox sinico-annamitica est nota vel catalogus; unde dien ba est nota agrorum. Dinh ba, catalogus virorum.

Ba co ba, Concubinæ magistratuûm. Thui ba, linguâ vulgari. Chù bai, patruus minor et major.

Bᴀɪ, argentum. Xuy bai, dealgentare. Danh bai, ludere aleis. Nguoi co bai, aleator. Bai ra, albescere. Bai tinh, cor ingratum. Bai ai, impius, &c. Bai, patruus major.

Bᴀɪ, elychicum, seu materia alia quâ nutritur ignis in oleo.

Bᴀɪ, gradus. Bai, vel mo ban tho, gradus candelabrorum supra altari positus. Dang bai, ordo vel status. Vide vocem Dang.

Bᴀcʜ. Vox sinico-annamitica, albus, a, um. Raro est in uso nisi trang bach ra, albescere. Ngua bach, equus albus.

Bᴀɪ. Septentrio. Thuoi bai, medicina sinica. Bai cuoi, imperium Sinarum. Gio bai, aquilo. Sao bai dau, septem stellæ quæ ab astronomis Europæis vocantur urus septentrionalis.

Bai, an noi be bai, disertè loqui. Non est in vulgari.

BAI. Labefactari. Bai tran, victus bello. Bai chiu quien, amittere dignitatem. Bai canh tay, arescit brachium.

BAI. Inclinatio capitis pro reverentia. Khau dau bai ta, supplex gratias agere. Bai nganh, vale dicere in malam partem.

BAI. Variis rebus applicatur. Bai thuoi, certus modus medicinam conficiendi. Bai hoi, lectio scholasticorum. Danh bai danh bai, ludere chartis, aleis. Chay hoa bai, vel the bai, mandatum per cursorem ad varia loca mittere. Bai giang, concio. Ra bai, thema dare.

Bai, choi bai bai, præfractè negare. Voi vang bo bai, intempestè properare. Bay, septem. Boy vel bay, decipula avium.

Bay gio, nunc. Boy ba, homo numquam serius. Bay gio, tunc. Sum bay, tammultum. Cua bay, cancer excoriatus. Bay chim, agmen avium.

BAI. Congestus arenarum ex inundatione, vel arena acclivis in ripis fluminum vel maris. Bai bien, littora maris. Quan be bai, nebulones; idem est ac dan soi cuoi bai.

BAY, volare. Chim bay, avis volans. Chim dau, chim bat, bat chim bay, dicitur de eo, qui re certâ relictâ sperat incertam. Bay, vel chung bay, vox non est in usu, nisi ad infimos homines et contemptibiles alloquendo. Cai bay, instrumentum ad liniendum parietes.

Bay ra. Collocare vel effingere. Bay mom ra, collocare abacos. Thung Anio bay ra nhieu deu doi, Anius effinxit multa mendatia.

Bay bay, septem, septima, thu bay, &c.

Bam bam, fructus quidam.

Bam chi, extremis digitis compingere. Bam, carnem aut piscem crebro ictu minutim conscindere.

BAN. Concedere. Vox propria Regi. Vua chua ban cho, Rex concedit. D. C. B. ban cho tanh on lanh. Deus concessit nobis multa beneficia.

Ban ghat. elargiri. Ban ngay ban dem, diu noctuque. Phat ban, scabies.

BAN. Societas, socius. Ke ban, intimam inire amicitiam vel societatem, vel etiam matrimonium contrahere. Con da ket ban chua, Filius vel Filia jam esse conjugatus vel conjugata.

BAN. Vendere. Buon ban, mercari. Ban phan, media pars. Ban sinh, ban thiu, semicrudus, a, um.

BAN, vel ban luah, ban bai, censere, consultari. Ban chiem bao, somnium interpretari. Ban tay, vola manus. Co ke bon rang phai sai quan pha lang ai, sunt qui exercitum ad certandum cum luce excitandum censent.

BAN, materia ex quâ aliquid fit: vel summa capitalis. Vo ban bat lap, sine materia nihil fit. Saih ban, exemplum originale ex quo aliquid transcribitur. Ban do, mundi mappa.

BAN, ventus typhonius, typho; tempestas valida.

BAN, explodere globos ex tormentis bellicis, aut sagittas ex arcubus. Ban tin di, divulgatur fama. Hon da ban ra, exilit lapis. Ban han net, dura indoles.

BAN, implicare et impedire. Ao dai ban chan, vestis oblonga impedit gressum.

Ban lung, paupertas extrema. Ban nhan, pauperrimus.

BAN, sordidus, a, um. Ban thiu, idem est. Ban than, hebescere.

BANG, vox Sinico-annamitica, regnum.

Bang nhao, vel bang bo, irridere contemnere. Bang vao dau, digitis caput pulsare.

BANG, arbor quædam.

BANG, inscriptio magnifica, quâ declarantur ii, qui in publicis litterarum certaminibus lauream adipiscuntur.

BANG, æquus, a, um, vel æqualis, e.

Ba ngoi lung bang nhau, tres personnæ sunt sibi invicem coæquales. Bang lao, æquo animo. Lam bang, dicitur de omnibus rebus quæ fiunt ex aliquâ materiâ, ut chan neu lain bang go, candelabrum ex ligno.

Bang, juxta, sicut. Lam bang, vel sa dan su bang su giai, cives hostesque juxta interficere. Lam bang di, vel bang tri di, solo æquare. Ke cho Annam quang da bang tri di ca, metropolem Tunkini Cochinsinenses solo æquarunt totam. Nhuoi bang, quod si.

Banh, panis. Banh che, os rotundum intra genu super quo genuflectimus.

Banh voi, turricula dorso elephantis superposita.

Bap chuoi, flos ficûs indicæ quando nondum est apertus. Bap giua, flos ananæ sylvestris qui est valdè suavis. Quat bap giua, flabellum ad formam illius floris factum. Noi lap bap, loqui ineptè, sine meditatione.

Bat, vel *lieu bat*, dispergi tempestate vel aliâ calamitate.

Bat, porsulana, scutella. Bat su, scutella sinica. Bat da, bat tai, obstupescunt aures.

Bat, capere, cogere. Bat lam viei, cogere ad laborem. Bat chuoi, imitari, æmulari. Chang nen bat chuoi ke xau net, non licet æmulari malos.

Bat, *nin bat bat*, altum silentium.

Bat lam, aliquando dicitur pro benè, nimis.

Bat maga, virescere.

Bat, vox sinico-annamitica, non.

Bat phue, inobediens. Bat nhan, ingratus, a, um.

Bau, *chua bau*, pretiosissimus, a, um.

Bau, unguibus vulnerare.

Bau, *ruoi bau*, muscæ assident.

Bau chu, fidejussor.

Bau cu, intercedere.

Bau, cucurbita alba.

Be, *cai be* vel *cai ve*, vasculum. Be ruoi, vasculum vini. Con be, con me, vitulus. Be tan, latera navis.

Be, tegumentum arborum quæ multiplici cortice teguntur, quales sunt coco, areca, ficus indica, &c.

Be, parvulus. Thauy be, puer parvulus. Con be, puella.

BE, *be boi*, rates vel colligatura multorum lignorum. Sumitur etiam pro discordiis et factionibus. Trao nha chung ch nen sinh ra be boi, in communitatibus non debent fieri factiones. Ve be ue nhau, adjungunt sese factiosi. Buon be, exercere mercaturam lignorum.

BE, frangere. Be doi ra, frangere in duas partes. Be boi, vide supra.

BE, suffundi pudore ex repulsa. Lam be mat, suffundere pudore aliquem per repulsam.

BE, cai be, ferula. Con be, vide supra.

Be be, gestare infantem.

Be ngoai extra; *be trao*, intus. Be ngoai la con chien, be trao la soi rung; extra es ovis, intus vero lupus. San soi su be ngoai xem sao su be trao, procurare multum exteriora, interiora negligere.

BE, melius dicitur *bien*, mare. Ta con o noi bien ca la the gian noy, adhuc sumus in hujus mundi pelago.

BE, follis. Thoi be, sufflare follem.

Bech nguoi bech mat, homo crassæ faciei et largæ.

BEN, et dinh ben, adhærere. Chang nen dinh ben su toi, non licet adhærere peccato.

BEN, sed. Ben chua chung toi chung su du, sed libera nos à malo; non est tam in usu quam *sao le*.

BEN, una pars respectu alterius. Ben trao ben ngoai, pars interior et exterior. Ben nay hay la ben kia, nemo potest duobus dominis servire.

BEN, statio navium vel cymbarum. Ben sou, ripa fluminis ad quam appellunt naves vel cymbæ.

BEN, durare, durabilis. Su the gianch ben chang do, quæ sunt hujus mundi fluxa atque fragilia sunt. Ben lao, firmo et constanti animo. Vide *vung*.

BEO, *con beo*, tigris parvus.

BEO, carnem digitis convellere.

BEO, pinguis, crassus.

BEO, herba in superficie aquæ nata, pascendis porcis apta.

Xem ng ta nhu cai beo bat vay, deprimere alios ad infi-
mum gradum. Re nhu beo, quod est valde vile.

Beo, *chim cheo beo,* avicula quædam quæ tempore æstivo
circa auroram cantillare solet.

Bep, *mu bep,* biretum vetustate depressum. Nguoi ay da
bep mat, ad vilitatem vel paupertatem redactus.

Bep, focus. Lam bep, agere coquum. Dan ba nam bep,
mulier est in puerperio, quia post partum solet adhiberi
focum. Nha bep, culina vel coquus. Vua bep, Deus foci.

Bep, *nam bep,* decumbere lassus.

Bet, *nat bet,* confractissimus, a, um.

Bi, mantica. Bi, cucurbita. Bi tieu tien, calculus. Bi,
pellis. Binh, miles. Binh, vasculum. Binh huong, thuribulum.

Bia, inscriptio in lapide ad perpetuam memoriam. Hom
bia thien chua de tru yen, arca fœderis veteris testamenti.
Bia ban, scopus.

Bia, tegumentum libri. Nguoi va bia sach, homo literis
imbutus.

Biei, color cœruleus.

Bich mu bich, color plusquam cœruleus.

Biem, degradatio dignitatis.

Bien, notare litteris. Bien, discernere, excogitare. Phai
lai tui phon bien ra ma lam, oportet uti ingenio ad exco-
gitandum quid faciendum sit.

Bien di, evanescere. Tuy co ung bien, accommodare se
ad omnes fortunæ casus. Bien tra bien coi, variabilis,
fallax, mobilis animo.

Bien, mare. Vide supra *be.*

Bieng, *Lam bieng,* piger. Bieng tra, bieng rap, idem est.

Biet, scire. Biet la the nao, quomodo scimus.

Bim. Cay bim bim, herba quædam.

Bim di, silentio supprimere.

Binh, miles. Binh si, idem. Binh vue, defendere. Binh
phap, disciplinæ militaris severitas. Binh ki, arma.

Bɪᴘ. Chim bip bip, avis quædam a suo cantu sic vocata.

Bɪᴛ, celare. Guom bit bac, gladius argento celatus. Bit tat, tibiale.

Bɪᴜ, ventriculus cujuscumque animalis.

Biu moi biu mo, deducere labia in signum contemptus.

Bo, *giu bo bo*, tenaciter custodire.

Bo, vermis ex fœtore natus. Bo cua, lignum quo retinetur pessula portæ.

Bo, colligare. Mot bo, fasciculus vel ligatura. Bo, con bo, bos, vis. Bo duoi dat, rapere in terra.

Bo, abjicere, relinquere, repudiare. Ke muon an nan toi nen, thi ph bo lao yeu men su toi ra khoi tao minh, qui ɩ vult esse vere pœnitens debet abjicere amorem peccati corde suo. Cai Thanh Tou Do de bo moi su ma theo, D. J. C. Apostoli relinquerunt omnia et secuti sunt Christum. Vo chou ch' de lia bo nhau bao gio sot, nunquam licet marito et uxori se invicem repudiare.

Bo, *bo nuoi*, nutritus. Cho bo, ad satisfaciendum iræ. An cho bo lue doi, comedere ad compensandum famem.

Boɪ, decorticare fructum aut arborem. Boi ao, spoliare aliquem veste.

Bon, conquirere aliquid cineri aut pulveri commixtum. Hay bon ng ta, corrodere pecuniam aut quid aliud ab aliis avaritiæ causâ.

Boɴ, *mot bon*, una classis.

Boɪ, *Di boi*, sortilegium scrutari. Thay boi, sortilegus cœcus. Trou boi, tympanulum ex papyro factum ad puerorum lusum.

Boᴘ, digitis comprimere. Bop da lai, contrahere viscera sua more avarorum. Bop bep, vide *bep*.

Boᴛ, saliva, spuma. Nuot nuoi bot, deglutire salivam. Sau bot mieng ra, despumare.

Boɪ, *Quan thai boi*, dignitas quædam.

Boi lay, aliquid sparsum compressis digitis colligere. Boi sang, aliquem supplantare.

Bon, *an noi bom bom*, rusticè et ineptè loqui.

Boi, ungere, linire. Nguoi boi boi, homo versipellis vel simulatus. Dai boi, simulata urbanitas.

Boi, excessus cujuscumque rei. Boi thue, excessus gulæ. Mung boi phan, gaudere superabundanter. Toi da chiu onng van boi, cumulatus sum à te beneficiis satis superque. D. C. B. da thuong yeu ta boi phan, Deus dilexit nos maximè. Boi nghia boi bai, ingratus. Lam boi, parentare mense septimo.

Boi toi, coma capillorum, vel comare aut potius glomerare capillos more annamitorum. Boi roi, intricatio cujuscumque rei. Boi roi nhieu viei, intricari multis negotiis. Phat boi, ulcus mortiferum.

Boi cank boi, jusculum ex farina et oleo confectum. Giay boi, papyrus crassa et vilis. Boi phu, adaugere ad cumulum. Ta boi, protegere; non est vulgaris vox.

Boi rai, herba siccata ad tegendum domos. Trau boi, purgamenta frumentorum.

Bon, confusio aut concursus multorum; non est tam in usu.

Bon, quatuor. Hut bon, quartus, a, um.

Bon. Mam bon vel mam bun, abax ad subigendum vestes aptus. Bon chon, inquietns.

Bon, vide ben.

Bop go bop, lignum molle et leve.

Bot, farina. It bot quay cb nen ho, deficiente farinâ non fit gluten; dicitur de iis qui incipiunt ædificare, et non possunt consummare.

Bot gay, ferrum acutum baculo conjunctum.

Bou, gossipium. Keo bou vai, fila ex gossipio ducere. Bou lua, spica.

Bou ca bou, quoddam pisciculum.

Bou cai bou, instrumentum musicum duo capita majora medium constrictum habens. Bou be, vide be.

Bou, *chim bay bou*, avis altè volat.

Bou bang, variabilis et dissimilis.

Bou phou, repentè.

Bo vo, incertus, vagus, nulli rei nixus.

Bo, *tam bo*, mutuari pecuniam ab aliquo. Co bo, species avis. Rau bo, species herbæ.

Bo, *bo coi*, terminus, confinium. Bo ao, ripa stagni. Bo bai, vide *bai*.

Boi, *cai giam boi*, remus minor. Boi thuyen, agere cymbam illis remis minoribus. Xem boi, spectare remigantes. Is lusus sæpe in honorem idoli fit.

Boi, exagere terram. Boi moira, ex abdito educere.

Boi boi, viei boi boi, negotia obsident turmatim.

Boi, undè, ex, propter. Boi dau ma neu su nay, undè fit istud? D. C. B. ch' ph' boi dau ma neu, Deus à nullo provenit. Su na boi toi ma ra, istud à peccato procedit. Luciphe ph' phat boi toi no, Lucifer damnatus est è peccato suo, vel propter peccatum suum.

Bon, *con bom*, scortum.

Bon, *ca bon*, quidam piscis, Lusitanicè lingoa de bufra.

Bon rai, herba vel palea vetustate confracta.

Bop, nomen piscis.

Bot, *ao da bot ra*, vestis vetustate diffracta.

Bot, demere. Khi xung toi ch' nen them hay la bot, in confessione non licet addere vel demere numerum peccatorum.

Bu, *bu ga*, claustrum gallinarum. Chop bu, caput.

Bu, *con tre bu sua*, infans ex lacte materno crassus.

Bu, sugere lac. Phai cho con inh bu tri, oportet filium suum lactare priùs.

Bu, compensare. Lam bu lai, facere in compensationem rei omissæ. Phai lam bu lai nh' ngay gio da bo qua khou vo ich, oportet reparare tempora malè collocata.

Bua, *bua viei*, negotia. Viei bua quan, negotia rei publicæ.

Bua, securis, malleus. Thit nac dao phay, luong cang riu bua, molli carni cultro mensali, ossibus duris securi opus est.

Bua, medicina hominem dementans. Bo bua chong ta, hominem dementare. Bua, veneficii litteræ.

Bu bu, vultus tristis et squalidus. Giau ve vang, sang lich su, kho bu bu ma tra, divites divertunt se, nobiles politicè agunt; pauperes sedent tristes et squalidi.

Bui, tabulatum paulisper è terra sublatum ad conservandum aliquid ab humiditate.

Bui, *ao bui,* vestis lugubris.

Bua, arbor quædam.

Bui, calor magnus. Bui tranh, pictura.

But, panniculus.

Buoi, gradiri. Mot buoi, unus passus.

Bua. Cai bua, cai bua di, verbis per fas et nefas contendere.

Bua, tempus comedendi, vel ipsa comestio. Chua den bua an, nondum venit tempus comedendi. Da qua bua, præterit hora comedendi. Ch' du bua, non completur comestio. Lan hoi bua doi bua no, dicitur de pauperibus qui certum vivendi modum non habent.

Bui, pulvis. Loai nguoi hai nho may la bui, thi may lai blo ra bui ma cho, memento homo quia pulvis es, et in pulverem reverteris. Bui tre, arundinetum.

Bui, sapor carnis aut piscis ex pinguedine proveniens. Qua bui, quidam fructus sylvestris.

Bui vel *buoi,* malum citreum, Lusitanicè Jambua. Bun, lutum.

Bun, genus edulii ex farinâ in modum funiculorum facti.

Bung, venter. Bung quay, lusus aleæ.

Bung beo, tumescere ex infirmitate.

Bung, ferre manibus, Bung lai, afferre. Bung di, auferre. Bung bit, cessare. Noi bung bit, cessate loqui.

Buon, contristari, tristitia. Buon ngu, provocari ad somnum. Buon mua, provocari ad vomitum.

Buo, relinquere aliquid è manu.

Buo chim tha ca, avibus et piscibus permittere suam libertatem.

Buo, cellarium. Buo cau, ramus arecarum.

Bup, pellicula florum.

Buom, vela navis aut cymbæ.

Buom buom, papilio.

Buoi, colligare, obligare. Buoi toi, obligare sub peccato.

Buot, dolor acerbus. Buot dau, dolor capitis.

But, idolum. Dao but, idolatria.

Bo thun ma qui, abjicere cultum idolorum et dæmonum.

But, calamus, penicillus.

Bla, *doi bla,* mendax, fallax.

Bla vel tra, reddere, restituere. Bla cua chong ta, restituere bona ablata. Bla no su vo chou, reddere debitum
conjugale.

Blai xem thay vel *nhai xem thay,* primo aspectu.

Blai gai, istæ duæ voces immediatè junctæ significant rem
veneream. Ut toi blai glai, peccatum fornicationis.

Blau vel *trau,* betel.

Blam vel *nham,* errare, decipi.

Blai vel *trai,* juvenis, adolescens, vel masculinus sexus.

Blai vel *trai,* fructus. Trai mle, contra rationem. Trai
phep, contra jus. Mai ao trai, inducere vestem inverso
modo. Trai thoi, trai cach, contra mores, contra modum.

Blai hoa blai, flos quidam.

Blai vel *trai,* extendere vel explicare vestem, mattas, paleas,
&c. Nguoi da trai moi su, homo omnium rerum experientiâ doctus.

Blan vel *tran ra,* inundare. Toi loi da blan ra, kap mat
dat, peccatum inundavit totam terram.

Blan blo, vertere et invertere, ut carnem assando. Lap blo,
fortunæ vicissitudo.

Blat, insulsus. Cuoi blat vel nhat, insulsè ridere.

Blat lay vel *nhat lay,* colligere.

Blat, vel *nhat mot blat,* uno ictu, vel transacto uno mo-
mento.

Blang vel *trang,* pagina.

Blang vel *trang*, luna.

Blao blo vel *trao tro*, deceptor.

Ble vel *nhe gai*, educere spinam carni infixam.

Bᴌᴏ. Vide *blam*.

Blo vel *tro*, cinis. Le tro, cinerum.

Blo vel *nho*, cinere vel pulvere sordidatus. Blom blem, idem.

Blo vel *tro cua*, efficere portam.

Blo blang, situatio aut concavitas in ædificiis.

Blo vel *tro, lua blo*, exurgunt spicæ.

Bloi vel *troi, bloi da ra*, evellitur pellis.

Bᴌᴏɴ, integer, ra, rum; perfectus, a, um. Blon doi, tota vita. Gui dao blon, observare perfectè religionem. Blon tat, blon lanh, perfecte Donus.* Hay blon vay, omnipotens. Quia non potest inveniri verbum in hac lingua ad significandum omnipotentiam divinam.

Bᴌᴏᴛ, ferè idem est ac blot.† Qua blòt vel qua nhòt, quidam fructus valdè acidus.

Blo di blo lai, ire et redire: vide *blan blo*. Blo lai cu D. C. B. Converti ad Deum.

Bᴌᴏɪ, cœlum. D. C. B. Dominus Deus cœli.

Blon vel *uhon*, magnus, a, um. Blon len, grandescere. Noi choi blon tieng, loquere altâ voce.

Bᴌᴏɪ, commendare aliquid alicui in ipsa morte. D. J. C. da bloi thit mau minh nuoi thon ta, Christus Dominus relinquit carnem et sanguinem in cibum animæ nostræ.

Bloi vel *troi*, convulsio cum magno fragore.

Blot vel *cot blot*, jocari ineptè. Chang nen cot blot cu dan ba con tre, non licet ineptè jocari.

Bᴌᴏᴜ, plantare.

Blou blao, vecors, protervus.

---

* Sic in MS.   † Differentia fit ex apice.

C.

CA, genus carminis, vel tonus cantandi. Mieng doi ca tay dan loi, verba non correspondent factis. Ca xuong, cantare; non est vulgare.

CA, piscis. Lao chim da ca, dicitur de perfidis.

CA, herba cujus fructus sale conditus est maximè in usu apud annamitas.

CA, totus, a, um; magnus, a, um. Ca thay thay, totus, omnino, universi, omnes. Cha ca, Deus. Anh ca, frater natu major.

CA, pretium taxatum.

CAI, ad significandum numerum pluralem. D. C. B. phu ho cho cai an hem, Deusauxilietur vobis fratres. Ph xung cai toi da pham, oportet confiteri omnia peccata commissa. Chun bo cai, quædam avis. Cui cai, sonus amputantis.

CAI, regere. Cai quan, præesse militibus. So cai, milites præpositi alicui populo ad colligendum vectigalia. D. C. B. cai tri mai su, Deus moderatur omnia.

CAI, nomen genericum instrumentorum, vel sexus fœmineus in animalibus. Ut lon cai, porca. Cho cai, canis fœmina. Exceptâ istâ voce, ga mai, gallina. Ruou cai, oryza fermentata. Con cai, filii. Cot cai, columna major. Ngon tay cai, pollex.

Cai dap, subjicere pedibus. Cai dai do, religare angulos vestis more annamitorum.

CAI, *rau cai*, sinapi. Cai cach, modum vel mores mutare. Cai ten, mutare nomen. Cai ma, mutare sepulcrum.

CAI, contradicere, disputare. Cai mle, argumentari. Cai co nhau, rixari inter se.

CAIH, modus. Caih xa, distare. Caih mui caih non, sao lao chang caih, separari locorum distantiâ, sed non corde.

Cay, acrimonia quæ gustum molestè pulsat, qualis est in grano sinapi vel piperis. Cay dang lam, amaritudo amarissima. Cay dang cay, quædam arbuscula cujus folia sunt acria admodum.

Cay ra, ungue aut clavo aliquid extundere. Lo cay cay, sollicitudo magna.

Cay, species cancri minimi et timidissimi, unde venit dictum Nhat nhu cay, timidus ad instar illius cancri.

Cay, arare. Cay cay, aratrum. Mua cay cay, tempus colendi agros. Dua di cay, arator. Cay danh cay, lusus puerorum.

Cay, arbor. Cay cay, arbores. Cay hang sou, arbor vitæ.

Cay, sperare. Cay mot hai vi̇ei, commendare aliqua negotia. Cay ng, confidere alicui. Cay sue D. C. B. Deo fretus.

Cay, transplantare fruges.

Cay, animalia sylvestria minora.

Cam, malum aureum. Cho cam lao, ut satisfiat desiderio. Xin nguoi thua lai cho tai duoc lao, rogo ut des responsum quod satisfiat animo meo. Mau cam, sanguis è naribus fluens.

Cam, muscipula. Phai kham ph. cam, incidere in laqueum.

Cam, furfur. Cam on D. C. B. Gratias agere Deo. Cam canh, miserandum sanè. Xem thay thi cam canh, miserabile spectaculum.

Cam, *phai kinh cam,* invadi malignâ aurâ. Giao cam, exercere actum conjugalem.

Cam da da lau, dudum exacerbatus in animo.

Cam, *lou cam,* mistaces.

Cam vao, manu figere. Cam xuo dat, infigere humo.

Cam, mentum.

Cam, *cu cam,* genus tuberis.

Cam, *nguoi cam,* mutus. Cam mieng di, obmutescere. Cam trao luoi, urere aliquid igne non accenso.

Cam, prohibere. Cam chi, prohibere omninò. Chang nen

lam nh su thanh Igh.ª da cam, non licet ea facere quæ Ecclesia prohibet.

CAM, tenere. Cam vong, manducare. Vox propria Regi.

Cam thu, volatilia et quadrupedia.

CAM, *com lam cam,* oryza subcruda.

CAN, impedire, dehortari. Can gian, idem est. Chang can co gi, nihil refert. Giao trang can, pugio longior. Chang can gi den nay, nihil ad te.

CAN, *nuoi can,* aqua exhausta. Kho can, siccitas aquæ.

CAN, manubrium cujuscumque instrumenti. Can can, statera.

Can vel *can gio,* temerè, indiscretè. An can o gio, indiscretè, sine legibus vivere. Don can, vectis ad portandum spicas aut paleas colligatas.

CAN, prævalere viribus, consilio, aut verbis.

Can ban, radix, fundamentum. Mloi noi chang co can ban nao, dictum absque ullo fundamento.

Can vel *cán,* infima pars cujuscumque liquoris, aut excrementum. Can muou, excretum vini.

CAN, mordere. Cho can, canis mordet, vel ablatrat. Ca can cau, piscis capitur hamo.

CAN, *lan can,* querulus, a, um. Gia nua lan can, senex querulus.

CAN, pondus vel statera, pondere.

CAN, vox sinico-annamitica, propè, à latere. Quan can than, vir à latere regis, conciliarii intimi regis.

CAN, *can can,* quidam pisciculus.

CAN, necessarius, a, um. Can kip, urgens. Ke liet can vel kip, infirmus in extremo positus, ideò est urgens. Rau can, quædam herba.

Can than, cum magnâ curâ aliquid facere. Xem cho can than, circumspicere vel custodire cum magnâ curâ.

CANG, quò magis, eò magis.

Cang can thi cang lam, quò magis admonetur eò magis facit.

CANH, jus vel vigilia.

Canh gio, vigilias agere. Mot trou canh, una vigilia. Canh mot, prima vigilia. Canh cot, obliquis verbis mordere. **Canh, ala.** Canh tay, brachium.

Canh, ramus.

Canh, arbusculæ delectabiles. Vuon canh, hortus deliciarum.

Canh, *di canh*, suspenso vestigio incedere.

Cao, altus, a, um. D. C. B. rat cao, rat trao, Deus altissimus. Cao tri, acris ingenio. Thay cao cou, vel Dia ly, vel Tuong dia, sunt nefarii illius gentis mathematici qui cæteris ex superstitiosâ terræ ad sepulcrum electione, bona evenire; mala vero præcaveri posse mentiuntur. Cao tinh, animus ferox.

Cao, radere. Dao cao, novacula.

Cao vel *cao kien,* accusare. Ma qui se cao may tri toa D. C. B. Dæmon accusabit te antè tribunal Dei. Phat cao vel dau cao, dau kien, dau tung, accusator. Bi cao, bi kien, bi tung, accusatus. Cao kien nhau, vel cao cu nhau, movere lites inter se. Con cao, vulpes.

Cao, ungue lacerare aliquid, vel terram sulcare. Cai cao, instrumentum dentatum ad terram comminuendam.

Cao, codex.

Cao, contortus, a, um. Cai cao, vas fictile ad continendum aquam.

Cao tay, riget manus ex frigore.

Cao cua vel *gao cua,* chelæ cancrorum.

Cao, *cao lung,* dorsum curvum.

Cao, gestare aliquid super dorsum.

Cap, *mot cap tay,* unus manipulus.

Cap, codex papyri, vel ligatura multorum librorum. Noi cap gia, pertinaciter affirmare. Suffurari, non clam sed coram et subtiliter. Ke kap, qui subtiliter furantur præsertim in confusione hominum. Troi cap canh, duo brachia in unum simul revincire.

Cap, *cua cap,* cancer chelis suis apprehendit aliquid.

CAP, idem est. Ac kip, urgens.

CAT, arena. Duong cat, saccharum arenosum.

CAT, secare, tondere aut mittere. Phai cat toi, tonsura ec-
clesiastica. Phep cat bi, circumcisio Judaica. Cat nghia,
explanare, explicare, interpretari.

CAT, tollere, auferre. Cat xai, efferre funera.

CAT, dorsum, sæpè dicitur de animalibus. Loai vat sap cat
len bloi, animalia (scilicet ingrata) obvertunt dorsa cœlo.

CAU, cay cau, areca. Cau mat lai, rugare frontem. Cau,
periodus. Cau, juridicè vocare. Cau ca, hamare pisces.
Luoi cau, hamus.

CAU, avunculus major et minor. Chim cau, columba.

CAU, cau rat, crux.

CAU, ungue vellere aliquid.

CAU, ovare vel pons. Cay co, arbor quædam.

CAU, cau tho, versus.

CAU, sordes ex aquâ natæ.

CAU, lau cau, tristis et querulus.

CAU, luoi cau, hamus. Cau cau, ames.

Co láy, attrahere ad se. Co lai,* contrahere.

Co, abstergere aliquid asperum.

Co lua, dicitur de hominibus parcis, qui nolunt sumptum
facere properè cum desideratur.

Co, affirmatio esse vel habere. Ad rectè utendum istis vocibus co et la, vel phai la, non potest dari certa regula
nisi per longum usum; ideò aliquas phrases hic jungo.
Co nhieu D. C. B. chang? suntne plures Dei? Co mot
D. C. B. ma thoi, est unus Deus solùmmodo. Sed in sequenti phrasi jam non est utendum voce co, sed la: ùt
D. C. B. la tinh di gi, Deus est quænam substantia. D.C.B.
la tinh thieng lieng, Deus est spiritus. D. C. B. co may
ngoi? Deus quot habet personas? D. C. B. co ba ngoi,
Deus habet tres personas. Ou khou tu co phai la D. C. B.

* Differentia ex apice.

chang ?* Chang phai, non est. Vox verò *co*, habere, semper præponitur interrogationi, ut non co muon xung
toi chang? fili, visne confiteri, vel habesne desiderium?
et respondetur *co*, affirmativè, volo, vel habeo desiderium. No co den chang? ille venitne? Co o, esse vel
manere. Cu co o nha chang? pater estne domi? et tunc
respondetur affirmativè, *co;* vel negative, *khou* vel *chang co.*

Co, *cai co*, grus. Co sung, machina ad ignem excutiendum.

Co, herba ad pascenda animalia; herbæ verò quæ usui
humano esse possunt vocantur vau hoa co, fœnum.
Su sang trao the gian duong bang hoa co, nobilitas mundi
comparatur fœno. Mang co, præsepium.

Co, amita. Co ba, vide *ba.*

Co, *ou co*, proavus. Ba co, proavia. Lam co, plus laborare
quam ferunt vires. Cam co, dare aliquid in pignus.

Co, collum. Cung co, duræ cervicis.

Co, edulia. Mam co, abacus eduliis·instructus.

Co mun, inventiones ingeniosæ. Chuoc moi, stratagema,
machinatio. Khi danh giai ph' co co mun chuoc moi,
in bello debent adhiberi stratagemata et machinationes.
Co quan, cohors militum.

Co, *cho di lam co*, ut sit in testimonium et monumentum.
Lam chung co, facere testimonium.

Co, vexillum. Mo co lam giac, erigere vexillum rebelle.
Tinh co, casus fortuitus. Trao the gian nay chang co su
gi tinh co dau, in hoc mundo nihil accidit casu forte.

Coc, mergulus. Coc cho coc duoi, canis brevis caudæ.

Coo, bufo. Nguoi coc, homo brevis staturæ.

Coi, inspicere. *Coi soi* vel *xem soi*, curam habere.

Coi, herba ex qua fiunt mattæ, vel teguntur domus. Co cai,
quædam avis.

Coi, buccina parva ad convocandos milites.

Coi. Vide *bo coi.* (Antè, p. 198.)

* Deest interpretatio hujus phrasis in MS.

Coi, *mo coi*, orphanus, a, um. Coi re, radix, insitium. D. C. B.
la coi re moi su, &c.* Coi dam, mortarium. Coi xay,
molendina.

Coi, *cay coi da coi*, arbores jam veterant.

Coi, *cai coi*, theca ad apponendum betel.

Coi treu, ad contentionem provocare. Coi tac, adinvenire,
exordiri. Ai coi tac ra viei nay, quis est adinventor vel
auctor istius operis?

Coi vel *coi ao*, exuere vestem. Phai coi dao cu, ma mac
lay Adaoᴗmoi, oportet exuere veterem Adamum, et induere novum.

Çoi vel *cuoi*, sedere super dorso bovis, bubali, elephantis.
Coi vel *di ngua*, equitare.

Com, *gia nua chou gay lom com*, senex capularis baculo in-
nixus, testudineo gradu incedens.

Com, confici macie.

Com dang, obscurus aspectu. An mac com dang, vili et ob-
scuro indutus habitu.

Com, oryza viridis, igne tosta et pistillo contusa; quod cibi
genus est in delicias apud Tunkinenses.

Com, oryza cocta, quæ est quotidianus cibus. Com nan gao
day, dicitur de eo qui à multis annis enutritur ab aliquo.
Ta co com an, co ao mac thi da du, habens victum et
vestitum, his contentissimus.

Com, locus impervius solis radiis.

Com, in hominibus vocatur filius, vel filia; addendo vocem
blai pro masculino genere, et *gai* pro fœminino; ut
con blai, filius; *con gai*, filia: sed quando dicitur *con
nay*, semper intelligendum est de ista puella. Interdùm
fit adjectivum diminutivum minimus, a, um; et tunc bis
dicitur, *con con;* et semper postponitur substantivo, ut *con
be con con*, puella minima. *Thang be con con*, puer parvulus; et etiam dicitur, *con sach con con*, libellus. Com

---

* Deest interpretatio.

dao con, cultellus. *Nha con con,* domuscula. In animalibus verò, quando præponitur nomini particulari, fit nomen genericum animalium; ut *con cho,* canis, *con lon,* porcus, *con voi,* elephas. Quando verò postponitur illorum animalium nominibus, fit iterum adjectivum, ut, supra. v. g. *cho con,* canis parvulus; *lon con,* porcellus, et etiam dicitur bis sed separando, ut *con lon con,* porcus parvulus. In plurali numero, *con cai,* semper pro utroque sexu in hominibus; ut *ta la con cai* D. C. B. sumus filii Dei. Lam con ng ta chang nen a no the ay, non licet hominis dignitati taliter vivere. Con nguoi, pupilla oculorum. Con mat, oculus. Con nha quan, nobili genere natus.

Con, adhuc. Con sou chang, adhucne vivit? et semper separatur à particulâ *chang,* ut bay gio con con muon pham toi nua chang, adhuc vis amplius peccare? quando verò in oratione incipit sequens membrum per vocem *con,* tunc est *quoad verò;* ut, ay la su dao; con ve su doi the nao, hæc sunt de religione; quoad verò res politicas, quomodo?

Con, colligare aliquid in unum. Con be, colligare ligna, seu instruere rates.

Con, arenarum insula.

Con, *voc lao con,* fericum draconum picturis refertum.

Con, accessus vel commotio iræ, tempestatis, pluviæ, febris.

Con co, lascivus, a, um.

Cop, contraheri, decrescere. Tre no ra, gia co plai, pueri crescunt, decrescunt senes. Est etiam aliquod monstrum fictitium ad deterrendum parvulos; undè venit modus loquendi. Thay ng ta thi so nhu cop, ad conspectum hominum stupescere, tanquam ad horribile monstrum.

Cot, *lin cot ng ta,* corrodere aliquid ab omnibus.

Cot, *la cot,* crates ex arundine denso modo contextæ ad continenda frumenta: inde fit modus loquendi, nom nay may di moy la lua, hoc anno quantum frumentorum collegisti?

Cot, columna. Cot tau, malus navis. Ou tanh Phero la cot

27

cai thanh Igh.ᵃ S. Petrus est columna et firmamentum Ecclesiæ.

Coт, centrum. Gia cot, Pythonissa. Cot dui, viri qui fingunt se esse mulieres ad exercendum officium Pythonissarum apud Tunkinenses.

Coт, jocosè loqui. Noi cot hay la that, jocosè vel seriò.

Cot geo, ineptè jocari.

Cou, *cou lenh,* merces. Cou nghiep, meritum. Chim cou, pavo. Cou bang, justus.

Cou, *tinh cou lai,* additionem facere in arithmetica.

Cou, ductus aquæ subterraneus. Huong cou, gradus penultimus litteratorum.

Cou, instrumentum ex ære factum, quo utuntur Tunkinenses ad cœtum cogendum, vel ad venationem.

Cou, fores exteriores.

Cu, *chim cu,* turtur.

Cu, *ou cu,* proavus. Ba cu, proavia apud Christianos; ita appellantur sacerdotes.

Cu, cuculus.

Cu, *cu non,* leviter aliquem circa latera contrectare ad risum provocandum.

Cu, nomen genericum omnium tuberum aut leguminum.

Cu,ʼvetus, antiquus, a, um. Truyen cu, historia antiqua.

Cua, *cou cua,* cancer.

Cua, res; bona corporalia vel spiritualia. Cua cai, idem.

Cuo, tuberculum in corpore vel globus aliquis. Cuc gian, promptissimus ad iram.

Cuo, globuli ad clausuram in vestibus. Hoa cuc, flos quidam flavi aut albi coloris.

Cui, inclinare caput.

Cui, cortex crassior in malis citreis. Cui tay, vola manûs absque digitis, qualis et in leprosis. Chim dai cui, avis quædam.

Cui, ligna apta ad ignem. Hai cui, colligere sarmenta.

Cui tuoi rao lua thi cham chay, Lignum viride injectum igni tarde ardebit.

Cui, cavea. Dao cui, includi cavea, vel construere caveam.

Cum, compes. Dao cum, ligare compedibus.

Cum, congeries herbarum aut plantarum.

Cun, instrumenta ferrea qualia sunt cultri, gladii, pugiones, &c., vetustate consumpta. Cun tri, ingenium obtusum. Mle cun, ratio futilis.

Cung, arcus, vel domus regalis, palatium. Cung hat, tonus cantandi, modus musicus.

Cung, aliquid offerri Deo aut idolis. Cung dang, cung vai, idem.

Cung, finis, terminus. Vo cung, infinitus. D. C. B. cou bang vo cung, Deus infinitè justus. Ban cung, paupertas extrema. Est etiam particula cum vel simul. Lam ban cung ke lanh, societatem inire cum bonis.

Cung, ita etiam, et etiam. Nguoi lieu the nao toi cung the ay, quomodo disponis ita etiam ego. Cung nen, ita etiam licet.

Cup, deprimere. Non cup, galerus depressus. Ao cham non cup, vestis viridis et galerus depressus; est habitus lugubris apud Tunkinenses.

Cut, aliquid abscissum vel nimis abbreviatum. Hui an cut chan tay, pedes et manus leprâ exesi et abscissi. Toi cut, capilli abbreviati.

Cut, cai cun cut, species avis valde pinguis. Danh cun cut, lusus puerorum.

Cuo, cuo luo, anxius animo.

Cuo, ramusculi qui surtinent folia.

Cuo, cuo lai, temo gubernaculi. Cuo luoi, radix linguæ.

Cuo, delirare ex morbo. Cuo ngon loan ngu', loquacitas ex delirio.

Cuoc, vox sinico annamitica, regnum. Trao phip cuoc trieu, in legibus regni. Cuoc dat, fodere terram. Cuoc giat vao lao, naturaliter omnes omnia ad se trahunt. Cai cuoc, instrumentum rusticum.

Cʋoc, bravium. Danh cuoc, contractus inter duos aut plures initus pro solvendo problemate aut aliquâ re incertâ præsagiandâ.

Cʋoɪ, quidam ex fabulosâ traditione bubulcus mendationum artifex, qui in lunam conscendisse, et nunc inibi residere, à paganis creditur. Mo cuoi, cumulus terræ ad instar tumuli in ejus honorem à gentibus frequenter in viis constructus.

Cʋoɪ, in exitu alicujus rei. Cuoi nam, in fine anni. Cuoi sach, ad calcem libri, apponitur voci *dau*.

Cʋoᴍ, decipere, fallere. Chang khon ngoan chang rung ve; chang cho ai cuom chang he cuom ai, nec prudens nec imprudens; neque decipi, neque decipere alios velle.

Cʋoɴ, involvere. Cuon sach, volumen libri.

Cʋ, habitare. Gia cu, dien san, domus latifundia. Ngu cu, inquilinus.

Cʋ, magnus. Dai cu, maximus. Cu, trung, tieu, magnus, mediocris, parvus. Cu dich, resistere.

Cʋ, juxta, conformare, secundùm. Phai cu muoi su ra ma xet minh, oportet juxta Decalogum examinare seipsum.

Cʋ, *lu cu* et *lu cu*, morosus ex infirmitate.

Cʋ, aliquod tempus determinatum, decem aut septem dierum. O cu, mulier in puerperio.

Cʋᴀ, tenera servare. Cua sung lam nghe, servare ex leone agnum.

Cʋᴀ, movere se instinctu ad vitandam molestiam. Cua ga, spina in pedibus gallorum, quâ ad pugnam utuntur.

Cʋᴀ, serrare aliquid obtuso cultro.

Cʋᴀ, porta. Cua bien, portus. Cua thien dangh ep hoi lam, porta cœli est valde stricta.

Cʋc, extremè, supremè. Cuc lam, extrema miseria. Hac vox non adjungitur nisi cum adjectivis nobilitatis, bonitatis, voluptatis, calamitatis, &c. ut: Cuc cao cuc trao, summè nobilis. Cuc tot cuc lanh, summè bonus. Khon cuc, summa calamitas. Thai cuc, principium quoddam, quod pro Deo colitur à sinensibus.

Cui, *det cui*, texere telas. Khung cuioi, machina ad texendum telas. Nghe canh cui, ars texendi.

Cuoc, catenulæ ex ære. Benh cuoc khi, morbus quidam.

Cuoi, *dam cuoi*, convivium nuptiale. An cuoi, adesse vel celebrare nuptias. D. C. J. da cuoi lay thanh Igh.ᵃ Christus accepit Ecclesiam in sponsam sibi.

Cuoi. Vide suprà *coi*.

Cuoi, ridere. Cuoi nhao, irridere.

Cuom, *cay cuom cuom*, arbor quædam.

Cuong, durus, a, um. Khi cuong khin hu, quandoque durus, quandoque mollis. Day cuong, capestrum. Kim cuo, species gemmæ.

Cuong, violentus, a, um.

Cuong, resistere. Ta chang cuong duai phep D. C. B. Non possumus resistere potestati divinæ.

Cuop, rapere. Ke cuop, raptores. Ke trom cuop, latrones.

Cut, stercus.

Cuu, liberare, salvare, morbum ustione curare. Not cuu, cicatrix ex ustione. Thuoc cap cuu, remedium quoddam ad depellendos morbos efficacissimum.

Cha, pater. Cha ca, pater magnus; apud Tunkinenses intelligitur Deus, apud Cocisinenses Episcopus. Cha ca phu ho cho an hem, adsit vobis Deus, fratres.

Cha, pagus vel communitas parva. Chung cha, in communi.

Cha, *cha vang* vel *thep vang*, deaurare.

Cha, ligna aut arbusculæ in aquis submersæ ad retinendum pisces in vivariis. Cha gai, rami spinarum.

Cha, caro assata. Nuong cha, assare carnem. Etiam interdum usurpatur pro *chang*, non; urbanitatis causâ. Toi cha dam, non ausim.

Chac; in provinciâ Xung-he significatur *funis*.

CHAC, *mua chac*, emere. Ban chac, vendere.

CHACH, pisciculus quidam.

CHACH, *lach chach*, pugillus. Thap be lach chach, pugillus staturæ.

CHAC, solidus, a, um; securus, a, um. Phai lieu viei linh hon cho chac da, oportet priùs curare negotium salutis quam securissimè. Nguoi chac chan, homo fidelis et capax ad res agendas.

CHAI, *chai loi, an mac chai loi*, habitus ad ostentationem vanam ornatus.

CHAI, *chai nha*, appendix domus.

CHAI, rete. Thuy en chai, piscator vel cymba piscatoria. Vai chai, quang chai, nem chai, jacere rete.

CHAI, *chai dau, chai toi*, pectere capillos. Boi chai kiem an, excolere terram ad quærendum victum.

CHAY, jejunium. Au chay, jejunare; apud Christianos; apud verò paganos, cam chay, vel cam he.

CHAY, fugere. Chay tri, profugere. Chay tien, quærere pecuniam. Chay vuoi quan, pecuniam vel munera offerre mandarino ad impetrandum aliquid. Lam chay, oblationes et eleemosynæ, quas faciunt gentiles pro suorum defunctorum redemptione. Do chay, cibaria ad jejunium parata.

CHAY, ardere, incendi. Chay nha, incendium domûs. Ca chay, species piscis. Chay, currere.

CHAY, *cai chay*, pistillum quo tunditur et purgatur oryza. Chay ngay, per multos dies. Chay ken, diuturna deliberatio et electio.

CHAY, fluere, diffluere. Nuoi chay, aqua rapida. Nguoi bay chay, homo levis et ineptus.

CHAM, *cham phai*, offendere, impingere contra aliquid ex obscuritate vel inadvertentiâ. Cham hoa, vasa cælata. Tho cham, sculptor. Cham, cælare, sculpere.

CHAM, *cham lua*, apponere ignem. Da nam cham, punctum; insculpere flores in tabellis.

Cham sach, examinare scripturam. Cham, tardus. Cham chap, idem.

Cham, herba quædam, cujus succo expresso tinguntur vestes lugubres.

Cham, *cham cam, qui cham cham, ngoi cham cham,* genuflectere, stare, sedere immotus.

Chan, armarium in quo reponuntur vasa testacea, vel cibaria.

Chan chan, maxima multitudo.

Chan, fastidium. An da chan ngan, comedere usque nauseam.

Chan, pascere. Chan, operimentum quo utimur tempore frigoris.

Chan, numerus.par, cui opponitur le, impar. Danh chan le, lusus aleæ.

Chang, *chang thiep,* maritus et uxor; raro sunt in usu.

Chang, ne interrogatio; et semper ponitur post omnes voces, ut con hieu D. C. B. chang? Sunt ne plures Dii? Con muon xung toi chang? visne, fili, confiteri?

Chang, negatio ad præcedentem vocem, non. Chang co, non esse, non habere.

Chang, constringere aliquid fune.

Chanh, ramusculi aut surculi arborum.

Chanh nhau, gian nhau, contendere verbis inter se aut viribus; vel invicem præcipere. Cay chanh, arbor, aut fructus quem Lusitani vocant limao.

Chao, *chao xue,* capere pisciculos rotando cistam in aquâ.

Chao, *lam chao,* modus condiendi piscem aut carnem.

Chao, puls. Ke liet an chao, sumit infirmus pulmentum.

Chao, salutare aliquem in primo congressu.

Chao, sartago, vel cacabus.

Chao, funes quibus alligatur jugum bobus dum arant.

Chao, *trau chao, bo chao, lon chao,* sunt animalia viva aut occisa, et collocata in funeribus ad honorem mortuorum, aut vanam ostentationem.

CHAO, properare, properè. Di- cho chao fac, properè. Chao chao, lusus puerorum instar rotæ aut trochi.

CHAO, *cai chao*, lectulus.

CHAP, parentalia mortuorum mensæ ultimo: unde ultimus mensis ab annamitis dicitur semper thang chap, cham chap, morosus.

CHAP, multa ligna aut aliam materiam in unum, glutine aut fune, colligare. Mot chap, numerus quinque monetarum ærearum.

CHAT, acerbus, a, um. Qua chat, fructus immaturus, acerbus.

CHAT, sal conglobatum.

CHAT, abscindere, amputare. Istud verbum *chat* usurpatur pro abscisione membri alicujus aut rami in particulari; cum verò fit sermo de amputatione capitis aut totius arboris, tum utendum est verbo *chem:* ut chat chan tay, chem dau chem co, vi bang tay mat may lam hu minh may thi phai chat no, ma bo di cho khoi; si dextera tua scandalizat te, &c. Cai riu da de gan re cay; cay nao chang co blai thi chem va dot di ma cho; securis ad radicem posita, est, &c. Chem quach, decollatio capitis est maledictio apud annamitas. Cam cho chat, firmiter tenere.

CHAT, pronepos, proneptis.

CHAU, nepos, neptis.

CHAY, pediculi in capite. Dau ai chay nay, quisquis onus suum portet.

CHAM, acu perforare, aut aculeum infligere.

Cham chap. Vide supra.

CHAM, punctum. Cham sach, scripturam examinare, totis librum distinguere.

CHAN, pes. *day to chan toy*, famulus, pedissequus.

CHAN, obicem aut septum opponere ad impediendum ingressum aquarum, animalium, &c.

Chan chan, simplicissimus, a, um, aut ineptus.

Chap vel *chap phap*, sinistrè interpretari, aut pro culpâ habere. Xin nguoi dung chap, ne reprehendas; parvi facere.

CHAT, angustus, a, um, vel angustia ex confluxu hominum.

CHAT, vel *chot len*, accumulare. Toi loi chat len bang nui bang non, peccata congesta superant montes.

CHAU, Toparehia.

CHAU, pelvis, lanx.

Chau chau chau, locustæ. Ou thanh Juaó Baotisita an nhung mat ao cung chau chau, cibus Sancti Johannis Baptistæ erat mel sylvestre et locustæ.

CHAU, assistere Regi aut sanctissimo sacramento. Quan chau, custodiæ regiæ. Chau chuc, idem.

Chau chang, species ranæ.

CHE, tegere aliquid ab aëris injuriis. Cai che, prelum seu machina quâ exprimitur oleum aut aliquis liquor.

CHE, spernere.

CHE, theum. Che tau, theum sinicum. Do che, edulium quod theum comitatur. Banh che lu, capulum gladii. Banh che, vide supra.

CHE, findere aliquid cultro aut alio instrumento.

CHE, *don che*, parvum præsidium.

Chat che, tenere firmiter. Nguoi chat che, tenax pecuniæ.

CHEM. Vide *chat*.

CHEN, calix, poculum.

CHEN, *don chen*, insidiari in angustiis. Ao chen, vestis constrictæ manicæ.

CHEN, *chen nhau*, premere invicem pro angustia.

CHEP, scribere vel transcribere. Ou thanh Mattheu chep truyen D. C. J., Sanctus Matthæus scripsit historiam Christi. Ca chep, piscis quidam.

CHEO, quidam contractus seu solutio quâ publicè declaratur matrimonium esse factum. Nop cheo, solvere illum contractum communitati. Thu cheo, approbare et acceptare illum contractum.

28

Cheo, forma triangularis. · Cheo ao, appendix triangularis
vestis. Roi leo cheo, loqui acutâ voce.

Cheo, remigare, remus.

Chet tay, premitur manus. Chet tay moi ha mieng, sera
pænitentia.

Chet, aliquid confractum fune religare. Bo chet, vermiculi in canibus aut gallinis latentes.

Che, aspernari, irridere, parvi facere. Che choi, abdicare.
Che vo, che chou, repudiare uxorem, maritum. Gia khen
thi lai gia che, qui multum laudabit, multum et con-
temnet.

Che, miscere, temperare. Bao che, temperare medicinam.

Chech, et *chech lech*, quod non rectè collocatur. Lam chech
lech, ordinem pervertere, mutuam pacem turbare.

Chem, aliquod instrumentum laxatum, dissolutumve reficere.

Chep, *chep giay*, plicare papyrum.

Chet, mori. Su chet, mors. May chet, vox communi-
cantis.

Chi, classis, turba, pars, exercitus; vox militaris. Chi thuy,
classis navalis. Chi va, exercitus pedestris. Truong chi,
dux classis, exercitûs. Lam chi, ad quid? oujus rei gratiâ? Con den day lam chi? ad quid venis, fili? Est
etiam vox dehortantis. Ta pham toi lam chi nua? ad
quid ampliùs peccemus? Mam chi chi, species piscis
salsi.

Chi, soror major. Chi em vuoi toi, consanguinea mea.
Chi em, etiam intelliguntur moniales.

Chi. Vide *bam chi*, supra.

Chi, plumbum. Tieng chi tieng bai, irrisiones, querimoniæ.

Chi, notare, determinare, decernere. Chi quy et, chi doan,
idem. Chi phan, sententia regalis. Chi truyen, regium
edictum. Chi tro, monstrare digito. Chi etiam vocatur
filum quo conficitur vestis. Xe chi, nere. Lam cho chi
di, perficere.

Chia, dividere, partiri.

Chia ra, ostendere, prominere. Chia Khoa, clavis. D.C.J. ban cho ou th' Phero chia khoa nuoi thien dang, Christus Dominus contulit Sancto Petro claves regni cœlorum.

CHICH, *giac chich mau,* elicere sanguinem. Chich chich, passerculus, pugillus.

CHIEC, nomen genericum aliquarum rerum. Mot chiec tau, chiec thuy en, una navis, cymba. Chiec chieu, matta. Chiec dua, bacillus, &c. Doi, par; chiec, impar.

CHIEM, *mua chiem,* mensis quintimensis. Ruo chiem, agri qui dant fructus mense quinto. Chiem bao, somnium.

Chiem vi, chiem quien, usurpari personam, auctoritatem. Chiem xa, idem est.

CHIEN, ovis. Chan chien, pascere oves.

Chien sao, cancelli. Chien tran, pugna. Thuyen chien, navicula bellica. Ao chien, lorica.

CHIENG, instrumentum ex ære sonante.

CHIENG, loqui ad personam honorabilem.

CHIET, *chiet cay,* transplantare arbores abscindendo ramos. Noi chiet dap, exaggerando exprobare.

Chieu tap, dispersionem populi congregare. Tay chieu, manus sinistra.

CHIEU, storea. Trai chieu, explicare mattas. Chieu khai, edictum regium publicè per notarium legere.

CHIEU, vespere. Chieu hom, som mai, vespere et manè. Chieu lao, acquiescere alterius voluntati.

CHIM, avis.

CHIM, in profundum tendere.

CHIN, novem; coctus, a, um, vel maturus, a, um. Com da chin, oryza jam est cocta. Hoa qua da chin, fructus maturescunt.

Chin that, certo, certius.

CHINH, præcipuus, principalis. Xa chinh, publicus procurator in uno pago. Chinh the, uxor legitima.

CHINH, genus vasis fictilis.

CHIT, *chit lay,* capere aliquid apprehensâ manu.

CHIT, *ao chit*, vestis constricti collarii.

CHIU, pati, sustinere, recipere. Chiu kho, sustinere miserias, vel habere patientiam. Con phai chiu kho vay, fili, habe patientiam. Ta phai chiu kho o doi nay, debemus multa mala ferre in hâc vitâ. Chiu le, recipere communionem sacram.

CHO, dare, concedere; hæc vox varia significat; quando est sermo de Deo vel regibus, dicitur: ban cho xin D.C.B. ban sui manh cho ta, concedat Deus nobis vires seu suam gratiam. Ke chiu sac lenh vua chua ban cho, qui receperunt dignitates à regibus concessas. Cho duoc, ad vel ut possim, possis, &c.; et sic collocatur. Cho de roi linh hom, thi ph' giu dao blon, ad salutem consequendam oportet observare religionem perfecte. Cho ta di dep lao D. C. B. thi phai co nhan diu charita, ut possimus placere Deo oportet habere charitatem. Cho nen, undè, ideò, idcirca. Boi con da pham toi, cho nen phai lam viei den toi, quia peccasti, fili, ideò debes agere pœnitentiam. Postremò jungitur adjectivis, et facit illa adjectiva fieri adverbia, maximè cum verbis hortantis, urgentis, &c. ut, xin nguoi, xoi cho du, digneris satisfacere fami. Di cho chao, vade citò. Phai giu dao cho nen; moi di len thien dang, oportet rectè fidem servare ut possis ire in cœlum.

CHO, canis. Cho soi, lupus. Cho ma, canes stupidi.

CHOAI, *bo choai*, bos juvencus. Cho cay nha ga cay vuon, in claustro Domini fuit acrior ira catelli.

CHO, nomen arboris. Nay nhu go cho, aliquid rectum instar illius ligni.

CHO, *noi cho*, olla ad coquendam oryzam, solo vapore aquæ callidæ.

Choc vel *xoc* vel *thoc*, acumine aliquid pungere, vel perforare. Noi cham choc, bovem aculeis impellere. Chet choc, dicitur de multorum morte.

CHOI, *chim choi choi*, species aviculæ.

Cʜoɪ, pugna animalium.

Choi loi, resplendens, vel radium vibrans.

Cʜoɪ, ædicula in alto posita ad speculandum.

Cʜoɪ, septum quo nocte recluduntur jumenta.

Cʜoᴍ, congregatio parsa hominum aut aliarum rerum. Chom xom, conventicula.

Chom nui vel *dinh*, apex montis.

Cʜoɴ, eligere. Ke goi thi nhieu, ke chon thi it, multi sunt vocati, pauci verò electi.

Cʜoᴘ, summitas cujuscumque rei. Chot vot, summitas etiam.

Cʜoᴛ, *do chot*, ruberrimus, a, um.

Cʜoᴛ, levi dolore affici. Phai chot minh, pati parvum dolorem.

Chot cua, pessulus portæ. Chot cua lai, pessulo portam firmare.

Cʜoᴜ, murices. Danh chou cam chou, armare muricibus.

Chou bla, resistere. Chou len, levare aliquid suppositâ furcâ.

Cʜoᴜ, maritus. Chou len, super ponere. Chang de hon da nao chou len, non relinquetur lapis super lapidem.

Cʜoᴜ, subverti retrò. *Chou chenh* vel *chou chenh*, res est in proclivi et lapsui proxima.

Cʜoo, *mot choc*, unum momentum vel quadrantem. Mot choc nua, post unum momentum. Choc lo, ulcerari.

Cʜo, forum vel nundinæ. Hop cho, congregatur cœtus mercatorum.

Cʜo, noli, vox imperantis, hortantis. Thu cho gi et nguoi, non occides. Cho, expectare. Cho doi, idem.

Cʜo, capere, continere, dicitur de navibus et cymbis: de vasis et capsulis vero *chua*.

Cʜoɪ, *chat choi*. Vide *chat*.

Cʜoɪ, abnegare, abnuere. Choi dao, abnegare fidem. Choi ch' nghe, abnuere, non audire, non consentire. Choi, scopa.

Choi chanh, vide *chanh.*

Choi vel *cho day,* surgere è lecto, è somno, ex cathedra ;
et etiam significat abire.

Cʜᴏᴍ, *ngoi chom goi len,* sedere erecto genu. Chom cham,
an noi chom cham, rusticè loqui.

Cʜᴏɴ, sepelire. Chon cot xuo dat, figere columnam humo.

Cʜᴏɴ, locus. Chon chon, ubique. Chon chon, cai soc,
mustela.

Cʜᴏɪ, ludere. Choi boi, idem. Noi choi, jocari.

Chon cho, cuoi chon cho, immodestè ridere. Da chon cho,
rupes asperæ.

Cʜᴏᴘ, fulgur. Chop loe ra, fulgur resplendens.

Chop ngu, initio et quasi subitaneo somno correptus.

Chot thay, primo intuitu.

Cʜᴠ, antiquissima imperatorum sinarum familia, quâ regnante natus est Confucius. Tho chu, terra rubra. Chu
chu, cham cham, modestè.

Cʜᴠ, patruus minor.

Cʜᴠ, *chuot chu,* mus fœtidus.

Cʜᴠ, tabella superstitiosa. De chu, scribere super illam ta-
bellam.

Cʜᴠᴀ, commentari, explicare.

Cʜᴠᴀ, acidus, a, um. Chua chat, acerbus, a, um. Nguoi
chua chat, homo acerbus. Chu bau, pretiosissimus, undè
fit locutio ambigua. Cua blai chua, id est homo ille tanquam fructus, vel pretiosissimus, vel acerbissimus. Sinici
chu gia chu.

Cʜᴠᴀ, Rex secundarius in regno vel Dominus cujuscumque.
Sic, chua bloi, Dominus cœli, idest Deus. Chua nha, Dominus domus. Chua tau, navarchus. Chua cua, Dominus rei. Ba chua, filia regis.

Cʜᴠᴀ, fanum idolorum. Thay chua, custos fani. Chua
chien, etiam fanum. Chua mieu, delubra.

Cʜᴠᴄ, *mot chuc,* una decas. Cai chuc chuc, species ostreæ
parvæ.

Chuo, orare, benè precari, optare. Van chuc, oratio precatoria apud Ethnicos. Chui chuc, vivere in angusto loco.

Chui, per angustum foramen transire.

Chui, *nga chui·di*, corruere in faciem.

Chui, abstergere aliquid.

Chui nhuc, summa patientia.

Chum, vas testaceum magnum, seu hydria magna et vasti corporis.

Chum, *ngoi chum lai,* sedere conjunctim.

Chum vel *gium,* racemus.

Chun vel *chun,* contrahere se. Miet chun, tibiale Europæum.

Chun, *thap lun chun,* homo brevis staturæ.

Chuoc, redimere. Chuoc toi, redimere à peccatis.

Chuoi, capulum cultri.

Chuoi, ficus Indica.

Chuom, fossa in agris.

Chuon chuon, genus papilionis.

Chuot, mus.

Chuot, *bao chuot,* benè expolire. Vang duc chuot, aurum purgatum.

Chut, abnepos; abneptis. Mot chut, modicum quid; parum, paulisper.

Chu, littera.

Chua, nondum. Con da xet minh chua? fili, examinastine conscientiam? Si respondetur *chua,* nondùm.

Chua, capere, continere. Chum chua nuoc, vas continet aquam.

Chuo, compare. Chinh chuo, rectus, a, um.

Chung in, communis, è. Nha chung, communitas. Chung cha, idem.

Chung toi, nos; inferiores loquendo ad superiorem. Chung bay, vos; superior ad inferiores alloquendo. Ao chung, vestis oblonga. Chung vi chung, quia.

Chung, testis. Lam chung, testimonium facere, aliquando

significat modum; ut, No lam chung nao thi lam, quo quomodo velit, faciat.

CHUA, emendari in melius. Con phai doi lao chua cac toi, fili, debes emendari et abstinere ab omni peccato.

CHUA, prægnans. Vox rustica et magis accommodata animalibus quam mulieribus; ut, Trau chua, cho chua, bubula prægnans, canis prægnans. De mulieribus verò dicitur, Dan ba co thai, mulier habens conceptionem, et ideo non potest dici, trau bo ca thai, bubula aut vacca habentes conceptionem.

CHUA, liberare, salvare, sanare. Chua thuoc, curare infirmos aptis remediis. Chua chung, idem. Lay khi giai na chua minh, armis se protegere.

CHUO, expectare, inhiare. Chau chuc, assistere. Vide *chau.*

CHUC, dignitas, ordo. Chuch dich, munus dignitati annexum. Chuc tuoc, vel chuc pham, idem est. Chiu chuc lam, vel vo, Episcopum consecrari.

CHUOI, maledicere, convitiari. Chuoi rua, imprecari mala. Mloi chuoi, contumeliosa dicta.

Chuoc lam, vox lusoria, pulchrè satis.

Chuoc moc, mua chuoc, stratagema, machinatio, dolus. Bat chuoc, vide *bat.*

CHUONG, tumor et fœtor post mortem. Van chuong, carmen, littera.

CHUONG, *day chuong,* indigestio cibi.

CHUONG, *ou chuong,* centurio. Chuong phu, præses palatii regalis.

Chuyen can, constans diligentia.

CHUYEN, *mot chuyen,* una profectio.

Chuyen dou, movere, motus.

CHUO, stabulum. Chuo, amare, magni æstimare.

Chung quanh, in circuitu.

CHUNG, *banh chung,* genus edulii.

CHUNG, circa, species panis ex oryza.

CHUO, estimare, amare, magni facere.

CHUO, receptaculum animalium.

D.

D**a**, pellis, corium. Lot da, excoriare. Cay da, arbor quædam. Da lon, tela lanea.

D**a**, pars interior hominis. Nguoi lau da, homo malevolus.
Dau da, dissenteria, et etiam vox respondentis inferioris
ad superiorem: adsum, domine. Da, sumitur etiam pro
ingenio.

D**a**, *vao da*, rete quo portantur magnates, aut etiam infirmi.

D**ao**, *doi rach dach dai*, fame et nuditate consumptus.

D**ac**, pars pejor in lignis.

D**ach**, *cho dach*, canes minores.

D**ai**, cibus aut quid aliud molle quidem sed non facilè rumpitur.

Dai dot, stultus, amens, imprudens. Cho dai, canis rabiosus. Kinh dai, venerari.

D**ai**, longus, a, um. Dai ngay, longi dies. Ao dai, vestis
oblonga.

D**ai**, salarium appensum pro aliquo labore. Dai ao, ansulæ
vestis. Cai dai, testudines majores et feroces; etiam
honestè vocantur zonæ, quibus sese cinguntur Tunkinenses.

D**ai**, exponere aliquid pluviæ et soli ut purgetur. Dau suong
dai nang, omnibus cœli injuriis et incommodis expositus.
Dai dot vel *bot dai*, sputum seu saliva.

D**ay**, docere. Day do, instruere. Khuy en day, cohortari.
Sumitur etiam pro præcipere, jubere.

D**ay**, *do day*, turpis, e. Su do day, res turpes. Truyen do
day, confabulatio turpis.

D**ay**, *cho day*, surgere è lecto, vel somno. Don day, fama
percrebrescens.

D**ay**, crassus, a, um. Ao day, vestis crassa.

D**ay**, *day dot* vel *nhay nhot*, saltare. Mung day dot, gestire
gaudio.

Dam, audere. Est urbanitas apud Tunkinenses, quando invitantur ad aliquid officium, vel præstatur eis obsequium, recusare dicendo : Toi chang dam, non ausim ; vel quomodo ausim ?

Dam, leuca annamitica, quæ est multò brevior leucis Europæis.

Dam, statio cymbarum, ubi defenduntur à fluctibus et vento.

Dan tay nhau, junctis palmis incedere aut stare.

Dan, *bao dan,* audax, magnanimus.

Dan, conglutinare aliquid, aut emplastrum vulneri applicare.

Dan, arbor quædam, cujus cortex amarissimus est, et veneratus.

Dan, *dan bao,* commendare aliquid alicui. Dan do, idem.

Dan, calcare aliquid pondere.

Dang vel *dang,* species seu externa apparentia. Lam dang, affectare externam apparentiam ad vanitatem. Xau dang, mala apparentia ; malum præsagium. Nguoi vo dang, homo nullius valoris.

Dang, *chim dang,* avis quædam.

Danh, nomen. Nhan danh cha, va con, va Spiritô Sancto, in nomine Patris, et Filii, et Spiritûs Sancti. Danh hieu, idem. Vo danh hieu, sine voce. Cau danh tieng xam am, quærere.

Dao, culter. Mua dao, pluvia magna.

Dao, *bao dao* vel *dao nou cho,* liberalis, liberalitas ; privilegium speciale. Hinh dao, vultus. Tho dao, faber ferrarius. Dao day, homo delicatus.

Dao, linea, ordo. Dao chu, linea litterarum. Dao sou, linea aquæ currentis seu fluminis. Dao ou Thanh Duminhgo, ordo Sancti Dominici. Lap dao, institutor, vel instituere religionem. Dao doi, prosapia.

Dap, *viet dap ra,* prima elucubratio seu scriptura.

Dat, timidus, pusillanimus, vecors.

Dat nhau, prius convenire ad cœcum, infantemve.

Day. Vide *choi day.*

Day, funiculus.

Day, *nuoi day*, aqua est in accessu.

Dam tuc, vel *ta dam*, fornicatio.

Dam dia, inungere. Nua dam, pluvia diuturna. Dan, comprimere.

Dan, populus. Dan da, paulatim.

Dan, ducere aliquem viæ ignotum.

Dat vel *dut*, serrâ secare; vel frangere funiculos.

Dang, offerre.

Dau, *con dau*, nurus. Cay dau, morus.

Dau, *gio dau*, hora circiter sexta serotina.

Dau, nota, signum. Dau vet, cicatrix. Nam dau thanh D.J.C. Quinque vulnera Christi. Lam dau cau rut, se crucis signo munire.

Dau, oleum. Dau vay, patientiam habere. Est in imperativo solum modo. Ke kung lao muon dam dia mai trao chon toi loi, peccator induratus vult usque et usque se ingurgitare in volutabro peccatorum.

De, *con de*, caper, capra. Ke chang muon lam con chien D. C. J. thi ph' lam con de ma qui ma cho, qui renuit esse ovis Christi, certò debet esse hircus diaboli.

De, *cai de*, grillus.

De, facilis, faciliter. De lam, facile factu. De o, commoda habitatio. Nguoi de an o, homo suavis in conversatione. Nguoi de dang, homo comis, liberalis. Lay lam de, parum curare.

De dat, an uo de dat, parce uti escâ et potu, in futurum prospiciendo.

Den, *cai den*, aranea. Vang den, tela aranearum. Den quay to, aranea texens telas.

Det vai, texere telas. Det chieu, texere mattas. Det, obdurare.

Deo, aliquid molle quidem, sed quod non facile rumpitur. Deo dang, infatigabilis.

Dep, sandalia annamitica. Dop, debellare.

De, *khinh de duoi*, idem significant; despicere; parvi facere.

Di, *chim di*, passerculus.

Di, *di mui*, depressus nasus.

Di, matertera.

Di, *mot di*, modicum quid.

Dich, ferre onera publica de loco in locum. Dich ra, recedere. Dich ra tieng, traducere in aliam linguam.

Dip, occasio. Phai lanh cai dip toi, dare occasionem aliis peccandi. Dip dang danh hat, concentus harmonicus. Loi dip, dissonantia.

Dip, *cai dip*, forceps ad evellendas barbas. Lim dim, oculi lippidi.

Dit, *dit thuoc*, applicare remedium vulneri.

Diu dang, suavis, e.

Diec, *chim diec*, avis. Diec doc, exprobare.

Diem, nitrum. Lua sinh lua diem, ignis sulfureus.

Diem man, appendix cortinae. Du diem, umbella.

Dien, genus serici rari et rubri. Sang dieng, vicinus.

Diep, *rau diep*, lactuca.

Diet, vincere, extinguere, interficere, percutere, ab stirpe evertere.

Diet di, fugere.

Dieu, *dieu hau*, milvus. Choi dieu, ludere ave papyraceâ. Dieu tha qua mo, maledictio annamitica.

Dieu quanh, circumcidere.

Dinh ben, vide *ben*.

Dinh vel *danh quan*, prætorium. Hang danh, milites ejusdem prætorii.

Do xem, explorare. Do lam sao? quâ ex causâ?

Dò, idem est ac *do*. Hoi dò la, interrogando paulatim explorare. Est etiam laqueus, undè dicitur: Cai co mac do ma chet, grus capta laqneo moritur.

Doo, vide *diec*.

Doc dang, in viâ. *Doc*, opponitur *ngang doc*, quod est linea

recta à capite ad calcem.   *Ngang*, est linea transversa à
sinistrâ ad dexteram.

Dom, *dom vao*, introspicere.   Ou dom, tubulatum conspicil-
lum.

Don, parare.   Don minh xung toi, disponere se ad confessionem sacramentalem.   Don dep, idem est.

Dou, *con dou*, tempestas minor.   Dou lam, nimis infaustè.
Di dou dai, stolidè discurrere; incertis sedibus vagari.

Dou, alloqui regem secundarium.   Dou be tren man nam,
vivat vex ad mille annos.

Do, allicere verbis.   Cam do, allicere ad malum; tentare.
Day do, vide *day*.   Do danh, idem est.   Do tre, demulcere parvulos.   Do danh, solicitare.

Doc, subvertere.   Doc lao, decernere, proponere in animo.
Doc lao chua cac toi, proponere emendationem omnium
peccatorum; decernere vitam emendare, et ab omni peccato abstinere.   Cho doc, locus proclivis.

Doi lai, resilire.

Doi, fallere.   Noi doi, mentiri.   Phai bo cac su doi bla,
oportet relinquere omnia vana et superstitiosa.

Doi, *lam doi*, modus condiendi cibum.   Doi vao, infarcire.

Don, tumultus ex concursu hominum.   Don da, idem est.

Don lai, ad brevitatem reducere.

Dot, indoctus.   Dot nat, valdè ignarus.   Dot, furunculus.

Dot, stillare, stillicidium.   Nha dot, stillat domus.

Do, sordes.   Trai chieu dap do, quærere artem malitiam
tegendi.   Lam ra do, polluere.

Do dang, nguoi do dang, homo imprudens, importunus.
Viec bo do, opus interruptum.   Do viec, impeditus negotio.

Do nha, destruere domum.

Doi, *cai doi*, vespertilio.   Lam doi lam chuot, dicitur de
homine versipelli qui varium et mutabilem se exhibet.

Doi di, alid ire.

Dot vel *nhot ca*, sordes ad instar sputi quæ adhærent piscibus.

Du, *ngao du*, otium, felicitas. Du, idem.

Du, umbella. Du ma, quamvis. Semper debet jungi istis vocibus Mac lao: et in sequenti membro semper ponitur unica vox *du* cum *mac lao*. Thi du, verbi gratia, parabola.

Du lao thuong, exhibere misericordiam, liberalitatem, quando est sermo de regibus ad populum. Du man xuo, deponere velum.

Duc, vide *dam*. Blai muc duc, renes.

Dui, furtis, vel ictus verberis; lignum quo pulsantur instrumenta.

Dum da, vel *dùm dà, cay dum da*, arbor pulchrè frondescens.

Dum, *nguoi dum chan*, qui habet pedes ex morbo tumidos.

Du yen, pulchritudo in vultu. Du yen do lam sao, vide *do lam sao*.

Dung, uti. Dung chang nen, abuti.

Du, superesse.

Du, *may la du nao*, cujus ordinis es tu? vox interrogantis per contemptum. Chang vao du nao, nullius ordinis, nullius valoris est.

Du, crudelis, inhumanus. Nguoi du ton, homo crudelis. Cho du, canis ferex.

Dua hau, pepo aqueus. Dua chuot, cucumis. Dua gang, etiam. Species peponis. Dua, olus sole* conditum.

Dua, inniti columnæ. Gummi etiam vocatur *dua*.

Dua, nuces Indicæ, Lusitanicè *coco*.

Duc lac, elatâ voce loqui moræ objurgantis. Sumitur etiam pro objurgare, reprehendere.

Dung vel *dong*, offerre aliquid Deo aut regi. Dung lai, sistere gradum. Nguoi dung, extraneus. Dung dung trao lao, nullo modo moveri corde.

Duoi chan ra, extendere crura.

Dut. Vide *dat*.

* Sic in MS.

Duoi, infra. Tren bloi duoi dat, in cœlo et in terrâ. Kinh ke be tren, yeu ke be duoi, venerari superiores, et amare inferiores.

Duom de, nguoi duom de, homo gravis et mansuetus.

Duong nao, quomodo? D. C. B. phep tac la duong nao, ta suy chang di, quomodo sit divina potentia, comprehendere non possumus. Tren thien dang vui ve la duong nao, in cœlo quale gaudium est. Am duong, vide *am*.

Duong, nutrire, fovere, indulgere. Duong duc cha sinh, me duong, pater genuit, et mater nutrivit. Chang nen duong xac qua, non licet indulgere corpori plus quam oportet. Dao duong, favere.

Da, *cay da* vel *cay da,* arbor quædam. Da lam, multum, nimis. Chim da da, perdix.

Dai khach, bene excipere hospites. Noi dai buoi, magnificis verbis absque re promittere. Dai gao, purgare oryzam.

Da, lapis. La da, idem est. *Da den* vel *da phai,* tangi vel tangere. Chang nen co y trai ma da minh ng ta, hay la cho ng ta da den minh, non licet ex malâ intentione contrectare alios, aut ab aliis contrectari. Mua la da gran da. Da, etiam significat calcitrare, undè ambigua locutio est. Voi da, elephas lapideus vel elephas calcitrans.

Da, adminiculum ad aliquid trahendum.

Da, jam. *Da doan* vel *da roi,* vel etiam *do an roi,* quæ si diriguntur ad interrogantem, nihil aliud significant quam, jam absolutum est, jam peractum est. Sed etiam significant post vel postquam, et in oratione disjunctim sic collocantur. D. C. J. da sou lai doan, roi thi len bloi, Christus postquam resurrexit, ascendit in cœlum. Est etiam adjectivum sanus, a, um; ut, Con da da chua? fili, esne jam sanus? Ai da chua may da? quis jam fecit te sanum?

Dac, *mot dac ruo,* latifundium.

Dac, aliquid solidum, ut lignum.

Dac, invenire, posse. Tra cho doi that, inquirere veritatem.

Dai, cingulum latum ex corio, vel ex duro serico.

Dai, magnus, a, um; vel præcellens cæteris in aliquâ re.

Dai thanh, magnus sanctus. Dai lam bieng, summè piger. Dai hang, ruburba.*

Dai, mingere. Urbanius dicitur *tieu tien*. Muoc tieu, urina.

Dai, pelliculæ florum. Cai dai, turricula. Chuc dai, columna super quam crematur incensum in honorem cœli.

Day, species herbæ.

Day, tegere. Che day, idem.

Day, exilium. Day di, mitti vel mittere in exilium.

Day vel *tui day*, mantica magna.

Day, hic. D. C. B. co day chang? Deus est ne hic?

Day, illic. No lam di gi day? Quid facit illic? Dau day, passim. Dau day deu tho phuong D. C. B., passim colitur Deus.

Day, plenus, a, um. Day garassa, gratiâ plena. Day lao chung toi, impleantur corda nostra. Day to, discipulus, famulus. Day day, abundanter, abundare.

Day, pellere. Noi dun day di, conari verbis difficultatem aliquam à se repellere.

Day, crassus, pinguis. Day da, idem est.

Dam, contendere pistillo vel pungere. Dam guo, xay lua, tundere et molere oryzam. Coi dam, vide *coi*.

Dam dap, idem est *day da*.

Dam, pugnare sine armis. Mot cai dam, unus pugnus. Cai dam dam, avicula quædam.

Dam, stagnum magnum. Dam am, vide *am*.

Dam, concursus vel celebritas aliqua. Dam ma, exequiæ. Dam hat, publicæ comediæ. Dam ben dai, solemnitates infidelium. Dam dat, cumulus terræ. Dam may, nubes densæ.

* Sic in MS.

Dam, fel. Nguoi dam lam, homo benè audax, cordatus.

Dam, *dam tau*, naufragium. Dam duoi, mergi vel capi. Dam duoi nhau, turpi suipsorum amore capi. Lao con chang nen duoi nhung su the gian, cor tuum non debet immergi rebus mundanis.

Dam, *trau dam*, bubalus se aquis aut luto immergens.

Dan, texere cistas aut alia instrumenta.

Dan, globi tormentorum. Dan duoc, globi et pulvis tormentarius.

Dan, instrumenta musicæ, aut pulsare illa instrumenta. Lap dan, erigere aras ad sacrificandum diis. Dan ou, vir. Dan ba, mulier. Dan trau bo, grex animalium. Dan chim, agmen avium. Bach dan, sandalum.

Dan, *bat dan* vel *bat da*, scutella seu porsulana annamitica.

Dan don, tardus ingenio.

Dang, dùm aliquid actualiter fit; et semper sequitur nominativum antè verbum, ut, D. C. J. dang giang, thi co mot ba kia khen nguoi, Christum actualiter prædicantem laudavit quædam mulier. Dang khi, cùm vel dùm; hæc particula semper præcedit nominativum; ut, Dang khi Duc chua Jesu o trao vuon Getsemani, thi thang Juda dem quan du den bat nguoi, cum Christus esset in horto Getsemani, Judas duxit cohortem militum ad eum capiendum. Cau dang, actor negotiorum. Xem chang dang, horret visus.

Dang, dignus, a, um. Xung dang, idem.

Dang, familia imperatorum sinarum, secundùm illustrissimi Agathopolitani computum, decima tertia; regnavit annis 283. Est etiam saccharum. Dang phen, saccharum petrosum. Dang cat, saccharum arenosum. Di dang ca dem, totam noctem iter facere. Con, phai ra suc di dang roi linh hon, conare, fili, ingredi viam salutis. Thien dang, paradisus. Dang len thien dang thi·hep, via ad paradisum est angusta. Dicitur etiam *duong*. Phu dang,

30

palatium regis secundarii. Dang ngoai, omnis provincia
à Xu thanh. Dang trao, omnis provincia à Xu thanh,
usque regnum Cambodiæ.

Dang, *ke dang*, societas malorum.

Dang, nassæ crassiores ad capiendos pisces. Thuyen dang,
piscatores qui utuntur illis nassis ad piscandum.

Dang, amarus, a, um. Cay dang lam, amaritudo amarissima.

Dang, mensa, altare.

Dang bac, ordo statûs. Nguoi ba dang, cua ba loai, tres
sunt ordines hominum, et tres ordines rerum. D. C. B. la
dang dung nen bloi dat muon vat, Deus est creator cœli,
terræ et omnium rerum. Dang lam Thay ca, est ipse
sacerdos.

Danh, verberare, capere, pugnare. Danh giac, pugnare
contra hostes. It quan danh di giac to lam, maximas
hostium copias parvâ manu fundere. Danh co bac,
ludere aleis. Danh ca, danh chim, capere pisces, aves.
Danh luoi, jactare rete. Danh toi, castigare corpus pro
pœnitentiâ. Danh com, manducare oryzam. Danh vo,
frangere. Chui danh, abstergere, et sic de cæteris. Danh
chuo, pulsare campanam. Di tanh giac, adversùs hostem
abire. Ke danh to danh giac, malo intentus.

Danh, *viei ay da danh*, illud jam certum est.

Dao, *ma dao*, gladii lati et longi quibus armantur equites.

Dao, religio Christiana. *Giu dao* vel *di dao*, observare, sequi religionem. Con, muon di dao chang, vis, fili, ingredi
religionem. Bon dao, Christiani. Vo dao, meliùs sic dice-
retur. Ngoai dao, infideles. Hai dao, via maritima.

Dao, lusus puerorum.

Dao, *cay dao*, quædam arbor, Lusitanicè vocata *pesco*.
Mui dao, color roseus. Dao dat, fodere terram.

Dao, metiri frumenta. Chung bay dao cho an hem dau nao,
thi Tao loi dao cho bay dau ay, quâ mensurâ mensi
fueritis fratribus vestris, eâdem remetietur vobis.

Dao, remoratur fluxus aquarum aut aliquid. Con dao nhieu viec, multa negotia remorantur.

Dao, construere aliquid ex multis tabulis aut lignis, ut, Dao tau, dao thuyen, dao hom, construere navim, cymbam, capsulam. Figere, vide *danh*. Dao don, castrametari. Dao cua, claudere januam. Dao quan gan ke cho, exercitum vel copias considere propè urbi.

Dao, lancea. Luoi dao, mucro lanceæ.

Dap, conculcare, conterere calce. Dap lua, triturare. Ga dap mai, gallus copulat se gallinæ. D. Ba dap dau cai ran, Beata Virgo conterit caput serpentis.

Dap, ferire. Ou Moysen dap vao hon da ba lan, Moyses percussit ter lapidem.

Dat, ponere. Dat len, superponere. Dat xuo, deponere. D. C. B. dat ke khiem nhuong leu, ma bo ke kieu ngao xuo, exaltat Deus humiles, et humiliat superbos. Dat ten, imponere nomen.

Dat, *ban dat, mua dat lam,* quod avidè venditur et emitur. Noi chang dat deu, non proficiunt verba.

Dat, terra. Dat thit, terra argillosa.

Dau, dolere. Om dau, ægrotare.

Dau, ista unica vox pro ubi, undè, quò, quà. O dau, ubi est; ubi manet. O dau ma den, undè venire. Di dau, quò ire. Qua dau, quà transire. Interdùm est vox admirantis vel dubitantis, ut, Co dau the ay? quomodo est sic? Postremò sæpissimè jungitur negationi ad majorem vim, ut, Chang co dau sot; chang thay dau sot, nullibi; nullibi apparet. Cay xoan dau, arbor quædam.

Dau vel *do*, faba vel faseolus. Benh nen dau, variolæ. Dau sinh do, adipisci ultimum gradum litterarum. Chim dau, avis residens. Dau nha, hospites.

Dau, mensura ad metiendum grana. Vide *dao*.

Dau, caput. Dau het, triticum; primò. Dau ke cuop, dux latronum. Ou thanh Phero la dau cai thanh tou do, Sanctus Petrus est princeps apostolorum. Man dau ra truoc, exordiri.

Dᴇ, minari, intentare malum.

Dᴇ, calcare supra aliquid. Noi de nen cho nguoi ta, imputare alicui culpam ex malâ suspicione.

Dᴇ, parere.

Dᴇ, *de cu rut,* basis crucis.

Dᴇ, inscribere. De thu, obsignare epistolam.

Dᴇ, servare. De danh, servare aliquid in futurum usum. De linh, præfectus vigilum urbis. De, ad. Lam den thanh de tho D. C. B., erigere ecclesiam ad colendum Deum.

Dᴇᴍ, ferre. Dem di, auferre. Dem lai, adferre, educere, adducere.

Dᴇɴ, niger, ra, rum. Den si, nigerrimus; sumitur etiam pro infaustâ fortunâ.

Dᴇɴ, lampas, lucerna. Den nha ai rang nha nay, quisquis res suas meliùs cognoscit.

Dᴇᴘ, formosus, a, um. Dep de, idem. Dep lao, placere.

Dᴇᴍ, nox. Dem hom, tempus nocturnum. Ban dem, vide *ban.*

Dᴇᴍ, stragulum.

Dᴇᴍ, numerare. Dem xem, numerare ad cognoscendum numerum.

Dᴇɴ, venire usque ad. Ai den day? quis venit illùc? Den bao gio con moi blo lai? quando nam tandem reverteris? Significat etiam *de.* Dung noi den su ay, noli loqui de illâ re. Chang nen tuong den su do day, non licet cogitare de rebus impuris. Nho den toi cung, memento mei.

Dᴇɴ, satisfacere, reparare. Den toi, satisfactio pro peccatis. Den va, reparare damnum. Den tho, templum. Den vua, palatium regis. Bat den, exigere reparationem.

Dᴇᴏ, gestare aliquid in corpore.

Dᴇᴘ, *dep trau,* theca betel.

Dᴇᴜ, sermo vel sententia. Deu nhau, hat cho deu nhau, cantare æqualiter. Deu lao nhau, junctis animis et viribus. Deu ngam, meditatio. Deu, etiam est articulus in libris.

Dɪ, ire. Tray di, proficisci. Di dao choi, vel Di bach bo, deambulare. Est etiam imperativus, ut, An di, comede. Con, xung toi di, fili, confitere peccata tua. Di ngua, vide *cuoi*. Di tro di, progredi.

Di gi, quid? Con noi di thay chang hieu, quid loqueris? non intelligo. D. C. B. la tinh di gi? quid est Deus? Et etiam est, ut quid. Con chang muon chua, ma xung toi di gi? non vis emere, ut quid conferis?

Dɪ, scortum.

Dɪᴀ, hirundo. Dia, paropsis.

Dɪᴄʜ, certare. Dich lai, repugnare. Dai dich, idem est.

Dɪᴇᴄ, surdus, a, um. Dicitur, Nang tai, aures graves. Qua diec, fructus qui ex aliquo casu evadit inutilis.

Dɪᴇᴍ, domuncula erecta ad excubias agendas. Diem phu lieu, senatus supremus. Diem trang, fucare faciem.

Dɪᴇᴘ, mandatum imperatoris. Trung trung diep diep, innumerabilis.

Dɪᴇᴜ, ducere reum ad judicem vel ad supplicium.

Dɪᴇᴜ, *cai dieu*, pipa. Mot dieu thuoc, buccella tabaci.

Dinh ba, tridens.

Dinh vel *dinh lieu*, disponere, ordinare. Cha ca da dinh lieu lam vay, sic Deus ordinavit. Dinh ki, constituere tempus.

Dɪɴʜ, cacumen.

Dɪɴʜ, bulcuterium, seu locus negotiis publicis destinatus. Ngua dinh pho, veredus.

Dɪᴛ, crepitus ventris. Danh dit, pedere. Rusticè *ram*.

Dɪᴛ, clunis.

Dɪᴜ, *ran diu diu*, quidam serpens.

Diu dit, molestia, quam patiuntur qui infantes et pueros secum ducunt.

Do, metiri cubito aliquid.

Do, componere vel comparare aliquas res ad invicem, ad sciendum earum longitudinem vel qualitatem.

Do, genus assæ. Day do, illic, istic.

Do, linter ad trajicienda flumina. *Lam do* vel *gia do*, simulare se.

Do, ruber, ra, rum. Thang do, infantulus recens natus. Cai do, infantula.

Do, lusores qui pugnam agunt ad populi recreationem. Kinh do, aula.

Do, gradus geometricus. Do ba bon ngay, circiter tres quatuorve dies. Toi bo dac kinh do nam sau lan, omisi recitare preces plus minusve sexties.

Do, *cai do*, ligna quibus construitur paries. Deu do, problema. Tao do may, etiam provoco te, jubeo, aude.

Do, omnia instrumenta aut res materiales. Do le, res ad sacrificium pertinentes. Do an, res comestibiles, seu cibaria. Do le, instrumenta. Do xoi, coquere oryzam solo vapore aquæ calidæ. Sinh do, ultimus gradus litteratorum. Tou do, apostolus.

Do, infundere, effundere. Xin D. C. B. do garasa xuo day lao chung toi, infundat Deus gratiam cordibus nostris. D. C. J. da do het mau minh ra, Christus effudit totum sanguinen suum. Do, vide *dau*.

Doa thai, fœtus effusus ante tempus ex imperitiâ medici. Thuoc sa con, medicina ad procurandum abortum.

Doc, recitare, legere. Doc kinh, apud Christianos, recitare preces. Si gentiles recitant suas preces, dicitur, Doc canh, doc hanh, legere libros. Doc thu cho ng ra nghe, recitare litteras.

Doc, *ban doc*, altare. Lao doc, malevolentia. Doc du, crudelis. An doc, qui solus devorat omnia, nihil dando aliis. Nguoi doc dinh, qui est unicus absque fratribus. Thuoc doc, venenum. Cætera omnia quæ sanitati nocent dicuntur *doc*, ut *nuoc doc*, aqua pestifera, khi doc, aër insalubris, &c.

Doc ra, degenerare. Doc chung ra, mutari in pejus.

Doi den, lanx parva quæ in lampadibus adhibetur.

Doi, esurire. Doi khat lam, fames magna. Kho khan doi

khat, pauperes esurientes. Doi cho an khat cho uo, cibare esurientem et potum dare sitienti. Ai doi khat sa phup duc, ay la phuc that, beati qui esuriunt et sitiunt justitiam.

Doɪ, repetere. Doi no, repetere debitum. D. C. B. se doi no nguoi vou va lai thang lam, Deus repetet debita sua exactissimè. Sumitur etiam aliquando pro vocare. Doi no den day, vocare illum hùc. Sed convenit superiori solùmmodo.

Doɪ, contendere verbis. *Doi co* vel *doi choi*, idem significant. Doi xet, respondere in judicio. Mot doi, unum par.

Doɪ, gerere aliquid super capite. Doi mu, gerere biretum. Doi on, gratias agere Deo vel superiori. Doi quan, cohors militum. Bay doi, ordinare aciem.

Doɪ, correspondere ad alterum. Cau doi, versus qui habent sensuum correspondentiam.

Doɪ, colles. Blai doi, idem est.

Doɪ, commutare. Ta phai doi sou doi nay ma lay sou doi sou, debemus commutare hanc vitam præsentem pro alterâ futurâ. Doi doi, vicissitudo sæculorum.

Doɪ, expectare, opperire. *Doi trau* vel retrò *trau doi*, expectare cum spe. Cai thanh to Tou doi tran chua cuu the ra doi, Patriarchæ expectabant adventum Messiæ. Trou mao, expectare ardentèr. Doi dang, spatium itineris.

Do, *ban do*, vendere cum pactu restituendi.

Do, juvare, sufferre.

Doɪ, sæculum, vita. Ca doi, tota vita. Blon doi, tota vita usque mortem. Con D. C. B. ra doi, filius Dei incarnatus. Doi doi vo cung, in sæcula sæculorum, sine fine.

Doᴍ, faces. Dom duoc, idem. Tay cam dom, chan dap do, qui tenet lucernam et sibi non illuminat. Cai dom dom, lampiris vel noctilux.

Doᴍ, *lam dom*, idem est ac *lam do.*

Doᴍ, cibum abaco apponere. Dom com, apponere oryzam.

Dom ou ba, ou vai, cibum offerre suis mortuis. Noi dom
dat ra, multa mendacia loquendo effingere.

Dom vel *dom danh*, flegma. Thuoc dom, medicina ad dis-
sipandum flegma.

Don, obviare. Don ruoc, ire in occursum ad recipiendum
aliquem. Don dang an cuop, obsidere viam ad rapien-
dum. Noi don, occludere viam loquendi.

Don, verbera. Don ngoi, sedile ex ligno integro. Don
khieng, don ganh, vectes ad onera ferenda. Significat
etiam ictus verberis.

Don tri, obtusum ingenium. Thay khoa don, sortilegus.

Don, divulgare. Tieng don ra, fama, rumor. Tieng may
don khap mai noi, fama tua vulgatur per omnia loca, vel
longè latèque diffunditur. Iste modus loquendi potest
sumi in utramque partem, id est, bonam vel malam. *Don
thu* vel *don quan dao*, præsidium, arx. Daong don, cas-
tra ponere.

Don, morbus quidam. Ao don, vestis simplex.

Don, vide *dau don*. Nguoi don mat, homo vilissimus. Don
chiec, solus, sine adjutore.

Dot, incendere. Dot nha, incendere domos. Ao dot, mui
dot, apes et culices pungunt.

Dou, *ben dou*, oriens. Mua dou, hiems. Gio dou, Eurus.
Nguoi ta dou lam, hominum concursus magnus. Dou lai,
congelari. Nuoc dou lai, congelatur aqua.

Dou vel *dou dat*, motus. Bien dou, motus maris. Danh
dou, commovere. Dou dat den tai be tren, fama fert ad
aures superiorum. Do kinh, morbus comitialis. Lao
dou, lao lo, motus cordis.

Dou, cumulus. Danh dou, accumulare. Nguoi sou hon
dou vang, vita hominis superat cumulum auri.

Dou, æs vel ager. Dou tien, moneta ærea. Mot dou, una
moneta. Dou bac, pateca. O ngoai dou, est in agris.
Dou khou, agri inculti. Dou hoang, idem est. Dou trinh,
virgo. Dou ho, horologium. Thay dou, magus.

Du, *danh du*, lusus quo juvenis unus et una puella, funibus innixi, sese in altum ejaculantur; quod valdè inhonestum est ac periculosum, ac ideò graviter prohibitum à missionariis est. Cai du du, quædam arbor, Lusitanicè *papaja* vocata.

Du hon vel *du hoi*, lascivire. Convenit magis animalibus quam homini.

Du, sufficere; vel *cho du*, sufficienter, satis. Aliquando usque ad: Con, phai doc mot ngay ba kinh thien chua, cho du muoi ngay, debes, fili, recitare unâ die ter Pater noster, et sic usque ad decem dies.

Dua, æmulari. Dua nhau tham dat bo loi, æmulantur invicem in amplectendo terrena, et despiciendo cœlestia. Cheo dua, contentio in remigando.

Dua, *cai dua di*, per fas et nefas contradicere.

Dua, bacilli quibus ad comedendum utuntur. Be dou tien chiec dua, testimonium repudii apud Tunkinenses.

Duc, perforare lignum scalpello. Cai duc, scalprum. Nuoc duc, aqua turbida.

Duc, conflare aliquid ex ære, auro, argento, &c. Tho duc, furor.

Dui, cœcus, a, um. Mu toi mat, idem sonant.

Dui, femur.

Dui, *den dui*, nigerrimus, a, um.

Dui, tela ex serico rudi.

Dum, *hat dum*, cantus amatorii gentilium, pariter prohibiti Christianis ac lusus *du.*

Dun, cumulus palearum vel spicarum. Dun lam, granarium.

Dun day, vide *day*, pellere.

Dung dung, sonitus tormentorum.

Duoc dom, vide *dom.*

Duoi, *chet duoi*, mori aquâ suffocante. Noi duoi deu, fluctuant verba. Ca duoi, piscis, Lusitanicè *Raja.*

Duoi cau da, finis. Opponitur *dau*, caput, initium.

31

Duoi, fugare et fundere; persequi hostem fugitivum, præ-
dam. Duoi di, expellere.

Dut, intromittere aliquid in foramen. An dut, manducare
oryzam per alium in os intromissam, more infantium vel
infirmorum. An dut, etíam intelligitur de judicibus qui,
pecuniâ corrupti, sententiam perversam contra justitiam
ferunt.

Dua, tradere, comitari.

Dua, hoc nomine appellantur pueri, puellæ aut homines infimæ conditionis, aut per contemptum, sicut nomen
thang; sed *thang* pro masculino genere solum, *dua* verò
pro utroque.

Dua, comitari in egressu; opponitur *ruoc,* quod est recipere
in egressu.

Dua cho, corrigere.

Duc, virtus, probitas. Hoc nomine appellantur omnes virtutes, sive naturales sive supernaturales; ut *duc tin,* fides.
Duc cau bang, justitia. Sed sæpiùs invenitur juncta ista
vox *duc* cum voce *nhan,* ut *con phai di dang cai nhan duc,*
fili debes ingredi viam virtutum. Quando verò præcedit
ista nomina Dominus, Rex, &c.; tunc non potest aliter
explicari quam adjectivum excellentissimus, a, um; ut
D. C. B.,* Excellentissimus Dominus cœli; Duc nua, excellentissimus rex; Duc vitvo, excellentissimus episcopus;
Duc ba, excellentissima domina, id est regina. Duc hanh,
pietas.

Duc, hâc voce nominatur omne genus masculinum in animalibus, exceptis gallis gallinaceis, qui semper appellantur *ga sou.* Vide *cai.*

Dung, stare. Dung lai, sistere gradum.

Dung, continere. Istud verbum convenit vasis minoribus,
ut, Bat dung di gi, scutella quid continet?

Dung, noli, nolite. Est in imperativo solùmmodo.

* Hæ litteræ sonant *Duc Chua Bloi.*

Duoc, posse, invenire, assequi. Chang duoc, non posse, non invenire. Ad rectè utendum istis vocibus *chang duoc*, in linguâ annamiticâ, magnâ opust est attentione, et non nisi per longum tempus; et in hunc scopulùm incidere solent hujus linguæ tyrones. Itaque quando quis ex propriâ sua impotentiâ aliquid facere non potest, istæ voces *non potest* semper debent postponi alteri verbo, ut, *an chang duoc*, id est morbo impeditus manducare non potest. Di chang duoc, ire non potest ex infirmitate vel aliâ causâ. Quando verò aliquâ lege vel mandato impeditus agere non potest, seu non valet, tunc *chang duoc*, debet præcedere illud verbum; ut, Ngay le chang duoc lam viec xai toi an thit chang duoc; id est ex infirmitate non possum manducare carnem. Toi chang di an thit, id est, prohibitus aliquâ lege manducare carnem non possum.

Duom nhuan, tempus suaviter temperatum. Mua duom nhuan, pluvia verna. Duom nom, ululatus.

E.

E, *duom e*, vili vendere.

Eoh, *cai ech*, rana.

Em, suavis, e; suaviter. Em ai, idem. Em so, revereri.

Em, frater minor et soror minor.

En, *chim en*, hirundo.

Ep, cogere, premere. Ep xuo, deprimi.

E chan vel *te chan*, tepescit pes. Dau e om, lentus dolor.

G.

Ga, gallina et gallus gallinaceus. Nguoi toi ga, homo luscus. Biet ga ga vay, scire aliquid subobscurè. Ga choi, gallus pugnax. Ga co, gallus enormis.

Ga, tradere filiam nuptui. Bon dao chang nen ga con cho ke khau dao, non licet Christianis filias suas tradere nuptui gentilium.

GAC, cornua cervorum.

GAC, appendere vel superponere aliquid ligno. Dao danh gai cu rut, clavis affixus cruci. Gac viec ay ra, suspendatur illud. Gac, est etiam tabulatum.

GAC, *cay gac*, quædam arbor cujus fructu tingitur oryza ut pulchra appareat.

GACH, lateres. Nung gach, coquere lateres. Xay gach, ædificare aliquid ex lateribus. Gach cua, pinguedo cancri.

GAI, spina. Gai goc, multæ spinæ. Dang nhung gai goc, via spinis plena. Noi gai ra, loquendo obicem ponere.

Gai dao, cultrum leviter ad cotem fricare.

GAI, *con gai*, filia puella. Sed quando per contemptum nominantur mulieres, tunc per unicam vocem *gai*. Chang nen danh ghen vuoi gai dai lam chi, non decet virum rixari cum mulierculis.

GAI, fricare.

GAY, occiput. Ga gay, gallus cantat.

Gay dan, tangere instrumenta musicæ. Gay no ra, proscribatur ille.

GAY, baculus.

GAY, macer, cra, crum. Gay dung ra, exordiri. Gay dung cho con cai, necessaria suppeditare filiis ad familiam instituendam.

GAY, lignum aut tabula confracta in duas partes. Danh gay, frangere.

GAM, sericum. Ao gam di dem, musica in luctu.

Gam thet, rugitus leonis aut tigridis. Bien gam, fremitus maris.

GAM, meditari, considerari.

GAN, jecur. Ca gan, magnanimus.

GAN, colare aquam, vas in unam partem inclinando. Hoi gan, diù sciscitando quærere.

Gan bo, enixè commendare; pice conglutinare. Gan, nemus. Gan, propè.

Gang, mensura quæ duanti æquivalet. Gang, est etiam genus ferri fragilis et crudi.

Gang, *noi gang*, verbis repetitis in memoriam refricare.

Gang, conari. Gang suc ra, exercere vires.

Ganh, solus per vectem aliquid portare. Si cum aliquo per vectem ferre, dicitur *khieng*. Solus humere sine vecte gerere aliquid, dicitur *vac*, ut D. C. J. vac cu rut, Christus bajulans crucem. Portare aliquid humero aut collo appensum, dicitur *mang;* manu gestare, dicitur *xech*.

Ganh nhau, dissentire invicem.

Ganh, *ganh nui*, dorsum montis.

Gao, oryza cruda.

Gap, occurrere. Gap nhau giua dong, occurrere invicem in viâ.

Gap, aliquid capere per bacillos. Gap lua bo tay, calumniari.

Gap vel *xép*, complicare vestem. Gap phai nhieu su, multis malis exagitatus.

Gat ra, manu repellere. Cai gat di, aliorum sententiam contendende repellere.

Gat, metere. Tho gat, messores. Gat ngay, urget tempus.

Gat gao, asperrimus, a, um.

Gat dau, annuere. Ngu gat, dormiturire.

Gau, *con gau*, ursus. Co gau, herba quædam cujus radix est medicinalis. *Chiendent* agrestis.

Gau, situla seu instrumentum ad hauriendam aquam.

Gen, *rau gen*, blitum.

Gen giao vel *cot gen*, ineptè jocari.

Gieo, seminare. Ai da gieo giou nao thi gat giou ay, quod semina serit homo, et metet.

Ghem, *rau ghem*, olera cruda, quæ cum jusculo comeduntur.

Ghe, *ghe rang*, horrent dentes.

Ghe, cathedra, sedile. Ge thay, terribile.

Ge, pannus vetus. Tam ge, frustum panni veteris.

Gie, scopa.

Giau mat, oculus lippitudine obductus.

Ghe ga, crista galli. Ghe su la, multa admiranda.

GHEN, invidia. Ghen ghet, invidia, et o dium. Ma qui hang ghen ghet loai nguoi ta ch co khi dung, dæmon implacabili odio prosequitur genus humanum.

GHE, *ghe con mat lai*, convertere oculos. Ghe non, deprimere galerum in unam partem. Tau chay ghe buom, obliquo velo navigare.

GHET, odium.

GHE, *cai ghe*, vasa.

GHE, scabies. Me ghe, noverca.

Gheo gat vel *treu gheo*, provocare aliquem ad lusum vel ad iracundiam.

Gheo gat dan ba, solicitare mulieres.

GHI, inscribere, notare.

GI, *ret gi, lo gi*, rubigine obduci.

GIA, pretium. Gia cao, pretium charum. Gia thuong, pretium ordinarium. Gia ha, pretium vile.

GIA, senex, senescere. Ou gia, titulus honoris.

GIA, falsus, a, um. Falsum testimonium. Chung doi gia lam, simulare se. Gia hinh, hypocrita. Gia, naviculæ onerariæ vel piscatoriæ. Hay gia hinh lam, cujuslibet rei simulator.

GIAO, bellum, hostes. Lam giac, rebellare contra regem suum. Chiec danh giac, sumere bellum. Danh giac, pugnare contra hostes. Ta ph danh giac vuoi ma qui, the gian, xac thit, mai cho den chet, debemus continuò pugnare contra dæmonem, mundum et carnem usque ad mortem.

Giai ran, sæpiùs apud Christianos Deu ran, mandatum. Thay giai, monachus idolatriæ. Sæpiùs *thay tu*.

GIAM, detinere in carcere vel custodiâ. Kien giam, perpetuò detineri in carcere.

GIAM, demere, subtrahere. Giam bot, idem.

GIAM, *cai giam* vel *cai gay*, festuca. Cai giam trao con mat

anh em thi may xem thay, ma cai xa trao con mat may,
thi may chang xem thay, festucam de' oculo fratris tui
vides, et trabem in oculo tuo non vides. Noi dam giam
vao, seminare zizaniam.

GIAN, spatium inter duas columnas. Nha nam gian, domus
quæ habet quinque ejusmodi spatia. Tho gian, mundus.
Nguoi gian, homo furax vel ipse fur. Noi gian, mentiri.
Gian doi, furax et mendax. Gian nan, tribulatio.

GIAN, *cai gian*, blatta.

Gian mat, sustinere conspectum. No chang dam gian mat
toi sot, non sustinet meum conspectum.

Gian ra, dissolvitur structura, vel differre opera in aliud
tempus.

GIANG, extendere brachia vel pedes. D. C. J. chiu dao danh
giang chan tay ra tren curut vi toi thien ha, Christus cru-
cifixus est pansis manibus et pedibus pro peccatis totius
mundi.

GIANG, prædicari, concionari. Thay giang, catechista.
Pho giang, nauclerus.

Giang nhau, præripere inter se ad se attrahendo. Gianh
nhau, idem.

Giang vel *blang* vel *trang*, luna.

Gianh vel *blanh* vel *tranh*, paleæ contextæ ad tegendas
domos. Nha tranh, domus ejusmodi paleis tectæ.

Giao cho, tradere. Giao nhau, contractum inter se facere.
Giao hua, promittere cum conventione. Giao hieu cung
nhau, societatem inire cum aliquo, fidem mutuam sibi
promittere, fœdus inire, fidem dare et accipere.

GIAO, pugio. Noi giao cho giac, suppeditare hostibus arena.

GIAO, *giao luat*, supplicium suffocationis. Giao giao, furax.

GIAP, propè. Giap tran, in ipso conflictu.

Giap gio, thi thuyen giap gio, homo variabilis, fallax.

GIAT, ejici fluctibus. Giat vao bai bien, ejici ad littora.

GIAT, lavare vestes, telas femorales, et cætera quæ fiunt ex
telis.

Giat, appendere aliquid alicui.

Giao, sopor.

Giay, momentum. Mot giay nua ma bay chang thay tao; mot giay nua ma bay lai thay tao, modicum et non videbitis me; et modicum et iterùm videbitis me.

Giay, papyrus. Giay sac, papyrus ad scribendum diplomata. Giay thi, papyrus ad scribendum mandata aliqua. Giay canh, papyrus latior. Giay so, papyrus ordinaria. To giay, folium papyri.

Giay co, eradicare herbas. Giay ma, sepulchra renovare; quod solet fieri apud Tunkinenses antè annum novum.

Giam, plantas novellas limo figere.

Giam, pede humum pulsare more irascentis. Dao giam, quædam secta, cujus assectæ, preces suas recitando, pede humum pulsant.

Giam, acetum. Giam thanh, acetum purum.

Giam boi, vide *boi*.

Giam, irasci. Sot gian, accendi ira. Con gian len, vide *con*. No mat ngon, gian mat khon, satietas saporem, ira prudentiam tollit.

Giap, suffringi.

Giap, herba quædam.

Giat, attrahere ad se fortiter.

Giau, abscondere aliquid.

Giau, dives. Giau co, idem est. Lam giau, conquerere divitias. Tham giau bo nghia, præferre divitias pietati.

Giec, *ca giec*, piscis valdè salubris.

Giem, *gian giem*, vide *giau*.

Gieng, *thang gieng*, mensis primus apud annamitas sic nominatur; secundus, *thang hai;* tertius, *thang 3*, et sic de cæteris juxta numerum ordinarium usque ultimum, qui vocatur *thang chap*.

Gieng moi, basis vel fundamentum aliarum rerum.

Gieng, puteus.

Giu, excutere. Giua, limare.

Giuc, instigare. Khi ma qui giuc lao con, quando dæmon instigat cor tuum.

Giui, perforare. Cai giui, subula.

Gium, turmatim. Ngoi gium nhau, turmatim sedere.

Giup, alicui auxiliari, opem alicui ferre, subvenire alicui; adjuvare, ministrare. D. C. B. giup sui cho nguoi, adsit tibi gratia Dei.

Giu, custodire, observare. Ke giu viec, præses òperis vel procurator. Ge giu, cautè circumspicere. Giua, medius, a, um.

Giuong ma tra, micare oculis.

Guong, maritus materteræ.

Giuong, lectus. Giuong luoi, basis sagenæ.

Giuong gianh, giuong nhau, invicem præripere.

Giet, occidere.

Gio, ventus. Gio thoi, ventus sufflat. Dung gio, quando nullus est ventus.

Gio, pedes gallinæ vel porci. Xem gio, genus sortilegii ex observatione pedis gallinæ.

Gio, cista piscatoris quâ continentur pisces capti.

Gio, spuere. Gio, terrere verbis aut factis.

Gio, parentalia quæ fiunt ipsomet die mortis. Moi gio, superstitio quâ suos defunctos ad convivia illa parentalia invitant. Gap gio, contribuere ad parentalia illa peragenda.

Gio, porrigere aliquid extra, vel prominere.

Gio, hora. Phai dung ngay gio cho nen, oportet tempus benè collocare.

Gioc, nectere funes aut capillos.

Gioi bo, vide *bo*. Gioi gion, quod est valdè fragile.

Gioi, abluere.

Giot, percutere æs aut ferrum lento ictu.

Gion, *hum gion nhau*, ludunt inter se tigrides.

Giou, semen, genus, species. D. C. B. da dung nen giou nao thi cu giou ay, creavit Deus omnia juxta genus suum

32

Pro genere humano semper utendum est voce *loai*—Loai nguoi ta. Loai, etiam potest dici de animalibus, arboribus, et aliis creaturis. Est etiam adjectivum similis, e. Con giou cha, filius similis patri. Giou nhau, sibi invicem similes.

Go, *go ca*, pecten piscis.

Go, insula; cogere. Go cho no bla no, cogere aliquem ad debita reddenda. Troi go lai, strictim ligare.

Go, *go cua*, pulsare fores. D. C. P. Santo go cua linh hon ta, spiritus sanctus pulsat ad fores animæ nostræ. Luoi go, genus retis. Thuyen go, cymba quæ piscatur illo reti.

Go ghe, via inæqualis.

Go vel *cay go*, lignum. Lam go, lignari. Deo go, dolare ligna.

Go, septum dimissum ad impediendum porcos aut canes.

Go, *quai go*, monstrum; horribilis, e; genus monstruosum. Giou xuai go, solvere tricas aut eximere, aut eximere aliquid à laqueo. Con, chang muon go minh cho khai tay ma qui ru, fili, non vis te eximere à manu dæmonis. Goa, viduatus, viduata.

Goc, angulus. Goc nha, domus. Ca goc, nomen piscis.

Goc, truncus. *Coi goc* vel *coi re*, vide *coi*.

Goi, vocare. Goi la, nominari. Ten con goi la lam sao? nomen tuum quomodo vocatur? Toi goi la Phero, vocor Petrus. Con, goi Phero den day, voca Petrum ut veniat.

Goi, involvere; involucrum; fasciculus. Goi thu, fasciculus litterarum.

Goi, piscis frustatim concissus; sed crudè sumitur.

Goi dau, lavare caput.

Goi dau, supponere aliquid capiti; sed *dau goi* est genu. Cai goi, cervical. Qui goi, flectere genu.

Goi lua, manipulus frugum.

Goi, incipere, exordiri. : Noi goi ra, primo verba facere ad inchoandum aliquid.

Gom ghiec, abominari, abhorrere. Con, phai lay su toi lam

gom ghiec hon su chet, debes, fili, abhorrere magis à peccato quam à morte. Khi chung bay xem thay su gom ghiec tra nha tho thi phai ten nui ma an, cùm videritis abominationem desolationis in templo, fugite ad montes.

Gom lai, per compendium aliquid dicere vel facere.

Gon, succinctus, a, um. Gon ghe, succinctè, clarè, perfectè.

Gon, sao gon, undæ crispantes. Gai gon, quod detinctur aliquo impedimento.

Gop, contribuere. Gop liem viec than phat, contribuere ad superstitiosa. Gop gio len doi, contribuere ad parentalia superstitiosa. Gop viec ho, vel Gop viec dao, contribuere ad negotia Christianorum.

Got, cultro decorticare fructus aut arbores. Got dau, tendere caput.

Got chan, calx pedis. Tu dau den chan, à capite ad calcem.

Got, maculam in veste abluere.

Gou, genus tormenti, quod ad collum appenditur reo recens deprehensus, et judici sistendo.

Gou, ganh gou, gestare aliquid per vectem, sed una vectis parte alteram propter pondus prævalente.

Gu guc, gemitus columbæ aut turturis.

Guc dan, inclinare caput.

Gung, *ca gung,* quidam piscis.

Guoc, lignipedium.

Gui, mittere, committere. Gui lay, salutem dicere ad superiores. Gui kinh, salutem dicere æqualibus. Gui tham, salutem dicere inferioribus.

Guom, gladius. Guom trang, gladius longior. Vo guom, vagina.

Guong, speculum. Sach guong phuc, libellus de imitatione Christi. Ke o nha D. C. B. phai lam guong cho bon dao, ministri domus Dei debent prælucere cæteris Christianis exemplo, vel debent cæteris specimen virtutis præbere Guong tot, bonum exemplum. Guong xau, vel Guong mu, scandalum.

Gung, zinziber.

H.

HA, prima imperatorum sinarum familia, de quâ novus
auctor è seminario Parisiensi missionariorum ad exteros
protulit verba hæc: Prima hæc familia ad 458 annos imperium administravit, numerando ab eo tempore quo *Vu* in
imperii consortium ab imperatore *Thuan* assumptus est;
eodem tempore vini ex oryza confecti usus incepit. Hujus
familiæ imperator VI.ᵘˢ *Kiet*, vir ad omne sceleris genus
profligatus, à potentissimo dynastâ *Thang* dirutus est, qui
secundæ familiæ initium dedit, ducentis circiter annis
antè Moysis nativitatem. Ha xuo, deponere. Thuong
giai, ha giai, cœlum et terra. Thien ha, mundus. Mua
ha, sed magis *mua he*, æstas.

HA, genus conchilii parvi, quod naves perforat. Ha tien,
avarus.

HAC, avis quæ secundo nobilitatis loco numeratur post
phuong hoang, quæ est regina avium, juxta eorum existi-
mationem, plus fabulis quam veritate fundatam.

HAC, coram et superbè arguere.

HAI, duo, duæ, duo. Ca hai, totidem duo. Thu hai, secundus, a, um.

HAI, damnum. Ton hai, thiet hai, idem. Chang nen lam
hai cho ai bao gio, nunquam licet alicui damnum inferre.

HAI, falx messoris.

HAI, genus calcei mulieris.

HAI, mare. Hai nam, insula sic vocata. Hai duong, una
provincia parva in Tunkino.

HAI, revereri, pavere. So hai, kinh hai, idem. Est etiam
modus hortantis aut urgentis, ut, Con, hai cay trau D. C. B.
va lam viec lanh, spera in Domino et fac bonitatem.

HAY, significat hæc vox nimiam cordis ad aliquam rem in-
clinationem, aut potentiam animi, aut etiam dotem sive à
naturâ sive arte acquisitam, et variè accommodatur, ut

infra videre est. D. C. B. hay blon vay, Deus est naturâ
suâ perfectissimus. D. C. B. hay thuong vo cung, Deus
est infinitè misericors. Nguoi hay an hay uo, homo edax
et bibax. Hay chu, litteris instructus. Hay thuoc, peritus in arte medicâ. Ngua hay cha, equus acer in cur-
rendo. Meo hay chuot, feles apta ad capiendos mures;
et sic de cæteris. Et hæc vox semper præponitur aliis
verbis aut adjectivis aut etiam substantivis; aliquando
sumitur pro nosse. Ai hay chang la, nosciturne? Chang
hay la, inopinatè. Toi ngo la co ba nguoi xung toi; chang
hay la co nam nguoi, putabam esse tres pœnitentes, sed
inopinatè adsunt quinque.

Ham, sed *tham* est frequentiùs in usu. Nimia cupido.

Ham rang, mandibula. Rang ham, dentes molares.

Ham, cohibere. Ham no trao nha, cohibere aliquem in claustro. Ham tinh me xac thit, cohibere naturam corruptam.
Ham minh, mortificare membra.

Ham, præruptus. Nui ham, mons præruptus. Ham ho, anhelare.

Ham, calefacere. Ham ham vay, tepidus, a, um.

Han, *cay han*, arbor quædam, cujus folia sunt valdè vene-
nata; ad quorum tactum intumescit cutis.

Han, infortunium. Toi phai cai han nay, hoc patior infortunium. Nam han, annus infaustus. Dai han, siccitas
agrorum.

Han, quinta sinarum imperatorum familia, cujus rege *Ai de*
regnante, est natus salvator mundi. Sach han, liber his-
toricus qui gesta ab hujus familiæ imperatoribus bella
continet.

Han, ollas æreas aut ferreas pertusas reficere. Tho han,
fusor qui illas ollas recudit; ærarius.

Han, statuere.

Han, *ban han net*, natura iracunda.

Han, in provinciâ Xu nghe, dicitur pro ille, illa, illud.

Han thu, ulcisci; odium execrabile.

HAN, omninò certum est. Da han voi, jam omninò certum est. Nguoi han hoi, homo bonæ indolis, fidelis.

HANG, spelunca, antrum. D. C. J. sinh ra trao hang da: den khi chet lai tang vao hang da, Christus natus est in speluncâ; in morte suâ denuò in speluncâ sepultus est. Hang ho, idem.

HANG, *ke dan hang*, purus plebeius absque ullâ dignitate.

HANG, inguen.

HANG, caupona, apotheca, merces. Hang pho, emporium. Hang ruu, venditor vini. Tau cho hang di gi? navis vehit quas merces? Quan hang co hang doi, milites, commilitones. Lai hang quan giac, hosti se dedere vel tradero, deditionem facere.

HANG, odor.

HANG, semper. Cay hang nien, arbores quæ omni anni tempestate dant fructus. Cay hang sou, arbor vitæ.

HANG, *co hang*, inceptum opus deserere, propositum mutando; non est frequens in usu.

HANH, arbor aquilonis.

HANH, *duc hang*, pietas. Hou hanh, fructus quidam. Doc hanh, vide *doc.*

HANH, cepa. Quan Judeu o tren rung sao le con nho hanh cu thit motra onuoc tchito, Judæi in deserto desiderabant cepas et carnes Ægyptiacas. Noi hanh, detrahere, famam alicujus lædere. Toi noi hanh, detractio. Luoi ke noi hanh la con ran doi, lingua detractoris est serpens venenatus. Hanh ly, facere iter. Tien hanh ly, pecunia pro viatico.

HAO, vel *hao ton*, paulatim consumi. Lam hao ton, consumere, magnos sumptus facere.

HAO, minima pars in monetâ. Xe hao, facere canales ad munitionem.

HAO, bonus, a, um. Benè, (vox sinica.)

HAO, *oau hao*, fauces.

HAO, frustrari spe.

Hap, *hap lay,* **aliquid per os capere.**

Hat vel *hot,* granum. Trang hat, corona Beatæ Mariæ vel rosarium. Lan hat, recitare rosarium. Con, phai lan hat tram ruoi, fili, debes recitare rosarium integrum. Lan hat nam chuc, recitare quinque decadas rosarii.

Hau, ostreæ magnæ. Da hau, jamjam ferè; et ponitur pro præterito et futuro, ut, Chung toi phai khon nan da hau chet, ita affecti sumus ut jamjam ferè mortui. Den khi da hau chet moi blo lai, jamjam ferè moriturus, tandem conversus est.

Hauh, elementa.

Hat, cantare. Con hat, cantatrix. Quan hat boi, mimus. Hat vot kiem an, adulari.

He, *menh he,* fatum. Moi su boi menh he, omnia ex fato pendent. (Opinio Ethnicorum.)

He, *chang he,* nunquam; vel *chang he co,* idem. Ke o trao dia nguc chang he co thay D. C. B., damnati in inferno nunquam videbunt Deum. Chang he co bao gio sot, idem est.

He ai ai, vide *ai ai.* He bao gio, vel He lan nao, quotiescunque. D. C. J. phan rang: he lan nao chung bay lam su nay thi nho den tao, Christus dixit: hoc quotiescunque feceritis, in mei memoriam facietis.

Hen, ostrea parva. Hen aun, morbus quidam.

Hen, infirmus, vilis. Ra hen, probro haberi.

Hep, *chat hep,* angustus, a, um. Phai di dang chat hep o doi nay, oportet incedere per viam angustam in hâc vitâ. Kep hoi, idem.

Het, finis. absolutè totus, a, um. Omninò. An cho het, absumere totum. Khap het moi nguoi, omnes omninò homines. Kinh men D. C. B. tren het moi su, diligere Deum super omnia omninò. Tho phuong cha het lao het suc, colere Deum toto corde, totis viribus.

Het cung nhau, concordare omninò; sibi invicem simillima.

Het, avis quædam. Muon an het, thi dao trun, vis rosas, fer spinas.

Hɛo, arescere. Cay chang co re thi heo di: lao ng ta chang co gratia D. C. B. thi cung vay, arbor sine radice arescit: sic et cor hominis sine gratia Dei.

Hɪɛм, rarus, a, um. *Hiem co* vel *cua hiem*, res non vulgaris. *Hiem thu*, odium capitale.

Hiem ngheo, periculum. Dang hiem, via periculosa.

Hien ra, apparere. Se hien xuo, Pentecostes.

Hien lanh, mansuetus.

Hiep dan ba, vim inferre mulieri. Ha hiep ng ta, pervim extorquere pecuniam aut alias res.

Hɪɛv, pietas in parentes. Con bat hieu, filius impius in parentes.

Hɪɛv, *danh hieu*, signum militare. Hieu, signum ad aliquod opus. Len hieu, dare signum.

Hi mui, emungere nares. Hi ha, gaudere. An uo hi ha, convivari cum lætitiâ.

Hɪɴн, species, figura. Hinh tuong, effigies, simulacrum. Hinh tuong nay la hinh tuong ai, cujus est hæc imago? Loai ng ta da dung nen giou hinh tuong D. C. B., homo creatus est ad imaginem et similitudinem Dei. Hinh nhu, quasi. Hinh nhu the vay, quasi sic esset.

Hɪᴛ, indagare naso more canis venatici. Thuoc hit, tabacum pulverisatum. Hon hit, osculari.

Ho, tussire, tussis. Thuoc ho, remedium contra tussim.

Ho, familia, consaguinitas, tribus, confraternitas, Christianitas. Con trao ho cung nhau, adhûc esse in eadem consaguinitate. Con da vao ho duc ba chang? jam esne adscriptus confraternitati rosarii? Con la nguoi ho nao, es cujus Christianitatis?

Ho, conclamare ad invicem urgendum.

Ho han, exclamare.

Ho, *phu ho*, auxiliari. Cha ca phu ho cho anh em, adsit vobis Deus. Ho dang, ho nuoc, impedire inundationem aquarum.

Ho, præcipitium. Sa ho, cadere in foveam.

Ho, gluten ex farina factum ; locus et vas vini.

Ho, tigris. Nguoi hung ho, famosus audaciâ et fortitudine.

Ho, applicare aliquid ad ignem.

Ho, apertus, a, um. Ke co net na chang nen an mac ho hang, modestum non decet habitus apertus seu dissolutus.

Ho, vox rusticè respondentis.

Hoa, flos. Hat hoa tinh, canere cantilenas. Mloi hoa tinh, verba turpitudinem sonantia. Nguoi hoa nguyet, mulier compta et suspecta.

Hoa, *la hoa, hoa la,* rarò et non nisi per accidens. Viec ay hoa la gap, illud negotium rarò et non nisi per accidens contigit.

Hoa ra, transsubstantiari, accidere. Vung tu kheo hoa, qui malè incepit sed benè finivit.

Hoa, pax. Hoa thuan, pacificus, a, um. Lam hoa thuan, pacificare. Hoa tap nhau, jungere se ad aliquod malum peragendum. Hoa, diluere.

Hoac, vel *hoac la,* si, quod si fortè.

Hoai di vel *lien di,* aliquid evidentissimo exponere periculo. Chang nen hoai linh hon minh di lam vay, non licet sic exponere se periculo æternæ damnationis. Lam hu hoai cua cai, dissipare substantiam aut abuti rebus suis.

Hoan lai, reddere debitum.

Hoan, castrare. Hoan minh di vi D. C. B., castrare se propter regnum cœlorum. Tho hoan, artifex castrandi.

Hoang dam, fornicatio. Lam hoang huy, devastare. Vuon hoang, hortus desertus. Dou hoang, agri inculti.

Hoang, deliquium mentis.

Hoang, *con hoang,* cervus minor.

Hoang, *thoi hoang,* fœtor intolerabilis.

Hoc, studere. Hoc tro, scholasticus. Hoc doi tinh net, incitari indolem. Ke co dao thi ph hoc doi tinh net D.C.J., Christiani debent æmulari charitatem Christi. Hoc truyen lai, referre historiam. Hoc tieng latinh, litteras latinas discere.

Hoc, suffocari, esse fauci hærente.

Hoc, certa mensura.

Hoc, devorare more helluonis.

Hoɪ, odor lactis.

Hoi dau, tendere caput.

Hoɪ, *hep hoi,* vide *hep.*

Hoɪ, interrogare. Hoi han, idem.

Hoi vo, primus contractus matrimonii.

Hoɪ, fœtor agrestis.

Hoɪ, *keo hoi,* publicæ processiones gentilium cum suis idolis.

Hoɪ, *hap hoi,* in agoniâ positus.

Hoɪ, redire. Mot hoi trou, semel. Dau hoi nha, duæ extremitates domûs.

Hoi oi, interjectio miserantis. Su hoi oi, res miserabilis.

Hoɪ, spiritus, habitus. Da gan het hoi, jamjam ferè expirare.

Hoɪ, ultima hora quæ est ferè circa mediam noctem. Ac hoi, lascivire.

Hoɴ, ossa. Sæpiùs dicitur *xuong.*

Hoɴ, arca, capsula.

Hoɴ, vesperè. Vide *chieu.*

Hoɴ, globus. Hon da, lapis. Hon nui, mons. Com hon, oryza conglobata. Hon bang, globus ex morbo congelatus in ventre.

Hoɴ, osculari.

Hoɴ, anima. Dicitur in tres ordines, et sic annamiticè dicitur; Linh hon, anima spiritualis, seu anima humana; 2.ª Giac hon, anima sensitiva, seu anima brutalis; 3.ª Sinh hon, anima vegetativa, seu anima arborum. Sic Christiani; Ethnicorum verò opinio est, unicuique homini inesse tres animas et novem *viea,* quæ vox juxta eorum mentem non potest aliter explicari quam spiritus quidam aut habitus; undè in unius cujusque morte, sæpè sic invocant: Ba hon chin via o dau thi vue; id est, O tres animæ et novem spiritus, ubicumque estis, venite. Et post illam invocationem constringunt sericum album quod vocatur Hon bach, id est anima alba; et realiter animam mortui illic inesse credunt.

Hon, vel *hon hao*, tumultus. Hon don, idem.

Hon, magis, plus, et ponitur semper cum adjectivis positivis ad faciendum illa fieri comparativa; ut, Trao nhung nguoi nam chang co ai trao hon Jùao Baotisita, inter natos mulierum non surrexit major Joanne Baptista. Sic cum verbis collocatur. Toi an hon anh, comedere plus quam tu; ponitur etiam pro adverbiis, sed semper post verbum et adverbium, ut, Juao di mau hon Phero, Joannes ibat citiùs Petro. Mot ngay mot hon, in dies magis ac magis. Ta phai kinh men cha ca mot hon, debemus amare Deum in dies magis ac magis.

Hon, ex odio negare loquelam, vel vitare consortium.

Hop, congregari, concilium facere. Hop hanh, idem. Hop cung nhau lam mot trai, in unum vicum convenire.

Hop, primis labris circiter haurire. Chin le doan cung nen hop mot chut nuoc cho di nuot di, post communionem sacram decet haurire ore modicum aquæ ad deglutiendam hostiam. Mot hop nuoc, haustus aquæ.

Hop mot y, convenire, simul intendere. No chang hop y vuoi toi, non consentit mihi.

Hot lay, grana sparsa manu colligere. Chim kheo hot, avicula suaviter cantat. Noi nhu khuou hot, vanè loqui ad instar cantûs avium.

Hou, lumbi.

Hou, *cay hou*, quædam arbor. Hou, color rubeus.

Hou, *ho hou*, clamosè loqui.

Hu nhau, per clamorem invicem vocare. Tu hu, avis quædam sic vocata ex cantu sic edito.

Hu, vas fictile. Hu ruou, vas vini.

Hua nhau, vide *tao hoa nhau*.

Huc nac, protervus; duræ cervicis.

Huc, *bo huc*, ferit per cornu bos.

Hui, lepra. Thang hui, leprosus.

Huy, destruere, occidere. Pha huy, idem.

Huy, *tieng huy,* vox vitanda. Huyen, ballivatus.

Hum, tigris. Hum tha, tigris aufert.

Hun, fumare. Hun cua nha, fumo malum aërem domo expellere.

Hung, furiosus. *Hung hang* vel *hung bao,* andax, trucu-
lentus.

Hung, *rau hung,* mentum.

Huo chi, vel *huo lo la,* vel *chang lo la,* idem significant:
quanto magis? Ke hien lanh nhau duc bay gio di roi con
kho lam ; huo lo la ke co toi, justi et sancti vix salvabun-
tur; quanto magis peccatores. Sed *chang lo la,* quando
invenitur pro etiam si non ; ut, Chang lo la anh phai noi,
toi da biet roi, etiam si non loquaris, jam scio.

Hup, vide *hop ;* sed *hup,* frequentius est.

Hut, ferè ac *hup ;* sed *hup,* pro rebus liquidis ut aqua, jusculum ; *hut,* attrahendo spiritum ut fumando tabacum
dicitur. Hut thuoc, thuoc hut, tabacum ad fumandum.

Hu, corruptus, perditus. Lam hu, corrumpere, perdere.
Mloi hu tu, verbum otiosum. Su hu khou, nihilum.

Hu, vox negantis, abnuentis.

Hu, vox rusticè respondentis, sicut *ho.*

Hua, promittere. Khan hua thanh trai, oris promissum
evadit in debitum. Khan hua, vovere. Con, da khan hua
su gi eu D. C. B. thi phai giu mloi da khan ay, quod vovisti
Deo, debes illud implere.

Hung, *conh hung,* rex è primâ familiâ, quo regnante Cocixi-
nenses Tunkinum invaserunt.

Hung, excipere aliquid sursùm dimissum. Hung nuoc mua,
excipere aquam pluviæ.

Huong, incensum. *Dot huong* vel *thap huong,* cremare incensum. Nhu huong, thus. Binh huong, thuribulum.
Huong hoa, vigesima pars hæreditatis primogenito assig-
nanda, ad incensum progenitoribus adolendum. Huong
am, communitates unoquoque pago institutæ ad negotia

publica sustinenda. Vao huong am, inscribi albo communitatis.

Huong, situs versùs. Nha lam huong nam, domus sita versùs austrum.

Huong, frui. Huong phuc vo cung, frui felicitate æterná.

Huou, *con kuou*, cervus.

Hua, *ban hua*, amicus.

Huyen, pendens; funis; niger.

Y. I.

Y, intentio, voluntas. Theo thanh y cha ca, conformare se divinæ voluntati.

Ya, cacare. Urbanè dicitur, *di dai tien*.

Ich, utilitas. Vo ich, inutilis, e.

Yem, thorax quo induuntur omnes mulieres annamitæ ut à viris distinguantur.

Yem, *tha phu thuy yem bua*, magi maleficio suo obsignant domos contra dæmonum infestationem.

Yen, pax, tranquillitas.

Yet, *yet than*, sacrificare diis.

Yeu, amare, ad inferiores vel æquales: sed ad Deum vel superiores dicendo, semper dicitur *kinh men* vel *cam men*. D. C. B. yeu ke lanh, justi sunt Deo grati et accepti.

Yeu, debilis, infirmus. Om yeu, vel yeu duoi, idem.

Yeu dieu, delicatus, a, um. Chet non, chet yeu, mors immatura. Est maledictio.

It, parùm, modicum. Mot it chut, idem est.

In, imprimere. Sach in, liber impressus. Ban in, typus. In tri rang, aliquid alicui in animo hærere.

K. Vide C.

Kᴇ, milium. Ke so, conficere catalogum, notare.

Ke no, relinquatur arbitrio suo. Quando est sermo de infimo nomine.

Kᴇ, jungere, succedere. Vo ke hau, sine successione.

Kᴇ, addere ad cumulum.

Kᴇ, nominare, numerare, memorare. Ke cho, vox approbantis vel laudantis. Annumeretur *ke le,* idem. Tieng tu toi dai ke toi, quod supra memoravi.

Kᴇᴄʜ, crassum, magnum. Kech dau ma dai, vesanum caput. Ken, texere raro modo.

Ken ken, vultur.

Kᴇᴛ, conjungere, componere. Ket ngh, ket ban, vide *ban.*

Kᴇᴜ, clamari, conqueri, vocare. Keu reu, idem.

Ke, vel *co ke con mat,* lippitudo oculorum.

Kᴇ, *cay ke,* herba quædam. Danh ke vao, miscere se aleatoribus. Ke nhe, homo ineptus, et importunus.

Kᴇ, æquivalet voci *nguoi,* homo, quicumque. Khiem nhuong thi dep lao D. C. B., humilis placet Deo. Ke dang chi, lineam ducere. Ke, rima.

Kᴇᴍ, *quan kem dau,* custodes frumentorum tempore messis.

Kᴇᴍ, minus, opponitur *hon.* Et est semper adverbium, et potest ad libitum poni antè vel post verbum; ut, Nguoi ay lam kem lam; vel Nguoi kem lam lam, ille minus laborat. Invenitur etiam cum substantivo solo; ut, Nguoi ay kem suc lam, minus valet.

Kᴇᴍ, aditus angustus.

Ken vel *chon,* seligere. Ken hinh, seligere milites. Ken an, delicatus qui debet seligere cibum. Cai ken, nidus bombycis ex quo serica fiunt.

Kᴇɴ, tibia. Thoi ken, canere tibiis. Quan thoi ken, vel ba lenh, tibicines. Ken cua, invidia : rarò usurpatur.

Keo, gluten ex corio factum. Keo lua, secare fruges tortâ falce.

Keo, mel percoctum.

Keo, trahere, extrahere. Keo nhau di, turmatim ire. Cai keo, forfex.

Keo lay, harpagare. Keo neo, harpago. Keo cu, parcus; qui quod jam dedit vult rursùs repetere.

Keo, ne. Con, phai giu minh, keo sa chuoc qui, vigila, fili, ne succumbas tentationi. Keo ma, idem est.

Ket, *nghien rang ket ket,* stridor dentium.

Ket, *chim ket,* coturnix.

Ket, conjungere.

Kep, premere. Treo kep ng ta, suspensio et tortura.

Kep, duplex. Ao kep, vestis duplex. Kep nha tro, consocius mimi. Lam kep, socium esse, adjuvare.

Kha, benè. Cung kha, satis benè, satis multùm. Chang kha, non benè, non decet. Ke khon ngoan chang kha an o lam vay, sapientem non decet taliter vivere.

Khao, diversus, a, um; alius, a, ud. Nguoi khai, alius homo. Chang khac gi, quasi. Con ph don mh xung toi, chang khai gi ke don minh chet vay, debes parare te ad confessionem, qui moriturus ad mortem.

Khao, execrare. Khac, quadrans.

Khaoh, hospes.

Khai, fœtor urinæ.

Khai, appellare regem secundarium.

Kham, examen mercium in teloniis; perlustrare.

Kham, *ngua bat kham,* equus indomitus.

Kham, insculpere; inserere.

Kham, *phai kham,* laqueis irretitus.

Khan, *kho khan,* siccus, a, um. An no kho khan, victus frugalis. Khan co, raucitas. Noi cho den khan co, loqui usque raucitatem.

Khan thu, præses seu custos in uno pago auctoritate publicâ constitutus.

Khan. Vide *kua.*

Khan, sudarium linteum. Kho khan, pauper. Khan khan, firmus in proposito.

Khang kien, prosperitas.

Khanh, campana lapidea.

Khao quan, exercitum magno convivio tractare.

Khao, conferre. Khao sach, conferre librum. Khao hoc tro, scholasticorum profectûs experimentum capere.

Khao ken, laudare.

Khap xuong, junctura ossium.

Khap, *khap moi ng,* omnes omninò homines. Khap moi noi, omnia omninò loca.

Khat, sitire. Khat khao, multum sitire; ardenter desiderare.

Khat, *khe khat,* parcissimus, a, um. Com khe, oryza tosta et ideò gravè olens.

Khe, *van khe* vel *van tu,* chirographum. Qua khe, fructus quidam, carambola.

Kheu, pus ex ulcere educere. Noi kheu ra, verbis provocare. Kheu den, emungere lampadem vel lucernam.

Khe, rivulus.

Khen, laudare. Nguoi khen, laudibus celebrare.

Kheo, machina ex duobus lignis erectis, quibus tanquam pedibus innixi prominentes incedunt; grallæ.

Kheo, peritus, a, um. Kheo hat, peritè cantare. Kheo lam, peritè efficere aliquid. Tho kheo, artifex peritus.

Khep ao, vestem honestè aptare. An mai khep nep, habitus modestus.

Khet, odor gravis ex carne assatâ, aut lampade extinctâ.

Khi, quando, cùm; et sic in oratione collocatur cum particula *thi* vel *thi moi.* Khi D. C. J. xuo phan xet thi moi su ba giai ra het thay thay, quando Christus Dominus judicaturus veniet, omnia patebunt. Khi con sach toi thi moi di nghia cu D. C. B., cùm conscientiam mundam haberis, tùm tandem Deo placebis. Khi nao, idem.

Kℍɪ, aër, humor; semen in corpore. Khi lanh, aëre frigidus. Khi dat xou len, humor ex terrâ erumpens. Khi
huyet da hu, semen et sanguis labefactati. Noi khi ng
ta, verbis alios deterrere.

Kℍɪ, con khi, simia, æ.

Khich nhau, vel *khich vac nhau*, invicem discordes.

Kℍɪᴇɴ, proponere, jubere. Sai khien, mandare, mittere.
D. C. B. chang co khien ta lam nhung su qua suc, Deus
non jubet impossibilia. Toi da khien xung toi; sao le tro
nhieu viec lam, proposui confiteri peccata; sed multis
negotiis impedior.

Khiem nuong, humilis, e. Duc khiem nhuong, humilitas.
Con, phai o khiem nhuong thi moi trou D. C. B. thuong di,
debes esse humilis ut misericordiam à Deo consequaris.
Duc khiem nhuo la nen cac nhan duc khac, humilitas est
fundamentum aliarum virtutum.

Kℍɪᴇɴɢ, portare aliquid grave per duos aut plures homines.

Kℍɪᴇɴɢ, *di khieng chan*, ambulare uno pede contorto.

Kℍɪᴇᴘ, perterritus, a, um.

Khienh de, contemnere. Vide *de*. Ai de duoi bay, thi no
de duoi tao, qui vos spernit, me spernit.

Kℍɪᴛ, de rebus arctè conjunctis.

Kℍᴏ, horreum, granarium; armamentaria. Ke giu kho,
custos horrei armamentariorum, vel cellarius. Kho ca,
coquere pisces multo sale.

Kℍᴏ, difficilis, e; difficulter. Kho lao, molestus, a, um.
Lam kho lao, molestiam inferre. Kho chiu, ægrè ferre.
Kho khan, vide *khan*. Chiu kho, ærumnas perferre. Hay
chiu kho, corpus patiens inediæ, vigiliæ, laborum.

Kℍᴏ, vel *kho khan*, aridus, a, um; siccus, a, um. Bao gio
con thay kho khan nguoi lanh trao lao, thi phai cay trou
keu van than tho cung D. C. B., cùm ariditatem in corde
sentis, debes cum magnâ fiduciâ Dominum invocare.

Kℍᴏ, zona quâ cinguntur omnes annamitæ viri.

34

Kho, instrumentum quo texitur tela. Kho the, fastus superbiæ.

Khoa, *khoa thi*, certamen litterarum quod semel intra quodcumque triennium fit, magno populi concursù.

Khoa lai, obserare. Cai khoa, sera. Chia khoa, clavis.

Khoac ao len vai, vestem ad humerum appendere.

Khoac khoai, ingenuitatis vocibus postulare.

Khoai, tuber.

Khoan khoan, lentè, graviter. Khoan thai, idem. Nguoi khoan dao, homo gravis, modestus. Noi khoan thai vay, loquere graviter et distinctè.

Khoan, decretum publicum in pago ad aliquod malum inhibendum, vel bonum efficiendum. Khoan uoc, idem est. Lap khoan, instituere ejusmodi decretum.

Khoan, *khoan sach*, forma aut mensura libri.

Khoan, *ban khoan*, inquietus ex multis curis, aut magno dolore.

Khoang, *khoe khoang*, vanè ostentare, jactare. Khoe minh deu no, deu kia, ostentare se de hâc, de aliâ re. Cho khoang co, canis maculatus collo.

Khoanh, in coronam flectere.

Khoat dat, liberalis, magnanimus.

Khoe, flere. Khoe loe, idem. Chung toi o noi khoe loe, sumus in lacrymarum valle.

Khoe. Vide *khoang*.

Khoet lo, perforare. Chuot khoet, mus corrodit.

Khoi, fumus. Gian toi nhu khoi, divitiæ meæ comparantur fumo.

Khoi, evadere; liberari; transigere. Est etiam particula à, ex: D. C. J. da chin chet cho ta duoi khoi, Christus passus est mortem ut liberaremur à peccato. Khoi chet, evadere mortem. Di khoi day, ab hinc recedere. D. C. J. sou lai doan, khoi bon muoi ngay thi ng len bloi, Christus postquam ressurrexit, transactis quadraginta diebus, ascendit in cœlum.

Khoi, globus. Khoi bac, sumitur pro talento, quia non est apud illos talentum.

Khoi chung, longum spatium vel temporis vel loci. Bien khoi, mare altum.

Khon, prudens. Khon ngoan, idem. Cho khon, canis sagax; sumitur etiam pro difficile, ut, Khon noi cho het, difficile est recensere omnia.

Khon nan, miserabilis, e; miserè. Khon kho, idem. Ma qui chiu phat khon nan vo cung trao dia nguc, dæmones patiuntur pœnas et miserias æternas in inferno. Lay lua ma thu vang, lay su khon kho ma thu su phuc duc, quemadmodum ignis probat aurum, ita calamitas hominem justum. Su vui suong thi mot giay mot phut: su khon kho thi vo cu vo tan, momentaneum est quod delectat; æternum quod cruciat.

Khop ngua, frænum equi. Xac thit nhu con gua bat kham, phai tra khop moi tri di no, natura corrupta ad instar equi indomiti, opus est fræm ut regatur.

Khou, non. Khou lac, nequaquam. Khou co chang khou, duæ negativæ faciunt affirmationem, non nihil. Khou, est etiam vacuus, a, um. Tau khou, navis vacua. Sinh khou Tu lai hoan, nudus nasci, nudus mori.

Khou phu tu, vel per syncopen, *Khou tu* vel *Ou Khou*, Confucius, natus Sinarum philosophus qui eò usque apud Annamitas et Sinenses in honore sit, ut ab eis pro Deo colatur; maximè à litteratis et litterarum alumnis. Con, co gop tien te Ou Khou chang, debes ne, fili, contribuere pecuniam ad sacrificandum Confucio? Con co phai gop tien Dou mon lam mot vuoi nhung tro khou dao chang, debesne contribuere societati scholasticorum gentilium?

Khua lao, strepitum facere.

Khuat, obtegere, vel obsequi aliquâ re interpositâ. Khuay khuat, oblivisci. Lam khuay lam khuat di, per oblivionem deleri.

Khuc, gyrus anfractus. Ran nam guòn khuc, serpens sese in gyrum componit. Khuc sou, confractus fluminis. Khuc ca, frustum piscis.

Khuya, *dem khuya*, nox alta. Thuc khuya day som, diù vigilare et maturè surgere. Khuya som, serò et manè.

Khuyen bao, cohortari. Khuyen chu, apponere notas litteris.

Khuyet, deesse, deficere. Mat blang ray tron, mai khuyet, luna hodie est integra, cras deficiet. Hanh khuyet, occidere.

Khung, *kinh khung*, magno metu concerti.

Khuynh chan tay, pedes, manus, ex morbo contorti.

Khuon, forma ad faciendum hostias pro sacrificio missæ, aut ad conflanda alia instrumenta. Khuon phcp, forma legum. Phai an o cho co khuon phep, oportet vivere secundùm disciplinam.

Khuo anh, quadratum cui appenduntur imagines.

Khuoc, participare virtutem potentialem. Est vox et imaginatio Gentilium, quâ ducti sic credunt; ita ut carnem tigridis manducando aut alias vanas observantias faciendo, aliquid boni inde sperent, et dicant: *An cho khuoc*, vel *lam cho khuoc*, id est, manducamus vel faciemus ut aliquam virtutem supernaturalem indè participemus.

Khuou, avicula, cujus cantus varius est et valdè delectabilis.

Kin hau, aliqua res est contraria alteri. Kieng ki, abstinere. Kieng thit, abstinere à carne. Kieng su vo chou, abstinere ab actu conjugali.

Ki, committere. Da ki tai ai, cui committere.

Ki, tempus determinatum. Da den ki D. C. B. dinh, venit tempus à Deo constitutum.

Ki, exactè, diligenter. Phai xet minh cho ki, oportet examinare conscientiam diligenter.

Kia, quidam, quædam, quoddam; vel alter, altera, alterum. D. C. J. ph rang: co mot nguoi kia co mot tram con chien, Christus Dominus dixit: quidam homo habebat centum oves. Et solet poni cum voce *nay* vel *no*, ut *nguoi no nguoi kia*, iste, alter. Noi no, noi kia, hinc, illic; hunc, illuc. Chay can noi no noi kia, vagatur huc illuc. Hom kia, nudiustertius.

KIA, *hom kia*, nudius quartus, dies præcedens immediatè nudiumtertium. Kia no, ecce ille.

KICH, *sao kich*, bidens.

Kiem tri, duarum provinciarum curam habere simul.

Kiem an, quærere victum.

Kien cao. Vide *cao.*

KIEN, formica. Chung kien, testes.

KIENG. Vide *ki.*

KIEP, ista vox, juxta locutionem Gentilium nihil aliud significare videtur quam sæculum. Undè, quando dicunt, phai tu cho den chin doi muoi kiep; id est, oportet vitam religiosam ducere usque novem sæcula et decem *kiep,* quod est sæculum aut transmigratio. Et sic *doi doi kiep kiep,* in sæcula sæculorum.

KIET, totus consumi. Kiet luc, totis viribus.

KIET, *dau kiet,* infirmitas quædam.

KIEU, gestatorium; lectica; gestare. Kien minh thanh, processio cum sanctissimo sacramento.

KIEU, excusare se. Toi xin khieu, excusatum me habere digneris.

KIM, acus. Con, camelu di qua tron kim thi de hon ke giau vao cua thien dang, facilius est camelum intrare foramen acûs, quam divitem intrare in regnum Dei.

KIM, *cai kim,* forceps. Nghia sat kim, fides inter maritum et uxorem.

KIN, *kin nuoc,* advehere aquam. Su kin viec kin nhiem, res secreta. Chang co, noi nao, kin nhiem ma che di con mat rat sang D. C. B., nullus est locus ita secretus qui possit Dei intuitum obtegere.

Kinh vel *so,* timere. Doc kinh, recitare preces. Khiep kinh, vide *khiep.*

KINH, venerari.

Kip. Vide *can.*

Kip, advenire in tempore. Den chang kip, non posse advenire intempore. Chet tuoc an nan toi chang kip, mori morte repentinâ absque ulla contritione.

L.

La, *la loi*, clamorem edere.

La, incognitus, a, um. Toi la chang biet, mihi incognitus est. Khach xa la, hospites peregrini et incogniti. Kach la khoan cha, incognitos obligatio non est salutare.

La, folia arborum. La co, vexillum.

La, esse, vel vocari. Ten anh la di gi, nomen tuum quodnam? vel quomodo vocatur? Vide *co.* Cai la, instrumentum ad complanandnm vestem. La ao, complanare vestem illo instrumento.

La, longâ inediâ lassus. Chet la, mori fame.

La, *nuoc la*, aqua naturalis et frigida.

Lao, herba quædam junco similis. Benh lac lao, impetigo.

Lac, errare. Lac dang roi thon, errare à viâ salutis. Lac hoa sinh, pistacium. Phu dao lac, carmina cujusdam litterati Tunkinensis, qui multa præcepta moralia tradidit; quædam identidem citantur in libro cui titulus est: Sach giang dao that.

Lac, *luc lac*, agitare aliquid. Lac dau, abnuere. Do lac, ruberrimus, a, um.

Lac ra, aliquid velatum aperire. Lac man, lac ao, aperire velum, vestem.

Lac lao, nguoi lac lao, immodestus, qui huc illuc stolidè circumspicit.

Lach, alveus flumnis, vel ipsum flumen.

Lah, *len lah vao*, in confertam turbam conari intrare.

Lai, *cay lai*, quædam arbor è cujus fructibus oleum educitur.

LAI, iterum; vel quod repetitâ vice fit, ut D. C. J. chet ban gay lai sou lai, Christus mortuus per tres dies, denuò resurrexit. Den ngay tan the lai xuo phan xet ke lanh ke du, in fine sæculi iterùm veniet judicaturus bonos et malos. Noi di noi lai, eadem verba iterùm iterùmque repetere. Sed quando monetur quis ut repetat suum verbum, quia nondum satis intellectum est, sufficit dicere: Con, noi lai.

LAI, gubernaculum. Cam lai, gubernare. Banh lai, idem. Luoi nhu banh lai, lingua biceps.

LAI, vel *lo lai*, vel *loi lai*, lucrum. Duoc lai, lucrari. Ai di lo lai ca va the gian, ma thon no lo no lo von phai thiet hai, thi nao di ich gi, quid prodest homini, si universum mundum lucretur, animæ vero suæ detrimentum patiatur? Cho no lai, vel Cho no lay lai, dare mutuum cum usurâ.

LAY, agitari vento. Noi lay lo, verbis impetere.

LAY, adorare; salutare. Lay cu, salve, pater. Guoi lay, mittere salutationem; ad æquales vel superiores. Le lay, festa de observatione. Le lay ca, festa de observatione primæ classis. Ngay nhat le lay, dies dominicæ. Sic distinguuntur in calendario.

Lay lay, decerpere fructus.

LAY, contrahere morbum. Tat lay, morbus communicativus; pestis.

LAY, accipere. Chin lay, recipere. Bat lay, capere. Et sic jungitur multis aliis verbis. Lay lam de, lay lam nhe, lay khinh, parvi facere. Lay lam trao, magni ducere. Lay vo, lay chou, nubere, &c.

LAY, revolvere aliquid grave. Con tre biet lay, infans sese revolvit. Lay no, machina in balistis. Lung lay, clamosus aliquis vel famosus ex bene vel male factis.

LAM, *banh cha lam*, genus edulii.

LAM, *gian lam*, injustus minister qui plus exigit quam jus postulat.

Lam, facere vel fieri; et variè accommodatur verbis, ut
Lam viec, operari. Lam toi, servire. Lam vua, esse
rex. Lam vay, hoc modo, sic aliqua exempla. Lam
nguoi phai o co duc, qui vult esse verus homo, debet
habere virtutes. Ngoi hai xuo the lam nguoi, verbum
caro factum est. Ta phai lam toi D. C. B. het lao het suc,
debemus servire Deo toto corde, totis veribus. Con, chang
nen noi lam vay, vuoi dang be tren, non debes sic loqui
ad superiorem. Lam sao, quare. Lam an, operari ad
quærendum victum vel parare comestionem.

Lam, aliquid diù in animo intendere.

Lam, *lam lam; nhieu lam*, multum, nimis, multitudo copiosa.

Lam dau, præsagium. Mat lam dau, malum præsagium.
Tot lam dau, bonum præsagium. Son lam, mons et sylva. Lam loc, bona quæ proveniunt ex montibus.

Lam, vel *lam lap*, luto conspurcari.

Lam, *ca lam*, quidam pisciculus.

Lam, *dun lam*, granarium vel acervi frumentorum.

Lan, *co ma lan ra*, herbæ luxuriantes. Lua lan, ignis serpens; metaphoricè pro familiariter, ut, chang nen o lua lan
cung dan ba con tre qua mle, non licet vivere familiariter
cum mulieribus, et puellis plusquam oportet.

Lan, revolvere aliquid rotundum super planitie terræ.

Lan, mergere se in aquam. Mat bloi lan, sol occidit. Lan
moc khiem an, terrâ marique victum quærere.

Lan, *than lan*, lacerta. Danh lan mh len, ictus verberum
corpori impressi.

Lan vao minh, secretè abscondere aliquid in corpore. Lan
can, vide *can*.

Lan day, palpando funem percurrere. Lan hat, recitare
rosarium.

Lan, *lang ng ta*, decipere. Thua lan ng ta, decipi aliorum
fraude.

Lan lat, paulatim vincere; vel usurpare bona, vel auctoritatem alterius.

Lan, vicis, is. Lan hoi, in dies.

Lan di, clam se subducere.

Lan, vel *lu lan,* errare ex deliquio mentis, vel senectute. Lan lon, idem.

Lang vel *annona,* stipendium militare. Phat lang cho quan, dare stipendium militibus. Minh thanh D. C. J. la luong cuc sang cuc trao moi lhon, corpus Christi est alimentum pretiosissimum nobilissimumque animarum. *Lang y* vel *ou lang,* medicus. *Khoai lang,* vel sola vox *lang,* significat etiam tubercula quæ Lusitanicè *tael.*

Lang vel *tuan lang,* telonium quod tributum à navibus aut cymbis mercatoriis exigit.

Lang, pagus. Lang nuoc, idem est. Lang nuoc bat bo, pagus capit vel punit propter aliquod delictum.

Lang ra, paulatim se subducere. Noi lang di dang khai, sermonem alio divertere.

Lang nhang, nguoi lang nhang, homo futilis. Noi lang nhang, ineptè loqui. O lang nhang, vivere sine lege.

Lang muong, sepulchra regalia. Ve qui lang, mortuus rex defertur ad sepulchrum. Quan thu lang, custos sepulchrorum regalium.

Lang, tranquillus, a, um; silentium. Bien lang, mare tranquillum. O lang, silere. Nin lang, idem.

Lang tai, auscultare.

Lang lo, immodestus, a, um.

Lang, *cai lang,* corbula.

Lanh chai, agilis, strenuus.

Lanh, frigidus, a, um. Nuoc lanh lam, aqua algida.

Lanh nguoi, frigidus, a, um; frigus.

Lao nguoi lanh, cor frigidum et tepidum; à bono opere torpere. Bao gio con nguoi lanh trao lao, thi phai o khiem nhuo ma xin D. C. B. thuong den con, quando es frigido corde, debes humiliter petere a Deo ut tui misereatur. *Nguoi di,* differt à voce *lanh,* quia *nguoi* significat illud quod erat calidum sed postea refrigeratum, ut com *nguoi,* oryza refrigerata. Canh nguoi, jusculum frigeratum. Sed *lanh* significat frigus ipsum, et quod ex se frigidum est.

LANH, ex odio vel metu declinare. Con, phai lanh ke xou net, debes vitare malos.

LANH, bonus, a, um; salubris, e; sanus, a, um. Con, phai lam ban cung ke lanh ma lanh ke du, debes associari bonis et vitare malos. Lanh khi, salubris aër. Tay da lanh, manus jam sana. Cha ea cho con di moi su lanh, Deus det tibi omnia prospera.

Lanh tieng, vel *tieng lanh loi,* vox alta et acuta.

LAO, jaculum. Benh lao, morbus quidam.

LAO, *lon lao,* confusio. Do lon lao, confundere, commiscere.

Lao dao, quan lao dao, nebulones.

LAO, *nuoc lao,* regnum Laos. Quan lao, Laocenses. Thuoc lao, tabacum. Bi lao, cucurbita rubra.

Lao ou, senex. Ba lao, vetula. Tuoi lao, senectus. De animalibus et arboribus semper dicitur *gia.*

LAO, draco. Hom da lao, arca laxata. Dao lao, culter dissolutus; et sic de aliis instrumentis laxatis.

LAO, cor, voluntas, affectus, animus. Sumitur etiam pro actibus virtutum, ut, Lao tin, lao cay, fides, spes. Lao doc, malevolentia. Co lao vuoi nhan, invicem benè affecti. Chia laong va, animus distrahitur.

LAO, laxus, a, um. Chao lao, pulmentum liquidum. Lao leo, idem.

LAP, *noi phet noi lap,* loquax absque veritate.

LAP, *noi lap,* balbutire vocem repetendo. Lap vao, construere instrumenta disjuncta in suum locum.

LAP, instituere collegium, congregationem, &c.

LAP, humo tegere. Chon lap, sepelire. Lap sou, replere flumen terrâ. Lap cua, lap ngo, aditum intercludere. La lap, obliviosus ex hebetudine vel senectute.

LAT, ligamen. Lat mem buoc chat, ligamen molle ligat arctius; id est, mollia verba proficiunt plus quam dura.

Lat, *lat van,* tabulis coöperire.

Lat vel *blat* vel *nhat,* colligere.

Lat, vertere.

Lat, *gao lat,* oryza nondùm pilo purgata.

Lau, *cay lau,* arundo. Chui lau, abstergere pulverem panno.

Lau, diu; quod fit per longum tempus. Dau lau, vide *dau.* Bao lau, quamdiù.

Lau, *benh lau,* morbus qui facit semen distillare.

Le, familia primaria regalis Vua, quæ Tunkinum rexit nomine *Chieu Thou* plusquam 200 annis; cujus rex ultimus anno 1789, persequentibus Cocisinensibus rebellibus, ad Sinarum Imperatorem confugit.

Le, consuetudo inveterata.

Le, funiculi quibus compinguntur libri. *Le luat* vel *luat phet,* lex.

Le, sacrificium. Te le, sacrificare. Lam le, celebrare missam. Cua le, oblatio. Do le, res ad sacrificium pertinentes vel munera.

Le, *le luoi ra,* exerere linguam.

Le, numerus impar.

Le, *vo le* vel *vo mou,* concubina.

Lech, quod non rectè et æqualiter collocatur. Vide *chech.*

Lech, *choi lech,* ulcera.

Len. Vide *lach.*

Len, ascendere. Len chuc, provehi ad dignitates. Conjungitur omnibus verbis quæ significant motum de infra ad supra, ut, Dat len, præponere. Treo len, suspendere. Xem ten, suspicere, &c.

Lenh, mandatum regium; vel rex ipse; imperator.

Leo, *noi mach leo,* qui creditum sibi secretum non servat.

Leo, *lanh leo,* frigidissimus, a, um; frigidè admodùm.

Lep, *lua lep,* granum frumenti vacuum.

Lep, *ca lep,* pisciculi.

Li, pars minima monetæ.

Li, dissenteria.

Ly, *dia ly*, geometria. Thay dia ly, vide *dia*.

Li, *say li ra*, vino immersus. Ngu li ra, somno sepultus.

Lia nhau, separari ab invicem. Linh hon nao lia khoi D. C. B. thi mat moi su lanh, anima separata à Deo, omnia bona amittit.

Lich, calendaria. Lich su, urbanus, a, um. An o lich su, urbanè tractare.

Liec, *liec ngang, liec ngua*, hinc indè obtutum vertere, curiositatis causâ.

Liem, *cou liem*, justus, a, um.

Liem, recondere cadaver loculo.

Liem, lambere, linguere.

Liem, falx minor quâ frugues et herbæ secantur.

Lien, continuè, incessanter, vel *lien*, idem. Thanh nhan lien, felicitas semper. Dau lien lai, cicatrix curata.

Liep, crates magnæ ex arundine contextæ ad regendum portas.

Lieng, *thieng lieng*, spiritualis, e. D. C. B. la tinh thieng lieng, Deus est spiritus. Ke me tinh xac thit chang hien duoc nhuong su thieng lieng, qui deditus est rebus carnalibus, non intelligit spiritualia; animalis homo non percipit ea quæ sunt spiritûs Dei.

Liet, infirmari. Ke liet, infirmus. Ruoc cu lam phuc cho ke liet, accersare ægro confessorem; quærere sacerdotem administrandum sacramenta infirmo. Ke liet kip, infirmus in periculo mortis. Liet giuong liet chieu, ita infirmari ut non possit surgere è lecto.

Lieu, *phu lieu*, primus senatus in regno. Quan phu lieu, senatores vel membra illius senatûs, cujus caput est *chua*, secundus à rege, penès quem summa rerum est.

Lieu, providere. Dinh lieu, ad nutum divinæ Providentiæ.

Lieu, exponere aliquid periculo, vel perdere. Lieu minh, exponere se periculo. D. C. J. da lieu minh chiu chet vi ta, Christus Dominus, exinaniens semetipsum, mortuus est propter nos. Con, cho lieu linh hon di lam vay, noli sic, fili, perdere animam tuam.

Lieu, quædam arbor.

Lim, arbor sylvestris cujus lignum durissimum est.

Linh hon, vide *hon.* Phep linh nghiem, potentia supernaturalis. Uy linh, majestas terribilis.

Linh, miles. Quan linh, idem est. Di linh, adscribi militiæ. Linh xac, miles egenus.

Linh di, idem est ac *an di,* clam se subducere. Linh, petere à mandarino.

Liu lo, lingua barbara.

Lo, sollicitus, a, um. Lo lang, idem est. Lo so, anxius cum timore.

Lo, *cai lo,* urceolus; vasculum. Chang lo la, vel per syncopen *lo la,* etiam si non. Toi da san lao cho chang lo la anh ph xin, paratus sum dare etiam si non petiisses. Ke pham mot toi trao da du ma sa dia ngue chang lo lanh, qui grave peccatum committit, necessariò debet damnari ad infernum, etiam si plura non commisisset.

Lo, fornax, clibanus.

Loc, colare. Loc nuoc lay cai, dicitur de cupidis qui corrodunt. Khon bay, vi bay gan loc cai muoi ra; ma nuot blot con camelu vao, væ vobis, qui colatis culicem, et camelum deglutitis.

Loc, *ca loc,* piscis repens.

Loc, frondes; beneficia. Phuc loc, felicitates. Vo phuc, xau loc, infelix. Ke chiu gian nan khon kho thi co phuc loc, beati qui persecutionem patiuntur; et divites sunt infelices. Quan ay day mat loc, ille marinus mortuus est. Loi loc, vide *loi.*

Loc, *lua loc,* frumenta quæ semel seruntur in terrâ siccâ ad maturitatem.

Lo, revelari. Viec ay do lo ra, negotium illud jam est revelatum. Lam lo ra, revelare. Moi su truoc mat D. C. B., thi bay giai to lo het thay thay, omnia nuda et aperta sunt oculis Dei.

Lo, *an cua thu lo*, vel *an dut*, judex pecuniâ vel munere corruptus.

Lo, foramen; fossa. Giui lo, duc lo, perforare. Dao lo, facere fossam in terra. Coi lo, mortarium pertusum. Lo von, detrimentum facere.

Loa, tuba, Thoi loa, canere tubâ. Cai loa goi ke chet sou lai, tuba quæ clangens revocabit mortuos ad vitam.

Loa lo tran truo, nuditas. Ta thay D. C. J. chiu chet tren cay curut loa lo tran truo thi ta run so, dùm contemplamus Christum crucifixum in cruce nudum, trepidamus.

Loa, caligare præ senectute vel nimio solis splendore. An mac loa lo et, habitus splendidus qui intuentium oculos offuscat.

Loai, *bi loai*, ejectus è numero bonorum.

Loai, genus. Loai vat, animalia. Loai nguoi genus humanum. Chang vao loai nao, nullius valoris.

Loan, tumultus, rebellio. Thi tuy et loan lac, tempus tumultuosum.

Loat, classis.

Loe ra, resplendere.

Loi, *choi loi*, offuscare oculos.

Loi ra, quod præ multitudine aut vi illatâ prominet extrà. Loi mat ra, eruti sunt oculi maledictionis.

Loi, funiculi quibus colligantur monetæ.

Loi, trahere super terrâ. Keo loi di, idem est.

Loi, natare. Loi qua sou, nando flumen transire.

Loi, *dang loi*, via. Loi, idem est ac *loi*.

Loi, delictum; error; errare.

Loi, gingiva. Loi loi, lucrum. Loi khau, facundus, eloquens; satis loquentiæ.

Loi, dicitur etiam pro *le do loi*, numera.

Lom, decrescens. Opponitur *loi*, eminens.

Lon, *cay lon*, animalcula sylvestria.

Lon, *van lon*, expostulare veniam, deprecari.

Lon, porcus.

Lon vel *blon*, magnus, a, um.

Lop, *lua lop*, spicæ siccitate arescunt. An noi lop lap, loquax sine veritate.

Lop nha, domum tegulis aut paleis contegere. Noi lop nguoi ta, quando inferior contradicit sententiæ superioris aut senioris, &c.

Lot, quod rotundum per foramen excidit; dicitur etiam pro abstergere. Lot nuoc mat di, abstergere lachrymas.

Lot, *lot ao*, duplicare intùs vestem.

Lot, extrahere pellem aut vestem.

Lou, pilus; pluma; penna.

Lou, *bien lou*, mare agitatum. Lou, cavea.

Lu, *vo'lu*, genus vasis. Lu lan, vide *lan*.

Lu, ensis.

Lu, turba hominum. Keo di co lu, turmatim ambulare. Nuoc lu, inundatio ex montibus.

Lua, tela ex serico tenuissimo.

Lua, segetes, fruges, frumenta. Lua thoi, idem.

Lua, *go lua*, lignum vetustate exesum.

Luc, *ki luc*, scriba. *Luc* vel *luc lao*, versare ad scrutandum aliquid.

Luc, *luc ay*, illo instante, illo casû.

Lui, vel *lui lai*, retrocedere. Ke da vao dang nhan duc mot lan; thi chang nen lui lai bao gio sot, qui semel ingressus est viam virtutis, non debet regredi unquam.

Lui, *cay lui*, arbor quædam arecæ similis, sed multò illâ minor.

Lui, dimisso corpore et quasi clanculùm incedere. Sumitur etiam pro fugere.

Luy, submittere se. Chin luy, obedire. Su chin luy, obedientia.

Luy, murus, septum. Thanh luy, mœnia. Luy tho, murus ex terrâ constructus.

Luyen thuoc, admiscere mel medicinæ ad conglobandum. Luyen tap, exercere.

Lun, *lun mat bloi, lun trang,* ad occasum solis, lunæ.

Lun, superari.

Lun, decrescere. Nguoi lun, homo brevis staturæ.

Luoc, lixare aliquid. Thit luoc, caro solâ aquâ cocta.

Luon, subductus aliquâ re ambulare; se aliquò insinuare.

Lut, eluvio. Lut doi Ou Noë, diluvium.

Lu, *con lu,* animal leoni simile.

Lu, *ngot lu,* dulcissimus, a, um. Luong lu, anceps, dubius.

Lu, *lu thu,* tristis vultus, taciturnus.

Lu, *nhoc lu,* valdè fatigatus.

Lua, seligere. Lua vao, aptare.

Lua, classis. Cung mot lua vuoi toi, ejusdem classis mecum
vel mihi coæqualis.

Lua, *con lua,* asinus. Lua dao, lua coi, co lua, sagaciter
agere, ac alterius fraudem cavere. Lua vao, intromittere.

Lua, ignis. Thoi lua, sufflare ignem. Danh lua, elicere
ignem è silice. Tat lua, extinguere ignem. Lua giai toi,
ignis purgatorii.

Lue si, fortes in bello. Khi lue, spiritus vegetativus. Lung,
dorsum.

Luoc, *cai luoc,* pecten. May luoc, sertura rara. Noi luoc
di vay, loqui per transennam. Hoi thay giai co luoc,
aquam è pumice postulas.

Luoi, lingua. Guom hai luoi, gladius anceps, homo bilinguis.
Giu luoi, moderari linguam. Le luoi, vide *le.* Luoi dao,
acies cultri. Luoi cau, hamus. Luoi cay, vomer. Luoi
ken, lingula.

Luoi, sagena. Dang luoi, laxare sagenam.

Luoi, *luoi lam, luoi than,* dissolutus, impudens.

Luom tay, duo brachia in unum constringere. Luom lua,
colligere; colligere spicas sparsas in unum. Mot luom
lua, manipulus. So toc, luom tay, resolutis capillis, con-
strictis brachiis. Est signum reverentiæ.

Luom mat, iniqui oculi.

Luon, anguilla. Nguoi luon bun, homo rusticus fallax.

Luon, *sao luon*, fluctus lentè tumescens. Sao luon lai, fluctus sese contra volvens.

Luon, *thuyen luon*, cymba ex uno ligno fabricata. Luon ga, pectus gallinæ.

Luong thuc vel *lang thuc*, vide *lang*.

Luong, cogitare; intellectu comprehendere. Luong chang ra, cogitare, comprehendere non posse. Vo luong vo bien, vide *bien*.

Luot, *lan luot*, vide *lan luot*.

Luot, *gio luot cay*, ventis conquassatæ arbores.

Luu, *phung luu*, otiosus, a, um. Nhan duc o nhung phung luu; ay la nhan duc gia, virtus otiosa est virtus falsa. Luu lai, quod relinquitur ab antecessore. Do luu lai, res ab antecessore datæ.

Luu, *thach luu*, malum granatum.

Lung lay, vide *lay*.

M.

Ma, phantasma. Ma nat, phantasma terret. Thay *ma*, cadaver. Dam ma, funus. Cat ma, efferre cadaver ad sepulchrum. Ma qui, dæmon.

Ma, oryza germinans quæ semper vocatur nomine isto ma; usque dùm, finito plusquam uno mense, evellatur et denuò transplantatur. Ruo ma, ager inq uo ejusmodi oryza primo seritur. Giou ma, instrumenta ad id apta.

Ma, genæ. Ma hou, genæ roseæ.

Ma, autem, verò. Ista particula variè accommodatur, et diversos sensus efficit. Du ma, quamvis, licet, etiamsi. Ou thanh Phero noi rang: Du ma toi phai chet cung thay thi toi cung chang choi, Sanctus Petrus ait: Etiamsi oporteat me mori tecum, non te negabo. Neu ma, quod si. Neu ma con chang doi lao chua that; thi chang di

36

khoi toi, quod si non habeas verum propositum emenda-
tionis, non impetrabis remissionem peccatorum. Ai ma,
qui verò. Ma thoi, solùmmodo. Ke giu dao nen moi di
roi thon ma thoi, soli legis observatores solùmmodo sal-
vabuntur. Cho lam ma co toi, noli facere, ne committas
peccatum. Boi dau ma ve, unde venis? Con, phai xem
guong lanh ma bat chuoc, debes videre bona exempla ad
imitationem. Ma ca, convenire de pretio.

MA, tumulus. Mo ma, idem. Cai ma, vide *cai*.

MA, *ao ma giap*, lorica. Ma la, genus instrumenti musici
ex ære. Phu ma, gener regis. Dot ma, incendere res
papyraceas pro mortuis.

MAC, *ve mac lay hinh*, pingere juxta formam propositam.
Mat mac, larvæ. Cha mac, majores pagi.

MAC, *dao mac*, culter cuspidatus.

MAC, impediri; impingi; adhærere alicui rei. Mac tro
nhieu viec, impediri multis negotiis. Mac cui, disponere
telarium ad texendum. Tau mac da, navis in syrtes acta.

MAC, *mac ao*, induere vestem. Mac lao, mac y con, ad libitum, juxta voluntatem filii. Ma doi bay gio, juxta oppor-
tunitatem temporis. Su loi ay mac anh, delictum illud
imputabitur tibi.

MACH, vena. Mach nuoc, fontes aquæ scaturientes. Xem
mach, vel an mach, tentare pulsum. Moc mach, genus
frumenti. Mach nha, hordeum.

MACH, secretum aliquod revelare ex odio; accusare. Mach
leo, vitium garrulitalis puerorum vel muliercularum. Noi
mach tuc, vel mach dap, proferre verba turpia.

MAI, cras. Ngay mai, dies crastina. Mai som, cras manè.
Som mai, manè. Cai mai, pala ferrea. Mai viet chu,
regula lineata ad scribendum. Hoa mai, ignis priùs funis.

MAI, *cà mai*, quidam pisciculus.

MAI, tectum domus, vel ala tecti. Man mai, velum quo
cooperiuntur tecta ecclesiæ. Mai ga, gallina. Mai cheo,
remus.

Mai, acuere. Mai thuoc, atterere medicinam fricando. Cu mai, genus tuberis. Giui mai kinh sach, acuere ingenium litteris.

Mai mot, unicè intentus alicui operi.

Mai, semper, continuò; continuare.

May ao, sarcire vestem. May ao cho, facere vestem alicui. May toi, fortunatè mihi accidit. Chang ma, infaustè. Gio may, aquilo.

May, genus cancri parvi.

May, machina artificiosè facta. May mieng, os loquax. May tay, manus inquieta.

May, tu, (ad minimos loquendo.) Lou may, supercilium Ran may, ran mat, perfrictæ frontis homo.

May, *mot may,* unum modicum. Chang co mot may, nihil est omninò.

May, nubes; vimen. Dam may, nubes densa.

May, quot. May lan, quoties? May nguoi, quot homines? Con, da bo doc kinh may lan, fili, omisisti recitare preces quot vicibus? Con, da noi hanh tri mat may nguoi, detraxisti, fili, coram quot personis? Chang blon may, non est adeò magnus.

May, pinguis. Lua may, granum plenum. Mih may, corpus.

Mam, pisciculi sale conditi. Mam tri, intendere animum. Mam muoi, gulæ irritamenta.

Mam, abacus. Mam co, abacus eduliis instructus. Bung mam di, auferre abacum. Mam banh xe, abacus rotundus ad instar rotæ. Mam dien tu, abacus quadratus similisque litteræ *dien.* Mam co bon, abacus superpositus basi. Mam che, abacus ad apponendum theum. Mam bun, abacus ad subigendam farinam vel lavandas vestes. Mam ban, abacus et mensa.

Mam, *moi mam,* granum germinans.

Mam, *rau mam mam,* barba recens.

Mam, *tinh da mam chac,* aliquid putatur certò consequendum.

MAN, vel *muon*, decem millia. Man di, barbarus. Man muon, fallax.

MAN, *kink man*, contemnere.

MAN, spatium terræ. Mien man, vicinia.

MAN, peristroma; velum.

MAN, plenè. Man tiec, absolvitur convivium. Man tai, cymba benè onerata.

MAN, salsus, a, um. Man ma nhau lam, multùm invicem diligere.

MAN, *go man con*, gallina quæ multos pullos et sæpissimè parit.

MAN, arbor quædam; primus.

MAN, in provinciâ *Xung he an*, dicitur pro *lam*, facere.

MAN, *nguoi tan man*, homo parvi animi. Me man, æger delirans.

MAN, *can man*, mica ex oryza fracta.

MANG, gestare aliquid collo vel humero appensum. Ke lam su nay thi mang toi vao nih, qui hoc fecerit, peccatum in se admittit. Ran ho mang, serpens venenatus. Mang ca, branchiæ piscis.

MANG, reticulum quo circumdatur theæ capsula vel vas. Dan mang, texere illud reticulum.

MANG, lignum excavatum ad recipiendam aquam è tectis stillantem, vel ad pascenda animalia. Mang co, præsepe.

MANG, idem est ac *mai*. Mang tim danh loi, unicè quærunt famam et divitias.

Mang xang, adeps tenuis. Anh em mang xang, consanguinitas jam a longâ lineâ. Mang den, vide *den*.

MANG, surculi arundinis. Tre gia, mang moi, arundine senescente, crescunt surculi, id est, senibus mortuis, nascuntur pueri.

MANG, vel *mang mo*, increpare acriter. Mang diec, idem est. *Mang tin* vel *mang tieng*, accipere nuntium.

Manh ao, vestis. Manh gie, frustum panni veteris. Chieu manh, matta fracta. Ao manh, vestis lacera.

Manh, fortis; fortiter. Sac manh, vires. An cho manh, audacter comede.

Manh, *noi manh kieo*, dolore loqui. Tim dang manh kheo, quærere viam alios dolo circumveniendi.

Manh manh, velum rarum ex arundine textum. Thuyen manh, onerarius.

Manh, fragmentum vasorum. Manh bat, fragmentum scutellæ. Mao manh, subtilis, gracilis.

Mao, *mao ngua*, jubæ equorum. Mu lou mao, galerus militaris pilis rubri coloris coöpertus.

Mao xung, falsè confiteri aliquid; fallere; mentiri.

Mao, *meu mao*, motus oris plorantis.

Mao, operimentum mulierum funus comitantium. Mao ga, crista galli. Chim chuc mao, vel Chao mao, avicula quædam cristam habens.

Mao, *trou mao* vel *mao moi*, ardenter expectare. Linh hon noi lua giai toi, trou mao ke o the gian cau nguyen cho minh, animæ in purgatorio ardenter expectant ut homines in mundo orent pro se. Mao linh thi, mox moriturus. Mao lam viec no viec kia, proposui facere hoc illud.

Mao ruou, succus oryzæ fermentatæ ad coquendum vinum. Chin mao, fructus valdè maturus.

Mao, unguis; ungula. Mai mao, instrumentum ad fodiendam terram.

Mao, *choc mao*, diu noctuque vehementer expectare.

Muo manh, vide *manh*.

Map, *con tre map vu*, infans labiis suis versat ubera.

Map, canis marinus. Map tap, canis marinus rapiat. Maledictio est.

Mat cua, fragmenta minutissima quæ ex ligno excidunt, dùm serrâ secatur. Nguoi mat doi, homo infelicissimus.

Mat, amœnus, a, um; refrigerans. Mat me, idem est. Bo mat, vermiculi in gallinis.

Mat, carus, a, um; carè. Con mat, oculus. Mat ca, talus. Mat mo, (Deest explicatio in MS.)

Mᴀᴛ, facies, vultus. Truoc mat, coràm. Ph nho co D. C. B, o tri mat lien, recordare semper præsentiæ Dei. Biet mat, noscere ex facie. Ra mat, apparere. Vang mat, abesse; absentia. Chang nen lay cua ng ta khi vang mat no, non licet accipere rem alienam in ejus domini absentia. Ph* chao mat, affici vertigine capitis. Dou mat ng* ta, in multorum præsentia. Sumitur etiam pro parte anteriore cujuscumque rei, ut, Mat dat, superficies terræ. Mat chien, pars superior mattæ. Mat ruo, ager. Dau mat, nodus arborum.

Mᴀᴛ, amittere, perdere. Danh mat, vel lam mat, idem. Mat ruo, perdere operam. Mat via, stupefieri. Mat lao, offendere. Da mat, jam mortuus est.

Mᴀᴛ, mel. Tot thi vang son, ngon thi mat mo, pulchritudinem aurum et minium, saporem dant mel et butyrum. Fel etiam dicitur *mat*, vel *trai mat*.

Mᴀᴜ, festinanter; age; agedum. Di mau, festinare. Luoi mau, rete densum. Luoc mau, pecten densus.

Mᴀᴜ, sanguis. Con hoi mau mu, adhùc consanguineus à longâ lineâ.

Mau vel *mui*, color. Lay mau lai, denuò tingitur. Mau nhiem, mysterium. Su mau nhiem, res ineffabilis. Trao dao co nh* su mau nhiem tri ta tuy chang den, in fide sunt multa mysteria intellectum nostrum superantia.

Mau ni phat, nomen idoli.

Mᴀᴜ, vox sinico-anamitica pro *me*, mater. Octo sunt apud anamitas ordines matrum quæ dicuntur *bat mau:* 1.ᵃ Tu mau me sinh de, genitrix. 2.ᵃ Ke mau, me ghe, noverca. 3.ᵃ Dich mau, em me, da nuoi ngay sau, matertera quæ sororis filium nutrit. 4.ᵃ Duong mau, me nuoi, mater alimenta præbens. 5.ᵃ Ga mau, me da lay chou khac ma con nuoi con, mater quæ secundo viro nupsit, et filium adhùc nutrit. 6.ᵃ Thu mau vo man cha, concubina patris.

* Hæ sunt abbrevationes quæ frequenter occurrunt in MS.

7.ª Xuat mau, me con nuoi con khi chou da bo ra, mater quæ parvum nutrit, à viro dismissa. 8.ª Nhu mau, me cho bu, nutrix. Duc thai mau, mater regis.

Mɛ, deditus alicui vitio. Me an uo, deditus gulæ. Me su blai gai, deditus vitio carnali. Me muoi, ignarus. Tinh me xac thit, concupiscentia carnalis vel natura corrupta. Boi tinh me xac thit thi sinh ra cai toi khac, ex naturâ corruptâ nascuntur omnia alia peccata. Me an ngu, deditus ventri atque somno.

Mɛ, ventriculus.

Mɛ, vasa aliqua parvâ parte fracta. Mat me, vide *mat.*

Mech lao, leviter aliquem offendere.

Mem moi, suaviter. An noi mem mai, loqui suaviter.

Mɛɴ, diligere Deum vel superiores. Men dang nhan duc, diligere virtutes.

Mɛɴ, *ao men,* vestis brumalis.

Mɛɴ, fermentum.

Mɛɴ, incedere per angustum locum.

Mɛɴ, genus campanulæ.

Mɛɴʜ, *mou menh;* nuoc lut mou menh, aqua innundans omnia coöperit.

Menh he, fatum; divina ordinatio de unoquoque homine inevitabilis.

Mɛo, *gio meo,* hora circiter octava ante meridiem.

Mɛo, contortus; non ex omni parte rotundus. Khi gio meo mieng, maligna aura quæ hominem corripit ex improviso et os contorquet.

Mɛo, felis.

Mɛᴘ, vox jubentis elephanti ut sese incurvet.

Mɛᴘ, prima tabella. Mep giay, margo papyri. Moi mep, labia; os.

Mɛᴛ, *mo met,* somniare.

Mɛᴛ, fatigatus valdè; lassus, a, um. Met nhau, amore inviceta lassi. Nhoc met, idem.

Mɛᴛ, *met dao,* fricare leviter cultrum.

Met, vannus.

Mi, tu, in provinciâ *Xung he* ad inferiores.

Mi, *lou mi mat*, palpebræ.

Mi, *hoa mi*, speciosus, a, um. Mi vi, sapidissimus, a, um.

Mia, canna dulcis.

Mia mai, an noi mia mai, egregiè exaggerare. Gia mia, bonis verbis demulcere.

Mien, *Cao Mien*, Cambodia. Quan cao mien, Cambodienses.

Mien, consarcire aliquid.

Mien, vicinia. Mien nay, vicinia hæc. Mien ay, vicinia illa.

Mieng cai, appellare regem, mandarinos.

Mieng, os; orificium. Mieng noi, orificium vel os ollæ. Chiu mieng, fidejussor. Ha mieng, os hians. Ngam mieng, claudere os. Kheo mieng, os eloquens.

Mieng, buccella. Mat mieng, amittere loquelam, vocem; loquelam alicui deficere.

Miet, genus calceorum.

Miet, instrumento aliquid obliniendo complanare.

Mieu, domus spiritui tutelari dicata.

Mim moi, claudere labia.

Min, ego. (Vox superbi.)

Min, *quan min*, nebulones.

Min cuoi, subsidere.

Min, argilla. Dat min, terra argillosa.

Minh, clarus, a, um. Dai minh, ultima imperatorum sinentium familia, sic dicta; aquâ etiam idem nomen accepit totum Sinarum Imperium. Nunc verò regnat Tartara familia, cujus quartus imperator nomine *Can Lao*, actualiter præsidet, mutato vocabulo *dai minh* magna claritas, in *dai tanh*, magna seremtas.

Minh, corpus. Mot minh, solus, a, um. *Minh* est adjectivum suus, a, um. Con, muon di dang nhan duc cho bien, thi tri het ph ham nih con cung bat no theo y D. C. B. dung theo y xac thit, vis perfectus esse in viâ virtutum, antè omnia debes mortificare corpus tuum, et cogere illud sequi divinam voluntatem, non naturam corruptam. Chang nen cai y Be tren, ma theo y rieng minh, bao gio sot, nunquam licet spretâ voluntate superioris, sequi proprium suum libitum. Phai yeu ng ta nhu bang minh vay, oportet amare proximum sicut se ipsum.

Minh tinh, domus papyracea inqua inscribitur nomen defuncti.

Mɪᴛ, *mu mit,* obscurissimus, a, um.

Mɪᴛ, *cay mit,* arbor quam Lusitani *jacam* vocant.

Mɪᴀ, *mia mio,* errare. Tinh xac thit yeu daoi hay mla mlo, caro fragilis, defectis obnoxia.

Mʟᴇ, ratio. Chang co mle nao, nulla est ratio. Ph mle, consonum rationi. Vi bang con chang muon chua toi thi chang co mle nao cho con duoc roi thon dau, nisi emendaveris vitam tuam, nulla ratione salutem consequeris tuam. Ta o khien nhuong thi ph mle moi dang vi ta la ke co toi, est conforme rationi omninò ut humiliemur, quia peccatores sumus.

Mʟᴏɪ, verbum; sermo. Mloi noi ph hop vuoi viec lam, verba debent consonare actioni. Vang mloi, obedire. Su vang mloi chiu luy th dep lao cha ca hon cua le, obedientia plus placet Deo, quam sacrificium. Toi xin cuop mloi, nguoi, bonâ tuâ veniâ loquar, domine.

Mᴏ, cortex quo arbores arecarum coöperiuntur; et quo leviter extenuato utuntur ad res quaslibet papyri loco involvendas. Chet bo mo, bo chieu, morere, infelicissime. Maledictio.

Mᴏ, leviter contrectare. Co y trai ma so mo ng ta thi co toi, ex malâ intentione alios contrectare, peccatum est.

Mᴏ, contrectando quærere aliquid in aquis latens. Noi mo, loqui per conjecturam.

Mᴏ, rostrum avium. Tre mo, pueri et puellæ. Mat mo, vide *mang mo.* Mo neo, anchora. Mo ac, vide *ac.* Mo rang, mo bac, folia auri et argenti.

37

Mo, crepitaculum ex ligno, quo vocantur ad negotia publica.
Go mo, pulsatur signum. Rao mo, publicare. Danh mo
chang bang go thot, citiùs vocantur sonitu mensæ quam
crepitaculi.

Mo, cumulus terræ elevatus ut defendat aliquid à diluvio.
In Xung he, di mo, quò ire.

Mo, desiderare. Ai mo, amare cum veneratione.

Mo ma, sepulchrum. Tin dia li cat mo cat ma, ex vanâ
observantiâ transferre ossa mortuorum in varia sepulchra.
Thay dia ly lay ngoi ma, nefarii Tunkinenses geographi
quærunt terram ad sepulchrum.

Mo, extentare. Chem mo do di, sermo gentilium, id est,
mala abeant. Ga mo, gallus suo rostro pulsat.

Mo, quispiam. Ten la mo, nomen est. Lo mo, sine ordine,
indiscretè.

Mo, somniando loqui. Noi mo noi mo, loqui per somnium
vel quasi somnians.

Mo, uxor avunculi mei; respectu *mei* debeo vocare *mo*.

Mo, pugillus; vel numerus decem millia.

Mo, *mo mo*, subobscurus, a, um.

Mo, aperire, explicare. Mo dao, propagare religionem.
Mo cua ra, aperire januam.

Mo, butyrum; adeps, pinguedo.

Moc, germinare. Mat bloi moc, sol oritur.

Moc, extrahere. Moc rach ra, lacerare. Cay moc, arbor
cujus funiculis ligantur galeri, vel fiunt funes anchoræ.

Moc, mucus; mucidus, a, um. Moc ra, mucescere. Banh
da moc, thi chang nen dung ma lam le, hostiâ mucidâ
non licet uti in sacrificio.

Moc, spiritus malignus quem gentiles credunt venire ex lignis, quia *moc*, linguâ Sinicâ, significat lignum. Moc ui,
tabella superstitiosa. Moc, clypeus.

Mot, pisciculi minutissimi in mari.

Moi, omnis, e. Moi nguoi moi co, omnibus, singulis diebus
est. Moi ng moi phai giu minh cho khoi chuoc ma qui,

quisque debet cavere se ab insidiis diaboli. Ro moi, inurbanus.

Moi, piscis quidam.

Moi, ex labore fatigatus. Moi met, idem.

Moi, labium. Cai mói, cochleare culinarium. Con moi, explorator; vel statua venefica ex paleâ.

Moi, tinea. Lam moi manh, viam aperire vel auxilium præbere alicui ad aliquid faciendum. Chang nen lam moi manh che ke lay vo mon, non licet auxilium præbere concubinariis. Gieng moi, basis aut fundamentum alicujus rei. D. J. papa cam giuong moi th Ighsa, sanctus pontifex tenet gubernaculum totius ecclesiæ. Bay moi toi dau, septem articuli peccatorum capitalium. Moi chi, capita filorum.

Moi, *doi moi*, testudo magna ex cujus pelle seu cortice, pulchrè elaboratâ, multa fiunt instrumenta; sicut *huoc doi moi*, pecten illâ testudine factus. Moi cau, esca in hamo, illicium. Ao moi, vestis splendidior. Moi lua, palea ad accipiendum ignem. Moi nhui, fomes.

Moi mot, unusquisque, unaquaque, unumquodque. Moi mot nguoi co mot linh hon ma thoi, unicuique inest unica anima.

Moi, novus, a, um; recenter; tandem. Sam truyen moi, testamentum novum. Con co an nan toi that moi duoc khoi toi, per solam contritionem veram remittuntur tibi peccata. Moi lam, recenter incipere facere.

Moi, invitare. D. C. B. moi ng ta vao nuoc thien dang: sao le co it nguoi nghe, Deus invitat omnes ad regnum cœlorum; sed pauci audiunt ejus verba. Moi ou ba ou vai moi gio moi chap, invitare progenitores mortuos ad convivia parentalia. Moi thay phu thuy chua chung, vocare magos ut per sua veneficia sanent.

Mom mem, edentulus.

Mom, os animalium. Mom cho, os canis.

Mom, cibum præmansum infanti instillare. Ba nam bu mom

muoi thang cuu mang, Tribus annis nutrire et lactare;
et decem mensibus gestare in utero infantem. Sic prædi-
catur labor matrum.

Moɴ, parvus, a, um. Hen mon, abjectus, a, um. Toi mon,
peccatum leve. Vo mon, concubina.

Moɴ, pars separata ab alterâ. Phai chia ra tung mon,
oportet segregatim ponere partem separatam ab alterâ.

Moɴ, quod atteritur vetustate. Moi su cang lau thi cang
mon nat; sao le net xau thi cang lau thi cang vung cang
ben, omnia atteruntur vetustate, sed vitia vetustate fir-
mantur.

Moɴ, janua. Dou mon, condiscipuli. Nha mon, ministri
justitiæ. Pha mon, veneficus. Thien mon dou, radix
quædam medicinalis.

Moɴ, demulcere animalia.

Moɴ, mon nuoc, vestigium aquæ.

Moᴛ, mot ya, mot dai, urget necessitas corporalis. An may
an mot, mendicare, vel colligere spicas post messem.

Moᴛ, vermiculi qui ligna corrodunt.

Moᴛ, unus, a, um; solus, a, um. Co mot D. C. B. ma thoi,
est unus Deus solùmmodo. An mot minh mot mam,
manducare solus in unâ mensâ. Lam mot, unà, simul.
Ke chiu minh thanh D. C. J. cho nen, thi di hop lam mot,
qui ritè communicat, efficitur unus cum Christo. Di lam
mot, simul ire.

Moᴛ, unus, a, um; ut, Hai muoi mot, viginti unus.

Mou, mou tron, nates.

Mou, germen. Moc mou, germinare. Mou mat, glaucoma,
tis.

Mou, mou tren bloi, signum in cœlo. Mou tre, arundo pul-
lulans. Chet cut mou, mori sine filio.

Mou, sic vocantur apud Anamitas omnes dies mensis lunarii.
1.° Usque diem decimum inclusivè; qui dies decimus vocatur mou muoi; et tunc incipit nominari dies undecimus,
ngay mou mot, usque diem decimum quintum; qui semper

vocatur *ram* vel *ngay ram.* Post illum dies decimus sextus iterum vocatur ordinario numero *ngay muoi sau,* usque diem trigesimum, qui dicitur anamiticè *ngay ba muoi,* si mensis habet triginta dies; et mensis triginta dierum vocatur *thang no.* Si mensis habeat viginti novem dies, ultimas erit vigesimus nonus *ngay hai chin;* et mensis vocatur *thang thien,* mensis defectuosus.

Mυ, conchilium, tegumen. Mu ba ba, tegumen testudinis.

Mυ, mulier. Dom ba mu, sacrificare deæ partûs. Ba mu, apud sorores religiosas, vocatur superiorissa.

Mυ, *cai lu mu,* species sinapis.

Mυ, obscurus, a, um; obscurari. Mu bloi, cœlum obnubilatum.

Mυ, pileus, biretum. Mu trieu thien, corona. Doi mu, gestare biretum. Cat mu, tollere biretum ex capite.

Mυ, pus.

Mυᴀ, emere. Mua lao ng ta, captare benevolentiam hominum.

Mυᴀ, saltare, gesticulare; choreas ducere.

Mυᴀ, quatuor anni tempora. Mua gat, messis. Nua mua, medio in tempore quo opus agitur. Giu dao nua mua lai bo, mediâ in vitâ fidem abjurare. Cho gi bay biet duoc ray la mua vieng bay, utinam cognosceretis tempus visitationis vestræ. Ruo mua, ager qui fructificat mense decimo; etiam vocatur *gao mua; com mua.* Que mua, rusticus. Mua lang, pecuniâ se eximere vel redimere ab operibus pagi superstitiosis.

Mυᴄ, aliquid liquidum cochleari exhaurire. Muc nuoc, haurire aquam.

Muc luc, index. Muc kinh, perspicillum. Muc ban, edictum scriptum in tabulâ. Muc dou, bubulcus. Go muc, lignum putrefactum.

Mυɪ, tectum cymbarum aut navicularum.

Mui vel *mun,* reliquiæ mensæ. Co mui, mensa instructa ex reliquiis.

Mui, particulæ quas in se continent fructus.

Mui, color; odor; sapor. Mui do, color rubeus. Mui thom, odor suaveolens. Mui thoi, odor graveolens. Mui ngon ngot, odor sapidus, dulcis. Rau mui, coriandrum. Chang co mui gi, nullius valoris est.

Mui mun muc, lignum putrefactum.

Mui, nasus, vel mucus e naribus stillans. Lo mui, nares. Di mui, nasus simus. Hi mui, emungere nares. So mui, solvitur mucus. Ngat muoi, naris rheumate obdurata. Mui dao, aciem acuere cultri.

Mun, *go mun*, ebenum.

Mun, frustulum, mica, modicum quid. Mun mat, verruncula in facie.

Mung, gaudium.

Muoi noi, fuligo ollæ adhærens. Me muoi, ignarus, a, um.

Muoi, sal; salire. Ca chang an muoi thi ra thoi, piscis sine sale putrescit; sic et homo sine correctione. Muoi, culex.

Muon, decem millia.

Muon, tardè, serò. Muon tuyet, tarda tempestas.

Muon, velle; cupere.

Mut, surgere; exsurgere.

Mut cai vel *vou cai*, surculus sinapis.

Mua, pluvia. D. C. B. lam mua xuo cho ke lanh va ke du cung bang nhau, Deus pluit super justos et injustos æqualiter. *Mua phun* vel *mua hi*, pluvia tenuissima instar pulveris.

Mua, vomere. Lom mua, provocatur stomachus ad vomitum.

Mua he, noli. Rarissimè est in usu.

Muc, atramentum. Mai muc, diluere atramentum. Ca muc, piscis marinus, qui aliquid modicum atri in suo corpore habet. Muc tau, amussis. Go vay chang ua muc tau, prava indoles odit correctionem.

Muoi, decem. Sed ad viginti usque nonaginta dicitur *hai muoi, ba muoi, &c.*

Muom, *cai muom*, cochlear. Moc muom, arbor quædam, Lusitanicè *manga*.

Muon, commodato accipere vel mutuari. Cho vay muon, commodare vel mutuo dare. Thue muon, conducere operarios.

Muon, conducere operarios. Lam thue, lam muon, operam locare. Ke lam thue, operarius.

Muo, catulus. Muo chim, animalia et volatilia. Cam thu, quadrupedes et aves.

Muo, *rau muo*, herba quædam.

Muong, *Quan muong*, homines montani quorum lingua ad Siamicam linguam accedit.

Muong sanh, testa.

Muop, species cucurbitæ.

Muot, madefieri sudore.

Muo, *cay muo*, papaver.

N.

Na, *cay na*, arbor Lusitanicè *atta*. Net na, indoles. Co net na, bonam habere indolem. Kho net kho na, austerus, rigidus.

Na, *trau na*, bubala catulos habens. Con na, ca nuoc, filius matrem, piscis aquam quærit.

Na, sæpiùs. Na, balista.

Nac, *ca nac*, pisciculus quidam.

Nac, *thi nac*, caro sine pinguedine. Nac in provinciâ Xung he, dicitur aqua.

Nach, axilla.

Nac no, singultire.

Nai, *con nai*, cervus major.

Nai, pannus ex serico rudi.

Nai, flagitare. Cao nai, acriter accusare. Nhi nai, appellare ad superiorem judicem. Chang nai, vel chang ne kho nhoc, non recusare laborem.

Nai chuoi, pars rami ficûs Indicæ. Tre nai, valdè piger.

NAY, *ngay hom nay*, hodiè. Dem nay, hâc nocte. Xua nay, ab initio usque nunc. Man nay, hoc anno.

NAY, *ay nay trao lao*, sollicitus, a, um.

NAY, hic, hæc, hoc; et semper debet postponi substantivo, ut *ou nay*, iste dominus. Viec nay, negotium hoc. Si præcedit substantivam, fit particula ecce, en; ut D. C. J. phan rang; nay tao, quan Judeu lien nga ra het, Jesus respondens ait: ecce Ego sum, abierunt Judei retrorsùm. Nay lay nguoi ay, ecce homo.

NAY, cadere; excidere. Nay muc tau, imprimere amussim ligno. Nay muc cam can, dicitur de judicibus, qui debent omnia ad trutinam et amussim examinare.

NAY, *khi nay*, modo antè, vel paulò antè. Su chung bay da tha khi nay, thi cho noi cu ai cho den khi tao sou lai, visionem quam vidistis modò, nemini dixeritis, donec à mortuis resurgam.

Ney lon, abdomen porci.

NAY, *ai nay*, quispiam vel ipse, ipsa, ipsum. Ai giu dao nen; di roi linh hon nay, quis perfectè fidem custodierit, consequetur ipse salutem suam. Ai co, nay an, qui habet victum, ipse edat.

Nay bun, locus plenus luto.

NAM, vir. Nam nu, vir et mulier. Anh em bon dao nam nu thay thay, O Christiani fratres et sorores omnes. Phuong nam, vel ben nam, plaga australis. Gio nam, auster. Ki nam, columbarum lignum. An nam, vide *an*.

NAM, annus. Nam nay, iste annus. Nam ngoai, anno præterito. Nam kia, annus plusquam perfectus. Nam truoc, anni præteriti. Sang nam, annus futurus. May nam, quot anni. Sed annus ætatis in homine dicitur *tuoi;* undè si rogetur quis, quot annos ætatis seu vitæ suæ haberet, dicendum est: *co may tuoi*. Postremò *nam* est etiam numerus quinque. Sic quinque anni dicitur *nam nam;* sed quindecim dicitur *muoi lam;* et à viginti usque ad nonaginta, quinque dicitur *lam*, ut *muoi lam*, quindecim; *hai muoi lam*, viginti quinque, &c.

Nam tay lai, contrahere digitos in pugnum. Mot nam, unus pugillus. Nam lay, capere aliquid pressis digitis.

Nam, jacere, cubare. Nam nghieng, jacere super latera. Nam ngua, jacere supinus. Nam sap, jacere pronus. Nam sai tay ra, decumbere extensis brachiis.

Nam, fungus, i.

Nam ruou, vas testaceum ad continendum vinum.

Nan, virgula elaborata ad texendum.

Nan, infortunium, calamitas. Khon nan, miserabilis; miseria. Chin nan, pati miserias. Anh chiu nan, imago crucifixi. Cuc nan, extrema miseria. Nan nou nan, procax.

Nan, meticulosus, a, um.

Nan, herba cujus radix amarissima est. An nan toi, pœnitere de peccato. An nan chang kip, sera pœnitentia.

Nan, premendo exprimere. Bop nan kiem an nguoi ta, dicitur de iis qui pauperum sanguinem sugunt.

Nan, digitis contrectando et palpando ad scrutandum quid intùs lateat. Nang nan, vel Nang no, sedulus, diligens.

Nang, *ha nang*, morbus qui virile membrum relaxat.

Nang, furca.

Nang, fœmina. Nang hau, ancilla vel concubina mandarinorum.

Nang, sæpè. Sieng nang, sedulus. Ta phai lam toi D. C. B. cho tieng nang, debemus esse diligentes in servitio Dei.

Nang, gravis, e. Toi nang, peccatum grave. Nang ne, idem. Lam nang lao ng* ta, esse gravis aliis. Quo mloi nang, reprehendere gravibus verbis. Nang tai, graves aures; surdus, a, um. Dao nang tay, metiri; mensura copiosa.

Nang, splendor solis. Nang boi, æstus solis.

Nanh, dentes animalium. Ke nanh vuot trao lang, qui est robustus in pago.

* Abbreviatio pro *nguoi*.

38

NANH. *ti nanh nhan*, ex pigritiâ laborem et difficultatem à se rejicere, et in alios derivare conari.

NANH, *dau nanh*, species fascoli vel ciceris.

NAO. *ph nao chang*, quid impedit. Ne chang ph nao, nihil refert, vel nihil impedit.

NAO, quis, quae, quod. Vide *ai*. Muon lam the nao, thi lam the ay, quoquo modo velit, sic facit. Nao ai lam di gi cho may, quid tibi fecit? Nao cu o dau, ubi est pater?

Nuc nuc, inquietus ex desiderio videndi aliquid.

Nao dua, ungulis dolare fructus.

NAO, *sau nao*, valdè afflictus. Nao ruot, exhauriuntur viscera.

NAO, vannus ad siccandum aliquid.

NAO, calidus, a, um. Nao ret, calor et frigus, id est febris. Nao nay, idem.

NAO, ellychnium in candelis. Nao noc, pisciculus quidam cujus jecur est valdè venenatum. Khan nao noc, sudarium multis coloribus distinctum.

NAP, operculum. Nap hom, arcæ operculum.

Nap sung, infundere fistulæ pulverem tormentarium; (charger un fusil.)

NAP, gladius minor.

NAP, latebra. Nap nom, è latebris videre.

NAP, *den nam nap mai*, sine cessatione venire.

NAT, terrere. Tan cho nat, comminuere; in pulverem redactus vel putrefactus. Dot nat, illiteratus.

NAT, incutere metum, vel simulare iram.

NAU, manere in secreto per aliquod tempus propter metum, vel ad insidiandum.

NAU, vel *bo nau*, quidam fructus sylvestris instar tuberis, cujus liquore tinguntur vestes, retia, sagenæ.

NAU, *ao nau*, vestis ex lanâ à Rege custodibus suis data.

NAU, coquere. Nau muong ng ta, valde molestus et gravis aliis esse.

Nau ra, dicitur de fructibus putrefactis.

N**ɛ**, *thuyen ne*, elevare cymbam, suppositis lignis.

Ne vel *le*, revereri ne sit alteri molestus.

N**ɛ**, *ne voi*, oblinire calce. Tho ne, cœmentarius. Chang ne, non recusare, non dedignari. D. C. J. xuo the gian chang ne chiu tram nghan su khon kho vi ta, Christus descendit in mundum, non dedignatus ferre tot mala pro nobis. Xin nguoi cho ne, ne recuses, rogo.

N**ɛ**, respectum hominis habere, personam respectare vel acceptare. Vi ne, vel ne nang, idem. Ch nen vi ne nguoi ta ma pham toi mat lao duc chua bloi, non licet ex reverentiâ hominis peccare contra Deum. Ne lao nguoi ta, revereri ne sit alteri molestum. To ne, progenitores.

Ne ga vao chuo, reducere gallinas in gallinarium.

N**ɛ**, *ne nhau*, metuunt invicem.

Ne ra, rimas agere. Ne bung, talitrum impingere.

N**ɛм**, *nem xem*, præustare cibum ad experimentum.

N**ɛм**, cuneus. Nem, protrimenta.

N**ɛм**, jacere. Nem da, lapidare.

N**ɛɴ**, licet, expedit. Nen viec, aptus ad negotia gerenda. Con nen viec, adhùc est utilis. Nen muoi tuoi, agit annum decimum. Cai nay nen bao nhieu tien, vel gio bao nhien tien, istud quanti constat? Nen cai, nen hoa, furunculis, variolis laborari. Dung nen, creare.

N**ɛɴ**, crebro ictu humum pulsare ad eam complanandam.

N**ɛɴ**, *cay nen*, candela. Duc nen, conflare candelas. Thap nen, accendere candelas. Tat nen, extinguere candelam. Chan nen, candelabrum.

N**ɛɴ**, fundamentum. *Xay nen* vel *dap nen*, jacere fundamentum.

N**ɛɴ**, decem taëlia. Nen vang, nen bac, mensura decem taelibus auri vel argenti constans. De nen, comprimere.

N**ɛo**, anchora. Bo neo, jacere anchoram. Gieo neo, jacere anchoram, vel esse in periculo.

N**ɛo**, contorquere prelo; tortura.

N**ɛo**, ferè idem est ac *nai*, flagitare.

Neo, semita. Dang neo, via.

Nep, *gao nep*, oryza viscosa. Nep ao, plicatura vestis.
Mu mat nep, pileus sine plicaturâ id est homo sine lege
vivens.

Nep, contracto corpore sese occultare.

Nep giau, asserculi quibus firmatur septum.

Net, vel *net na*, vide *na*.

Net chu, ductus calami; apex litteræ. Chang li mot net,
apex non præteribit. Bat net, reprehendere.

Net, *bo net*, vermis venenatus.

Neu, pertica, hasta. Len neu, attollere aliquid hastâ, signum erigere.

Neu, *neu ma*, si, quod si. Neu co lam, thi hay lam, si ita
res se habet, optimè est.

Nga, *sao nga*, otiari nihil faciendo.

Nga, contemptus cibi. An no nen nga, saturatus fastidit
cibum.

Nga, ebur.

Nga ba dang, trivium. Nga tu, quadrivium. Nga ba sou,
trivium fluminis. Nga xuo, cadere. Nga nuoc, labi in
morbum ex insalubri aquâ. Nga lao, despondere animum.

Nga ra, reclinare vel explicare aliquid in terram. Nga
trau bo, occidere animalia.

Ngac, *ngo ngac*, stolidus, a, um. Ngan ngac, confusè positus.

Ngac ngu, agitare caput et collum.

Ngach, lignum quod parietem sustinet. Ngach tua, limen.

Nganch sou, aditus fluminis.

Ngai, sedes regalis.

Ngai, vereri, vel potiùs deterreri labore, vel difficultate aliquâ. Ai ngai, idem.

Ngai, arbor quædam. Dang xa dam ngai, longa distantia.

Ngai, herba cujus folio siccato utuntur ad adustionem in
morbo curando.

Ngai vel *nghia*, amicitia, gratitudo. Nhan nghia, amicus, a, um.

Ngay, rectus, a, um. Ngay that, sincerus, a, um; simplex. Lao ngay, conscientia recta. Ngay nhau, rectè correspondere ad alterum; ex adverso alterius.

Ngay, stertere.

Ngay, dies. Sang ngay, diluculo, primâ luce radiante. Nua ngay, meridies, media dies. Ban ngay, de die. Than ngay, totâ die. Ngay ray, nunc; his diebus. Ray la ngay lam viec lanh, nunc est dies salutis. Ngay sou, postea. Ngay sou se hay, postea vibebitur. Hang ngay, quotidiè; vel *ngay ngay*, idem est. Gian ra ngay nay ngay khoi, differre de die in diem. Chang khoi may ngay, non transactis tot diebus; (de præterito.) Khoi mot it ngay nua con lai den, post aliquot dies denuò venies. Da khoi, vel da duoc may ray, jam ab hinc quot diebus? Hen ngay, assignare diem.

Ngay muoi, hebes, ignarus.

Ngay, fastidium ex cibo nimis pingui.

Ngam, humectare aliquid in aquâ, macerare.

Ngam, tenere aliquid ore clauso. Ngam mieng lai, recludere os.

Ngam nuoc vao, aliquid siccum aquam imbibit; vel aqua sensim penetrat.

Ngam, aliquid in aquâ latet immersum. Cung co ngam, protervus, sed non apertâ fronte; latens superbia.

Ngam nga, identidem laudare.

Ngam, meditari. Nguyen ngam, oratio mentalis. Mle ngam, meditatio.

Ngam, *dang ngam ngam*, valdè amarus, a, um.

Ngan, sylvæ. D. C. B. la ngan moi su lanh, Deus est congregatio omnium bonorum. Ngan ngac, vide *ngac*.

Ngan, impedire. Ngan ra, separare. Ngan hom, separamentum capsæ. Ngan tro, idem.

Ngan, brevis. Van, idem est.

Ngan, modulari.

Ngan, modus, mensura certa. Ngan nao, quantum. Ngan
ay, tantum. Sicut et *bao nhieu*, *bay nhieu:* et sic collocantur in oratione. Muon ngan nan, thi lay ngan ay,
quantum volueris, tantum accipe. Ke co toi da duoc vui
ve doi nay bao nhieu, thi lai phai chiu phat trao dia nguc
bay nhieu, peccatores quantò fuerunt feliciores in huc
mundo, tantò graviores dant pœnas in inferno. Chang
co ngan, sine modo, sine fine. Ke lanh o tren thien dang
kinh men D. C. B. chang co ngan: lam ban cung D. C. B.
chang hay no, sancti in cœlo amant Deum sine fine; con-
versantur cum Deo sine fastidio.

Ngan ngo, stolidus morosus.

Ngang, *be ngang*, latitudo; linea transversa, vide *doc*. Lam
ngang ngua, aliorum consilio contraire vel obicem ponere.
Cai ngang ra, aliorum sententiæ contradicere.

Ngang lai, cohibere obstaculo.

Ngang nghiu, arbor gibbosa. Dat xau tron cay ngang
nghiu: he nguoi tho tuc noi deu pham phu, sicut mala
terra procreat arbores gibbosas, sic rusticus semper rustica verba profert.

Ngang, *that ngang*, sic dicitur omne genus quod habet mediam partem constrictam. Ca nganh ngang, quidam
piscis spinosus. Nguoi nganh hoa, homo dolosus.

Nganh vel *canh*, vide *canh*.

Nganh mat di, avertere faciem. Nganh mat lai, faciem
convertere.

Ngao du, otiosus; felix. Cho ngao, canis enormis.

Ngao, *kieu ngao*, superbus, a, um. Toi kieu ngao, superbia.
Ca ngao, quidam piscis.

Ngao, balbutire. Nguoi noi ngao, homo balbus.

Ngao co ma xem, arrecto collo de longè intuere.

Ngao coi, axis mortariis.

Ngap, oscitare; fastidire.

Ngam ngap, di ngam ngap, irc per multam moram tardando.

NGAP, aqua superans aliquid. Lut doi ou Noë nuot ngap len khoi nui muoi lam thuoc, tempore diluvii Noëmi aqua superabat montes quindecim cubitis. Ngap ngung nuoc mat, erumpentes lachrymæ.

NGAT, *ngat keo,* claviculus forficis. Ngat mui, vide *mui.*

NGAT, *thom ngat,* suavis odor spargitur. Tieng don ngat het moi roi, fama suavis spargitur per omnia loca.

NGAT, intercipere lumen, obscurare.

NGAT, frangere aliquid. Cao ngat ngheo, insolitæ altitudinis homo.

NGAU, *mam ngau,* piscis a longo tempore conditus sale jam benè detritus.

NGHE, animal simile leoni.

NGHE, crocus, i. Nghe, tingere aliquid croceo colore. Kien nghe, formica flavi coloris. Xung he, provincia Tunkini proxima Cocisinæ.

NGHE, ars, officium. Nghe nghiep, idem. Con lam nghe nghiep kiem an, quas exerces, fili, artes ad quærendum victum?

NGHE, quædam herba.

NGHE, audire. Nghe mloi, obedire; consentire. Con dung nghe chuoc ma qui, noli consentire tentationi dæmonis. Nghe thay, auribus percipere.

NGHE, *con nghe,* vitulus.

Nghe mieu, domus spiritui tutelari dicata. Ou nghe, vel tien si, doctor. Do ou nghe, vel do tien si, doctoratum adipisci.

Nghech dau, caput vesanum, insanum.

NGHEN, suffocari cibo faucem premente.

NGHEN, *dan ba co thai nghen,* mulier gravida.

Nghenh ngang, di nghenh ngang, incedere superbo fastu, magnâ pompâ.

Ngheo dang, via tortuosa.

NGHEO, expositus miseriis, paupertati. Benh ngheo, morbus periculosus. Su hiem ngheo, periculum.

Nghet, quod est valdè constrictum. Lam nghet lam, rigidè
agere; arctè constringere.

Nghi, *ho nghi*, dubitare. Chang nen ho nghi su gi ve dao,
non licet dubitare aliquid de fide. Uy nghi, terribilis
majestas. Nghi hoac, dubius, a, um.

Nghi, *quan bat nghi*, truculenti, latrones.

Nghi nghoi, quiescere. Giac nghi, quies, somnus. Ou quan
ay da ngoi, ille mandarinus jam mortuus est. Nguoi
nghi, in lecto quiescit vel dormit.

Nghi, sumitur etiam pro ille homo, sed dicendum est solùmmodo de infimo homine.

Nghi, putare, cogitare. Ta nghi the nao, quomodo cogita-
mus, quid facto opus est? Quando est sermo de consilio
capiendo, quid fertis sententiæ; quidnam consilii capitis?

Nghia, amicitia. Lam nghia, vel ket nghia, inire amicitiam. Bat nhan bat nghia, ingratus; significat etiam
sensum. Nghia la di gi, sensus quis est? Cat nghia,
explicare sensum. Hay qui nghia cung D. C. B., diligenter divinam amicitiam colere.

Nghich, *ke nghich*, inimicus, hostis. Nghich nhau, invicem
adversari. Lam nghich cung D. C. B., agere contra
Deum.

Nghien, atramentarium annamiticum.

Nghien rang, stridere dentibus. Gian nghien ngam, irasci
tacitus; ira intus latens.

Nghiem, *nhiem nghi, nhiem trang*, magna majestas.

Nghiem quan, nghiem khi giai, exercitum instruere; arma
comparare.

Nghiem, *phep linh khiem*, medicina divina. Minh thanh
D. C. J. la thuoc linh nghiem chua cac tat nguy en linh
hon, corpus Christi est divinum pharmacum contra omnes
animæ langueres. Nghiem nhan menh, authenticè actum
homicidii conscribere.

Nghieng, latus anteponere. Lam nghieng lech, quod erat
benè situm pervertere. Nam nghieng, decumbere super
latere.

Nghiep, *ac nghiep*, vide *ac*.

Nghiep, *nghe nghiep*, vide *nghe*. Toi nghiep, delictum. Cou nghiep, meritum. That nghiep, mendicus.

Nghin, mille. Dou nghin nghit, numerus hominum confertus.

Nghinh, *ngung nghinh*, leviter aversari.

Ngo, *gio ngo*, hora duodecimam et primam pomeridianam complectens. Ngo duoc, fortè posse.

Ngo xem, arrigere collum ad videndum.

Ngo, apertus, a, um; patens. De ngo cua, relinquere portam apertam. Ngo mloi, declarare suum intentum.

Ngo, fores exteriores. Ngo ngang, homo capax. Hien ngo, sapiens, prudens.

Ngo, regnum sinarum. Thang ngo, sinensis, (per contemptum.) Urbaniter dicitur *chu kach*.

Ngo, furiosus, amens. Cho ngo, canis rabiosus. Giac ngo, hostes irrumpunt.

Ngo, surculus nimpheæ.

Ngo ngan, insanus, stolidus.

Ngo, existimare, putare. Chang nen ngo su trai cho ng ta vo co, non licet malè suspicari de proximo absque fundamento. Ngò la, idem est ac *ngo la*, puto quod. Con, ngo su nay la toi nhe ru, putas hoc esse leve peccatum?

Ngoa, hyperbole. Noi ngoa, loqui per hyperbolem. Dan ba ngoa nguya, mulier linguosa.

Ngoac di, vide *ngoai*.

Ngoai, extra. Ho ngoai, familia matris. Anh em ben ngoai, consanguinei ex parte matris. Ke ngoai dao, extra fidem, id est infidelis. Ngoai kinh, ngoai thu, extra libros, seu traditio incerta.

Ngoai, *nam ngoai*, annus immediatè præcedens. Ngac ngoai y, ultimos spiritus ducere.

Ngoay, *ngoay vao*, ferro acuto fortiter perforare.

Ngoay, *cho ngoay duoi*, canis caudâ suâ adblandiens.

Ngoai, extra. Be ngoai, extùs. Chang nen lay mot su be

39

ngoai khou ma tho phuong D. C. B. pha co viec be trao
lam mot, non expedit colere Deum solis operibus exteri-
oribus, sed comitari debent opera interna. *Ngoai* opponitur *trao*, intùs.

Ngoan, officiosus; fidelis. Ngoan dao, fidelis Christianus.
Ngoan net o, urbanus.

Ngoap, ranuncula.

Ngoat tri, tro lai, illicò reverti.

Ngoc, gemma.

Ngoc dau len, erigere caput, dicitur de piscibus.

Ngoi, innatare undis, dicitur de serpentibus aut avibus quæ
fluitant super aquâ. Ca ngoi, supernatat piscis.

Ngoi, tegulæ. Nha ngoi, domus tecta tegulis.

Ngoi, *con ngoi,* rivus. Ngoi but, acumen penicilli. Gi et
ng ta bang ngoi but, dicitur de iis qui suis scriptis alteri
nocumentum afferunt.

Ngoi, sperare aliquid ab aliquo: sed non dicitur nisi per
contemptum. Tao chang ngoi may dau, quid à te spero?

Ngoi, persona. Ngoi thu, ordo aut dignitas in quâ aliquis
constituitur. Ngoi sao, sydus. Cao ngoi, tonsura in
fronte quam solent facere nebulones. Tho ngoi, tonsor.

Ngoi, sedere. Ngoi xep bang, sedere decubitis cruribus,
qui modus apud eos honestus est. Ngoi dung cung nhau,
dicitur de cohabitatione viri et mulieris.

Ngoi, vide *nghi.* Dai ngoi, expectare à rege responsum.

Ngom, stultus, vecors; qui non est dignus vocuri homo.

Ngon, sapidus. Mui ngon, sapor. Ngon lanh, sapidus et
salubris.

Ngon lua, flamma. Ngon cay, cacumen arboris. Ngon
dau, monticulus mensuræ confertæ.

Ngon cai, pollex. Ngon tro, index. Ngón ut, digitus ultimus. La ngon, folium quoddam venenatum.

Ngop, *trou ngop len,* suspicere tantisper.

Ngot, dulcis, e; suavis. Ngot ngao, idem. An o ngot,
suaviter conversari. Ngot ngot voy, parùm dulcis.

Ngot xuo, detumere, decrescere. Com an da ngot, oryza sumpta jam digesta est.

Ngot nang, peruri calore solis.

Ngot mua, pluvia sese paulisper remittens.

Ngou, anser. Thang xac ngou, loquaculus nebulo.

Ngu cu, vide *cu.* Ngu tam mot it cau, hospitari per breve tempus.

Ngu, dormire. Ngu gat, vide *buon ngu,* gravari somno. Nua ngu, nua nuc, semisomnus.

Ngu, quinque. Ngu sac, quinque colores, scilicet: Do, ruber; Den, niger; Vang, flavus; Trang, albus; Xanh, viridis. Ngu quan, quinque sensus corporales, scilicet: Con mat xem, visus; Tai nghe, auditus; Mui ngui, olfactus; Mieng noi, locutio; Chan tay lam, tactus. Ngu tang, quinque interiora hominis, scilicet: Tam, cor; Can, jecur; Ti, ventriculus; Phe, pulmo. Than tem, cai ngu, mensura quinque cubitorum.

Ngu, vox propria regi. Ngu tri, præsidere. Ngu ra, exire. Ngu vao, intrare. Ngu di danh giac, proficisci ad bellum contra hostes. Ngu kinh li, proficisci ad lustrationem sui regni.

Ngua, equus.

Ngua, prurire. Ngua mieng, pruriens os, id est, loquax.

Ngua, supinus, a, um. Ngua mat len, sursùm faciem erigere. Ngua tay mat ra, dextræ palmam extendere.

Nguc, carcer. Dia nguc, infernus.

Nguc, pentus.

Ngui ngui, commotus misericordiâ, vel desiderio alicujus.

Ngui, olfacere; odorari.

Nguy, rebellis. Lam nguy, conjuratio facta.

Nguyen, *nguyen lam sao?* quâ ex causâ? Nguyen boi, ex.

Nguyen, orare. Mloi nguyen, oratio. Sach nguyen, breviarium.

Nguyen, *the nguyen,* vovere; jurare. Nguyen rua, malè precari.

Nguyen, familia quædam in Tunkino antiquissima.

Nguyet, luna. Mloi nguyet hoa, verbum turpitudinem redolens. Nguyet thuc, vide *thuc*.

Nguoc, contrarius, a, um. Di nguoc sou, navigare adverso amne. Nguoc gio, ventus contrarius. Noi nguoc, loqui confuso ordine verborum.

Nguoi, tepescere; defervere. Nguoi gian, defervet ira. Nguoi su dao, tepor in fide.

Nguoi, tu: ad infimos et cum irâ loquendo. To se xem nguoi, ego te videbo. Con nguoi, pupilla oculi. Ho nguoi, erubescere. De nguoi, protervus homo. Treu nguoi, insidias struere.

Nguoi khen, laudare.

Nguoi, homo. Nguoi ta, alii, cæteri. Lam nguoi, esse homo. Sumitur etiam pro secundâ et tertiâ personâ, quando est sermo de honorabilibus personis. Chang nen lam hai nguoi ta, non licet aliis nocere. D. C. B. sinh ra ta lam nguoi o the gian nay cho duoc tho phuong nguoi, Deus creavit nos esse in hoc mundo ut illum colamus. Nguoi, noi di gi, Domine, quid loqueris? Nuoc nguoi, regnum extraneum seu exteræ nationes.

Nguon, mons; sylva.

Nguong, revereri conspectum hominum.

Nguong cua, limen portæ inferius.

Nha, domus. Nha xe, ædicula ex lignis pulchrè elaborata ad efferendum cadaver ad sepulchrum. Nha tang, domus papyracea ad sepulturam destinata. (Tang, propriè est sepelire.) Nha que, petria. Nha phu, nha huyen, judices in balliviatibus. Vao an may nha D. C. B., domum Dei ingredi.

Nha mon, sedes tribunalis vel ministri justitiæ, vel etiam telonarii. Mach nha, vide *mach*. Nhuoc nha, magno pudore affici.

Nha, leviter manderè.

Nha ra, ejicere cibum ex ore.

Nha ra vel *lao ra*, liquefieri vel dissolvi.

Nhac, campanulæ collo equi aut canis appensæ. Le nhac, cæremonia, urbanitas civilis.

Nhac nhuoi, segnis, vecors.

Nhac, attollere aliquid. Nhac can, appendere aliquid stateræ. Nhac di nhac lai, aliquid in memoriam iterùm iterùmque refricare.

Nhac, *nhoc nhac*, movere se; qui incipit se movere; resistere alicui.

Nhai, mandere.

Nhai, sibilando contemnere; contemptim verba aliorum repetere.

Nhai, ranulæ in arbustis frequentes.

Nhai, *hoa nhai*, flos quidam albi coloris valdè suavis. Nhai quat, claviculus quo compingitur flabellum.

Nhay, quod celerrimè concipit ignem.

Nhay, connivere. Mot nhay mat, in ictu oculi. Nhay nhau, sibi invicem signum facere connivendo.

Nhay, saltare. Nhay khoi vao, evadere laqueum.

Nham, *goi nham*, acetarium ex olere et pisce confusis.

Nham, *nham nhuoi*, quod fit cum magnâ confusione. An da nham, fastidium cibi.

Nham, *ca nham*, mustela marina.

Nham, asper, a, um; quod pellem sæviter pungit. Ao nham minh, cilicium.

Nham ruou, temperare vinum. Do nham ruou, esculentum quod vini vim temperat. Nham con mat lai, claudere oculos.

Nham, collimare. Nham, meliùs *mlam*, errare, decipi.

Nham, præsidere.

Nhan, avicula quadam.

Nhan ha, otium. Thanh nhan, beatitudo.

Nhan, arbor quædam. Nhan hon, ob oculos.

Nhan, vel *nhan nho*, rugæ. Nhan mat lai, rugare frontem. Cho nhan nanh, canis rugens.

Nhan, denunciare. Nhan tin, mittere nuntium.

Nhan nghia, gratitudo, pietas. Nhan duc, vide *duc.* Nhan the, eâdem operâ. Nhan sao, quare. Nhan xuo, calcare. Nhan, agnoscere.

Nhan, annulus. Tu ay nhan nay, ab illo tempore usque modò.

Nhang, *mot nhang*, in ictu oculi.

Nhang, *lang nhang*, vide *lang.*

Nhang, *cai nhang*, muscæ magnæ.

Nhang, *quan nhang*, homines sylvestres.

Nhao, irridere; illudere.

Nhao, rotare vel volvere se.

Nhao, *com nhao*, oryza multâ aquâ cocta.

Nhao, ordo, gradus.

Nhap, intrare. Qui nhap vao no, diabolus intravit in illum.

Nhap con mat, leviter oculum claudere. Thuc nhap, vigilare et interdùm leviter dormire.

Nhat, meliùs mlat, insulsus, a, um. Ruou nhat, vinum debile. Cuoi nhat, ridere sine sale.

Nhat vel *dat*, timidus, a, um; formidolosus; vecors. *Mot nhat* vel *mot blai*, unum momentum, vel unus ictus in amputando.

Nhat vel *blat lay*, colligere. Nhat ph, rigida disciplina. Cam nhat, rigidè prohibere. Chay nhat, jejunium rigidum seu sub peccato obligans.

Nhat, unus, a, um; primus, a, um. Nhat la, maximè, præsertim. Con, ph lo buon ghet cai toi nhat la toi trao, debes, fili, dolere de omnibus peccatis, maximè mortalibus. Nhat thuc, eclipsis solis. Nhat ban, Japonia.

Nhau, invicem. Cung nhau, simul cum. Ta phai cau nguyen cho nhau, debemus orare pro invicem.

Nhe, levis, e.

Nhe vel *mle*, vide *mle.*

Nhech, anguilla cujus càro est valdè sapida.

Nhet lo, obdurare rimas.

Nheo, *ca nheo*, piscis quidam. Nheo nhoc, orphani.

Nhich, *nhuc nhich*, lentè movere.

Nhiem, *sau nhiem*, idem est ac *mau nhiem*, vide *mau*.

Nhiet, calor. Lam nhiet lam, angustiare.

Nhieu, multus, a, um ; multùm.

Nhieu cho, eximere aliquem ab oneribus publicis. Nhieu sinh, vitam servare. Ou nhieu no, à publicis oneribus liber vel exemptus.

Nhim, *cai nhim*, histrix.

Nhin, tolerare. Nhin nuc, tolerantia.

Nhin, idem est ac *nhan*, recognoscere ; contemplari.

Nhiu, *noi nhiu*, error in loquendo ex inadvertentiâ.

Nho, vitis. Chu nho, littera sinica. Hoc tro nho, scholastici qui litteris sinico-annamiticis operam dant; qui student litteris sinicis. Hoc tro nho thou phai lam, litteris sinicis doctissimè eruditus.

Nho, macula ex cinere vel fuligine aut atramento contracta. Da nho mat, sub obscurà luce.

Nho, parvus. Thang nho nho, puer parvulus. Nho xuo, distillare.

Nho, tollere aliquid humo infixum. Nho co, eradicare herbas.

Nho, inniti auctoritate, viribus, divitiis alterius. Nho dip, fretus occasione. O nho, vel dau cho, hospitari. Nho nho vay, aliquo colore non benè tinctus.

Nho, recordari; teneri desiderio. Con, ph nho co D. C. B. o tre mat lien, recordari, fili, semper præsentiam Dei. Nho moi diu nay, hoc in pectus tuum dimitte.

Nhoc, vel *nhoc nan*, fatigari. Nhoc met, idem est. Kho nhoc, labor.

Nhoc, elevare.

Nhoi vel *mloi*, vide *mloi*.

Nhom nham, an noi nhom nham, proferre rustica verba; sine ordine et sensû effundere verba.

Nhon, quod in mucronem desinit.

Nᴏɴ, *di nhon chan len*, incedere suspenso pede. Nhon tay
cat lay, capere aliquid extremis digitis.

Nᴏᴛ, arbor quædam cujus fructus valdè acidus est.

Nᴏᴛ, furunculus. Nhot moc len, furunculi oriuntur.

Nhot vel *dot*, vide *dot*.

Nᴏᴛ, pallescere; pallidum fieri vel lividum.

Nhop nhua, sordidus, a, um; impurus.

Nhu bao, commovere.

Nhu thuo, thus. Nhua, pix.

Nᴜ, sicut. Cung nhu, sicut et similis; similiter; ita. . Nhu
vay, ita, sic.

Nᴜ, quod benè percoctum est. Danh du no nhu ra, verberibus contusus, a, um.

Nᴜ, extrahere illecebris. Nhu ga, escâ allicere galli-
nam.

Nᴜᴏᴄ, *nhin nuc*, vide *nhin*.

Nhuc nhich, vide *nhich*.

Nᴜᴏᴄ, *mu nhuc*, vide *mu*.

Nhuc dau, dolor capitis; dolere capite. Nhuc ca va mh,
dolor per totum corpus.

Nᴜɪ, *mui nhui*, fomes, igniarium.

Nhuy hoc, pulchritudo florum. Nhuy tieng, suavitas vocis.
Hing ng noi co nhuy nhang, verba suavia.

Nᴜᴀɴ, *nam nhuan*, annus lunaris tredecim mensium.
Thang nhuan, mensis additus vel duplicatus, intercalaris.

Nᴜᴍ, *mot nhum*, unus captus digitorum.

Nhung cho, eximere ab onere publico, sicut verbum *nhieu*.
O nhung, otiosus, a, um. Nhung ma, sed, verùm.

Nᴜɴɢ, omnes. Chang nhung la, non solùm. Nhung phai
su kho lien, semper incidere in calamitates.

Nhuoc nha, vide *nha*.

Nᴜᴏᴄ, *da nhuoc*, valdè debilitatus. Nhuoc bang, quod si
verò.

Nᴜᴏᴍ, tingere aliquo colore. Tho nhuom, tinctores vestium.

Nhuo sao doi so, vana observantia et superstitio, quâ gentiles credunt se posse sortem sen fatum commutare.

Nнuo, cedere alteri. Nhuo cho, idem est. Khiem nuong, humilis, e. O kiem nhuong, humiliare se. Duc khiem nhuo, humilitas.

Nнut, *dao nhut,* culter obtusus, cujus ferrum hebescit. Nhut tri, obtusum ingenium; truncus.

Nнut, condimentum salsum ex pisce et fructibus, aliisque generibus.

Ni, bonzia, mulier templo idolorum serviens.

Ni, *nan ni,* leviter conqueri de se vel de aliis.

Nia, instrumentum vimineum ad purgandum oryzam; vannus rotundus ex arundine contextus.

Niem phat, precari idolum; recitare preces in honorem idoli.

Nieng, vermis in aquis natus.

Ninh than, aulicus; adulator.

Nieu, olla parva. Nieu huo, olla parva in quâ crematur odoramentum.

Nin di vel *nin lang,* silere, tacere, reticere, premere vocem.

Nip, *cai nip,* corbula ad continendum vestes.

Nit, *con nit,* puer; puella.

Nit, *ao nit,* vestis stricta. Nit sang, constringere loculum mortui.

Niu, *nang niu,* molliter tractare.

Niu lay, fortiter apprehendere; stringere.

No, saturatus, a, um. Fastidium cibi vel alterius rei.

No, iste, a, ud; alter, a, um.

No, ille, a, ud. Ay no, ecce ille est.

No, balista; exsiccatus, a, um. Cui no, lignum aridum.

No, cuneus.

No nhau, æmulari invicem; certatim et turmatim aliquo occurrere vel confluere.

40

No, irasci. Nat nò, vide *nat.*

No, crepare, disrumpi cum strepitu. No sung, crepitus tormentorum bellicorum. No tai ra, maledictio.

No, *ay no no,* ille homo, vel illud nègotium.

No, debitum. Mac no, debitorem esse, debere. Doi noi, vide *doi,* mutuum repetere ab aliquo. Ke lam no lam, aere alieno oppressus.

No, germinare, pullulare. No mat, famam gloriamve acquirere.

No, non sustinere. Chang no mang mot deu nang, non sustinuit ut aliquod grave verbum excideret ex ore.

Noc nha, fastigium domûs. Ca noc, piscis quidam cujus jecur est venenosum.

Noc, venenum; aculeus animalium.

Noɪ, *ho noi,* familia patris. Quan noi, eunuchus.

Noɪ, jungere. Noi dao, succedere in ordine progeniti.

Noɪ, olla.

Noɪ, emergere ex aquâ. Ganh noi, par ferendo oneri. Lam noi viec, optimè negotium peragere; cumulari divitiis.

Noi ay, eò usque. Chang den noi ay, non eò usque.

Noɪ, incedere super ponte. Noi giua, sequendo custodire. Noi neo, sequi vestigia. Noi, loqui. Chang ai noi den may, de te siletur.

Noɪ, gallus ex genere pugnaci.

Noɪ, locus. O noi, tai noi, pendere. Su sou chet ta o noi D. C. B., vita et mors nostra pendent à Deo.

Noɪ, relaxare, remittere; recedere paululum.

Noм, *chu nom,* Litterae Annamiticae, vel Sinico-Annamiticae, ad exprimendas vulgares voces, seu ad referenda Annamitica verba. Tieng nom, lingua vulgaris; verbum in linguâ Annamiticâ.

Noм, acetarium.

Noм, aspicere.

Noм, instrumentum ex arundine contextum ad piscandum.

Non, immaturus, a, um ; recens ; quod ad perfectionem
nondùm pervenit. Sinh non, abortus. Nui non, montes.
Nuoc non, montes et aqua. Non not, idem.

Non, galerus.

Non chuoi, pars intima arboris Indicæ.

Non, *cu non,* contrectando molestiam inferre. Non nao
trao da, stomachum movere ad vomitum. Timidus, formidolosus. Lam non nao, inquietare ; facere ut hùc illùc
cursitent perturbatim.

Nop, tradere judici. Nop thue, solvere tributum. Nop rua,
maledicendo tradere diabolo.

Not, finire aliquid. An not di y, finire comedendo.

Not bung lai, contrahere ventrem.

Nou, pauca aqua. Bien nou, mare modicam aquam habens.
Canh nou, arare, colere terram. Bo nou, avis, quædam.

Nou, ardor calcis. Nou nan, protervus, a, um.

Nou, sufferre sustentaculum.

Nu, calix floris.

Nu, fœmina.

Nua, *gia nua,* senex decrepitus.

Nua, arundo indica.

Nua, medius, a, um.

Nua, ampliùs. Mot it nua, modicum magis. Doi mot it
nua, expectare paulisper.

Nuc lai, torquere funem.

Nuc may, ligare aliquid vimine. Nuc lao, inflammatum cor
alicujus rei desiderio.

Nuc, calor magnus.

Nui, mons.

Nuoc, aqua, liquor ; regnum.

Nuoc, nodus. Lam den nuoc, rigorosè agere.

Nung, coquere lateres, vel vasa testacea. Tho nung noi,
figulus.

Nuoi, nutrire. Duong nuoi, idem est.

Nuong eay, sperare in aliquo, vel niti alicujus potentiâ divitiis.

Nᴜoɴɢ, assare.

Nᴜoᴛ, deglutere; absorbire.

Nᴜᴛ, nodus; obduramentum. Nut ao, globuli in veste.

Nᴜᴛ, disrumpi, hiscere, rimas agere.

O.

O, *ca o,* nomen piscis. Chim o, avis quædam milvio major.

O ue, sordidus, a, um. Su o ue, res turpis.

O, *ao o ra,* vestis vetustate maculata.

O, nidus gallinæ. O ho, exclamatio magis adhibita in libris. Heu! proh dolor!

O, eructare. O, manere; esse.

Oᴀɴ, quod fit injustè alicui. Oan gia, hostis; inimicitia; infortunium.

Oan thu, ulcisci injuriam, vindicare.

Oᴀɴ, edulium ex sola oryza factum, quod in primâ quâque lunâ et plenilunio cujusque mensis, idolis offerri solet; quodque pro sancto cibo à gentilibus habetur.

Oai linh vel *oai vao,* idem est ac *uy linh* vel *uy vao.* Vide *uy.*

Oo, cerebrum. Dau oc, caput.

Oo, cochlea. Oc tu va, cochlea marina magna. Oc nhoi, cochlea parva.

Oo, eructare.

Oɪ, graviter olens. Do an da oi, cibarium jam graveolens. Est etiam interjectio: Heu! eia! Hi oi, idem est.

Oɪ, genus pyræ, quædam arbor Lusitanicâ *goava.*

Oi oi, goi oi oi, vocare magnâ et repetitâ voce, ve lclamare.

Oᴍ, amplecti, amplexari. Om nang, veretrum.

Om dau, om yeu, ægrotare.

Oᴍ, *nau om,* percoquere aliquid ore ollæ, abstracto et lento

igne. Dau om ca va minh, lentus dolor serpet per totum
corpus.

Oɴ, gratia, beneficium. Ta on, gratias agere Deo. Gia on,
agere gratias æqualibus vel inferioribus. Ta da chiu
nhieu on D. C. B. xuo cho, multa recepimus beneficia à
Deo concessa.

On dich vel *khi dich*, pestis.

Oᴘ, granum frumenti vel quid aliud macrum et vacuum.

Op ep, mollis, e; putrefactus, a, um.

Oᴛ, *cay ot*, pimentum.

Oᴜ, avus; dominus. Ou ba, ou vai, progenitores. Duc ou,
princeps.

Oᴜ, internodium; tubus. Ou nhoi, tubiculus pulvere tor-
mentario repletus, et bene obstructus, ad sonitum eden-
dum, cùm accensus fuerit. Ou to, pensum sericum.

P.

Pha vao, vel *pha phach vao*, commiscere. Noi giem pha,
zizanias disseminare.

Pha vel *pha phach*, destruere, diruere, vastare. Pha thanh,
vastare urbem. Danh chay pha, expugnare armis.

Pʜᴀᴄʜ, crepitaculum. Ho phach, crystallum.

Pʜᴀɪ, decolorari, amittere colorem.

Pʜᴀɪ, debere, oportare, incidere, tangere. Phai mle, consonare rationi. Ai muon roi linh hon thi phai chiu kho,
qui vult suam salutem consequi debet habere patientiam,
vel multa pati. Phai tay ma qui, incidere in manus dæmonis. Tau phai da, navis tangit vel incidit in saxa, syrtes.
Phai lao, amare, capi amore venereo. Phai khi, contigit.
Chang phai nao, nihil mali accidere.

Pʜᴀʏ, *dao phay*, culter ad secandas carnes aptus.

Pʜᴀʏ, *mot cai phay*, unus ductus calami. Quat phe phay,
ventilare leviter.

PHAM, facere contra aliquem. Pham toi, committere peccatum. Pham deu ran, violare præceptum. Noi pham den D. C. B., blasphemare in Deum. Pham su thanh, sacrilegum esse, violare sacra. Phai dau pham, vulnerari graviter.

Pham hen, ignobilis homuncio.

PHAM, *chuc pham,* dignitas, ordo.

PHAN, *lang phan,* annona, oryza.

PHAN, vel *phan day,* eloqui, præcipere. (Vox propria regi vel Deo.) Phan xet, judicare.

PHAN, tabulatum in modum lecti. Lam phan cung ai, agere adversùm aliquem. Phai phuc, fallax, maliciosus, dolosus.

Phan nan, pœnitere.

PHAN, fimus, i. Phan chia, dividere.

PHAN, fucus; cerussa. Gioi phan, fucare faciem.

PHAN, sors. So phan, fortuna. Dia phan, districtus. Chuc phan, dignitas. Phan phuc, bona opera exercere: de sacerdotibus intelligitur administrare sacramenta.

PHAN, pars. Phan ai nay lay, partem suam quisque accipiat. Chia phan, partiri, distribuere in partes.

PHAN, excrementum.

PHAN, operimentum ollæ magnæ.

PHANG, culter magnus.

PHANG, *cai phang,* tela serica.

PHANG, complanatus, a, um. Lam cho phang, complanare. Bang phang trao lao, animo quieto.

PHAO, lignum supernatans in sagenis.

PHAO, igniculus pyræus sonum edens.

Phao vel *phung, tat phao* vel *benh phao,* lepra. Nguoi co tat phung, leprosus.

PHAO, *phao vo ra,* repudiare uxorem. To phao, libellus repudii.

PHAO, cubiculum; thorus. Viec cam phao, exercitia spiritualia recollectionis. Benh pham phao, morbus ex intemperantiâ rei venereæ.

Phao, opinari, conjectare. Phao len, inflari ex vento. Phao minh, providere sibi in futurum.

Phat, punire, damnare. Chiu phat, luere pœnas. Phai phat, damnari.

Phat ra, depromere; elargiri. Vox mandarinis conveniens. Phat lang cho quan, dare stipendium militibus. Quien thu phat, officium promuscondi.* Phat sung, explodere tormenta bellica.

Phat, idolum. Phat giao, vel dao phat, idolatria. Ke di dao phat, idolatra.

Phat pho, vento agitari.

Phau bay, exponere. Trang phau phau, candor niveus.

Phe, subscribere. Bang phe, subscriptura mandarini. Phe chu vao, subscribere.

Phe, aliqua pars in communitate pagi. Lang phe, idem. Phen le, æmulari.

Phen vel *buc phe*, cratis contexta.

Phen, alumen.

Pheo, *tre pheo*, arundo.

Phep, *quien phep, phep tac*, potestas, virtus, auctoritas. Le phep, cæremonia, civilitas. Chiu phep, obedire, subjici; recipere sacramenta. Lam phep, benedicere aliquid, aut administrare sacramenta. Anh phep, nuoc phep, imago benedicta, aqua lustralis. Phep la, miraculum. Ra phep tac, exercere auctoritatem; condere leges. Thoi phep, mos.

Phet ho, glutinare. Danh phet, lusus pueri.

Phet, percutere. Noi phet, loquax, jactabundus.

Phi cua, profusus, prodigus. a, um. Phi ton, idem.

Phi ra, emittere ventum.

Phi lao, satiare animum. Phi chi, phi da, idem sonant. Phi, est interjectio.

Phien cho, successio nundinarum. Phien thu, juxta succes-

---

* Sic in MS.

sionem. Phien len loa tren, appellare superiorem judicem. Phien quan tren, idem.

Phiah pho, adulari.

Phien, mœstus. Phien da, phien lao, mœstus animo. Phien den ng ta, aliis gravis esse vel laborem afferre.

Pho sach, volumen, vel auctor librorum. Ngua dinh pho, vide *dinh.*

Pho cua, ostentare divitias. Pho mac, pho an, ostentare luxum in veste et victû. Pho truong, exponeres opes suas publico conspectui ad vanam gloriam, quod facere solent gentiles in suorum mortuorum exsequiis.

Pho, taberna; emporium. Hang pho, idem.

Pho, commendare, committere. Toi pho linh hon toi o tay chua toi, in manus tuas, Domine, commendo spiritum meum. Con, da pho cho ai, cui, fili, tradidisti?

Phoi, pulmo. Ca phoi, magnanimus, liberalis.

Phoi, siccare aliquid in sole.

Phou, simulacra hominum facta ex papyro aut aliâ materiâ.

Phu lao, æquo animo esse ex percepto aliquo emolumento. Phu dam, bajuli. Phu trao, remiges. Binh phu, militum bajuli. Nou phu, agricola. Phep nat phu nhat phu, sacramentum matrimonii. Cou phu, labores.

Phu ko, adjuvare, protegere. D. C. B. phu ho cho, con, Deus adsit tibi, fili. Verbum frequens in ore patrum ad Christianos Tunkinenses. Phu vua, militare regi. Thay phu thuy, veneficus. Phu phep, veneficia. Ve phu, depingere schedulas et characteres veneficos. Dan bua, deo bua, appendere, gestare res veneficas. Benh phu, hydrops. Phu tay vao, admovere manum operi.

Phu, dives. Phu qui, dives et nobilis. Su phu qui, opes, dignitates.

Phu, operire. Phu ca minh, coöperire totum corpus. Phu, significat etiam balliviatum majorem post *Xu* provinciam. Quam nha phu, vel ou phu, judex in illo balliviato majori. Dicitur pro copulâ quoque animalium. Con duoc phu

con cai, masculum animal copulat se fœminino. Am phu,
Avernus apud gentiles.

Phu phang, homo crudus, crudelis. Phu on, phu nghia,
tinh phu, ingratus. Phu nhung on D. C. B. xuo cho,
qui abutitur donis Dei est ingratus ei.

Phuc, virtus, meritum, bonum opus; præmium; felicitas.
Lam phuc, vide *phan*. Huong phuc, frui felicitate.
Nguoi vo phuc, infelix; reprobatus.

Phuc, obedientiam dare, subjicere se, venerari. Phuc mle,
consentire rationi. Le phuc sinh, resurrectio Domini seu
pascha. Phục mo, latere in insidiis.

Phuc thom, suavis odor.

Phun, aliquid ex ore spirando fortiter emittere. Ran phun,
serpens sibilat. Phun ra nhung deu dai, effutire verba
stulta.

Phung vel *phao*, vide *phao*. Phung chuc, vel phao chuc,
dignitatem conferre. Phao vuo, inaugurare regem.
Phao thu, claudere litteras.

Phung truyen, edictum regis. Phung sai, legatus.

Phung ma, os tumidum. Phung dam ma, aliquid ad cele-
brandum exsequias offerre.

Phuo, plaga mundi. Phuo dou, plaga orientalis seu Asia.
Phuo tay, plaga occidentalis seu Europa. Phuo nam,
austrum. Phuo bac, aquilo seu septentrio. Phuo chi,
quanto magis. Phuo the, modus.

Phuo tho, colere. Phuong duong cha me, nutrire parentes
cum honore.

Phuong, societas. Phuong mac, idem.

Phuon vao, vexillum in quo scribitur nomen defuncti. Cay
phuon, vide *phuon*.

Phung ba, tempestas et fluctus. Phai phung ba, pati tem-
pestatem. Phung luu, otiosus, a, um. Phao tuc, mos,
politicæ res. Phao chi, confiscare; sigillum publicum
apponere rebus alicujus.

41

Q.

Qᴜᴀ, fructus.

Qᴜᴀ, transire. Hom qua, heri. Thau qua, pertransire, penetrare.

Qᴜᴀ, corvus. Qua mo, corvus dilacerans.

Qᴜᴀ, excedere; excessus; extra. Khach qua giang, vectores. Qua do, extra modum. Qua phep, extra legem præscriptam. Quay qua, indecens; exlex.

Qᴜᴀ, munusculum; fructus vel aliquod edulium.

Qᴜᴀᴄʜ, radix quædam sylvestris quam mandunt cum betel in defectu arecæ.

Qᴜᴀɪ, ansulæ cujuscumque rei.

Quai go, quod est insolitum, monstruosum, horrendum. Qui quai, sagax, astutus.

Qᴜᴀɪ, offerre cibum progenitoribus aut diis falsis.

Qᴜᴀʏ, rotare, in gyrum agere. Dau quay quat, vertitur caput.

Qᴜᴀʏ, gestare aliquid humero.

Quay boc vel *vay boc*, vide *boc*.

Qᴜᴀɴ, magistratus, mandarinus. Viec quan, negotia publicæ rei. Quan chuc, in dignitate constitutus. Quan thay, patronus, fautor. Cau lam quan, vel cau chuc quien, ambire dignitates. Quan tien, ligatura monetarum. Quay, movere. Quay quat, infestare.

Qᴜᴀɴ, diversorium, caupona. Do quan, hospitari.

Qᴜᴀɴ, inhumare mortuum ad aliquod breve tempus.

Quan cai, præses. Quan voi, ductor elephantis. Quan but, calamus penicilli.

Qᴜᴀɴ, crispus, a, um. Toc quan, capilli crispi. Dau quan, caput hirsutum.

Qᴜᴀɴ, miles. Dai quan, exercitus. Cat quan di, ducere exercitum. Quan va, exercitus pedestris. Quan thuy, exercitus navalis. Quan hau, milites servientes. Quan sumitur etiam pro nationibus gentium, ut: Quan ngo, Sinenses. Quan quang, Cocisinenses. Quan hoa lang, Lusitani.

Quan, omnes nepotes regis *chua* nomine hoc appellantur. Vide *chua*. Quan cou, primus gradus magistratuum.

Quan, involvere aliquid panno aut fune. Quat quit, multis nexibus involvere.

Quan, femorale. Quan tu, congregare se in unum. Danh quan, quidam lusus.

Quan, *di quan lai*, repetitis vicibus molestè ire, redire. Noi lan quan, obliviosus, qui multoties et ineptè idem repetit.

Quang sang, claritas. Hao quang, radius. Noi quang sang, locus patens, clarus. Noi quang que, locus spatiosus absque ullo impedimento. Quang, significat etiam funes connexos ad ferenda onera.

Quang mat, offuscantur oculi. Quang ga, oculi subobscurati.

Quang lay, circumligare in modum crucis. Lam quang di cho chao, facere per transennam ut citò absolvatur opus. Lam quang quay, agere imprudenter, vel lam can gio, idem.

Quang nam, provincia principalis in Cocisinâ, quæ et toti illi terræ nomen dedit; undè Tunkinenses per syncopen vocant Cocisinam Nuoc quang, vel Dang trao, id est pars (terræ) interior; quia pertinebat etiam ad Tunkinum, et non fuit ab eo separata nisi per ducentos solùmmodo annos.

Quang, spatium locorum, agrorum, itinerum.

Quan di, fortiter projicere.

Quanh, circuitus. Di quanh, per varios viæ anfractus ire. Chung quanh, in circuitû. Di chung quanh, circumire.

Quanh, *dou quanh*, agri solitarii.

Quanh, *go quanh*, lignum induratum. Dat quanh, terra indurata. Quat dieu, inquietare, molestare.

Quao, rapere unguibus.

Quat, ventilare; ventilabrum.

Quat, increpare altâ voce.

Quat, reflectere aliquid.

Quat lai, dao quat lai, reflectitur acies cultri.

Que quat, captus pedibus, manibusve.

Que, patria. Que mua, inurbanus. Que D. C. J. la thanh Nazaret, patria Christi Nazaret. Nha que, idem est. Ve que, redire in patriam; vel mori.

Que, cinnamomum. Nhuc que, cinnamomum aromatizatum. Que quan, cinnamomum secundum in suo genere. Que chi, cinnamomum ramosum.

Que, frustulum sarmentorum. That lung bo que, cingere latera.

Que sau lung, abscondere aliquid à tergo.

Que boi, sortilegium.

Quen, oblivisci. Quen on D, C. B., ingratus erga Dei dono. Bo quen, relinquere ex oblivione.

Quien, reducere alliciendo, attrahere. Quien du, idem.

Quen, assuetus, a, um; assuescere; notus, a, um. Con, phai tap cho quen, fili, debes exercere te ut assuetus fias. Toi da no, no da quen toi, ego notus illi, et ille mihi. Quen thuoc, idem est. Ke da, quen da, locorum sciens. Chang quen lam nghe xau, insolens malorum artium.

Quet phai, leviter aspergere.

Quet, verrere. Quet tuoc, quet nha, domum verrere.

Qui, nobilis, e; nobilitas. Qui gia, pretiosus, a, um.

Qui, genuflectere. Qui goi, idem.

Qui, dæmon. Qui quai, callidus ingenio; ingenium versutum; subdolus; varius.

Qui, *hoa nguyet qui,* heliotropium.

Qui ve, redire; redigere in unum.

Quien, auctoritas. Quien phep, potestas. Quam quien, *Quien sach,* tomus libri. Thoi quien, sufflare fistulas. mandarinus.

Quiet, decernere, statuere.

Quit, malum aureum minoris generis.

Quo, increpare.

R.

R<small>A</small>, exire, egredi. Ista vox jungi solet omnibus verbis quæ
motum de interiore parte ad extra vel mutationem in
aliam formam significant; ut *lay ra*, depromere Dem ra,
educere. Noi ra, eloqui, &c. Ra khoi thanh, egredi ex
civitate. Hoa ra xau, factus est malus. Ra xem, visum;
procedere.

R<small>A</small>, palea. Rom ra, idem est.

R<small>A</small>, cista crassa ad lavandam oryzam.

Ra mat, oculi lippitudine pleni.

R<small>AC</small>, purgamentum. Nha rac, domus pulvere et sordibus
plena. Lam rac nha ra, sordidare domum. Rech rac,
idem est.

Rac rai, nuditate et fame tabescens. Tu rac, carcer.

R<small>AC</small>, *nuoc rac*, aqua est in recessû.

R<small>AC</small>, spargere. Rai rac, sparsim.

R<small>ACH</small>, laceratus, a, um. Danh rac, vel lam rach, dilacerare.
Ao rach ruoi, vestis vetustate dilacerata.

R<small>ACH</small>, secare per rectam lineam.

R<small>AI</small>, *con rai*, lutra. Kiem an nhu rai, qui omnia sibi rapit
et verrit.

Ray rut, dissecare ventibus. Noi ray rut, mordere verbis
exaggerando.

R<small>AY</small>, nunc. Ray mai, post aliquod tempus. Ray ray, molestiam inferre auribus.

Ray tai, sordes in auribus. Cu ray, colocasia.

R<small>AY</small>, aspergere. Ray nuoc thanh, aspergere aliquod aquâ
benedictâ.

Ray vo, repudiare uxorem. Lon chou, dicitur virum suum.

R<small>AY</small>, cribrare farinam. Cai ray, cribrum.

R<small>AM</small>, *don ram*, vectes quibus affertur cadaver ad sepulchrum.

R<small>AM</small>, herba quædam valdè acris.

Ram, plenilunium, seu dies decimus quintus mensis lunaris.

Ram, crepitus ventris.

Ram, *cay ram*, arbor quædam.

Ram, densitas sylvarum, arborum. Rung ram, sylvæ condensæ. Ram rau, barba spissa. Ram rap, densæ arbores.

Ran, sonus resonans per loca.

Ran, *da ran*, scopuli in mare.

Ran mo, coquendo adipem exprimere. Ran ra, frigere piscem adipe ferventi.

Ran, prohibere sub legibus. Deu ran, mandata.

Ran ra, eniti pariendo. Noi ran ro, loqui cum magnâ emphasi.

Ran, *cai ran*, coluber serpens. Et etiam adjectivum durus, a, um. Ran gan, induratum cor; intrepidus. Ran may, ran mat, homo perfrictæ frontis. Ran roi, formosus.

Ran, *can ran* vel *lan can*, vide *can*.

Ran, pediculi in veste.

Ran suc ra vel *gang suc ra*, exigere vires.

Rang, torrere. Gao rang, oryza tosta.

Rang ngay, dilucescente die; aurora.

Rang bloi, offuscatum cœlum aliquid præsagiens.

Rang rit, multis nexibus aliquid colligare.

Rang, aiens, dicens.

Rang, dens. Rang ham, dens molaris.

Ranh, opinio gentilium, qui credunt quod quidam dæmon soleat intrare in infantulos, dùm adhùc sunt in utero matris; undè tenellos infantes quos immatura mors absumit, vocant *ranh*, id est obsessos ab illo dæmone; et pueris imprecando dicunt: *ranh bat may*, dæmon ille rapiat te.

Ranh viec, cessant negotia. Ranh, canalis.

Rao, publicare aliquid.

Rao, siccus, a, um. Kho rao, idem. Ran rao, serpens quidam.

Rao, sepire. Rao giau rao luy, septo circumdare.

Rao, *rau rao*, herba quædam comestibilis.

Rao, *nuoc rao*, reflexus maris.

Rap, domus ad aliquam solemnitatem pro brevi tempore constructa.

Rap, asper, a, um. Lam rap rua, fortiter aut durè agere.

Rap, statuere. Rap lao, statuere in animo. Rap ranh, idem.

Rap, genus retis.

Rap, *rap xuo dat*, aliquid cadit humo fixum.

Rap loi di, intercludere iter.

Rap, ardere. Rap rua, magno ardore torqueri.

Rat di, projicere aliquid.

Rat, aliquid integrum in suo genere et non admixtum alteri.

Rat, particula ad significandum superlativum, ut, ou San sao rat manh, Samson fortissimus. Rat cuc, summa miseria.

Rau, vel *rau co*, olus. Rau thom, mentha. Rau diep, lactuca. Rau sam, portulaca. Dau rau, lateres trini ex quibus fit focus ad coquendum.

Rau, barba. Rau bac, barba cana. Rau sam, barba densa per totum mentum. Rau ria, barbæ et mystaces.

Rau ri, molestissimus, a, um. Lam rau ri, molestiam inferre.

Re lua, purgare frumentum flante vento aut ventilabro.

Re, cista contexta ad sustinendam ollam.

Re, gener. Lam re, servire socero ad probandam generi indolem antè matrimonium; qui mos a missionariis improbatus est, propter multa mala. Anh em re, maritus sororis magnæ et parvæ.

Re, radix, truncus; initium, origo, vide *coi*. Tinh me xat thit lai coi re moi toi loi, cupiditas est origo omnium peccatorum.

Re, *go re*, quoddam lignum.

Re, *gao re* vel *gao te*, oryza ordinaria.

Re, sonus campanæ fractæ.

Re, quod vili pretio venditur vel emitur. Re quat, basis flabelli.

Re, separare, separatim. Phan re, idem.

Ren, gemere.

Ren, vectigal. Ista vox à voce Lusitanicâ, *renda*.

Ren, cudere ferrum. Tho ren, ferrarius. Tap ren, exercere se ad aliquam rem.

Reo, *ho reo*, acclamare. Reo ro, idem.

Reo quanh, circumcidere.

Rep, cimex.

Ret, frigus. Run ret, frigore tremere. Ret, est etiam rubigo ferri.

Ret, *cai ret*, centipes.

Reu, mucus in aquâ aut in terrâ humidâ. Ri cot ri, pythonissa.

Ri, *ru ri* vel *ri ram*, submissâ et lentâ voce loqui.

Ria, *rau ria*, vide *rau*. Ria quanh, in circuitu aut margine cujuscumque rei.

Ria ba ba, margo testudinis.

Ria, *chim ria lou*, avis suas pennas vellicans.

Rinh, insidiari ad furandum vel capiendum aliquid. Rinh mo, idem. Di rinh rich, strepitus multorum ambulantium. Rinh sinh thi, propè mortem.

Rieng, particularis, e; particulariter. Viec rieng, opus particulare. Viec rieng, intelligitur etiam de salute cujusque propriâ. Con, phai lieu viec rieng con hon moi viec khac, debes ,fili, procurare salutem tuam antè omnia. Y rieng minh, propria voluntas.

Rieng, species zinziberis majoris.

Rim, condire cibum lento igne et per longum tempus.

Riet, arctè constringere. Lam riet lam, rigorosè agere.

Rit, aliquid induratum rubigine.

Riu, *cai riu* vel *cai rui*, cratis contexta ad capiendos pisciculos.

Riu, *cai riu*, securis.

Ro, cista ad capiendum porcos.

Ro, *bi ro*, mantica ex sacco. Ro lay, surripere.

Ro, vel *ro rang*, clarus, a, um; clare. Noi khoan ro rang, loqui lentè et clarè.

Ro, *ca ro*, pisciculus quidam.

Ro, *dou ro*, dementatus.

Ro, cista ad lavandum pisces vel olera.

Ro, *mat ro*, facies variolis notata.

Ro moi vel *man di*, vide *man*, genus boum agreste.

Ro, appetitus inordinatus mulieris prægnantis. Chua ro, prægnans.

Roc, secare papyrum aut telam aut tabulam in duas tresve partes.

Roc, expolire quod est asperum.

Roc, *cua roc*, cancer in agris natus.

Roc, *ruo roc*, ager aquosus.

Roi, virga. Roi vot, verbera.

Roi, multis nexibus implicare. Chi roi, filum implicatum. Roi nhieu viec, implicatus multis negotiis. Ke roi dao, hæreticus.

Roi, vide *doan*. Sau khi ao da noi roi, postquam loquendi finem fecit.

Roi, quies post laborem; salus. Roi viec, cessant negotia; functus negotiis.

Roi, *buon roi*, mercatura piscium.

Roi ra, excidere. Roi xuo, cadere.

Roi, *mat roi*, refrigerium.

Roi, quod non est conjunctum. Roi roc, idem.

Rom, *sau rom*, vermis pilosus, foliis arborum inhærens, **valdè** venenatus; undè dicitur *gan sau rom*, id est **malevolus**. Rom, vide *ra*.

Rom, *ngua rom ca va minh*, prurigo serpit per totum corpus.

Ron lai, aliquid jam ad paucitatem redactum.

Ron vel *don*, tumultus ex concursu multorum hominum. Ron ra, idem.

Ron, umbilicus. Lam ron, vel lam gang, conari perducere opus ad finem.

Ron moi, tepor et dolor.

Rop, *bao rop,* quod est obumbratum. Rop nang, radii solis intercepti.

Rot ra, effundere. Rot vao, infundere quod est liquidum. Rot ruoc, miscere vinum.

Rot, ultimus, a, um. Rot bet, idem.

Rot, *roi rot,* vide *roi.*

Rou, draco. Cay xuong rou, lactaria.

Rou, vastus. Rou rai, pecuniæ liberalis.

Ru con, demulcere infantem ut dormiat. Ngoi ru ru, sedere tristis.

Ru, convocando attrahere invicem. Ru, est etiam particula *ne, non ne?* Con, muon xung toi ru, visne, fili, confiteri?

Ru, *chet ru,* mori senectute vel ariditate.

Rua, genus testudinis.

Rua, maledicere imprecari. Chui rua, idem.

Rua, *dao rua,* culter magnus.

Rua, lavare. Dicitur de lotione instrumentorum, et aliarum rerum, vel alicujus membri in corpore. Quando lavatur totum corpus, dicitur *tam;* de pannis vero et vestibus dicitur *giat.* Phep rua toi, sacramentum baptismi. Rua toi, baptizare. Chiu phep toi, baptizari; sacro regenerari lavacro.

Ruc ngay, ruc thang, pauci supersunt dies, et exiguus mensis. Viec da ruc lam, negotium valdè urgens.

Ruc rich; don ruc rich the vay, sic fert fama. Don ruc, idem est.

Rui, *rui nha,* scandula in tecto domûs.

Rum, *cay rum,* planta ex cujus flore exprimitur color purpureus. Ao rum, vestis purpurea.

Rum vel *ram,* species cancri minoris.

Run, tremere. Run so, tremor et timor.

Rung, de lapsu florum et foliorum ex arbore. La rung, folia decidunt.

Rung, sylva; deserta loca. Rung xanh, nemus, sylva, saltum.

Rung cay coi, agitare arbores. Noi rung, verbis terrere.

Rung mat bloi, ante ortum solis.

Ruoc, obviare; recipere; accercere.

Ruoi, vermis subterraneus qui propè Novembris calendas ex humo prodit, quemque in deliciis habent Annamitæ.

Ruoi, *ruoi mat*, facies tristis.

Ruoi, media pars alicujus rei. Gio thu nhat ruoi, sesqui prima hora. Mot dou bac ruoi, una pataca cum dimidio.

Ruoi, arbor quædam.

Ruoi, musca. Cut ruoi, nevus. (*Sic;* q. nervus?)

Ruoi, *xo ruoi*, aliquid in sertum ducere.

Ruo, ager. Lam ruo, colere agros. Mau ruo, sau ruo, thuoc ruo, sunt variæ mensuræ agrorum. Ruong tor, ager frugum fertilis. Ruong tor ma muoi bo tray, ager bonus pecori.

Ruot, viscera. Ruot gia, viscera majora. Ruot non, viscera minora. Anh em ruot, fratres uterini. Ruot don, substantia dicæ vel actionis in jure.

Ruou, cicera. Say ruou, inebriatus cicerâ seu vino ex oryzâ facto.

Rut, contrahere; educere. Rut ra, extrahere. Rut quan ve, reducere exercitum.

Rut chan lai, contrahere pedem.

Rut, *cat rut*, morsu lacerare.

S.

Sa, cadere. Suong sa, res cadens. Sa con, abortus. Nuoc sa, inundatio aquarum tempore pluviæ, montibus ad mare decurrens. Hang ha sa so, multitudo innumerabilis.

Sa, *cai sa sa*, genus cancri valdè sapidi.

Sa sao, chang sa sao ba nhieu, non curare de re tantillâ.

Sa vao da vao do, intrat hùc illùc sine modestiâ.

Sa ra, partiri, dividere in partes.

Sao, color. Ngu sac, ngu sac thuoc, coquere medicinam. Nau sac lai, coquere usque ad siccitatem. Dao sac, culter benè acutus. Nhan sac, pulchritudo in vultû. Sac duc, concupiscentia venerea. *Sac* vel *sac chi,* edictum, diploma.

Sac so, tela multiformis coloris. Sac so, idem.

Sach, liber. So sach, catalogus, nota. Sach Ou Khou, libri qui Confucii dicuntur.

Sach vel *sach se,* mudus, a, um (*sic*); castus. Nhan duc sach se, virtus castitatis. Giu minh sach se, castitatem servare.

Sai loi, sai mlam, sai lac, ista tria verba significant errare, aberrare à scopo; agere contra illud quod jussum est. Sai, mittere. D. C. B. sai thien thanh truyen tin cho D. B. Maria, Deus misit angelum ad nuntiandum Beatæ Mariæ. Phuong sai, commissarius regius. Sai vien, minister missus. Cay sai qua, arbor onusta fructibus.

Sai, scabies vel morbus parvulorum.

Sai, *noi sai,* error in loquendo.

Sai, duo brachia extensa, seu ulna. Nuoc sau may sai, aqua est profunda quot ulnis? Bo sai tay ra, extendere brachia.

Say, inebriari. Say me nhau, inebriari impuro suipsorum amore.

Say ra, purgare frumentum ventilando.

Sai, Bonzii, sacrificuli, vel custodes fanorum. Item, senes qui officium habent parvulos mortuos inhumandi; undè pueris maledicendo aut increpando dicunt *sai quay,* id est, senex ille deferat te ad sepulchrum. Thay sai, magister et sacrificulus.

Say chien, excutere mattam. Say vay, desquamare pisces. Say moc ca minh, papulæ oriuntur toto corpore.

Say vel *sut da ra,* laceratur pellis.

Say, arundines minores et molliores.

Say, *thit say*, caro exsiccata igne.

Say, *say thay*, aliquid excidit è manu. Say chan chua duoc, say mieng chang chua duoc, lapsus pedum est reparabilis, sed lapsus verborum est irreparabilis. Sinh say, abortus.

Sam, *rau sam*, portulaca.

Sam, dicitur de avibus quæ faciliter capiuntur escâ.

Sam nha, construere ligna jam apta ad structuram domûs. Vo sam, tudes magna, quâ utuntur fabri in construendâ domo. Rau sam, barbæ per totum mentum crescentes, quales habent Europæi.

Sam, tonitru. Sam set, tonitrua et fulmina. Sam truyen cu, vetus testamentum; vel *kinh thanh*, scriptura sacra. Sam truyen moi, novum testamentum. Sam ki, prophetia apud gentiles.

Sam, *sam sam vao*, irrumpere in aliquem.

Sam, *so sam*, palpitare et contrectare manibus.

Sam san, Lam cho sam san, facere diligenter et celeriter.

Sam et sam sua, comparare, præparare.

San, tabulatum propè terram.

San, *sinh san*, gignere. San hau, morbus muliebris post partum. San vat, bona ex fructibus terræ.

San se, partiri, dividere. San dinh kinh quien, componere multos libros in usum scholasticorum.

San, *da san*, lapilli.

San soc, sedulus, a, um. Day san, funis fortiter contortus. Di san, venari. Cho san, canis venaticus. Quan san, venatores.

San, arbor cujus cortice obturantur cymbæ.

San, paratus, a, um; et in promptu. Con, da san cho duoc xung toi ru, fili, jam paratus es ad confitendum? Phai sam sua cho san, oportet parare ut sint in promptu.

San, atrium.

San vao, vim facere ad intrandum.

San, *san mat ra*, facies impudens.

SANG, transmigrare; transfretare; transire. Do sang, transfundere. Cat sang, transferre. Sang trao, nobilis; nobilitas.

SANG, clarus, a, um; lux. Sang lang, lux. Sang ngay, diluscente die; manè. Khi moi sang, ubi dies cœpit. Sang da, bona memoria, ingenium tenax. Sang ngay som lam, antelucanum tempus.

Sang gao, cribrare oryzam. Cai sang, cribrum.

Sang sot, omittere ex oblivione; obliviosus.

SANG, loculus. Co sang, herba quædam.

SANH, comparare unum ad alterum. Sanh lai, conferre unum cum altero.

SANH, testa. Phai sanh, offendere testam. Cam sanh, genus mali aurei.

SAO, *cai sao, ngoi sao,* quare? quomodo? Con, chang muon chua toi ma mu roi linh bom lam sao duoc, fili, non vis abstinere à peccatis, et quomodo salutem consequeris? Sao ma, con, chang blo lai cu D. C. B. cho kip, quare non vis converti ad Deum celeriter?

SAO, contus. Sao man, pertica quâ suspenditur velum.

SAO, fistula. Thoi sao, canere fistulis. Chim sao, avicula quædam.

Sao con ra, fœtum offendere antè tempus.

SAO, vel *sao le,* sed, verùm, tamen. Sao nguoi, ligna transversa super quibus cubamus in lecto. Sao may, vimen. Sao van, quoddam instrumentum musicum.

SAP, cera. Nen sap, cereus. Sap chay xuo, cera defluit.

Sap thuyen, tabulatum in cymbis.

SAP, disponere; collocare. Quan cuoc lay doi sap hang, milites per aciem et ordinem dispositi. Sap san, collocare dispositè.

SAP, pronus, a, um. Sap cat, vertere tergum alicui. Con, sap minh xuo ma doc kinh cao minh; thay se giai toi cho con, fili, prosterne te et dic actum contritionis; et dabo tibi absolutionem.

Sap bay xuo, recluditur laqueus seu decipula.

Sat se, idem est ac *san se,* vide *san.*

Sat ra vel *sat ra,* dehiscere, frangi.

Sᴀᴛ, ferrum. Nung sat, coquere ferrum. Cut sat, scoria. Mot chang an bi cut sat, tinea non potest exedere rubiginem. Dicitur de homine valdè avaro et tenax, à quo nihil unquam extorqueri potest.

Sᴀᴜ, postea; post. Sau nay, post hac. Ve sau, de futuro; in futurum; deinceps. Sau nua, deindè. Sau het, postremò. Ngay sau, tempore futuro. Doi sau, futuro sæculo. Tu nay ve sau, con, phai ra suc lam viec roi linh hon, ab hinc in posterum conaberis satagere saluti tuæ.

Sᴀᴜ, sex. Thu sau, sextus, a, um.

Sᴀᴜ, *sau bot ra,* despumare.

Sᴀᴜ, profundis, a, um. Sau nhiem, vel mau nhiem, mysterium. Thanh y duc chua bloi sau nhiem vo cung, divina voluntas est inscrutabilis. Sau bo, vermis. Cai sau bo cat rut trao tri khon, vermis corrodens conscientiam.

Sᴀᴜ, crocodilus. Giuong sau sanh ra, frontem ferream explicare.

Sau nao, mœror magnus; valdè mœstus.

Sᴇ, *da se lai,* aliquid parumper exsiccatum. Se, chim se, passerculus.

Sᴇ, particula affirmans aliquid certissimè de futuro. Ke co toi trao ma chet, thi se mat linh hon, reus peccati mortalis moritur impœnitens; certè peribit. Mai, con, se den, cras venies, fili. Noi se vay, loqui demissâ voce. Di se se, lentè ambulare.

Sᴇ, *sou se,* vel *sou sit, lam sou se,* vel *sou sit,* crudeliter vel crudè agere. An noi sou se, vel sou sit, cruda verba proferre, effutire verba; sine ullâ consideratione verba fundere.

Sᴇᴍ, *chay sem,* semiustus. Com sem, oryza semiusta.

Sᴇɴ, nymphea. Hoa sen, flores nympheæ. Toa sen, sedes

ornata nympheæ floribus, quam idolum *Thick ca*, promisit suis cultoribus.

Senh phach, senh lem, varia crepitacula, quibus utuntur histriones.

Seo, cicatrix. Seo trau bo, nasus bubalorum boumque perforatus.

Set, fulmen. Set danh, fulmen icit. Set danh·sen set, sonitus fulminis.

Seu, quædam avis.

Si, arbor quædam.

Si, *su si*, vel *su si*, asper, a, um.

Si luot nhau, succedere sibi invicem, unus post alterum.

Si, *tien si*, doctor.

Siec, *so siec*, timere.

Sieng nang, diligens, impiger; diligenter. Nang nan, idem est.

Siet, terere aliquid moliendo.

Sim, *cay sim*, myrtus.

Sinh de, nativitas. Phuc sinh, pascha. Sinh ki, tu qui, vita est iter peragere vel proficisci, mors autem est redire domum. Ke hau sinh, posteri. Sinh doi, infantes gemini. Sinh thi, mori. Sinh, sulfur. Lua sinh lua diem, ignis sulfureus. Sinh do, vide *do*.

So sanh, comparare, conferre.

So, calvaria. So, mytilus. So, caput. So con, so trau, de bestiis dicitur.

So phan, fatum. So he, idem. Xem so, sortilegium inquirere. Doi so, sortem mutare. Do so, numerus graduum astronomicorum.

So sach, vide *sach net so*, ductus penicelli desursùm descendens. So ten, vel so chu di, obliteratio nominis aut scripturæ. Cua so, fenestræ. So ra, disrumpere, dissolvere aliquid colligatum. So tren bloi, iris in cœlo.

So mo, so sam, vide *sam*. Doi so, vel doi xua, antiquiore tempore.

So, palpitare ex cœcitate.

So, *cay so*, quædam arbor. So cai, milites super populis præpositi ad colligenda vectigalia.

So, timere, metuere, formidare. Ke so hai lam, metu perculsus.

Soan lai, revisere, recensere, aut recognoscere aliquas res.

Soat, colligere vectigalia quæ defuerant ex superioribus annis. Khach soat, tributarii.

Soc tran, calvus. Soc vao, sacrificium quod offertur initio lunæ et in plenilunio. Coi soc, vide *coi*. Cai soc, mustela.

Soc ruo, spatium certum agrorum.

Soi, illuminare. Nen soi, lucerna. Soi guong, inspicere se in speculo. Soi bai, arenarium in flumine. Nguoi soi sinh, homo perspicax.

Soi, fervere. Bien soi, mare turbidum. Lam soi len, qui alios nimium urget et quasi fervere facit.

Soi tran, idem est ac *soc tran*, vide *soc*. Cho soi, vide *cho*.

Soi, lapilli. Dat soi, terra petrosa.

Soi, vel *soi nao*, ad exprimendum quod adhùc à fine longè distat; et sic solet dici: Soi nao chua mui gi, adhùc longè est finis; nullâ ex parte evacuatur opus.

Soi chi, filum.

Soi, morbilli. Nen soi, laborare morbillis.

Som, maturè, manè. Som muon, vel kip chay, ocyùs seriùs. Chay kip ta se den truoc toa D. C. J. phan xet, seriùs ocyùs omnes veniemus ante tribunal Christi judicantis. Con som, adhùc nondùm venit tempus. Som mai, summo manè. Mai som, cras manè. Lua som, frugis præcox. Khi con som lam chua sung, multò antè lucis adventum.

Som nguoi hon som cua, multitudo hominum melior est multitudine divitiarum. Giau som, valdè dives.

Som lai, macie confectus; macerrimus.

Som, *cho som*, canis hirsutus. Rau ria som sam, homo maximè barbatus.

Son, minium. Giam son, acetum forte. Dan ba son, mulier non maritata vel sterilis. Vo chou con son se, novi sponsi filium nondùm habentes.

Son son, sinh de son son, mulier sæpissimè filios pariens.

Son, sandaracha. Son hom, sandarachâ capsulas obtegere. Lo son, sandarachæ vapore infectus.

Son lao, relaxatur animus. Ao da son ra, vestis vetustate sublacera.

Son so, exhilarescere. Son gay len, horrent capilli.

Sot, cista rara ad capiendum aliquid.

Sot, calor; calidus, a, um. Sot ret, febris. Sot ruot, ardens animus; inquietus animo. Sot tinh, ardens in cupiditatibus. Sot buc, ardor solis. Chang co sot, nihil omninô. Dat sot lam, terra exusta solis ardoribus.

Sot, aliquid superest ex oblivione. Sang sot, vide *sang*:

Sou, fluvius. Sou van ha, via lactea.

Sou, vivere; vivus, a, um; vita; crudus, a, um. Sou doi doi, vita æterna. Ga sou, gallus. Thit sou, caro cruda. Rau sou, olera cruda. An noi sou sit, vide *se*. Xuong sou, os magnum in dorso quod sustinet omnes costas. Nguoi ay la xuong sou trao lang, ille est primarius in pago. Lai sou, resurgere ex mortuis. Sou sot, qui vix vivus evasit. Su sou ta chao qua chuong hu, vita quâ fruimur brevis est.

Su su, hirsutus, a, um. Dau su su ra, caput hirsutum.

Su, *ca su*, coracinus piscis.

Su, magister. Tien su, adinventor cujuslibet artis, qui pro deo a gentilibus colitur. Dom tien su, le tien su, sacrificare illis diis adinventoribus artium. Ton su, venerandi magistri. Sic etiam vocantur sacerdotes ecclesiæ. Su tu, leo.

Su vel *viec*, res immateriales vel negotia. Sic etiam possunt dici omnia nomina quæ a verbis fiunt; ut *su an*, comestio; su noi, locutio; su o nhung, otium. Chang su gi den may, nihil ad te pertinet. Res verò materiales vocantur do le, cua cai, san vat. Thou su, interpres. Dan su, populus.

Su, legatus. Chinh su, primus legatus. Pho su, secundus
legatus. Bat su, vide *bat.*

Su, historia. Su ki, historici. Sach su, libri historici Sinen-
sium. Quan ngu su, mandarini ex supremo senatû.

Sua, latrare. Mieng hum sua, omnis vis virtusque ejus in
lingua sua est.

Sua sang, disponere; moderari. Sua phat, corrigere. Sua
tri, regere.

Sua, lac. Banh sua bo, caseus.

Suc, abluere vasa. Luc suc, sex species animalium, scilicet,
elephas, equus, bos, ovis, canis, gallina. Sed nunc etiam
sumitur communitur pro omnibus animalibus ista vox
luc suc. Suc go, lignum enorme; lignum rude.

Suc, vis. Suc khoe, fortitudo, valetudo. Qua suc, supra
vires. Het suc, totis viribus. Ra suc, summâ ope niti.

Suy, cogitare, meditari. Suy di ng hi lai, cogitare iterùm
atque iterùm. Suy den su thuong kho D. C. J., cogitare
de passione Christi.

Sui, calefacere se.

Sum hop, congregare se; congregatim habitare. Sum nhau
vao, idem.

Sum lai, fructus contrahuntur, vel pellis contracta.

Sum rang, exesi dentes.

Sung suong, voluptas, voluptuosè. Cay sung, arbor quædam.

Sung, catapulta. Sung tru, sclopeta major, tormentum bellicum. Sung trung xa, sung het, sung trang ma, dai pha
qua son, varia sunt tormentorum bellicorum genera.

Sung, *kham sung, kinh xuo,* venerari, amare. Sung su dao,
diligens in fide, fervens Đei cultor. Sung phat, addictus
idolis.

Sung vel *thung,* perforatus, a, um. Noi thung, olla perfo-
rata. Thung thung, cista pertusa. Sung sung, strepitus
in loco aquarum profundo.

Sung, inflari; vel *phu,* idem. Ca va minh sung len, vel
phu len, totum corpus inflatur, tumescit.

Song, cornua boum. Sung sung, dung sung, sung gitta
dung, stat immotus et enormis in medio viæ.

Suoi, *khe suoi*, rivulus, fons.

Suon, vel *canh suon*, latus. Xuo suon, costæ.

Suong, ros. Hat suong, guttula roris. Suong muoi, ros
malignus.

Suong, vide *sung*.

Suot lua, evellere grana ex spicis.

Sut vel *sut*, dilabi. Dat sut xuo, terra dilapsa in profundum.

Sut da ra, laceratur pellis. Say sut, idem. Vel *sut so*,
etiam.

T.

Ta, vel *chung ta*, nos. Sic superiores ad inferiorem; sed
inferiores ad superiorem, semper *chung toi*.

Ta, injuriam illatam superiori aut etiam æqualibus reparare.
Ta on, gratias agere superiori aut Deo.

Ta vao, ma ta vao no, dæmon intravit in illum. Toi ta,
servus. Lam toi ta, servire.

Ta, perversus, inordinatus. Ta ma, ta than, dæmones.
Dao la, religio perversa. Ta dam, fornicatio. Gian ta,
iniquus.

Ta huu vel *mat trai*, sinister, a, um; dexter a, um. Benh
ta, fluxus ventris. Quan ta dao, latrones.

Tac tuong tac kinh, insculpere simulacrum.

Tac lai, nuoc tac lai, detinetur cursus aquarum. Tac hoi
lai, coercetur spiritus. Tac co, suffocentur fauces: maledictio apud Tunkinenses. Phep tac, potestas; majestas;
modestia. Vo phep vo tac, sine modestia, sine urbani-
tate. Tac luoi, sonitum per linguam edere in signum ad-
mirationis, doloris, iræ.

Tao, decima pars in cubito.

Tai, auricula. Lo tai, aures. Nang tai, graves aures seu
surdæ. Tai va tai ach, infortunium, calamitas.

Tai, dotes naturæ. Tai tri, dexter ingenio. Tien tai, divitiæ. Gia tai, omnia bona domestica. Thu gia tai, con-
fiscatio.

Tai mat, pallor in facie.

Tai, a, ex; propter, circa. Boi tai, idem est. Su nay boi
tai ta ma ra, istud provenit ex peccatis nostris. Toi ph
ke cuop tai noi ay, incidi in latrones circa illum locum,
vel propter illum locum.

Tay, manus. Canh tay, brachia.

Tay, *phuo tay,* occidens; Europa. Gio tay, zephyrus. Con
tay, unicornis. Rieng tay, injustitia in judicando ex re-
spectû personarum. Suscipere personam.

Tay, æqualis; æqualiter.

Tay, purgare se. Thuoc tay, purga.

Tam, *vo tam tinh,* homo non attendens ad sua negotia.

Tam, *cho tam tien,* mutuo dare pecuniam. Tam bo, lam
tam vay, aliquid facere pro brevi tempore. Tam te, ædicula ad tempus constructa, ubi collocantur cibaria mag-
nificè facta ad sacrificandum suis mortuis.

Tam, octo. Thu tam, octavus, a, um.

Tam, dentis calpium, vel spumæ ex immersione alicujus rei
in aquam; unde dicitur; Chang thay tam dang gi sot,
nulla umbra, nullum vestigium apparet. Toi tam, obscuritas magna. Ruou tam, sicera fortissima, spiritus vini.

Tam, lavare corpus totum.

Tam, bombyx. Ngo chan tam, ars serica producendi.

Tam, frustum, particula.

Tam thuoc, temperare medicinam. Tam tuc, gliscit animus.

Tan ra vel *tan tac,* diffrangi; dissipari. Vo tan ra, aliquid
fractum in varias partes. D. C. B. phat quan Judêu tan
tac khap moi noi, Deus punivit Judeos dispersione per
varia loca. Tan nat, fractio, ruina.

Tan ra, comminuere aliquid, pulverizare. Tan thuoc, comminuere medicinam. Tan tan, umbella. Tan lua, favilla.
Tieu tan, dispendia magna.

Tan, umbella circumdata velo. Xieu tan, dispersio. Tan
hai, vastatio, desolatio.

Tan, *khoi len tan bloi*, fumus ascendit usque cœlum. Deu
tan nha, venit ad domum.

Tan, *lan tan*, parvus pruritus.

Tan, finis. Tan the, consummatio sæculi.

Tan vao, tan den, concursus hominum.

Tang, luctus, habitus lugubris. Ao tang, vestis lugubris.
De tang, esse in luctû vel in veste lugubri.

Tang, sepelire. Nha tang, ædicula ad sepulturam destinata.
Tang, est sepelire cum honore. Cai tang, aperire sepulchra ad denuò inhumandum.

Tang, *cot tang*, columnæ domûs humo infixæ. Da tang,
lapides fundamentales. Tang len, augere, accrescere.

Tanh, vel *tanh tao*, fœtor piscis crudi.

Tanh, cessatio pluviæ. Tanh mua, cessat pluvia.

Tao, ego; superbè loquendo, vel superior ad inferiores.

Tao, creare. D. C. B. tao thien lap dia, Deus creavit cœlum
et terram.

Tao, *qua tao*, ziziphum. Tao bao, audax. Tao tinh, audax
natura.

Tao nap sung, replere et infarcire tormenta bellica.

Tap, *go tap*, lignum fragile. Ue tap, sordidus, a, um. Tap
an, comedere sordes: dicitur de piscibus. Do tap, cibaria
ex carne facta.

Tap, *con tap*, tempestas brevis. Bao tap, tempestas magna.
An tap, vel an thit tap, comedere carnem semicrudam.
Tam tap, lavare corpus.

Tap, exercere se, vel aliquid in aliquâ re assuescere. Tap
quan, exercere milites. Con, ph tap nhan duc khien
nhuong, fili, debes exercere humilitatem. Toi tap, rapere
aliquid celeriter.

Tat nuoc, exhaurire aquam de agro in agrum: haurire
aquam de vase in aliud vas, dicitur *mui;* de puteo verò

per situlam, dicitur *kin.* Mang nhu tat nuoc, acriter et multùm increpare.

TAT, *di tat,* per viam compendiosam ire. Noi tat, breviter dicere. Tat lua, extinguere ignem. Tat nghi, mori. Tat gio, cessat ventus.

TAT, vel *tat nguyen,* languor.

TAT, vel *bit tat,* tibiale; ocreæ.

Tau tanh, emere res magni pretii, quales sunt naves, agri, vaccæ, equi.

TAU, navis. Tau voi, tau ngua, stabulum elephantorum equorumque. Muc tau, vide *muc.*

Tau vel *tau,* alloqui vel appellare regem. Tau duc vua muon muon nam, vivat rex ad mille annos.

TE, genus retis.

TE, movere.

TE, tædium. Khi vui, khi te, modò gaudium, modò tædium. Com te, oryza ordinaria.

Te chan, stupent vel tepescunt pedes. Te moi, tepor et dolor.

TE, sacrificare. Te le D. C. B., offerre Deo sacrificium.

TE, secare aliquid æqualiter.

Tem blan, parate betel.

TEN, nomen. Ten thanh, nomen baptismi. Ten con la di gi, nomen tuum quod est? Dat ten, dare nomen. Dat ten thanh, dare nomen sanctum; dicitur pro baptizare. Cai ten, sagitta. Bat ten, sagittari.

TEN, pudorem pati ex repulsâ.

TET, solemnitas anni novi. Di tet, offerre numera anno novo. Tet lai, connectere.

THA, parcere. Tha toi, remittere peccata; donare veniam. Meo tha chuot, felis portat murem. Hum tha, ran can, rapiat tigris et mordeat serpens; maledictio. Tha ra, liberare aliquem à vinculis.

THA, malle. Toi tha chet chang tha bo dao, malo mori quam abjurare fidem.

Tha ra, solvere animal ligatum. Thao tha, otio fruens, libertate gaudens; immunis ab omni labore et dolore.

Thac ra, vel *thac co ra,* calumniam struere.

Thach nhau, provocare invicem ad certamen.

THAI, conceptio. Co thai, fœtu gravida. Khoan thai, paulatim, lentè.

Thai cuc, aër aut principium quoddam à quo omnia creata esse credunt litterati Sinenses. Thai rau, secare olera.

Thai ra, res veteres abdicare.

Thay doi, commutare; succedere unum post alterum. Thay mat, vel thay vi, gerere vicem alterius. Be tren la dang thay mat D. C. B., superior est qui gerit vicem Dei. Thay quien, succedere vel esse in potestate, loco alterius. Khoan thay, lam thay, valdè clemens; valdè multùm, in laudando. Thay thay, omnes, omninò, totum.

THAY, cadaver; per contemptum. Thay no, relinquatur ad nutum ejus.

THAY, oculis, auribus, naribus percipere. Xem chang thay, invisibile aliquid, vel visû percipere non posse. Tim chang thay, quærendo non invenire.

THAY, magister. Thay dao, missionarii et eorum ministri. Thay thuoc, medici. Thay phu thuy, magi venefici. Thay boi, arioli. Thay ca, sacerdotes. Duc thay, vel duc cu, episcopus.

THAM, et *tham lam,* cupidus, a, um; alieni appetens.

Tham thiet, res digna commisseratione. Cai tham hoa, Tapes.

Tham hoa, gradus litteratorum supra doctoratum tien si.

Tham vieng, visitare. Guoi tham, vide *guoi.* Hoi tham, inquirere de aliquo homine; vel nova nuntia. Bat tham, sortem mittere.

THAM, color niger. Nguoi den, homo niger. Ao le tham, casula nigra.

THAM, *mui tham,* color rubeus obscurus. Tham phai, maximè conveniens est. Tham cuc, maxima miseria.

THAM, *giay tham* vel *giay dam*, papyrus quæ atramentum diffundit.

THAM, vel *tham thi*, secretò, demissâ voce. Quan tien tham, exercitus secretè ducitur.

THAN, carbo. Than lua, carbo ignitus. Quan dot than, carbonarii. Than tho, suspirare, ingemere, lamentari. Mloi than, lamentatio; suspiria; oratio jaculatoria. Con, phai nang than tho cung D. C. B., debes, fili, sæpè elevare mentem, et suspirare ad Deum.

THAN, *thit than,* caro macra in dorso.

Than lan, lacertula.

THAN, vox ista variè significat. Than ou, alloquor te, Domine. Than lay cu, salve, pater. Trao than thich, in consanguinitate. Dou than, virgo. Mot than mot minh, solus; solitarius, absque fratribus. Than toi khon nan, corpus meum vel vita mea misera vel vita ejus.

THAN, spiritus. Thien than, angelus. Thanh than, sanctus spiritus. Qui than, dæmon. Thay vi, sedes spiritûs tutelaris. Quan dai thay, magistratus supremus. Noi than, eunuchus. Su than, legatus.

Than tho, vagus; stolidus.

THANG, scala. Bac thang, gradus scalæ. Vi thang, aconitum.

THANG, mensis. Cuoi thang, in fine mensis.

THANG, homuncio; sic vocantur parvuli vel homines infimæ sortis.

Thang ngua, ornare equum ephippiis. Thang tran, vincere, victoriam adipisci.

THANG, rectus; severus; extensus. D. C. B. rat cou thang vo cung, Deus infinitè justus et rectus. Lam cho thang, severè agere. Keo cho thang, extrahere ut sit extensum.

Thanh guom, ferrum; ensis. Thanh tre, frustum arundinis. Thanh nhan, felicitas, beatitudo. Thanh vang, solitudo. Thanh mui, color limpidus, vel sapor. Nha thanh, familia imperatorum tartarorum, qui nunc in Sinis regnant.

44

THANH, civitas; mœnia. Thanh luy, propugnaculum muri.
Ke o trao thanh, oppidani.

THANH, sanctus, a, um. Ou thanh, pro masculino genere.
Ba thanh, sancta. Cua thanh, sacra. Nen thanh, sanc-
tificari. Phao chuc thanh, canonizare. Thanh thot,
stillicidium.

THAO, cingulum seu ornamentum vestis mandarinorum.
Thao tui, ansula bursæ.

THAO, dissolvere; aperire; relaxare.

THAO, liberalitas. Cam thao, glycyrrhiza.

Thao kinh cha me, venerari parentes. Thao lao, urbanus;
liber in conversatione.

Thao tha, vide *tha*. Thao manh, captus lumine.

THAO, vasculum.

THAP, turris.

Thap but, theca penicilli. Thap nen, accendere candelam.

THAP, infimus; demissus, a, um. Thap nuoc, madefacere.
Thap tri, ingenium vulgare; parum ingenii.

THAP, decas. Vox militaris.

THAT, stringere. That co, strangulare. Noi that nguoi ta,
alios reprehendere in verbis.

THAT, vel *ngay that*, et *that tha*, rectus, sincerus et simplex.

That theu, titubare. That tan, profugus. That the, omni
auxilio egere.

THAU, æs. Chi thau, filum ex ære productum.

THAU, animalia juvenca. Viet thau, scribere abreviatè, vel
per compendium; ratio scribendi compendiosè per notas.

Thau dem, totâ nocte. Thau ngay, totâ die. Thau qua,
pertransire, penetrare.

THE, sericum rarissimum.

THE, inscriptio; mandatum. The bai, idem.

THE, modus; opportunitas. Cay quien the, niti auctoritate.
Tot the, bonus modus.

THE, jurare. The thot, idem. The doi, jurare falsa.

THE, ferè eadem est cum voce *the*, modus. The nao, quomodo. The nao the nao, quoquomodo. Nhu the, simili
modo, sicut. Nhan the, eâdem operâ. Phai the, honesto
modo; et sic collocantur: Con, lieu the nao, quomodo,
disponis, fili? Du the nao the nao thi con cu phai cu nhu
vay, etiam si res quoquomodo acciderit, sic debes observare. Con phai cu nhu thay da day, debes te gerere sicut
tibi præcepi. Con ph* dem thu nay di nhan the, affer illi
hanc epistolam eâdem operâ. Con ph an o cho ph the,
debes conversari honesto modo. Trao the, solemnis ritus.
Thou the, liberalis.

THEM, appetitus.

THEM, addere, suppeditare.

Them nha, additamentum domûs.

Theu cua, pessula.

THEU, pudore suffundi.

THEO, sequi. Theo chau, sequi vestigia.

Thep vang, deaurare aliquid.

THEP, chalybs. An may, an thep, mendicare.

THET, *voi thet*, elephas barrit. Keu thet, clamare altâ voce.

THET, vel *thet dai*, hospites liberaliter tractare.

THEU, acû pingere. Ao theu, vestis acû picta.

THI, certamen litterarum. Trang thi, palestra litterarum.
Thi nhau ma lam, certatim agere.

THI, arbor quædam. That qua thi, verissimè.

THI, elargiri; dare eleemosynam. Thi du, exempli gratiâ;
parabola.

THI, aliquid certi affirmans particula; et solet poni cum
moi vel *se*, ut, Con, co sach toi thi moi dep lao D. C. B.,
cùm es mundo corde, tùm Deo placebis. No ki thi lanh
khi thi, alternis bonus, alternis malus; modò bonus, modò
malus.

THICH, icere cubito. Thich chu, insculpere litteras. Thich

---

* Abbreviatio pro *phai*, debere, debes, oportet.

muon an, appetitus naturalis et proprius cuique. Ben thich, idolatria, religio idoli Thicæ; paganismus.

Thich thich, sonitus tundentis.

THIEC, stannum.

THIEN, cælum. Thien dia chan chua, cœli terræque Deus. Thien dang, paradisus cœlestis. Quan tu thien, magistratus mathematicus; astrologus regius.

THIEN, castrare animalia. Ga thien, gallus castratus.

Thieng lieng, spiritualis. Phep thieng, virtus supernaturalis.

THIEP, concubina. Thi thiep, mandatum; commissio. Thiep tinh, veneficus.

THIET, detrimentum. Hon thiet, lucrum vel damnum.

THIEU, incendere. Thieu sinh, vivus aduri.

THIEU, deesse, deficere. Nha nho thieu, inopiâ rei familiaris laborat.

Thieu chau, fenestella in altari.

THIM, uxor patrui minoris.

Thin net, bonæ indolis.

THIN, *noi thin*, adulari.

THINH, *thanh lam thinh*, dissimulare.

THINH, pax, prosperitas. Thinh su, prosperitas rerum. Thinh no, furor; ira principis vel regis.

THINH, farina ex oryza tosta.

Thinh thoang, rarò. Thung thinh, lentus.

THIT, caro. Lam thit, occidere animalia. Dat thit, terra argillosa. Ghe thit, horret caro. Dicitur jocosè de eo qui fecit quod facere non posse parebatur.

THIU, cibaria incipiunt fœtere.

THO, *thom tho*, odoriferus, a, um.

Tho ra, emittere aliquid; prominere.

THO, lepus.

Tho tuc, rusticus, a, um.

Tho ra, evomere. Tho huyet, sanguinem evomere.

THO, carmen, versus. Tho, faber, artifex.

Tho, colere, venerari. Nha tho, ecclesia, oratorium. Ke tho biet, idolorum cultor.

Tho, respirare; suspirare; anhelare.

Thoa lao buon, recreatur animus à tristitiâ et mœrore.

Thoat, vel *thoat choc*, statim; illicò. Thoat, primo intuitu; statim atque. Thoat xem thay; thi lien biet, statim atque vidi; illico cognovi.

Thoc, frumentum.

Thoi muc, frustum atramenti.

Thoi, mos. Thoi tuc, idem.

Thoi. satis esse; sufficere; cessare; quies.

Thoi, fœtere. Mui thoi, fœtor.

Thoi, sufflare, insufflare; canere instrumentis musicis. Thoi be, attrahere.

Thom, odor suavis. Thom lam, odorem mirè fragrantem emittere, vel diffundere.

Thon, pagus parvus.

Thot ra, eloqui.

Thot, tabula culinaria.

Thou thai, doctus, a, um; scientiis, litteris instructus, vel imbutus. Thou biet moi su vo cung, scientia divina. Thou cou, communicatio meritorum. Thou su, interpres.

Thu gop, colligere, congerere. Thu qui thue, colligere vectigalia. Mua thu, autumnus. An trung thu, celebrare convivium autumnale.

Thu, locus; habitatio. Vui thu, delectari habitatione in tali loco. Thu vui, locus delectabilis. Cam thu, vide *cam*.

Thu, inimicus. Ba thu, tres hostes animæ. Ma qui, dæmon; the gian, mundus; xac thit, caro.

Thu lo, vel *an dut*, vide *lo*.

Thu, *don thu*, præsidium. Tuan thu, custodes.

Thu, epistola. Thu tu, idem. Kinh thu kinh thi, libri veterum carminum quæ Confucius recognovit et emendavit.

Thu, ordo. Ista vox ponitur cum omnibus numeris ad distinguendum et faciendum, ut sint numeri cardinales; et

sic dicendum est, *thu nhat,* primus, a, um. Thu hai, secundus, a, um, &c. May la do thu nao, tu es cujus ordinis, seu gradus? Thu tu, ordo benè dispositus. Thu may,
quotus, a, um.

THU, *ngoi thu ra,* sedere tacitus.

THU, experiri, probare.

THUA, vinci, superari.

THUA, respondere, responsio. Semper ponitur cum vocibus
rang, et *vuoi,* ut *no da thua vuoi toi rang,* jam respondit
mihi dicens. Ponitur etiam pro accusare, denuntiare.
Phai thua den dang be tren cho nguoi lieu, oportet denuntiare superiori, ut provideat. Vai thua, tela rara.

THUA, superesse. Du thua, thua lua, magna abundantia.

THUA, *cai thua,* lima ad elaborandum ebur vel cornu. Kach
thua, hospites.

Thua tho lam, præmonere artificem ut aliquid meliùs faciat.
Thua ay, thua no, in tali loco.

THUC, vel *thuc tha,* instare ardenter, urgere. Thung thuc,
tela pilosa.

THUC, redimere. Thuoc, clarius.

THUC, vigilare. Danh thuc, excitare à somno. Thuc day,
evigilare à somno. Mot thuc, unum genus.

THUE, conducere. Cho thue, locare. Thue ng* lam, conducere operarios. Nguoi lam thue, operarii.

THUE, tributum, vectigal. Nop thue, solvere tributum.

Thuy nuoc, aqua. Dang thuy, via maritima. Dang va, via
terrestris. Hou thuy, diluvium. Thuy tinh, vitrum.
Thu vai, terrâ marique. Thuy, argentum vivum. Thuy
thung, hydropisis.

THUI, semiurere animalia occisa ut mundentur à pilis; et
sic rarò excoriantur animalia occisa.

THUYEN, navigium, cymba. Dam thuyen, cymba submer-
sa... Thung, vallis.

---

* Abbreviatio pro *nguoi,* homo.

Thung, cophinus; sporta.

Thung, dolium. Thung chua, dolium maximum.

Thung tinh, vide *tinh*.

Thuo, *thuo xua*, olim. Thuo truoc, prioribus temporibus. Thuo ay, illo tempore.

Thuoc, medicina. Thuoc hay, remedium efficax. Thay thuoc, medicus. Thuoc doi, venenum. Thuoc lao, tabacum. Thuoc sung, pulvis tormentarius.

Thuoc ve, pertinere, esse sub. Toi nay thuoc ve den ran thu nhat, peccatum hoc pertinet ad primum mandatum. Thuoc, vel thuoc lao, expertus, a, um; memoriâ tenere. Con, thuoc nhung kinh nao, quasnam orationes tenes memoriâ? Bon dai thuoc ve o thay, Christiani qui sub domino ipso sunt.

Thuoc ke, regula. Thuoc do, cubitus, mensura. Ke muc thuoc, homo ad regendum cæteros capacissimus.

Thuong, misereri. Lao thuong, hay thuong, misericordia, misericors. Thuong hai than toi, heu, me miserum! Nha thuong, domus misericordiæ. Thuong xot co muoi bon moi, misericordiæ sunt quatuordecim. Thuong yen, amare.

Thuo, remunerare pro aliquo labore aut aliquo negotio prudenter facto.

Thuo, sæpè; ordinarius, a, um. Le thuo, missa ordinaria seu privata.

Thuon vuoi dan anh, prosequi honore majores.

Thuong, mercedem consequi aut donare à rege, aut Deo. D. C. B. thuong ke lanh len thien dang phat ke du xuo dia nguc, Deus remunerabit justos, ascendendo in paradisum; et damnabit malos, præcipitando in infernum.

Thuot qua vel *thau qua*, vide *thau*.

Thut, *ou thut*, syringa. Ou thut thou quan, clysterium.

Ti, *tam ti*, tria tribunalia judicum, scilicet, Nha huyen, nha phu, nha thua.

Ti, vel *ti nhan nhau*, vide *nhan*.

Tɪ, prima hora nocturna, quæ est initium diei apud Sinenses et Annamitas, qui unicuique diei tribuunt duodecim horas, quæ sic nominantur: 1.ª ti; 2.ª suu; 3.ª dan; 4.ª meo; 5.ª thin; 6.ª ti; 7.ª ngo; 8.ª mui; 9.ª than; 10.ª dan; 11.ª tuat; 12.ª hoi. Quarum explicationem hic brevitatis causâ omitto. Quæque duodecim horæ, 24 horis Europæis correspondent: qui modus horas numerandi apud Hebræos quoque extat.

Tɪ, medulla. Da hu ti, corruptus usque ad medullam; omninò corruptus.

Tɪ, extremitas viscerum.

Tia mau, vena sanguinis.

Tɪᴀ, *mui tia*, color violaceus. Tia ca, examen piscium.

Tia rau, evellere olera condensa. Moi tia, invitare cæteros ad convivium particulatim.

Tich cua, conservare, congerere divitias. *Tich su gian*, vel *tich lao thu oan*, servare odium in corde diù et vindictam sumere. Dau tich, cicatrix. Vo tang tich, sine testimonio vel cautelâ, nihil indè probetur crimen.

Tɪᴇᴄ, convivium celebre.

Tɪᴇᴄ, dolere de jacturâ alicujus rei vel personæ. Thuong tiec, commisereri et dolere. Tiec lua chang muon ton, tenax, qui non vult exponere vitam suam periculo. Chang nen tiec minh vi D. C. B., non oportet recusare mortem pro Deo.

Tɪᴇᴍ, *da tiem xao*, jam ferè peractum vel compositum negotium. Tiem, paulatim; ferè.

Tɪᴇɴ, homo pulcherrimus, talis qualis est è cœlo elapsus, ut dicunt gentiles. *To tien* vel *tien nhan*, progenitores, antecessores. Tien binh, primum agmen.

Tɪᴇɴ, tornare. Tho tien, tornator. Con tien, opera tornata. Tien the, eadem opera. Tieu tien, mingere.

Tɪᴇɴ, offerre aliquid regi. Tien cung, offerre Deo. Cung dang, idem est.

Tɪᴇɴ, moneta. Tien bac, pecunia. Dou tien, moneta cuprea.

Tien khach, excipere hospites.

Tieng, vox; lingua; fama. Blon tieng, altâ voce Nho tieng, parvâ voce. Khan tieng, vox rauca. Trao tieng, vox canora. Em tieng, vox suavis. Co danh tieng, habere celebrem famam. Xau tieng, fama pessima. Noi tieng khoe nhau, dissimili linguâ loqui.

Tiep, carina. Tiep vao, adjungere.

Tiet, sanguis.

Tieu, digerere cibum. Tieu dung, impendere pecuniam. Ho tieu, piper. An chang tieu, ciborum indigestio.

Tieu, parvus, a, um. Thang tieu, parvuli Bonziorum ministri. Tieu hau, pedissequus. Cai tieu, sarcophagus.

Tim, *blai tim*, cor. Tim la, morbus venereus.

Tim mau, livor.

Tim, quærere. Tim toi, idem est.

Tin, credere, fidere nuntium. No chang tin, non credit. Co tin den, venit nuntium. Dem tin, nuntiare. Mang tin, audito nuntio. Tham tin, inquirere nuntia. Ng ta chang ke hay noi doi may, parum fides mendacibus est.

Tinh than, spiritus vitales. Hao ton tinh than, consumuntur spiritus vitales. Lau ting, vide *lau*. Tinh, etiam sumitur pro dæmonibus. Qui tinh, pejor dæmone. Tinh mui, vel son mui, os nasi.

Tinh, *thanh tinh*, castus, a, um; castitas. Tinh trai, jejunium naturale. Tinh khou, parûm, nihil.

Tinh, natura, substantia. Tinh giao, lex naturalis. Tinh net, indoles, propensio. Tinh lai, vel tinh loan lai, ad calculum revocare. Toi tinh the nay, sic puto. Ng tinh me net xau, vir ingenio malo pravoque.

Tinh, affectus cordis. Vo tinh, sine attentione. Tinh co, vide *co*.

Tinh, sanus, compos mentis. Tinh lai, redire ad se, animum revocare ad se.

Tit, callum parvum. No co tit trao minh, habet callum in corpore; aut conscius sibi alicujus sceleris.

45

Tɪᴛ, *be tit*, vel *nho tit*, minimus, a, um.

Tɪᴜ, *tuc tiu*, verba obscœna.

To, crassus, grassus, a, um; grandis, e.

To te, sciolus.

To, et *to tuong*, clarus, a, um; clarè; clarificare; prodere; clarè scire. Noi lai cho to, repetere clarè. Cu, da nghe to chua, jam ne clarè audiisti, pater. Viec ay toi da to, illud negotium jam clarè scio.

To lo, publicè, manifestè. Con dou, con to, tempestas levis.

To, nidus. To tou, progenitores. Cai Thanh to tou, sancti Patriarchæ.

To, sericum ex quo fiunt fila. Keo to, producere fita serica. Giou to, omnia quæ fiunt ex serico.

To, *to vay*, ferè similis, e.

To vel *tao*, vide *tao*. May tao, tu, ego. Nguoi to, idem. Sunt voces superborum et iratorum. Day to, discipulus, famulus.

To giay, folium papyri, scriptum. Guio to, mittere scriptum. Len to, scriptum conficere.

Toᴀ, *giao toa*, causidicus versipellis et vafer.

Toᴀ, thronus; tribunal.

Toᴀ, *la toa*, pulvinar ephippii.

Toa khoi toa ra, fumus spargitur. Hoa moi toa ra, flos sese explicans. Thiet toa, vinculum.

Toᴀɪ, *bat toai*, paralyticus.

Toᴀɴ, deliberare; decernere; aggredi; parare. Ao toan keu, parabat acclamare.

Toᴀɴ, arithmetica; computare. Con toan, calculi. Ha con toan, bo con toan, calculos ponere.

Toᴄ, capillus. De tang, vel de toc cho cha me, pullâ veste indui causâ luctûs; habitum lugubre induere pro honore parentum mortuorum.

Toᴄ, *tui toc*, statim, cæleriter.

Toɪ, pestis animalium, lues.

Toɪ, vinculum; catena. Loi toi, idem.

Toɪ, allium.

Toɪ, ego; meus, a, um. Cua toi, res mea. Chung toi, nos, noster, a, um. Toi ta, servus; ancilla.

Toɪ, peccatum; pœna; reatus. Pham toi, peccare. Chiu toi, pœnam luere. Phep giai toi, sacramentum pœnitentiæ vel absolutio sacramentalis. Xung toi, confiteri peccata. Den toi, satisfacere pro peccatis. Noi giai toi, purgatorium. Toa giai toi, confessionale. Thang rat ke co toi, homo omnium quos terra sustinet sceleratissimus.

Toɪ, obscurus, a, um; obscuritas, nox. Dem toi tam, nox obscurissima. Toi da, obscurum ingenium, homo parvæ memoriæ.

Toi tan, labefactus, a, um; desolatus; lapsus in ruinam.

Toɪ, *ao toi*, pluviale.

Toɪ, venire. O dau ma toi, undè venis? Buoc toi len, progredi. Toi len, progredi, regredi.

Toм, comprehendere. *Tom ve* vel *tom lai*, comprehendere ad. Muoi den ran D. C. B. tom ve hai su nay, decem mandata Dei ad hæc duo comprehenduntur.

Toм, locusta marina.

Ton kinh, honorare. Ton su, reverendus magister seu sacerdos.

Toɴ, expendere. Lam ton cua, prodigus.

Toɴ, *du ton*, crudelis; crudeliter.

Ton tac, pavidus, a, um; trepidè hùc illùc cursitare.

Tᴀɴɢ, contignatio. Tang bloi, gradus cœlorum.

Tang len lam quan, provehere ad dignitates. Bong tang, aurora.

Top mo, adeps decocta et expressa. Nguoi ra tung top, turmatim sedere.

Top lay, ore celeriter rapere.

Tot ra, citò foras elabi vel effugere. Tot truoc, fugere. Bo tot, unicornius.

Toᴛ, bonus, a, um. Tot lanh, formosus, a, um. Tot xinh, idem.

Tou chi vel *to tou*, progenies; progenitores. Tou do, discipuli.

Tou, deducere; comitari; adjudicare.

Tou, toparchia. Truong tou, procurator publicus in toparchiâ. Tou co, signifer.

Tra vao, promittere. Tra hoi, inquirere juridicè, interrogare. Quanh thanh tra, inquisitores. Tra do an, temperare cibaria.

Tra, *man tra*, vel *doi tra*, fallax, mendax.

Tra lua, ejusdem classis, occasionis.

Tra vel *blu*, reddere, restituere.

Tra, genus ollæ fictilis.

Trao, crepitaculum.

Trach, vel *trach moc*, conqueri. Trach vi su loi, delicta reprehendere.

Trai, ostrea. Con trai, vel con blai, puer. Trai gai, peccatum luxuriæ.

Trai, villa. Trai chan, vel truot chan, lapsus pedum; ferè labi, ferè lapsus est.

Trai, perverso modo. Tay trai, manus sinistra. Trai vel blai, fructus.

Trai vel *blai chieu*, explicare mattas. Da tra moi su, experientiâ omnium rerum doctus.

Tray lay vel *blay lai*, legere flores aut fructus.

Tray vao vel *blay vao*, respergere sordes aut vicem vestibus, aut aliis rebus.

Tray, proficisci. Chuyen tray, profectio.

Tray tro, quod difficilè fit.

Tram, pix, bitumen.

Tram, *mot tram*, centum. Tram lan, centies.

Tram, piscis, quidam. Tram, in aures.

Tran, certamen. Duoc tran, vincere. Thua, vel thoi tran, vinci.

Tran chau, gemmæ.

Tran, regere, moderari. Quan tran, gubernator provinciæ.

Tran, nudus, a, um; sine veste. Tran truo, nudus absque ullo velamine.

Tran trut, fugere laborem.

Tʀᴀɴ, frons. Soi tran, calvus.

Tran vel *blan ra*, exundare. Toi ng ta da blan kap dat, peccatum hominum jam exundat per totum orbem.

Tʀᴀɴ, coluber.

Tʀᴀɴ, *dai tran*, parva pocula quibus utuntur gentiles in suis sacrificiis.

Trang vel *blang*, pagina. Nghiem trang, majestuosus.

Trang nguyen, supremus gradus litteratorum.

Trang gio, pervius locus vento. Banh trang, genus edulii.

Tʀᴀɴɢ, palæstra. Trang hoc, collegium. Trang ao, collarium vestis. Tre trang, piger. Trang hot, rosarium. Trang hoa, serta florum.

Trang vel *blang*, luna.

Tʀᴀɴɢ, albus, a, um.

Tʀᴀɴɢ, *go trang*, lignum durissimum. Nguoi tro trang, homo durus, impudens. Tro trao, idem.

Tranh ve, tabula picta. Tranh, vel blanh lop nha, paleæ contextæ quibus teguntur domus. Tranh nhau, æmulari invicem.

Tʀᴀɴʜ, genus testudinis.

Tʀᴀɴʜ, decedere viâ aut paulisper declinare. Tranh trut, vel tran trut, vide *tran trut.*

Trao cho, tradere, præbere.

Trao ra, ebullire.

Tʀᴀᴏ, inter, intra; inter vos. Trao chung bay, intra arcam. Trao hom, trao lao, in corde. Trao nam, anno recenter elapso. Ra nan, anno proximè venturo. Nuoc trao, aqua limpida.

Tʀᴀᴏ, nobilis, pretiosus, gravis. Sang trao, nobilitas. Minh thanh D. C. J. la cua rat trao, corpus Christi est res pretiosissima. Toi trao, peccatum grave.

Tʀᴀᴏ, incunabula. Trao, laqueus.

Trap vel *blap*, aqua agitata exilit è vase.

Trap com, aliquid oryzæ calidæ superponere, ut calefiat.

Trap tai, canis depressæ auriculæ.

TRAT, oblinere parietem.

TRAT, *an trat*, manducare grana dente frangendo. Trat, occasio, tempus.

TRAU, bubalus.

TRAU, pellicula oryzæ.

Trau vel *blau*, betel. Tem blau, vide *tem.*

TRE, arundo indica. Tre pheo, idem. Bui tre, arundinetum.

TRE, vel *tre mo*, pueri, puellæ. Tuoi tre, adolescentia, juventus. Con tre, teneris adhùc annis, adhùc esse juvenis.

Tre nai, desidiosus; vide *tre trang.* Tre ao xuo, vestis ab humero pendens.

Trech ra, aliquid paulisper excedens è suo loco.

Trem moi, lambere labia.

TREM, *chay trem mot chut*, aliquid modicè semiustum.

TREN, superior; supra, super. Be tren, Deus; rex; superior. Tren bloi, in cœlo. Tren rung, in sylvis.

TREO, suspendere aliquid fune.

TREO, *ghe treo*, sedes plicabilis.

TREO, conscendere arbores.

Treu gheo, molestare, inquietare.

Tret vel *giet lo*, obturare foramen.

TRI, regere, imperare.

TRI, mens, ingenium. Tri khon, idem. Thuong tri, excellentis ingenii. Co tri tra, ingeniosus.

TRICH, *ca trich*, immotus.

TRIEU, decem milliones.

Trieu than vel *quan trieu*, curia, supremi consules. Mu trieu thien, corona regis.

Triet di, delere.

Tro vel *blo*, cinis.

TRO, *hoc tro*, scholasticus. Nha tro, histriones. Lam tro, representare comœdias. Noi truyen tro, narrare historias.

Tro, indicare.

Tro cua vel *blo cua,* portam facere.

Tro, vel *blo lua da tro,* vel *du blo,* spicæ exurgunt. Ngon lua tro len, exurgit flamma.

Tro trao, homo perfrictæ frontis.

Tro thi, pro circumstantiâ et instantiâ temporis ; ad tempus aliquid factum.

Tro di tro lai, vel *blo di blo lai,* ire, redire ; vertere, revertere. Tro nhieu viec, impediri multis negotiis. Nhieu su ngan tro, multa obtant impedimenta. Ngan tro viec doi bla, negotiis superstitiosis implicatus. Tro viec, intentus negotio aliquo.

Troc vel *bloc da ra,* evellitur pellis.

Troc dau vel *troi dau,* obtonsum caput.

Troc vel *bloc di,* convellitur arbor tempestate.

Troi, *cai troi,* cista rara ad capiendas ollas. Troi, ligare reum, vincire.

Troi di, ferri aquarum impulsû. Ca troi, quidam piscis. Qua troi, fructus quidam. Ma troi, igniculi nocte apparentes.

Troi len vel *bloi,* emergere, eminere.

Trom, clam, occultè. An trom, furari. Ke trom, fur. Chua cua ke trom, custodire res furto ablatas.

Tron, rotundus, a, um.

Tron vel *blon,* integer, a, um ; perfectus ; absolutus, a, um. perfectè.

Tron, vel *blan tron,* nates. Tron kim, foramen acûs.

Tron, vertere et revertere acetarium.

Tron, fugere. Tron tranh, idem.

Tron, lubricus, a, um ; labilis. Dang tron, via luto lubrica.

Tron trung mat len, micant oculi deductis superciliis.

Trot vel *blot,* integer, a, um ; totus, a, um. Lam viec blot ngay, laborare totâ die. Trot, aliquandò est vox excusantis se, ut : Toi da trot lam, xin anh tha cho, jam erravi, peto à te veniam. Su da trot, quod ex errore peractum est.

Trou doi, expectare. Trou cay, sperare, spem in aliquo ponere. Bo lao trou cay, despondere animo.

Trou, *cai trou*, tympanum. Danh trou, pulsare tympanum. Bung trou, fabricare tympanum. Trou, vel trou trai, patens; palam. Noi trou vay, generaliter dicere sine determinatione personæ, &c. Xung toi trou vay chang du, confessio generalis peccatorum, id est, absque circumstantiis requisitis, non satis est.

Trou vel *blou cay*, plantare arbores.

Tru len, ululare more canis aut lupi. Cho dai can tru len, canis rabiosi veneno infectus ululatus. Tru nha, columna domûs. Nen tru, cera paschalis.

Trou, *o tam tru*, hospitari per aliquot dies.

Tru tri, morari, morosus.

Trou, expellere; amandare. Tru qui, expellere dæmonem ex energumenis.

Trou, vel *tich tru*, conservare, asservare in futurum usum. Tru duong, conservare, favere alicui. Tru duong dao kiep, protegere latrones.

Trua, *da trua*, si dicatur manè, sensus est: jam est tardè; ut: Hom nay ta thuc day da trua, hodiè surreximus tardè. Si verò propè meridiem est sermo; tunc verò ferè meridies est. Bua trua, vel an com trua, prandium.

Truc trac, vox non apta ad orationis connectionem. Non est *porpolia* oratio. (*Sic in MS.*)

Truc tinh, natura fervida, zelosa. Truc doi, expectare, assistere, astare ut in promptu sit.

Trui, idem est ac *troc troi*, vide *troc.*

Trui vat, luctatores qui caput suum obtundent.

Truy tam, quærere, investigare.

Truyen, historia, confabulatio.

Truyen, mandare, præcipere; tradere posteris. D. C. B. phan truyeu lam vay, Deus præcipit sic. D. C. J. truyen bay phep sacramento, Christus instituit septem sacramenta. Chi truyen, vel phung truyen, edictum regis. Toi to tou truyen, originale peccatum.

Trum, *ou trum,* vel *lam trum,* caput esse in aliquâ societate, pago, confraternitate. Trum ca minh, coöperire totum corpus.

Trum, genus cistæ ad capiendos pisciculos, et locustas aquaticas.

Trum, *non trum,* galerus concavus.

Trun vel *blun,* lumbricus.

Trung phao, captus malignâ aurâ aut aliquâ aliâ infirmitate.

Trung, *trung diep diep,* numerus innumerabilis. Trung danh trung hieu, similitudo nominis.

Trung, ovum. Trung chay, lens. Trung ung, ovum urinum. Ga ap trung, gallina incubat ovis. Ga de trung, gallina parit ova. Vo trung, testa ovi. Lao trang trung, albumen ovi. Lao do trung, vitellus.

Truoc, antè. Truoc mat, coram. Khi truoc, vel truoc khi, antèquam. Doi truoc, priora tempora. Truoc het, antè omnia. Truoc khi D. C. J. chua co ra doi thi chang co ai duoc len thien dang sot, antè Christi incarnationem nemo ascendit in cœlum omninò. Toi chang dam hua truoc, non audeo priùs promittere.

Trung vel *sung,* vallis, loca demissiora.

Truo, major. Truong nam, primogenitus. Truong tou, major seu procurator in toparchiâ. Xa truong, vel truong toc, pater familias; familiæ princeps.

Truong, *pho truong,* vide *pho.*

Truong don, infligere verbera; cædere fuste vel verberibus. Mot truong, mensura decem cubitorum.

Truo, vide *tran.*

Trut ra, diffugere. Trut ao ra, exuere se veste.

Tu, congregare se; concrescere. Vide *quan tu.*

Tu hanh, monachus vel eremita. Thay tu, monachi idolatriæ. Cai thanh tu hanh, sancti monachi. Di tu, monachum profiteri. Dao tu hanh, religiones monachorum. Nha tu hanh, monasterium.

46

Tv, *nhieu tu*, sic vocantur filii privilegiati ex dignitate aut merito patris. Ou nhieu ou tu, idem.

Tu rac, vel *tu nguc*, carcer. Tu chan, pedes coercendo aut sedendo diù in uno loco fatigantur.

Tu vel *phu*, coöperire aliquid paleis.

Tv, quatuor, quartus, a, um. Muoi tu, quatuordecim. Thu tu, quartus, a, um, vel feria quarta. Tu thien, scientia mathematica. Quan tu thien, magistratus mathematici, quorum est conficere calendaria.

Tv, *y tu*, intentio; res intenta. Nguoi co y co tu, homo benè attentus ad sua opera.

Tv, à, ab, ex. Tu nha toi den day, è domo meâ hùc usque. Tu con xung toi lan truoc den ray, duoc may thang nay, fili, ex quo fecisti ultimam confessionem usquemodo, quot menses effluxerunt? Tu D. C. J. ra doi, à Christianâ salute, vel à Christi nativitate, vel à Christo nato. Tu bao gio, à quo tempore. Tu nay ve sau, con ph ra suc lanh cac dip toi, ex hoc in posterum debes, fili, vitare omnes occasiones peccandi. Tu con, abdicare filium. Chang nen tu con trai mle, non licet contra rationem abdicare à se filium.

Tv, vox Sinico Annamitica duas significationes habens, mortis aut filii. Undè cùm dicitur *sinh tu*, id est, vita et mors. Tu vi dao, mortuus vel mortua pro religione, seu martyris. The tu, uxor et liberi. De tu, famuli, discipuli. Quan tu, philosophus vel scientiis celeberrimus; sapiens.

Tv, *thu tu*, vide *thu*. Tu nhien, dao tu nhien, lex naturæ. Tinh tu nhien, natura. Nguoi nhien biet yen men cha me, homines à naturâ sicut parentes esse amandos. Nguoi tu nhien hay noi, homo à naturâ suâ seu ex seipso loquax.

Tva, radius. Sao tua, stella caudata.

Tua sach, præfatio libri.

Tuc, *thoi tuc*, mos, consuetudo. Xuat giang tuy tuy khuc, nhap gia tuy tuc, cùm Romæ fueris, Romano vivito more. Noi tuc, vorax.

Tuc, *chuot tuc*, vox muri propria.

Tuc thi, statim. Tuc gian, impetus iræ. Dau tuc, impetus doloris.

Tui, saccus, crumena.

Tui than vel *tui ho*, pudore et confusione plenus.

Tuy rang, etiam si licet.

Tuy, sequi, conformare se mori. Tuy tuc, sequi morem. Tuy ma cai minh, pro opibus. Tuy suc, pro viribus.

Tuyen, integer, a, um; totus, a, um. Lang nay da co dao tuyen, iste pagus jam factus est Christianus totus. Tuyen nien, toto anno. Tuyet, nix.

Tuoc, *quet tuoc*, verrere. Chut tuoc, dignitates.

Tuoi, annus ætatis. Tuoi tac, senex. Da co tuoi, accedere ad senectutem. Xem tuoi, vana observantia annorum ætatis.

Tuoi, viridis, recens. Ca tuoi, piscis recens. Chet tuoi, mors subitanea.

Tuoi, rigare.

Tuon vao, confluere.

Tuo, *pha tuo ra*, perfringere, destruere.

Tuo, forma. Tuo chu, forma litteræ seu scripturæ. Nguoi vo tuo, sine formâ homo, seu homo nullius formæ urbanitatis. Nguoi buo tuo, disolutus.

Tuong, condimentum ex fabis factum.

Tuong, statua, simulachrum.

Tuong, dux. Thuong tuong, supremus seu maximus dux. Dai tuong, magnus dux. Ta tuo, pho tuo, dux ad sinistrum cornu. Co tuo hieu, vexillum ducis ad commonendum.

Tuo, murus, paries. To luong, vide *to*.

Tuong, versare in mente aliquid. Tuong su chang nen, cogitare illicita. Tuong nho, vel to tuong, desiderare in animo.

U.

U, aliquid tegendo humectare.

U, respondentis et approbantis vox.

U bo, gilbus vaccarum, vel callum.

Uᴀ, folia flava ex ariditate.

Uᴀ, invicem amare, concordare.   No chang ua toi la bao nhieu, non multùm me amat.   U me, hebes.

Ua mau ra, sanguis per os fluit.

Uo, ca uc, nomen piscis.

Uc ich tra bung, motus et molestia in ventre.

Uc mo ac, pectus.

Uc di, sonus deglutientis.

Uo, lam uc lao ng ta, injustitiam facere aliis per vim.

Uɪ, *ca ui,* pisces supernantes fœtorem aquæ non ferentes.

Uɪ, *lam ui xuo,* supprimere.   Lam ui di, per vim facere.

Uɪ, *yen ui,* consolari.   Sach yen ui ke liet, liber legendus ad consolationem infirmorum.

Uy nghiem, majestas magna.

Uɴɢ, *trung ung,* ovum urinum.

Ung ung, genus solæ.

Uɴɢ, consentire.

Uoɪ, *banh uoi,* edulii genus.

Uoᴍ, rugitus tigridis.

Uong hot, seminare.

Uoc ao, impensè desiderare.

Uong uong, nondùm benè maturus fructus.   Homo non est perfectè prudens.   Inh uong, genus ranæ.

Uoᴍ, accommodare vestem, componere ad videndum.

Uop ca, respergere sal piscibus, ad conservandum per breve tempus.

Uoᴛ, madidus, a, um ; madefactus, a, um.

Uo, bibere.   Ung thu, ulcus.

Uᴘ, coöperire ollas suo operculo.

Uᴛ, ultimus, a, um.   Con ut, filius ultimus.

V.

Vᴀ, *vao dau*, impingere aliquid contra caput.

Vᴀ, reatus; pœna ex peccato.

Vᴀ, resarcire vestem. Cho va, canis maculatus.

Vᴀ, particula *et.* Va com vao mieng, intromittere oryzam ori per baculos. Ca va hai, simul duo. Ca va, totus, a, um.

Vᴀ, alapas dare. Cay va, ficus. Quo at va, genus umbellæ ad instar foliorum ficûs.

Vᴀ, *di va*, iter pedestre. An va, comedere obsonia absque oryzâ.

Vᴀᴄ, dolabro secare; dolare. Chim vac, luna splendidissima.

Vᴀᴄ, gerere aliquid solidum humero.

Vᴀᴄʜ, paries. Cai vach, centurio.

Vach voi, notare aliquid per calcem. Vach dat, terram per lineam cultro secare. Cai vach, instrumentum fartoris quo lineam facit.

Vᴀɪ, humerus.

Vᴀɪ, vasa ad continenda salsamenta.

Vᴀɪ, invocare. Vai bloi dat, invocare cœlum et terram. Khan vai, idem.

Vai va, duo tresque vel tria.

Vᴀɪ, tela, pannus ex gossipio. Vai gai, tela ex lino texta.

Vᴀɪ, bonzia. Vai thoc ra, spargere frumenta.

Vᴀɪ, *ou ba ou vai*, progenitores. Vay muon, mutuari. Cho vay muon, mutuo dare; vide *muon*.

Vᴀʏ, contortus, a, um; perversus, a, um.

Vᴀʏ, femorale mulierum.

Vay ten, ala sagittæ.

Vᴀʏ, squama. Danh vay, desquamare.

Vay tay, vocare per manum.

Vay ca, pinna piscis. Vay boc thanh, obsidere civitatem. Circumsedere urbem armis, circumdare urbem.

Vay, igitur. Ay vay, vay thi, idem. The vay, sic. Nhu vay, idem.

Van, *keu van*, expostulare, implorare. Con, phai nang keu van than tho cung D. C. B., fili, debes continuò suspirare ad Deum.

Van, vel *muon van*, decem millia. Muon muon van van, innumerabilis multitudo.

Van, tabula. Dau van, genus phaseoli.

Van, *viec da van*, opus jam est in exitû, vel jam paulò sese remittunt negotia. Van, est etiam prosa. Van bot ao, vestem minuere.

Van, littera; oratio. Van te, oratio precatoria in sacrificiis gentilium. Van thao, epitaphium. Van tu, chirographum. Van tho, carmina. Nguoi van vat, homo litteris benè instructus. Quan van, mandarini litterati.

Van, circumvolvere.

Van vel *ngan*, brevis, e.

Van, *hum van*, tigris maculatus.

Van nien, cyclus annorum. Van menh, fortuna, fatum.

Van van, et cætera, et reliqua.

Van vit vel *quat quid*, multis nexibus involvere.

Van quanh, circumagere, circumvolvere.

Van vo vel *vo van*, homo ineptus, imprudens, importunus.

Vang, aurum. Nhuom vang, tingere colore flavo.

Vang, obedire.

Vang, lignum ex quo elicitur rubeus color.

Vang, abesse. Vang nha, abesse domo suâ. Vang ve, locus solitarius, secretus.

Vanh vel *vao*, circulus; torquis.

Vao, vide *da*. Vao, intrare.

Vao, *trao vao*, vide *trao*. Tieng vao ra, echo.

Vat, res; brutum; animal. Vat gi, quid? quæ res? Muon vat, vel moi vat, omnes creaturæ. May la vat gi, tu quid es? Danh vat, colluctari.

Vat, *thuyen chay vat*, cymba fertur obliquo velo contra ventum.

VAT, duæ partes exteriores vestis.

Vat nuoc di, exprimere aquam ab aliquâ re ut exsiccetur.

Vat di vel *quang di,* projicere aliquid fortiter. Vat man len, velum relevare vel attollere.

Ve sau, cicadæ.

Ve van, versus quidam aut prosa.

VE, modus. Ve nay, ve no, isto modo, alio modo. Noi nhieu ve lam, multifariè loqui.

VE, pingere. Tho ve, pictor.

VE, de; in; redire. Cho ve nha, domum dimittere. Ph nang noi truyen ve D. C. J. cung cac thanh, oportet identidem sermonem facere de Christo et Sanctis. Su vui that ve mot D. C. B. ma thoi, vera voluptas est in solo Deo. Tu nay ve sau, posthàc, in posterum.

Ve lai vel *vien lai,* globos facere; rotundum aliquid reddere.

VE, vel *blai ve,* femur.

VEM, genus ostreæ magnæ.

Ven tuyen vel *blon ven,* integer, a, um. *Ven ao,* sustollere vestem. Ven quan len, elevare femorale.

VEN, *cho ven,* canis maculatus.

VEO, testus, a, um.

VEO, digitis carnem convellere.

Vet lay, colligere particulas vel aliquid residuum è mensis, vasibus, &c.

VET, psittacus. Vet, cicatrix, ærugo.

Vi bang, si.

VI, propter, eo quid, pro, quoniam, quia. Vi su ay, ideò, proptereà. Vi chung, quia. Vi toi, propter me; pro me. Vi lam sao? quare? Thay vi, loco alterius, vice alterius. Vi nha, arcus domûs. Than vi than chu, sedes animæ; tabella superstitiosa.

VIA, spiritus animalis; spiratio. Mat via, ex metû ferè exhalare animam. Hu via, revocare animam egressam ex metû. An via, celebrare natale.

VIEC, negotium, occupatio. Viec vieng, negotium particu-

lare; salus propria. Viec bua viec quan, negotia publica.
Viec doi bla, opera superstitiosa. Viec nen viec chang,
opera licita aut illicita. Ng nay nen viec, iste homo aptus est negotiis gerendis.

VIEN, globus. Vien thuoc, pillula medicinæ. Cha vien,
condimentum ex carne concisâ et globatâ. Quan vien,
majores in pago. Sai vien, ministri missi.

VIENG, vigilare. Tham vieng, idem.

VIET, vel *viet sach*, scribere.

VIOH, *cai vich*, testudo marina.

Vin xuo, deprimere ramum.

Vin lay vel *vo lay*, apprehendere aliquid in adjumentum.
Chet duoi vo lay bot, naufragus apprehendit spumam, id
est, vanas spes.

Vinh hien, felicitas, beatitudo.

VIT, anas. Vit bloi, coturnices.

Vo, rete parvum ad piscandum.

Vo, *cai vo*, dicta, seu vas mediocre. Vo lua, triturare.
Vo gao, lavare oryzam.

Vo, cortex arborum aut fructuûm.

Vo vang, pallidus; macer.

Vo, sine. Vo dao, sine religione, seu gentilis. Vo phep,
inurbanus. Vo y, sine intentione, ex inadvertentiâ. Vo
cung, sine fine. Vo thuy vo chung, æternus.

Vo, malleus; tudes. Vo, palma manûs.

Vo, suaviter demulcere. Noi vo ve, adulari.

Vo, uxor. Vo mon, concubina.

Vo van, vide *van*. Vo, vide *vin*.

Vo, quoddam insectum macerrimum; undè fit proverbium.
Xac nhu vo, id est, macerrimum sicut illud insectum.

Vo, codex. Sach vo, libri.

Vo, confractio; confractus, a, um. Danh vo, vel lam vo,
frangere. Chum vo, vas fractum. Vo tau, vel dam tau,
naufragium.

Voc, tela serica crassa.

Voc, manipulum.

Voi, elephas.

Voi voi, altissimus, a, um.

Voi, proboscis. Voi voi au, elephas proterit suis pedibus aliquid.

Voi, calx. Ne voi, calce parietem oblinire.

Voi, properanter. Viec voi, negotium urgens. Voi vang, idem. Voi gian, facilis ad iram. An noi voi vang, inconsideratè loqui.

Voi, *cay voi*, quædam arbor.

Voi, ex parte evacuari. Con voi, nondùm omninò impletus, a, um.

Voi sang, transfundere. Voi ra, evacuare.

Voi tay len, extendere in altum manum ad apprehendendum aliquid.

Voi, *xa voi*, longum spatium. Con xa voi, adhùc longè distare.

Von lai, aliquid conglobatur.

Von, summa capitalis. Iniro von lai, (*Sic in* MS.) summa capitalis et lucrum. Von no the vay, ex se sic est.

Von, *hum von nhau*, tigrides lasciviunt.

Vang, obedire; obtemperare. Vang mloi chiu luy, obedientia.

Vot, expolire aliquid cultro.

Vot, pertica, virga. Vide *roi*.

Vot, *cai vot*, reticulum.

Vot, *cai vot*, gladius qui habet manubrium longum.

Vot len, extrahere aliquid ex aquâ.

Vu tam, commodato dare.

Vu, ubera, mammilla.

Vu, *quam vu*, mandarini bellicosi.

Vua, rex.

Vuc lay, haurire aquam vasculo.

Vuc, stagnum.

Vui, lætus, a, um; lætitia. Vui ve, lætitia magna.

47

Vui, aliquid humo contegere.

Vun lai, accumulare. Vun trou, accumulare terram ad plantandum aliquid.

Vung, *cai vung*, operculum ollæ parvæ. Vung vang, rotare ad projiciendum.

Vung ve, imperitus, a, um; imperitè.

Vung nay, hæc vicinia. Vung vang, gestus irati.

Vung, *dao vung*, fossam facere.

Vung vang, firmus, a, um. Stabilis, e. O cho vung, esto confirmatus.

Vuo, quadratus, a, um. Vuo vuc, idem.

Vuon, *hum vuon ra*, tigris se erigens.

Vuon, species simiæ.

Vuon, hortus.

Vung, sesamum. Vung dat, globus terræ. Vung bloi, sphæra cœlestis. Vung cu mloi be tren day, jussa efficere.

Vuong mat chut, leviter detineri.

Vuot, unguis tigris aut leonis.

Vuot bien, navigare, currere maria. Vuot khoi, evadere; superare.

Vua phai, mediocriter. Vua, æqualis, conformis. Hai nguoi nhau, duo homines concordes inter se. Vua vua, mediocriter. Vua doan, vel vua roi, statim atque. Toi vua den, statim atque perveni.

Vuoi, cùm. Habet plures significationes. Thao vuoi cha, honorare parentes, &c.

X.

Xa, longus, a, um; longè distare. Bao xa, quanta distantia. Di xa, longè profiscici. Con xa ngay, adhùc restant multi dies. Xau xa, turpis, deformis. Cai xa keo vai, rota ad producendum fila.

Xa huo, moschus. Con xa, animal quod moschum producit.

Xa nhan, legatus ad inquirendum de bello. Xa qui thue cho dan, eximere à tributo populum. Pho xa, taberna.

Xa nha, tigrum. (*Sic in* MS. q. tignum?)

Xᴀ, pagus major. Xa truo, vide *truong.* Negotiorum pagi curator. In uno quoque pago magno sunt tres procuratores qui vocantur Xa truo; nempè Xa chinh, primus, Xa su, secundus; et tertius vocatur Xa tu. Lam xa, esse procurator in pago.

Xᴀᴄ, corpus. Xac thit, caro. Tinh xac thit yeu duoi, caro infirma, fragilis. Chang nen theo tinh xac thit, non oportet sequi naturam corruptam. Xac chet, cadaver. Liem xac, vide *liem.* Lam phep xac, benedictio tumuli. Xac ran lot, exuvia serpentis.

Xᴀᴄ, gestare aliquid per manum.

Xᴀᴄ, *thang lao xac,* nebulo.

Xᴀɪ, *so mat xai di,* ex timore perdere vires.

Xᴀʏ, ædificare. Xay di van lai, cursus et recursus.

Xᴀʏ, molere. Coi xay, molendina. Cay coi xay, malva.

Xay thay, ex improviso videre.

Xᴀᴍ, *mui xam,* color cineris.

Xam tau lai, oblinire iterùm bitumine navem.

Xᴀᴍ, rete ad capiendos pisciculos in aquâ rapidâ.

Xᴀᴍ, humum per acutum ferrum scrutari. Xam choc, idem est. Loan xam, bellum externum.

Xᴀᴍ, cœcus.

Xan dat, secare terram ligone.

Xang xit, imprudens. Lam xang xit, temerè agere absque ullâ prudentiâ.

Xᴀɴʜ, *cai xanh,* cacabus. Mui xanh, color viridis. Xanh mat, pallor in vult'.

Xao xac, perturbatio; perturbatus, a, um.

Xao vel *xuó,* condire aliquid celeriter.

Xao viec, opus perfectè factum; lis jam absoluta. Chi xao, filo expedire se ab aliquâ difficultate. Xao chon tay ra, extendere brachia et pedes. Xao gi ac roi, bellum paratum est.

Xap, *muon xap lay*, dare commodato aliquid; aut conducere operarios per breve tempus.

Xap nuoc aut *thap nuoc*, madefacere aliquid aquâ.

Xat muoi, fricare sale aliquid.

Xat rau, *xat thit*, secare olera, carnem et cætera.

Xau lai, papyrus aut tela rugosa.

Xau lay, colligare aliquid fune.

Xau ra, deformis, turpis.

Xau ho, pudor. Xau mat, rubor in facie. Ke xau net lam,
flagitiosissimus; pessimus.

Xe, currus. Xe chi, nere.

Xe, dilacerare. Danh xe, percutere et dilacerare.

Xe ra, scindere aliquid serrâ aut cultro. Cua xe, vide *cua*.

Xe vao, accedere. Xe ra, recedere. Xe den gan, accedere
propè.

Xem, videre, inspicere. Xem thu, probare. Xem soc, vel
coi soc, vide *coi*. Xem tuoi, vide *tuoi*. Xem xet, examinare. Ma chang xem sao, nec quidam pensi habere.
Xem ng nha cha, sibi loco patris aliquem ducere.

Xen vao, inserere; insertus, a, um.

Xen sach, secare librum. Xen toc, tendere.

Xeo dap, conculcare pedibus.

Xeo, frustatim secare. Toi xeo, supplicium quo reo caro
paulatim per frusta secatur ad majorem cruciatum.

Xep, plicare; complicare. Xep ao, plicare vestem. Nha
xep, ædicula, quâ tegitur cadaver, dùm ad sepulchrum
defertur; quia peracto exequiarum officio denuò com-
plicatur et asservatur. Ngoi xep bang, vide supra.

Xet, inquirere, examinare, judicare. Xet doan, judicare,
decernere. Quan xet, judex. Xet minh, examinare
seipsum, conscientiam discutere. Con da xet minh ki ru,
jam examinasti conscientiam diligenter?

Xi va, exprobare, contumeliis afficere. Xi bang, idem.

Xia rang, scalpere dentes.

Xich cho, revincere canem; vel catena quâ revincitur canis.

Xien, *cai xien*, veru. Xien qua, transfigere.

Xiet, recensere numero. Ai ke cho xiet, quis numerare potest? Toi toi ke chang xiet, peccata mea sunt innumera.

Xiet, *cai xiet*, reticulum quo pisces aut ranæ capiuntur.

Xieu, inclinari. Nha xieu, domus inclinata. Xieu bat, dispergi tempestate aut perturbatione. Xieu lao, attractus blanditiis.

Xin, petere, rogare.

Xinh, pulcher, a, um; formosus.

Xo, angulus. Xo xinh, locus abditus.

Xo vao, immittere. Xo tien, trajicere filo monetas. Xo chan vao dep, immittere pedem sandaliis. Xo gop, vel dao gop, contribuere.

Xo, impellere.

Xo xo, cay moc xo xo, plantæ crescunt confertæ.

Xoc, agitare. Gai xoc vao chan, spina pedi infixa.

Xoi dang chi, ducere lineam in tabulâ.

Xoi, oryza vapore aquæ ferventis cocta.

Xoi nha, imbrex.

Xoi, sume cibum aut potum: vox solis superioribus et honoratis personis conveniens.

Xoi dat, pastinare terram.

Xom, vicus.

Xom, *ngoi xom*, sedere super pedibus complicatis.

Xom, insolidus, a, um; fragile, quod non est solidum.

Xot, dolor acerbus. Xot ruot, ardor viscerum. Chua xot, miserabilis, e.

Xou vao, irrumpere, aggredi, invadere. Xou vao dinh quan giac, contra hostem invadere. Xou huong, incensare. Lua xou len, ignis erumpens. Di xou xao moi noi, discurrere per omnia loca.

Xou, femorale muliebris. Urbaniùs dicitur, *quan dan ba.*

Xu ao cap tay, vestis manicis manum operire.

Xu, provincia. Tunkinum dividitur in undecim provincias,

quarum nomina hic recensere juvat: *Nghe an; Thanh hoa; Thai nguyen; Son nam; Son tay; Hung hoa; Tuyen cua; Lang son; Kinh bac; Hai duong; Yen quang:* et duæ aliæ, scilicet, *Quang nam* et *Thuan hoa;* olim Tunkino subjectæ, sed à plusquam ducentis annis Regi *Chua nguyen* datæ, ut ex eis et aliis terris Cambodiæ adjacentibus, suum Cocisinæ conflaret regnum; quod à Tunkinensibus appellatur *Nuoc quang,* propter provinciam *Quang nam;* ideòque adhùc undecim superadictæ remanent Tunkino provinciolæ, quæ dividunt in balliviatus majores, *phu;* et balliviatus majores *phu* dividuntur in minores, qui appellantur *huyen;* et *huyen* dividuntur in toparchias appellatus *tou;* et *tou* dividuntur in *xa; xa* dividuntur in *thon; thon* dividuntur in *xom,* vicum; vicus dividitur in *nha,* familia.

XUA, expellere, abjicere.

XUA, olim, quondam. Xua nay, ab initio usque nunc. Nhu xua, ut olim.

Xuc lay, capere hauriendo.

XUC, ungere. Phep xuc dou thanh cho ke liet, sacramentum extremæ unctionis.

XUI, instigare, impellere.

Xuy vang, deaurare.

Xung khac, contrarius, a, um.

Xung xinh, di xung xinh, incedere gestû superbiam redolente.

XUNG, confiteri, declarare. Xung toi, confiteri peccata.

XUOI, *xuoi gio,* ventus secundus. Xuoi nuoc, secundum flumen. Chay xuoi nguoc, hùc illùc discurrere. Ut penitùs intelligatur iste modus loquendi *di xuoi di nguoc,* opus est hic aliquâ compendiosâ descriptioné.

XUO, descendere; descensus. Nga xuo, cadere. Con D. C. B. xuo the lam nguoi, filius Dei incarnatus factus est homo. Xuo tau, navim conscendere. O tau len dat, è navi in terram descendere.

Xuo, os, ossis. Xuo ca, spina piscis. Cay xuong rou, lactaria. Xuong sou, vide *sou.*

Xuo len, nominare, aut recitare nomina uniuscujusque.
Xuong kinh, incipere orationem.

Xuo tuy, armamentarium navium, cymbarumque.

ADDENDA.

Gнет, detestatio.
Gio chop, facere convivium.
Giua, medium.
Han, statuere.
Hanh, elementa.
Hua, vel *Ban hua,* amicus.

FINIS.

ERRATA.

Page 6, Note †, line 1, *for* suavity, *read* vanity.

" 10, line 8, *for* answers *read* answer.

" 13, Note †, line 6, *for* grant, *read* grand; and *for* appellens, *read* appellons.

" 44, Note *, line 1, *for* alganos, *read* algunos.

" 50, line 11, *for* Thebes, *read* Minerva at Sais.

" 56, Note *, line 5, *for* Adomah, *read* Adamah.

" 69, line 12, *dele* the.

" 90, line 13, *dele* which.

" 94, line 6, *dele* But.

" 137, Note *, line 1, *for* Romanum *read* Bomanum.

" 145, lines 3 and 5 from the bottom, *for* Dui, *read* Duc.

" 146, line 6, *for* Dui lin, *read* Duc tin; and *for* dui, *read* duc.

" 179, line 8 from the bottom, *dele* but most probably a goose.

" 187, line 4, *for* hc, *read* hic.

" 200, line 22, *for* fericum, *read* sericum.

" 223, line 6 from the bottom, *for* Chung in, *read* Chung, in.

" 267, line 8, *for* Khon nau, *read* Khon nan.